CHINA KNOWLEDGE SERIES

A BRIEF HISTORY
OF
CHINESE FICTION

LU HSUN

HYPERION PRESS, INC.
WESTPORT, CONNECTICUT

Library of Congress Cataloging in Publication Data

Chou, Shu-jên, 1881-1936.
   A brief history of Chinese fiction.

    Translation of Chung-kuo hsiao shuo shih lüeh.
    Reprint of the 1959 ed. published by Foreign Languages Press, Peking, which was issued as no. 7 of China knowledge series.
    1. Chinese fiction--History and criticism. I.
I. Title. II. Series: China knowledge series, no. 7.
PL2415.C513 1973]   895.1'3'09   73-870
ISBN 0-88355-065-2

Translated by
YANG HSIEN-YI and GLADYS YANG

Published in 1959 by Foreign Languages Press, Peking, China

First Hyperion reprint edition 1973

Library of Congress Catalogue Number 73-870

ISBN 0-88355-065-2

Printed in the United States of America

Publisher's Note

A Brief History of Chinese Fiction grew out of the lecture notes Lu Hsun used when teaching a course on Chinese fiction at Peking University between 1920 and 1924. In January 1923 a first volume was printed and in June 1924 a second volume. In September 1925 these were reprinted as one book. In 1930 the author made certain changes, but all subsequent editions have remained the same.

"The Historical Development of Chinese Fiction" in the Appendix served as notes for a series of lectures Lu Hsun gave at a Sian summer school in July 1924. The preface to the Japanese edition appeared first in the edition published in 1935 by the Sairosha Press, Tokyo, Japan.

This translation has been made from the *Complete Works of Lu Hsun* published by the People's Literature Publishing House: *A Brief History of Chinese Fiction* and "The Historical Development of Chinese Fiction" can be found in Volume 8, while the preface to the Japanese edition comes from the second series of *Essays of Chieh-chieh-ting* in Volume 6.

CHRONOLOGICAL TABLE OF CHINESE DYNASTIES

HSIA	c. 21st — 16th century B.C.
SHANG	c. 16th — 11th century B.C.
CHOU	c. 11th century —221 B.C.
Spring and Autumn Period	770—475 B.C.
Warring States Period	475—221 B.C.
CHIN	221—206 B.C.
HAN	206 B.C.—A.D. 220
Former (or Western) Han	206 B.C. — A.D. 24
Later (or Eastern) Han	25—220
THREE KINGDOMS	220—280
TSIN	265—420
SOUTHERN AND NORTHERN DYNASTIES	420—589
SUI	581—618
TANG	618—907
FIVE DYNASTIES	907—960
SUNG	960—1279
Northern Sung	960—1127
Southern Sung	1127—1279
YUAN (Mongol)	1279—1368
MING	1368—1644
CHING (Manchu)	1644—1911

CONTENTS

Preface to the New Edition

Preface

1. The Historians' Accounts and Evaluations of Fiction — 1
2. Myths and Legends — 10
3. Works of Fiction Mentioned in the *Han Dynasty History* — 23
4. Fiction Attributed to Han Dynasty Writers — 29
5. Tales of the Supernatural in the Six Dynasties — 45
6. Tales of the Supernatural in the Six Dynasties *(Continued)* — 61
7. *Social Talk* and Other Works — 71
8. The Tang Dynasty Prose Romances — 85
9. The Tang Dynasty Prose Romances *(Continued)* — 100
10. Collections of Tang Dynasty Tales — 113
11. Supernatural Tales and Prose Romances in the Sung Dynasty — 123
12. Story-Tellers' Prompt-Books of the Sung Dynasty — 139
13. Imitations of Prompt-Books in the Sung and Yuan Dynasties — 152
14. Historical Romances of the Yuan and Ming Dynasties — 163
15. Historical Romances of the Yuan and Ming Dynasties *(Continued)* — 180

16.	Ming Dynasty Novels About Gods and Devils	198
17.	Ming Dynasty Novels About Gods and Devils *(Continued)*	209
18.	Ming Dynasty Novels About Gods and Devils *(Continued)*	220
19.	Novels of Manners in the Ming Dynasty	232
20.	Novels of Manners in the Ming Dynasty *(Continued)*	245
21.	Ming Dynasty Imitations of Sung Stories in the Vernacular	256
22.	Imitations of Classical Tales in the Ching Dynasty	269
23.	Novels of Social Satire in the Ching Dynasty	288
24.	Novels of Manners in the Ching Dynasty	298
25.	Novels of Erudition in the Ching Dynasty	317
26.	Novels About Prostitution in the Ching Dynasty	337
27.	Novels of Adventure and Detection in the Ching Dynasty	355
28.	Novels of Exposure at the End of the Ching Dynasty	372

Postscript 389

Appendices:
    The Historical Development of Chinese Fiction 393
    Preface to the Japanese Edition 444

Index 447

PREFACE TO THE NEW EDITION

Nearly ten years have passed since I began to lecture on the history of Chinese fiction, and this brief outline was first printed seven years ago. Since then much research has been done in this field and new discoveries have cleared up certain points which were obscure. For example, the discovery by Professor Shionoya Akushi of the mutilated Yuan dynasty edition of *Illustrated Vernacular Tales* and Feng Meng-lung's three collections of popular stories, as well as his researches on these, are of major significance in the history of Chinese fiction; and the contention of some Chinese scholars that there should be separate histories for the fiction of different periods is a sound one. All this means that my brief outline should now be outdated; but since no new histories have yet been written, there are still readers for these notes. For a new edition, this book should by rights be revised, but since I started moving from place to place I have given up literary studies, and have nothing but a vague recollection of what I wrote in the past. So I simply made a few changes in Chapters 14, 15 and 21, keeping the other chapters unchanged as I have no new theories regarding them. Since great vessels take years to produce, this earthenware pot of mine still serves some purpose; but though this fact has prolonged the life of my book, I am disheartened by this dearth of new writing.

In a melancholy mood I have gone through these proofs, hoping that better scholars will soon produce a more authoritative book.

> Lu Hsun
> Night of November 25, 1930

Illustration from an old edition of *The Book of Mountains and Seas* published about 1615

PREFACE

There has never been a history of Chinese fiction, if we except the accounts in the histories of Chinese literature written by foreigners. Recently certain summaries have appeared in Chinese works too, but the space devoted to fiction is usually less than one-tenth of the whole. Hence we still lack a detailed account of the development of Chinese fiction.

Though this book is concerned entirely with fiction, it is nothing but a rough outline. I wrote it because three years ago, happening to give some lectures on this subject and fearing that my defects as a speaker might make it hard for my hearers to understand, I jotted down this outline and had it duplicated for my students. Then, in order not to give the copyist too much trouble, I compressed it by using the classical language, omitting certain examples but keeping the main outline which I have been using ever since.

These notes are finally being printed because they have been duplicated so many times and given those in charge so much trouble that printing appears to be more economical.

During the preparation of this copy for the press, four or five friends have lent me reference books or helped me with proofreading; indeed, for the last three years they have proved consistently helpful. I would like to thank them here.

Lu Hsun
Night of October 7, 1923, Peking

1. THE HISTORIANS' ACCOUNTS AND EVALUATIONS OF FICTION

Hsiao-shuo,[1] the name for fiction, was first used by Chuang Tzu[2] who spoke of "winning honour and renown by means of *hsiao-shuo*." All he meant by this expression, as a matter of fact, was chit-chat of no great consequence. So here the term has a different connotation from that acquired later. Huan Tan[3] said: "The writers of *hsiao-shuo* string together odd sayings and parables to make short tales which contain matters of use for daily life." This seems closer to our understanding of fiction. But Yao's[4] questioning of Confucius in *Chuang Tzu* and the account in *Huai Nan Tzu*[5] of how the giant Kung Kung made the earth quake were considered as "worthless *hsiao-shuo*." In these cases the term meant legends and fables having no basis in historical fact and counter to the Confucian tradition. Later there were many theories which we need not go into here; but we may as well see what the historians had to say about

---

[1] Literally "small-talk."
[2] A philosopher of the Warring States Period who lived in the fourth or third century B.C.
[3] A scholar of the first century A.D.
[4] A legendary sage king believed to have lived about 2000 B.C. He and Confucius lived centuries apart.
[5] A philosophical work by the protégés of Prince Liu An who lived during the second and first century B.C.

hsiao-shuo, since literary criticism has always been one function of Chinese historians.

In the Chin dynasty books were burned in order to keep the people ignorant. When the Han dynasty was established, records were collected and copyists hired by the state, while the emperors Cheng Ti and Ai Ti ordered Liu Hsiang and his son Liu Hsin[1] to edit the books in the imperial library; and Liu Hsin, having made a summary, presented his *Seven Summaries.* This work is lost now, but Pan Ku's *Han Dynasty History* preserved its main contents in the section on literature. The third part of this gives a brief account of the works of non-Confucian philosophers up to that time and ten schools are recorded, of which Pan Ku says: "Nine are worth reading," but works of *hsiao-shuo* were excluded; however he appended the names of these fifteen works in the end.

1. *The Sayings of Yi Yin* in twenty-seven *chuan*[2] or books
2. *The Sayings of Yu Tzu* in nineteen books
3. *Records of Chou* in seventy-six books
4. *Ching Shih Tzu* in fifty-seven books
5. *Shih Kuang* in six books
6. *Wu Cheng Tzu* in eleven books
7. *Sung Tzu* in eighteen books
8. *Tien Yi* in three books
9. *The Sayings of the Yellow Emperor* in forty books
10. *Notes on the Sacrifice to Heaven and Earth* in eighteen books
11. *Adviser Jao's Writings* in twenty-five books

---

[1] Han dynasty scholars in the latter part of the first century B.C.
[2] *Chuan*: literally "rolls." A physical unit of textual division in old Chinese works.

12. *Adviser An Cheng's Writings* in one book
13. *Shou's Account of the Chou Dynasty* in seven books
14. *Yu Chu's Chou Dynasty Tales* in 943 books
15. *Miscellaneous Writings* in 139 books
In all, this totals 1,380 books.

The *hsiao-shuo* writers succeeded those officers of the Chou dynasty whose task it was to collect the gossip of the streets. Confucius said: "Even by-ways are worth exploring. But if we go too far we may be bogged down." Gentlemen do not undertake this themselves, but neither do they dismiss such talk altogether. They have the sayings of the common people collected and kept, as some of them may prove useful. This was at least the opinion of country rustics.

By the Liang dynasty (505-556) *Ching Shih Tzu* alone of these fifteen works was left, and this book was lost too by the Sui dynasty. Judging by Pan Ku's comments, however, most of these titles were later works attributed to some ancient men, or anecdotes about ancient history. The first category bore some resemblance to early philosophic writings except that they were inferior, while the second resembled historical records, only they were less reliable.

During the first half of the seventh century the official *Sui Dynasty History* was compiled by Changsun Wu-chi and other Tang dynasty scholars. The bibliographical section was written by Wei Cheng, who based it on the record by Hsun Hsu of the Tsin dynasty, dividing books into four categories:
1. Confucian classics
2. Historical records

3. Philosophical writings
4. Miscellaneous works

Hsiao-shuo are included under philosophical writings. All the works in this section except the *Story of Prince Tan of Yen* date from the Tsin dynasty and include records of sayings as well as descriptions of various arts and games; while the definition of *hsiao-shuo* is based on that in the *Han Dynasty History:*

> *Hsiao-shuo* were the talk of the streets. Thus the *Tso Chuan*[1] quotes chair-bearers' chants while the *Book of Songs*[2] praises the ruler who consulted rustics. In days of old when a sage was on the throne, the official historians wrote records, blind minstrels made songs, artisans recited admonitions, ministers gave advice, gentlemen discoursed and the common people gossiped. Clappers sounded in early spring as a search was made for folk songs, while officers on tours of inspections understood local customs from the popular songs; and if mistakes had been made these were rectified. All the talk of the streets and highways was recorded. Officers at court took charge of local records and prohibitions, while the officers in charge of civil affairs reported local sayings and customs. Thus Confucius said: "Even by-ways are worth exploring. But if we go too far we may be bogged down. . . ."

In the first half of the tenth century, Liu Hsu and others drew up the bibliographical section of the *Tang Dynasty History* based on the *Record of Books Ancient*

---

[1] A commentary on the *Spring and Autumn Annals* by Tsochiu Ming, who was roughly contemporary with Confucius.
[2] A collection of songs compiled in the Chou dynasty.

and *Modern* by Wu Ching[1] and others, shortening it by cutting out the preface and notes. So we find no comments on books in the official Tang history. The *hsiao-shuo* listed here differ little from those enumerated in the *Sui Dynasty History*; but works no longer extant are omitted, while Chang Hua's[2] *Records of Strange Things*, formerly classified as miscellaneous writings, is added.

In the middle of the eleventh century, Tseng Kung-liang and other Sung dynasty scholars were ordered to edit the *New Tang Dynasty History*, and Ouyang Hsiu wrote the bibliographical section. His list of *hsiao-shuo* includes many additional works from the third to the sixth century: fifteen accounts of ghosts and fairies in 115 books from Chang Hua's *Tales of Marvels* and Tai Tso's *Discerning the Marvels* down to Wu Chun's *More Tales of Chi Hsieh*; as well as nine works in seventy books on divine retribution from Wang Yen-hsiu's *Tales of Divine Retribution* to Hou Pai's *Stories Exemplifying Marvels*. These works had previously been included in the section on historical works together with the biographies of local elders, hermits, filial sons, loyal officers and famous women. But from this time onwards these accounts of the supernatural were considered as fiction and ceased to be classed as history. Other works of the Tang dynasty added to the list of *hsiao-shuo* were moral admonitions like Li Shu's *Advice to My Son*, compendiums of knowledge like Liu Hsiao-sun's *Origin of Things*, Li Fu's *Corrections of Mistakes* or Lu Yu's *Book of Tea*. Thus this category became more diversified. When the *Sung Dynasty History* was compiled

---

[1] A Tang dynasty scholar of the eighth century.
[2] A Tsin dynasty scholar. See Chapter 5.

in the Yuan dynasty the same tradition was followed, though the connotation of *hsiao-shuo* became even more all-embracing.

Hu Ying-lin[1] of the Ming dynasty, judging the *hsiao-shuo* genre too indefinite, subdivided *hsiao-shuo* as follows:
1. Records of marvels
2. Prose romances
3. Anecdotes
4. Miscellaneous notes
5. Researches
6. Moral admonitions

During the reign of Chien Lung (1736-1795) of the Ching dynasty, when a general survey was made of the catalogue of books in the Imperial Manuscript Library under the direction of Chi Yun,[2] *hsiao-shuo* were divided into three main groups. But Chi Yun's views were based on earlier records:

> When we investigate the different types of *hsiao-shuo*, we find three groups: miscellaneous records, records of marvels, and anecdotes. Since the Tang and Sung dynasties there has been a great deal of literature of this sort. Though much of it is idle gossip or foolish superstition, intermingled with this are quite a number of useful pieces of knowledge, research and moral teaching. Pan Ku tells us that the *hsiao-shuo* writers were successors of the Chou dynasty officers who collected information, and a comment in the *Han Dynasty History* says that the task of these officers was to help the ruler to understand country ways and

---
[1] A scholar of the early seventeenth century.
[2] See Chapter 22.

morals. Evidently this was the ancient system for assembling miscellaneous information; hence these works should not be thrust aside as useless or spurious. We have selected only the better examples which serve to broaden knowledge, rejecting vulgar and extravagant writings which simply confuse people.

He goes on to list three categories of *hsiao-shuo*:

1. Miscellaneous writings
   The Western Capital Miscellany in six books
   New Anecdotes of Social Talk in three books, etc. . . .
2. Records of Marvels
   The Book of Mountains and Seas in eighteen books
   The Travels of King Mu in six books
   The Book of Supernatural Things in one book
   Records of Spirits in twenty books
   More Tales of Chi Hsieh in one book, etc. . . .
3. Anecdotes
   Records of Strange Things in ten books
   Accounts of Marvels in two books
   The Yuyang Miscellany in twenty books
   Sequel to the Yuyang Miscellany in ten books, etc. . . .

If we compare this with Hu Ying-lin's categories, we can see that there were actually two main groups: miscellaneous anecdotes and tales of marvels; but here those tales which are more complete are classified as records of marvels, the briefer and more miscellaneous are described as anecdotes. Prose romances are not included, neither are miscellaneous sayings, short studies and moral admonitions. From this time on, the *hsiao-shuo* genre seems to be more clearly defined. Since this was the first time works like *The Book of Mountains and Seas* and *The Travels of King Mu* had been classed as *hsiao-shuo*, the following explanation was given: "Works like *The Travels of King Mu* were formerly classified as biographies. . . . But in fact those tales are sheer fantasy, not to be compared with the *Lost Records of Chou*. . . . If we count them as authentic history, the concept of history becomes confused and the rules of history are broken. We have therefore put them down as *hsiao-shuo*, which seems more logical. We hope readers will not condemn us for altering time-honoured categories in this way." Since then, historical legends have been classed under *hsiao-shuo* as tales of marvels, and the section on history contains no more legendary accounts.

The Sung dynasty story-tellers' scripts and the Yuan and Ming novels have always been popular with the common people and very numerous, but they were never listed in official histories. Only Wang Chi and Kao Ju of the Ming dynasty in their bibliographies, *Hsu Wen Hsien Tung Kao* (*Sequel to Studies in Ancient Bibliographies*) and *Pai Chuan Shu Chih* (*Hundred Rivers Bibliographical Notes*), mention the *Romance of the Three Kingdoms* and the *Shui Hu Chuan*. Chien Tseng at the beginning of the Ching dynasty in his bibliography, *Yeh Shih Yuan Shu Mu*, mentions three popular romances including the *Romance of the Three Kingdoms*, and sixteen Sung dynasty tales including *Mother Lamp-Wick*. *Romance of the Three Kingdoms* and *Shui Hu Chuan* were considered as proper writings because they were printed by the censorate of the Ming government in the sixteenth century, and that was why they were included in Ming bibliographies; but subsequently they were omitted again. And Chien Tseng included those novels in his list simply because he was a collector who valued old editions of these works — not because he appreciated their true value and deliberately broke the old conventions. The historians' point of view has remained unchanged from the Han dynasty to the present day; and as bibliography is after all a branch of historical science, we cannot expect bibliographers to break their own rules.

2. MYTHS AND LEGENDS

Tales of marvels were first recorded according to *Chuang Tzu* by Chi Hsieh and according to *Lieh Tzu* by Yi Chien, but these are unsubstantiated legends. Though the *Han Dynasty History* attributes their origin to the Chou dynasty officers who collected folk legends, these men were collectors only, not authors. Tales which were "the talk of the streets" arose among the people and were not created by any single writer. In China, just as elsewhere, they must have sprung out of myths and legends.

When primitive men observed natural phenomena and changes which could not be accomplished by any human power, they made up stories to explain them, and these explanations became myths. Myths usually centred round a group of gods: men described these gods and their feats and came to worship them, singing hymns in praise of their divine power and making offerings in their shrines. And so, as time went by, culture developed. For myths were not only the beginning of religion and art but the fountain-head of literature. Though mythology gave birth to literature, poets were its greatest enemies; for when they made songs or stories they naturally touched things up till very little of the original myth was left. In fact, while it was the poets who preserved and developed myths, they were also the ones to change and weaken them too. For example, our existing myth about the creation shows a rather advanced imagination at work and can hardly be the invention of primitive man.

Heaven and earth were commingled like an egg in the midst of which Pan Ku was born and he lived for eighteen thousand years. Then heaven and earth split asunder: the pure and bright element became heaven, the impure and dark element earth, while Pan Ku within underwent nine transformations in one day, turning into a god in heaven and a saint on earth. Heaven grew ten feet higher every day, earth grew ten feet thicker every day, and Pan Ku grew ten feet taller every day. So it went for eighteen thousand years, till heaven was exceedingly high, earth exceedingly thick, and Pan Ku exceedingly tall. Then came the three divine emperors.

(A quotation from Hsu Cheng's
Ancient Chronology, now lost)

Heaven and earth are matter too, but there were deficiencies. So in ancient times Nu-kua melted coloured stones to fill out these deficiencies and cut off the feet of a giant turtle to prop up the four extremities of the earth. Later Kung Kung contended against Chuan-hsu for the mastery and in his rage crashed into Mount Puchou, breaking the pillars of heaven and earth's foundations. Then heaven tilted down on the northwest, and the sun, moon and stars all go that way. The earth has a gap in the southeast, and thither all the streams and rivers flow.

(*Lieh Tzu*)

As myths developed, the central figures became increasingly human till the myths turned into legends. The chief figures of legends had semi-divine attributes or were ancient heroes with outstanding intelligence and skill, braver than all ordinary men. They received special gifts from Heaven or were aided by the gods. Two examples out of many are the ancestor of the Shangs born to Chien Ti after she ate a swallow's egg, and the founder of the Han dynasty whose mother was possessed by a dragon.

In the time of King Yao ten suns appeared in the sky, scorching the crops and killing trees and plants. Then there was a famine in the land, and centaurs, wild boars, huge serpents and other monsters began to prey upon the people. Yao ordered Yi . . . to shoot down the ten suns and kill the centaurs. . . . Then all the people rejoiced and made Yao their sovereign.

(Huai Nan Tzu)

Yi had an elixir given him by the Queen Mother of the West. Huan Ngo stole it and went up to the moon.

(Huai Nan Tzu)

(A note by Kao Yu says: "Huan Ngo was Yi's wife. Yi asked the Queen Mother of the West for an elixir, but before he could take it his wife stole it and became immortal, flying to the moon to be the fairy of the moon.)

In ancient times Yao killed Kun at Feather Mountain. Kun's spirit changed into a yellow dragon and entered Feather Lake.

(Tso Chuan)

Shun's father, ordering him to climb up and repair the roof of the granary, set fire to it below. But Shun came down safe and sound, carrying two straw hats. Then his father ordered him to dig a well, which he

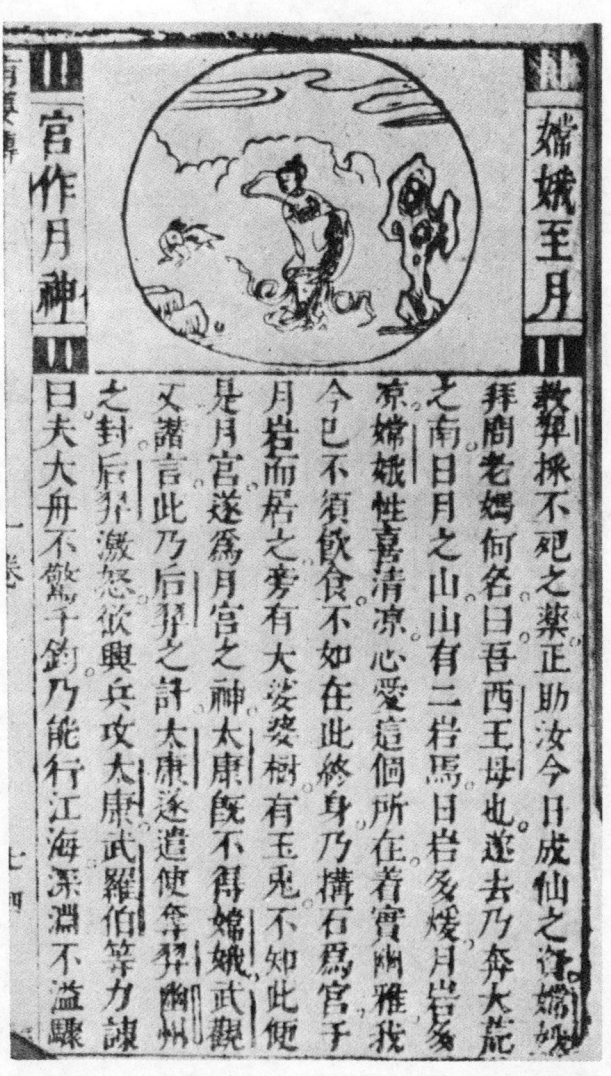

Among the books which contain the legend "Chang Ngo Goes to the Moon" this one appeared at a comparatively early date published about 1640

did. But he made an opening at the bottom by which he escaped again.

(Ssuma Chien's *Historical Records*)

No collections of myths and legends have yet been made in China, but these tales can be found scattered in ancient books, and there are many in *The Book of Mountains and Seas*. Our existing edition, in eighteen books, records strange phenomena and deities of the mountains and rivers, as well as the sacrifices to them. It is wrong to attribute the authorship to Yu and Yi,[1] equally wrong to claim that the work was written as a commentary for the Chu poems.[2] The use of rice in shamanist sacrifices is mentioned, and probably this work was meant for ancient shamans; but later legends were added in the Chin and Han dynasties. The best known and most quoted of all the myths in it are those about Mount Kunlun and the Queen Mother of the West.

Mount Kunlun is the lower capital of the Heavenly Emperor. It is guarded by Lu Wu, a deity having a tiger's body, nine tails, a human face and tiger's claws. He has sway over the nine regions of heaven and paradise.

("The Western Mountains")

In Jade Mountain lives the Queen Mother of the West. This deity bears resemblance to a mortal but has a leopard's tail, tiger's teeth, a shrill voice and matted hair, on which she wears a tiara. She controls the furies and avenging spirits of heaven.

("The Western Mountains")

---

[1] Ancient legendary king and minister.
[2] *Poems of the Kingdom of Chu,* some of its pieces by the great poet Chu Yuan.

Kunlun is eight hundred *li* square, hundreds of thousands of feet high. On its summit grows a tree forty feet in height which five men can barely span. There are nine wells with jade balustrades and nine gates guarded by the beast Kai Ming. Here all the deities live, on an eight-sided cliff by the Red Stream which Yi alone can ascend.

("The Western Regions Within the Seas")

The Queen Mother of the West wears a tiara and has a stool. In the south are three blue birds which fetch food for her from north of Kunlun.

("The Northern Regions Within the Seas")

In the Great Wilderness is a mountain called Fengchu Jade Gate, where the sun and moon go down. This is a holy mountain. Ten witches go up and down there, and there grow all manner of herbs.

("The Western Regions of the Great Wilderness")

South of the Western Sea by the Shifting Sands, behind the Red Stream and before the Black Stream, is a great mountain called Kunlun. Here lives a deity with a human face, tiger's form and white tail. Beneath him is the water on which nothing floats, beyond is the flaming mountain where all things are burned. A creature wearing a tiara, with tiger's teeth and leopard's tail, inhabits a cavern there. This is the Queen Mother of the West. Here is great abundance of all things.

("The Western Regions of the Great Wilderness")

In A.D. 279, during the Tsin dynasty, Pu Chun of the principality of Chi opened the tomb of Prince Hsiang of

Wei and found records written on bamboo strips: *The Travels of King Mu* in five books and nineteen other books. Today *The Travels of King Mu* exists in six books: the first five describe how King Mu of Chou went to the west on a chariot drawn by eight fine horses, while the last deals with the death and funeral of Lady Sheng, but this was originally a separate work. Though the Queen Mother of the West is mentioned here too, she does not have such a monstrous appearance but is more like a human sovereign.

On *chia-tzu* day the king called on the Queen Mother of the West, presenting her with white and black jade, a hundred lengths of coloured silk and three hundred of white. The Queen Mother bowed and accepted these gifts. On *yi-chou* day the king invited her to a feast at Jade Pool, and the Queen Mother sang this song for him:

"The white clouds in the sky float out from the mountains;
The way is long, hills and rivers lie between us;
If you do not die, you may come back again."

The king made reply:

"I must return to my eastern realm to govern the men of Hsia. When all our people are at peace I shall look to see you again. Three years from now I shall come back to your country."

Then the king rode to Yen Mountain, inscribed a record on the rocks there and planted ash trees, naming the place Queen Mother Mount.

(Book 3)

There was a tiger in the bushes, and the king was about to pass by. A guard named Kao Peng-jung asked permission to catch the tiger alive, and having done this presented it to the king. The king ordered a cage to be made and kept it in the east forest. That place was named Tiger's Cage. The king gave Kao ten teams of horses and a grand sacrifice, and Kao bowed his thanks.

(Book 5)

According to Ying Shao of the Han dynasty, the *Records of Chou* was the base of Yu Chu's[1] tales. Only four books in the existing text of the *Lost Records of Chou* abound in descriptive detail like a work of fiction. Among the writings on bamboo strips discovered in the Tsin dynasty were eleven books of miscellaneous works on divination, dreams and supernatural happenings; but all these have been lost. A few quotations only have been preserved in the Sung dynasty *Tai-ping Imperial Encyclopaedia*. A Tsin dynasty stone inscription in Chi County about the Patriarch Lu Wang[2] is based on the *Records of Chou* and speaks of dreams and divination in the manner of fiction. Possibly Yu Chu's tales were based on similar writings. Lacking proof, however, we cannot say for certain.

When Duke Ching of Chi set out to conquer the state of Sung and reached Chuling, he saw in a dream a short man who greeted him.

Yen Tzu asked him: "What was he like, sir?"

---

[1] A story writer of the time of Emperor Wu Ti of the Han dynasty.

[2] Chiang Shang, believed to have helped King Wu of Chou to overthrow the Shang dynasty.

The duke said: "He was very short, with a longer body than his legs. He spoke angrily and often lowered his head."

Yen Tzu said: "That must have been Yi Yin. He was broad and short, with a longer trunk than his legs. He was ruddy and bearded and often lowered his head, talking in gruff tones."

The duke said: "That's the man."

Yen Tzu said: "He is angry on account of your expedition. You had better not go on."

So the duke gave up his campaign.

(Tai-ping Imperial Encyclopaedia, Book 378)

King Wen dreamed that he saw the Heavenly Emperor in dark robes standing at Linghu Ford.

The god said: "I give you Wang."

King Wen bowed and so did Lu Wang, standing behind him, who was later styled the Patriarch. The same night that King Wen had this dream, Lu Wang dreamed it also. Some time later King Wen met Lu Wang and asked him: "Is your name Wang?"

He answered: "Yes, it is."

King Wen said: "Your face looks familiar."

Lu Wang repeated to him all that had passed, giving him the exact year, month and day, and explaining: "That is how Your Majesty saw me."

King Wen exclaimed: "True, true!"

He returned to his palace with Lu Wang and made him his minister.

(From the Tsin dynasty inscription on the Patriarch Lu Wang)

There were also historical works which contained legends, such as the *Story of Prince Tan of Yen* written probably before the Han dynasty, the *History of the Kings of Shu* by Yang Hsiung of the Han dynasty, *Annals of Wu and Yueh* by Chao Yeh and *Lost Records of Yueh* by Yuan Kang and Wu Ping of the end of the Han dynasty. The poems of Chu Yuan[1] also abound in myths and legends, especially "The Riddles." The poet asks: What virtue has the moon that it dies and is born again? Why is there a toad in the moon? What were the labours of Kun? What did Yu accomplish? Why did the giant grow angry and make the earth fall in the southeast? Where are the foundations of the Hanging Gardens of Kunlun? How high is the ninefold city? Where is the *ling* fish? Where is the *chi-tui* bird? Why did Yi shoot down the suns? Where do birds discard their feathers? . . . The Han dynasty commentator Wang Yi says: "After Chu Yuan was sent into exile, wandering through hills and marshlands he saw temples built to past kings and ministers where the walls had paintings of deities and spirits of hills and streams, depicting strange tales of ancient sages and monsters . . . so he wrote this poem on the wall, putting riddles to Heaven." Evidently such legends were not only commonly told but used as subjects for the decoration of temples. This tradition was handed down to the Han dynasty. Even today in Han tombs we can see stone bas-reliefs representing deities, monsters, sages and famous figures. After the bamboo writings were dis-

---

[1] The great poet of the kingdom of Chu in the fourth century B.C.

covered in the Tsin dynasty, Kuo Pu[1] wrote a commentary for *The Travels of King Mu* as well as for *The Book of Mountains and Seas* and appended short summaries. Chiang Kuan[2] after him did the same. So it seems that after the Tsin dynasty these ancient legends were still popular. But China has never had monumental works putting all these myths and legends together, as in the Greek epics. In our literature myths and legends serve merely as allusions and embellishments in poetry or prose. They left their mark, too, on later fiction.

It seems likely that Chinese myths remained separate fragments for the following reasons: First, the early dwellers in the Yellow River Valley were not an imaginative people; and since their life was hard and they devoted most of their energy to practical matters without indulging in flights of fancy, they did not combine all the old legends into one great epic. Secondly, Confucius appeared with his practical common-sense teaching about the way to cultivate individual morality, regulate the family, rule the state and bring peace to the world. Since he disapproved of talk of the supernatural, the old myths were not quoted by Confucian scholars, and instead of undergoing further development many of them were lost.

But a more fundamental reason was probably the absence of a strict division between gods and ghosts. In the earliest times though there was apparently some line of demarcation between the deities of heaven and earth and the ghosts of dead men, yet ghosts could become deities too. Since men and gods intermingled in this

---

[1] A scholar of the first half of the fourth century.
[2] A scholar of the second half of the fourth century.

manner, the early religion was never fully developed, and as more new legends appeared the old ones died out, and the new legends lacked lustre. Here are two examples of the way in which new gods were constantly created, and three showing that though the old gods might change their form and names there was no real development of myths and legends.

Chiang Tzu-wen, a citizen of Kuangling, was fond of drink and women, a thorough profligate. He boasted that because his bones were dark he would become a god after his death. At the end of the Han dynasty, when he was tribune of Moling, he chased a brigand to Mount Chung. When Chiang was about to tie him up, the brigand struck him on the temple and killed him. During the reign of Sun Chuan of Wu, some of Chiang's former officers saw him on the road. . . . Chiang's spirit said: "I shall be the tutelary god here to bring happiness to the people. Tell them to build a shrine for me if they want to avoid serious trouble." That summer there was a great outbreak of plague and moved by fear many worshipped him in secret.

(Records of Spirits)

There is a goddess called Tzu Ku. Tradition has it that she was once a concubine but she was so ill-treated by the wife, who made her do all the dirtiest work, that on the fifteenth of the first month she killed herself. So on this day every year effigies are made of her, and at night folk stand by the privy or pigsty to welcome her spirit. . . . When the one holding the effigy finds it grow heavier, that means her spirit has come. Then the man becomes possessed. They set out wine and fruit as sacrifice, while he shows approval and moves incessantly, giving portents concerning the raising of silkworms and mulberry crops. If he dances wildly it means success; if he lies down to sleep it means failure.

(The Garden of Marvels)

From the ocean rises Mount Tushuo and upon it grows a huge peach tree. . . . On its northeast side is the Gate of Spirits where a myriad ghosts pass to and fro. Above are two deities, Shen Tu and Yu Lei, who rule over the ghosts, catching evil spirits with a straw rope and feeding them to tigers. This is why the Yellow Emperor instituted rites to exorcize spirits in due season: men set up a huge peach-wood image, on the doors paint Shen Tu, Yu Lei and the tiger, and hang up straw ropes to guard against evil spirits.

(A quotation from a passage now lost in The Book of Mountains and Seas)

Southeast is Mount Taotu. . . . At its foot are two deities, the one on the left called Lung, the one on the right called Yu, and both hold straw ropes to catch evil spirits which they will kill. Nowadays at New Year men make two figures in peach wood to stand by the door . . . as images of these deities.

(The Heart of Mysteries)

The door-gods were two Tang dynasty generals: Chin Shu-pao and Hu Ching-teh. According to the records, when Emperor Tai Tsung was ill, ghosts started screeching outside his chamber and throwing bricks and tiles. . . . The emperor in alarm told his ministers.

Then Chin Shu-pao stepped forward and said: "I have killed men like chopping melons, piling up corpses like ant-hills: what have I to fear from ghosts? Let me and Hu Ching-teh stand guard outside your door in battle dress."

The emperor consented. That night there was no further alarm and the emperor was pleased to have portraits painted of both men . . . to hang on both sides of his palace gate. Then the ghosts ceased to disturb him. This tradition was carried forward into later years, and so these men became door-gods.

(The Compendium of Deities of the Three Religions)

3. WORKS OF FICTION MENTIONED IN THE *HAN DYNASTY HISTORY*

The bibliographical section of the *Han Dynasty History* describes the writers of *hsiao-shuo* as successors of the Chou dynasty *pai* officers. Thus Ju Chun comments: "*Pai* meant fine rice. This alluded to the trivial talk or gossip of the street. The ancient kings who wanted to know local customs appointed these officers to report on them." Since all the *hsiao-shuo* mentioned in the *Han Dynasty History* are lost we cannot make a study of them, but judging by their titles they can hardly have been collected from the people like the folk-songs in the *Book of Songs*. Seven of these works are attributed to famous men of early times, namely *The Sayings of Yi Yin, The Sayings of Yu Tzu, Shih Kuang, Wu Cheng Tzu, Sung Tzu, Tien Yi* and *The Sayings of the Yellow Emperor*. Two were ancient records, *Records of Chou* and *Ching Shih Tzu*. We do not know the date of these; but the following four were written in the Han dynasty: *Notes on the Sacrifice to Heaven and Earth, Adviser Jao's Works, Shou's Account of the Chou Dynasty* and *Yu Chu's Chou Dynasty Tales*. Though *Adviser An Cheng's Works* and *Miscellaneous Writings* are not dated, judging by their position in the list they probably date from the Han dynasty also.

Taoist philosophical works mentioned in the *Han Dynasty History* include *The Sayings of Yi Yin* in fifty-one books, which is no longer extant. *The Sayings of*

Yi Yin in twenty-seven books classified as *hsiao-shuo* is also lost. In a note to the "Life of Ssuma Hsiang-ju" in Ssuma Chien's *Historical Records* we find this quotation from Yi Yin's sayings: "East of Chi Mountain where the blue birds live are oranges that ripen in the summer." This must be the only fragment left. The *Works of Lu Pu-wei*[1] records that Yi Yin was introduced to King Tang after serving him delicious food; the quotation just given is also cited and there is elegant descriptive detail but actually very little content. That episode was probably also based on this lost work. Since Mencius in one discussion also refers to the legend that Yi Yin was introduced to King Tang as a cook, *The Sayings of Yi Yin* was most likely written in the Warring States Period.

Another Taoist work mentioned in the *Han Dynasty History* is *Yu Tzu* in twenty-one books of which one book only is left. Some critics have deduced from its lack of content that it was not the work of a Taoist philosopher; and fragments quoted by a Tang dynasty scholar are quite different from the existing text; so the deduction was probably correct:

> King Wu led his men and chariots against the Shangs. The king of Shang had a million picked troops in formation outside the city from Huangniao to Chihfu. They came on as fast as the wind with a noise like thunder, and King Wu's men were afraid. Then King

---

[1] A philosophical work by the protégés of Lu Pu-wei, prime minister of Chin in the third century B.C.

Wu ordered the Patriarch to wave his white banner at the enemy, and the army of Shang fled.

(Quoted in the *Tai-ping Imperial Encyclopaedia*)

Ching Shih Tzu was an early historian whose date is unknown. His book was lost by the Sui dynasty, and when Liu Chih-chi[1] described it as "a collection of street gossip" he was going by the *Han Dynasty History*, for this work had not reappeared in the Tang dynasty. Three fragments left deal with ancient ceremony, making it hard to understand why this work was classed as *hsiao-shuo*.

In ancient times a child's education began before it was born. When the queen was seven months with child, she went to the hall, and the annalist with his pipe would wait on the left of the door, the cook with his ladle on the right, the diviner with his instruments of divination would wait outside the hall, while the other officers waited within the gate, each busy with his different task. In these three months, if she asked for improper music the annalist would decline to play it, if she asked for improper food the cook would decline to prepare it, saying: "We dare not offer this to the crown prince." When the child was born and cried, the annalist would play his pipe at the befitting pitch, the cook would provide food of the befitting taste, and the diviner would read the stars. Then the ceremony to celebrate the prince's birth was performed.

(Quoted in the *Records of Rites*)

---

[1] An eighth century historian.

In ancient times, a boy would move to lodgings outside his home at the age of eight to learn the lesser arts and practise the lesser etiquette. When he bound his hair and undertook more advanced studies, he would learn the greater arts and practise the greater etiquette. At home he would study ceremony and literature, abroad his jade pendants would tinkle, and when riding in his carriage he would hear harmonious bells. Thus no improper ideas could enter his heart.... In ancient times carriages were built with round canopies to symbolize heaven, twenty-eight ribs to symbolize the zodiac, a square frame to symbolize the earth, and thirty strips of cloth to symbolize the moon. Thus looking up the driver could see heaven and looking down the earth; in front of him were the harmonious bells, at his side the evolution of the seasons. So education was brought into the carriage.

(Quoted in the *Records of Rites*)

The cock is a creature of the east. When the yearly cycle comes to an end, the new order begins in the east and the myriad things emerge. Thus the cock is used in sacrifice.

(Quoted in Ying Shao's *Popular Traditions and Customs*)

Works of military science and divination listed in the *Han Dynasty History* include Shih Kuang's work on divination in eight books. We know nothing of the contents of his *hsiao-shuo*, except that the commentator tells us they were based for the most part on the *Chou Dynasty Annals*. *Lost Records of Chou* relates that Shih Kuang once judged from the voice of a certain prince that this ruler would not live long, and the prince himself knew that three years later he would appear before the Heavenly Emperor. This certainly reads like fiction.

The only thing we know about Yu Chu, whose name appears in the commentary to the *Han Dynasty History*, is that he joined with others to lay curses upon the Huns and men of Ferghana: this is mentioned in the section on imperial sacrifices. He wrote nearly a thousand chapters of tales of the Chou dynasty, but all of these are lost. Three quotations from the *Records of Chou* in Tsin and Tang works are more reminiscent of *The Book of Mountains and Seas* and *The Travels of King Mu* than of the *Lost Records of Chou*, and Chu Yu-tseng[1] thought these might well be from Yu Chu's tales.

Mount Chieh is where the god Ju Shou lives. West of this mountain is the place where the sun sets, and a round aura is there. It is ruled over by the god Ching Kuang.

(From the *Tai-ping Imperial Encyclopaedia*)

Wherever the Heavenly Hound stops, the earth slopes down. Its light illumines the sky like shooting stars more than a hundred feet long. Its speed is like the wind, its noise like thunder, and its brightness like lightning.

(From the commentary on *The Book of Mountains and Seas*)

When King Mu went hunting, a black bird like a pigeon flew down to alight on his chariot. When the charioteer killed it with his whip the horses stampeded

---

[1] A nineteenth century scholar who edited the *Lost Records of Chou*.

and could not be controlled. The king stumbled and hurt his left leg.

(From Li Shan's commentary on the *Anthology of Literature*)

In his preface to the *Garden of Anecdotes,* Liu Hsiang comments on the *Miscellaneous Writings* classified as *hsiao-shuo*: "There are anecdotes of every description. . . . I cut out those which are redundant, and since the remainder are shallow and lack profundity I put these together as the *Miscellaneous Writings.*" His *Garden of Anecdotes* still exists, and all the tales in it concern deeds of ancient men from which morals can be drawn. Judging by his description of the *Miscellaneous Writings*, the tales in it probably serve no moral purpose.

We know nothing of the other works of fiction mentioned in the *Han Dynasty History.* It appears from their titles, that they were attributed to ancients like Yi Yin, Yu Hsiung, Shih Kuang and the Yellow Emperor and dealt with such topics as the prolongation of life and sacrifice; so probably all but *Ching Shih Tzu* were writings by alchemists. *Wu Cheng Tzu* is mentioned in *Hsun Tzu*, and *Shih Tzu* notes that he taught his disciples to avoid acting against nature. Sung Tzu's name appears in *Chuang Tzu*, *Work of Mencius* and *Han Fei Tzu* in slightly different forms, and Hsun Tzu quotes him as saying that if a man feels no shame when he is insulted, he will not become aggressive. This smacks of Taoist philosophy, though it is not the sort of thing the alchemists said.

4. FICTION ATTRIBUTED TO HAN DYNASTY WRITERS

Some writings of *hsiao-shuo* still in existence have been attributed to Han dynasty writers, but none of these are genuine Han dynasty works. From the Tsin to the Sung and Ming dynasties, scholars and alchemists forged "ancient" works. The scholars did this for their own amusement, to show off their talent or to claim that they had acquired some rare manuscript; the alchemists did this to spread superstition, utilizing these "ancient" texts to impress the credulous. After the Tsin dynasty these forgeries were ascribed to Han dynasty authors, just as during the Han dynasty various anecdotes and sayings were ascribed to the Yellow Emperor or Yi Yin. Of these *hsiao-shuo* alleged to be Han dynasty writings, two were attributed to Tungfang Shuo, two to Pan Ku, one to Kuo Hsien, one to Liu Hsin. Works about distant lands were attributed to Tungfang Shuo or Kuo Hsien, those about local affairs to Liu Hsin or Pan Ku. By and large, all these writings treat of the supernatural.

One work supposedly by Tungfang Shuo is the *Book of Deities and Marvels*. Written in the style of *The Book of Mountains and Seas,* this has fewer geographic details and more accounts of wonders, with an occasional jest thrown in. Since *The Book of Mountains and Seas* was little talked of in the Han dynasty, not becoming widely known until the Tsin, the *Book of Deities and Marvels* can hardly date from before that time. Certain repetitious passages are no doubt due to the fact that a mutilated text was re-edited and gaps filled in with material from Tang and Sung dynasty books. A commentary attributed to Chang Hua of the Tsin dynasty is also a later fabrication.

In the south are plantations of sugar-cane, which grows to a height of a thousand feet with trunks thirty-eight inches round. This tree has many knots and is full of juice as sweet as honey. This juice, sucked, imparts strength and vigour and helps to check worms. The tapeworms that infest the human body look like earthworms. They aid the digestion but too many are harmful, too few make for indigestion. This sugar-cane, like other canes, can adjust the number of worms in the body.

("The Southern Wilderness")

The Lying Beast lives in the mountains of the Southwest Wilderness. In appearance like a rabbit with a human face, it can speak like a human being. It often cheats men, saying east when it should be west and bad when it should be good. Its flesh is delicious, but eating it makes a man tell lies. Its other name is Rumour.

("The Southwestern Wilderness")

On Mount Kunlun there is a bronze pillar as high as the sky, and this is the pillar of heaven. It has a circumference of three thousand *li* and rises sheer. Underneath is a mansion with an area of a thousand square feet where live fairies who govern the region. Above is the giant bird Hsi-yu. This bird faces south, shields the Lord of the East with its left wing and the Queen Mother of the West with its right. The span of its back between the two wings is nineteen thousand *li*. Every year the Queen Mother of the West mounts one wing to meet the Lord of the East.

("The Central Wilderness")

The *Accounts of the Ten Continents,* also attributed to Tungfang Shuo, tells of the ten continents, Tsu, Yin, Hsuan, Yen, Chang, Yuan, Liu, Sheng, Feng-ling and Chu-ku. Emperor Wu Ti, having heard about these from the Queen Mother of the West, asked Tungfang Shuo to describe these regions to him. The style is also modelled on *The Book of Mountains and Seas.*

The continent of Hsuan lies in the North Sea in the land of Hsu-hai. It has an area of 7,200 square *li* and is 360,000 *li* from the southern coast. There is a great city governed by saints and fairies, and many hills besides. The Hill of the Winds facing the Northwest Gate of heaven rumbles like thunder. There are many palaces for the angels, each one different. Gold plants and jade herbs abound. It is here that the Three Lords of Heaven descend to rule, hence all is solemnity. . . .

In the third year of the Cheng Ho period (90 B.C.) when Emperor Wu Ti went to Anting, the west Scythians presented four ounces of incense as large as a sparrow's egg and as dark as a mulberry. Because this was unknown in China, the emperor kept it in the outer treasury. . . . In the first year of the Hou Yuan period (88 B.C.) hundreds fell ill in the city of Changan, and more than half of them died. But when the emperor burned some of this Scythian incense in the capital, all who had not been dead for more than three months came back to life. The fragrance also lingered for more than three months so that the emperor knew that this was a treasure. Yet though the remaining incense was carefully kept, some time later it was lost, and the next year when the emperor lay dying in Wu-tso Palace no Scythian incense was left. Had the envoys received better treatment, at the time of the emperor's death there would have been no lack of this wonderful incense. So it seems he was fated to perish!

Though Tungfang Shuo was noted for his jests, he could not have gone to such fantastic lengths. "The Life of Tungfang Shuo" in the *Han Dynasty History* tells us: "He loved a joke or any trick or prank, and his stories were so easy to understand and so popular that even children and cowherds spoke of them. Thus all kinds of strange tales and original sayings were attributed to him." So even during the Han dynasty tales were attributed to Tungfang Shuo. These two forgeries are listed in the bibliographical section of the *Sui Dynasty History,* and because the tales in them are rather unusual, writers of the Six Dynasties often referred to them. The *Book of Deities and Marvels,* though crammed with the fantastic talk of alchemists, is couched in the language of a literary man. The *Accounts of the Ten Continents* is rather naive, as can be seen from the story of the Scythian incense that restored men to life. In fact, at the beginning of this work we read: "Tungfang Shuo said: 'I am one who is learning to become an immortal, not one who is already a saint. In this magnificent and prosperous reign, the government is inviting all logicians, Confucians and Mohists to take part in the culture of our state and discourage the mysteries of the unworldly Taoists. So I have given up my hermit's life to come to court, setting aside my arts of longevity to wait in the palace.'" Obviously here speaks some alchemist who wanted to make himself known, impress readers and console himself.

One work ascribed to Pan Ku is the *Tales of Emperor Wu Ti*. Only a single book of this remains, which describes the emperor's birth in Yilan Palace, his death and burial and the reign of Emperor Cheng Ti. Though supernatural episodes are included, the writer does not believe in alchemists and the language is concise and fairly distinguished, showing it was the work of a scholar. According to the bibliographical section of the *Sui Dynasty History*, the *Tales of Emperor Wu Ti* consisted of two books, but no writer's name is given. Chao Kung-wu a bibliographer of the Sung dynasty was the first to say that it was attributed to Pan Ku. Though he also mentioned that Chang Chien-chih of the Tang dynasty in his postscript to *Penetrating the Mysteries* ascribed this book to Wang Chien who lived at the end of the fifth century, later critics regarded Pan Ku as the author.

The emperor was born in Yilan Palace on the seventh day of the seventh month in the cyclic year of *Yi-yu*. At the age of four he was made Prince of Chiaotung. A year or two later the Elder Princess, holding him on her knee, asked: "Do you want a wife?"

The prince intimated that he did.

The princess indicated the ladies-in-waiting who numbered more than a hundred, but the prince shook his head to them all. Finally she pointed to her daughter. "How about Ah-chiao?"

The prince laughed and said: "If I have Ah-chiao as my wife, I'll put her in a chamber of gold."

The Elder Princess was overjoyed and prevailed on the emperor to marry her daughter to the prince.

*

Emperor Wu Ti once went to the guardsmen's office. There he saw a white-bearded and white-haired old man in shabby clothes.

"How long have you served here?" asked the emperor. "How is it you are so old?"

"My name is Yen Ssu," was the reply. "I am from Chiangtu. I joined the guards in the reign of Emperor Wen Ti."

"Why have you never been promoted in all these years?"

"Emperor Wen Ti cared more for the arts of peace, while I was trained in those of war. Emperor Ching Ti preferred older men; I was too young for him. Now Your Majesty prefers younger men, and I have become too old. So for three reigns I have never been promoted, but am still an old guardsman in this office."

The emperor was moved and appointed him tribune of Kuaichi.

*

On the seventh day of the seventh month the emperor fasted in Chenghua Palace. At noon a blue bird came flying from the west and the emperor asked Tungfang Shuo what this portended.

Tungfang Shuo said: "The Queen Mother of the West will descend on the sacred image this evening."

. . . At night when the clepsydra struck the seventh note, though there was not a single cloud a rumble as of thunder was heard in the distance and a purple mist enveloped the sky. Forthwith the Queen Mother of the West arrived in a purple chariot with serving-maids on both sides. She wore a tiara and above her was a blue aura like a cloud. Two blue birds descended on both sides of the goddess. When she alighted, the emperor welcomed her and bowed. Having invited her to take a seat, he asked her for some recipe that would make him immortal.

The goddess said: " . . . Your Majesty is not yet free of worldly passion. You still retain too much lust to be ready for the elixir."

She took out seven peaches and ate two herself, giving the other five to the emperor. When he kept the stones she asked what he intended to do with them.

He told her: "These peaches are so delicious that I intend to plant them."

The goddess said with a smile: "This peach tree bears fruit only once in three thousand years, and cannot grow on earth."

She stayed till the fifth watch at dawn, and they spoke of worldly affairs, for she would not speak of the gods. Then she left suddenly.

Tungfang Shuo had been peeping from Red-bird Gate at the goddess, and she said: "This boy is a mischievous, foolish rascal. That is why he was banished from heaven for a time. But there is no harm in him and he will return to heaven eventually. You must look after him well."

After the goddess left, the emperor was melancholy for many days.

The other work attributed to Pan Ku is the *Private Life of Emperor Wu Ti* in one book. This also tells of the birth and death of the emperor, giving fuller details about the visit of the Queen Mother of the West. The language is magniloquent yet superficial, some Buddhist sayings are used, and certain episodes are borrowed from the last work and the *Accounts of the Ten Continents*; so this was obviously written later. The authorship was unknown in the Sung dynasty, but Ming dynasty critics attributed both works to Pan Ku simply because of his fame as a historian.

After the second watch that night a white vapour ascended suddenly in the southwest and this radiance approached the palace. Soon fluting and drumming could be heard in the clouds, and the clamour of men and horses. In half the time for a meal the goddess arrived. Deities alighted before the palace like a flock of birds, some mounted on dragons and tigers, some on white unicorns or white storks, some in carriages or on winged horses. There were several thousand of these angelic beings, whose splendour shed a radiance on all the court. Then this retinue of angels vanished and the Queen Mother of the West appeared! She had fifty attendants and was riding in a carriage of purple clouds drawn by nine-coloured dragons. . . .

The others remained outside while the goddess entered, supported by two maids. These were girls of sixteen or seventeen, clad in dark silk; they had alluring eyes, exquisite features, and were utterly ravishing. The goddess mounted the steps and sat down facing east. In her golden coat she was splendid yet dignified. At her waist she had a long belt and a sword, on her head a tiara over her knotted hair, and on her feet slippers embroidered with phoenixes. She appeared to be in her thirties, of medium height, and her beauty, divine and magnificent, was peerless. She was a true goddess!

The emperor knelt in thanks. . . . Lady Shang-yuan bade him be seated.

The Queen Mother rebuked her: "You will frighten the emperor by speaking so sharply, since he still lacks true understanding."

Lady Shang-yuan replied: "A man who desires to understand the Truth will willingly give his body to a hungry tiger, ignoring personal calamities, braving fire and flood, single-minded and fearless. . . . I spoke sharply to help him to make up his mind. If you wish to help him, you will give him the recipe for discarding his mortal body."

The Queen Mother said: "His mind has long been exercised, but for lack of a good master he is beginning to waver in his beliefs and suspect that no immortals exist. I left my celestial palace and came to the dusty world to strengthen his resolution and free him from doubt. Our meeting today is one that will be remembered. As for a recipe for leaving the earth, I do not grudge it him: in three years' time I shall give him one half of it. If I were to give him the whole, he would not stay here. But the Huns are not yet pacified and there are alarms at the frontier: why should he be so impatient to leave his throne and live as a hermit in the woods and hills? All depends upon his faith. If he mends his ways, I shall return." She patted the emperor on the back. "Follow Lady Shang-yuan's sound advice and you will become an immortal. Take good care!"

The emperor, kneeling, replied: "I shall have it written in gold and wear it on my person."

Penetrating the Mysteries in four books, ascribed to Kuo Hsien of the Later Han dynasty, consists of sixty anecdotes about fairies, magic and marvels in distant lands. The title is explained as follows in the preface: "Emperor Wu Ti was a perspicacious and remarkable monarch, and Tungfang Shuo in jest gave him good advice, going to the heart of the Truth so that mysteries were made manifest. Now I have assembled tales hitherto unrecorded in history, and produced this work in four books as one form of writing." So, just as in the other works, these legends were attributed to Tungfang Shuo too. Kuo Hsien or Kuo Tzu-heng was a citizen of Junan who became an imperial academician in the time of Emperor Kuang Wu (A.D. 25-57). Fearless and honest, he was noted for his frankness. The legend of how he extinguished a fire with wine was used by the alchemists, and when Fan Yeh compiled the *Later Han Dynasty History* he made the mistake of classing him as one of them. Kuo Hsien was first cited as the author of this work in the *Tang Dynasty History*, but the *Sui Dynasty History* speaks of the author as Kuo, not Kuo Hsien. During the Six Dynasties when tales of the supernatural were popular, they were often attributed to Kuo Pu of the Tsin dynasty. Thus *The Heart of Mysteries* and *Penetrating the Mysteries* were both ascribed to him. The former work is now lost, but judging by fragments which remain it resembled the *Book of Deities and Marvels*. *Penetrating the Mysteries* is still complete. Here are two extracts from it:

Huang An was a citizen of the prefecture of Tai, who served as a soldier in that district. . . . He ate cinnabar till his whole body was red. In winter he wore no furs but invariably sat on a holy tortoise two feet across.

He was asked: "How many years have you sat on this tortoise?"

He answered: "When divine Fu Hsi invented nets and snares and caught this tortoise, he gave it to me, and I have been sitting on it ever since. Its back is flat. This creature shrinks from the light of the sun and the moon, and puts out its head only once every two thousand years. Since I started sitting on it, its head has emerged five times. . . ."

(Book 2)

In the second year of the Tien Han period (99 B.C.) the emperor mounted Hoary-Dragon Pavilion and, longing to become an immortal, summoned alchemists to talk of distant lands. Then Tungfang Shuo left his seat and, pen in hand, advanced to kneel before the emperor.

The emperor asked him what he had to say.

Tungfang Shuo replied: "When I went to the northern extremities of the earth, I reached the Mountain of Fire-Seeds where the sun and moon never shine. A blue dragon holds a torch in its mouth to light the rare trees and herbs. There bright-stemmed grass shines at night like a golden lamp, and when plucked for torches reveals the form of ghosts. Because Saint Ning Feng used to eat this herb and at night you could see light shining through his belly, it is also called Penetrating-the-Dark Plant."

The emperor ordered men to pulp this herb and smear Bright-Cloud Pavilion with it, so that he could sit there at night with no need for candles. This was also called Ghost-Revealing Herb. A man who bound this under his feet could walk upon the water.

(Book 3)

The Western Capital Miscellany in two books contains anecdotes about worldly events. Our present edition in six books was made by some Sung dynasty scholar. A postscript by Ko Hung of the Tsin dynasty says that he had a copy of Liu Hsin's *Han Dynasty History* in one hundred books, and when he compared it with that of Pan Ku he found the latter almost entirely based on Liu Hsin's work, apart from minor modifications, though about twenty thousand words of Liu's text had been omitted; he was therefore copying these out as supplementary material for Pan Ku's history. But the bibliographical section of the *Sui Dynasty History* does not give the author of this work, and in the *Tang Dynasty History*, *The Western Capital Miscellany* is attributed to Ko Hung. Clearly no one at that time believed that Liu Hsin was the author. Tuan Cheng-shih[1] wrote in the *Yuyang Miscellany*: "Yu Hsin[2] in his poems used allusions from *The Western Capital Miscellany*, but later he cut these out, saying: 'Phrases like those of Wu Chun[3] are hardly suitable for poetry.'" Since then this work has also been attributed to Wu Chun. Yu Hsin may merely have been speaking of isolated phrases, however, not of this work. When Emperor Wu Ti (502-549) of the Liang dynasty

[1] A Tang dynasty scholar. See Chapter 10.
[2] A sixth century poet.
[3] A fifth century poet.

-ordered Yin Yun to compile some tales, he made a collection based on old texts including many quotations from *The Western Capital Miscellany.* So this book must already have been in existence, and it seems likely that Ko Hung wrote it. When some critics saw that the writer referred to Liu Hsiang as his father, they doubted Ko Hung's authorship; but since Ko Hung ascribed this work to Liu Hsin he would naturally pose as Liu Hsin — Liu Hsiang's son. According to a preface by Huang Sheng-tseng:[1] "This work has four characteristics: the anecdotes deal with insignificant and minor incidents, there are casual comments devoid of any moral purpose; there are also unauthenticated legends and matters that should not have been spoken about." This was the viewpoint of an official historian. Judged as literature, however, this is one of the better works of early fiction.

When Ssuma Hsiang-ju and Cho Wen-chun first returned to Chengtu, they led a life of poverty and care, selling their furs to Yang Chang in the market to buy wine and take their pleasure. Then Wen-chun threw her arms round her husband's neck and said with tears: "All my life I have been rich, but now I have to sell my furs to buy wine!"

They decided to become tavern-keepers in the city. Ssuma Hsiang-ju wore a short jacket and breeches and washed the cups himself to shame his father-in-law. At that, Wen-chun's father felt concern and gave his daughter such rich gifts that they once more became well-off. Wen-chun was a pretty girl with eyebrows like distant hills, a face like hibiscus flowers and a

---

[1] A sixteenth century scholar.

smooth, soft skin. Because she was romantic and unconventional, she had been struck by Ssuma Hsiang-ju's talents and so eloped with him.

(Book 2)

Kuo Wei or Kuo Wen-wei was a citizen of Maoling who was devoted to reading. He said that since *Erh Ya*,[1] supposedly compiled by the Duke of Chou, contained the name of Chang Chung, an upright and loyal subject of King Hsuan of Chou, it could not be by the duke.[2] When I questioned Yang Hsiung about this, he told me the work was compiled by disciples of Confucius in order to throw light on the classics. My father pointed out that the ancient historian Yi is related to have used *Erh Ya* to teach his son language, while Confucius also used this work to teach Duke Ai of Lu. So it seems that *Erh Ya* had an early origin, and that is why past scholars attributed it to the Duke of Chou. Passages like that concerning Chang Chung were later interpolations.

(Book 3)

Ssuma Chien during his disgrace wrote the *Historical Records* in one hundred and thirty books and the scholars of old praised his talent as a historian. He put the "Life of Po Yi" first of all the biographies because Po Yi though virtuous came to an unhappy end; he classed Hsiang Yu among the emperors because he felt that some men attained high position not necessarily owing to virtuous deeds; his accounts of Chu

---

[1] Ancient lexicon. The date of its compilation is not known.
[2] The Duke of Chou lived in the twelfth century B.C., King Hsuan in the ninth.

Yuan and Chia Yi are passionate, tragic yet restrained — he was certainly one of the greatest men of genius in recent ages.

(Book 4)

When Chu-chi, Prince of Kuangchuan, gathered together some ruffians to dig up the grave of Luan Shu, they found that the coffin and all the utensils in it had rotted. A white fox, startled by them, ran away. They tried to catch it but failed, only injuring its left paw. That night in a dream the prince saw a man with white hair and a white beard approach him. "Why did you hurt my left foot?" demanded this man. He struck at the prince's left foot.

When the prince awoke, his foot was swollen and he had a boil there which never healed till the day of his death.

(Book 6)

Ko Hung (circa 290-370) was a citizen of Kouyung in Tanyang, known for his scholarship even as a youth. He was widely read but particularly interested in the search for immortality and sainthood. In A.D. 302 he was made a general in some southern expedition, and after suppressing a rebellion was ennobled. He was a close friend of Kan Pao, who recommended him for the post of historian; but hearing that cinnabar was produced in the south, he asked for the magistracy of Koulou. When he reached Canton, he was detained by the local prefect and stayed in Lofu Mountain. He died in his sleep at the age of eighty-one. His biography appears in the *Tsin Dynasty History*. He left many works, some six hundred books in all. In his work *Pao Pu Tzu* he says that Chen Shih, a prefect of Taichiu in the Han dynasty, wrote a book called *Accounts of Marvels*. And he quotes a story from this about Chang Kuang-ting, a native of his own district who left his four-year-old daughter in an ancient grave during some war. Three years later he went back to find her still alive, in a state of suspended animation. But since this work by Chen Shih is not mentioned in other historical records and this story sounds like one of the alchemist's tales, it was probably spurious. Though Ko Hung lived not long after the Han dynasty, he was so obsessed by the search for immortality that not all his statements are reliable.

The Private Life of Lady Swallow, dealing with the famous Han dynasty imperial concubine[1] and her sister, was attributed to Ling Hsuan, tribune of Hotung. Since the Sung historian Ssuma Kuang used an allusion from this about water extinguishing fire in his *Mirror of History,* he no doubt believed it to be a Han dynasty record. I think it is more likely that it was written in the Tang or Sung dynasty. There was also the *Secret Tales of the Han Palace,* which describes how Liang Chi's sister came to be chosen as empress,[2] and this has a preface by the Ming dynasty scholar Yang Shen, who says that this ancient text was found in the possession of a prefect of Anning named Wan; but Shen Teh-fu[3] thought that this was written by Yang Shen himself for his own diversion.

---

[1] She became empress in 18 B.C.
[2] In A.D. 147.
[3] A seventeenth century scholar.

搜神記卷二

晉干寶撰　明沈士龍胡震亨同校

壽光侯者漢章帝時人也能劾百鬼衆魅令自
縛見形其鄉人有婦為魅所病侯為劾之得
大蛇數丈死於門外婦因以安又有大樹樹
有精人止其下者死鳥過之亦墜侯劾之樹
盛夏枯落有大蛇長七八丈懸死樹間章帝
聞之徵問對曰有之帝曰殿下有怪夜半後
常有數人絳衣被髮持火相隨豈能劾之侯

An old edition of the *Records of Spirits* published about 1603

5. TALES OF THE SUPERNATURAL IN THE SIX DYNASTIES

Shamanism was widespread in ancient China and during the Chin and Han dynasties there was much talk of spirits and saints, while the end of the Han dynasty saw a great increase in shaman worship so that superstition was rife. Then Hinayana Buddhism came to China to spread by degrees. Since these various religions had much to say about spirits and miracles, the fourth, fifth and sixth centuries produced many works dealing with the supernatural. Some were written by scholars, other by religious devotees. Though the scholars differed from the professed Buddhists and Taoists whose aim was to spread their religion, they were not writing fiction either. The men of that age believed that although the ways of mortals were not those of spirits, none the less spirits existed. So they recorded these tales of the supernatural in the same way as anecdotes about men and women, not viewing the former as fiction and the latter as fact.

The biographical section of the *Sui Dynasty History* mentions the *Tales of Marvels* in three books by Tsao Pei, Emperor Wen Ti of Wei.[1] Though this is lost, the abundant quotations from it in other works have preserved for us some of its tales, all of which, according to the *Sui Dynasty History*, dealt with ghosts and marvels. Some stories date from the middle of the third century

---

[1]Who ruled from A.D. 220 to 226.

after the death of Tsao Pei. Perhaps these were subsequent interpolations, or the book was written by a later man who used Emperor Wen Ti's name. The *Tang Dynasty History* gives the author as Chang Hua of the Tsin dynasty, but there is no evidence to support this view either. It seems likely that some later scholar, realizing the inconsistency in the date, made this arbitrary change in authorship. At all events, since this work was quoted by Pei Sung-chih[1] in his commentary to the *History of the Three Kingdoms* and by Li Tao-yuan[2] in his commentary to the *Book of Waterways*, it must date from the Wei or Tsin dynasty.

When Tsung Ting-po of Nanyang was young, he met a ghost one night as he was walking.

"Who are you?" he asked.

"A ghost, sir. Who are you?"

"A ghost like yourself," lied Tsung.

"Where are you going?"

"To the city."

"So am I."

They went on together for a mile or so.

"Walking is most exhausting. Why not carry each other in turn?" suggested the ghost.

"A good idea," agreed Tsung.

First the ghost carried him for some distance.

"How heavy you are!" said the ghost. "Are you really a spectre?"

"I am a new ghost," answered Tsung. "That is why I am heavier than usual."

---

[1] A fifth century scholar.
[2] A late fifth century scholar.

Then he carried the ghost, which was no weight at all. And so they went on, changing several times.

"I am a new ghost," said Tsung presently. "I don't know what we spectres are most afraid of."

"Being spat at by men — that is all." . . .

As they approached the city, Tsung threw the ghost over his shoulder and held it tight. The ghost gave a screech and begged to be put down, but Tsung would not listen and made straight for the market. When he set the ghost down it had turned into a goat. He promptly sold it, having first spat at it to prevent it changing its form again. Then he left the richer by one thousand five hundred coins.

(From the *Tai-ping Imperial Encyclopaedia*)

The goddess Ma Ku came down to the house of Tsai Ching of Tungyang, and she had finger nails four inches long. Tsai thought: "This woman has the most beautiful hands — I wish she would scratch my back for me." The goddess flew into a rage, and Tsai fell to the ground with blood streaming from his eyes.

(From the *Tai-ping Imperial Encyclopaedia*)

On the North Mountain of Hsinhsien in Wuchang is a stone boulder called the Waiting Wife, which looks like a woman. Legend has it that in ancient times a man was conscripted to fight far away from home. His devoted wife, leading their young child, saw him off to the hill and stood there gazing after him till she turned into stone.

(From the *Tai-ping Imperial Encyclopaedia*)

Literary forgers after the Tsin dynasty ascribed tales on wonders in distant lands to Chang Hua, just as those about saints and paradise were attributed to Tungfang

Shuo. Chang Hua or Chang Mao-hsien was a citizen of Fangcheng in Fanyang Prefecture. He was appointed a doctor of ceremony at the beginning of the Wei dynasty. During the Tsin dynasty he became minister of works and Lord of Chuangwu. In A.D. 300, at the age of sixty-nine, he was killed in the rebellion of the Prince of Chao and his clan was wiped out. His biography appears in the *Tsin Dynasty History*. Since Chang Hua was interested in mystic lore, read numerous books on magic and alchemy, could interpret good omens and bad and was known for his erudition, many legends were attributed to him. Wang Chia in his *Forgotten Tales* says that Chang Hua collected forgotten anecdotes from many sources starting with the beginning of language and going on to stories of spirits and marvels as well as the gossip of the villages. He compiled his *Records of Strange Things* in four hundred books and presented it to Emperor Wu Ti of the Tsin dynasty, who ordered him to cut out dubious passages and divide the work into ten volumes. The edition we have today, however, contains anecdotes about marvels, strange lands and ancient legends taken from other books, with nothing new. Hence it does not live up to its name. Perhaps this is not the original work but a later compilation. This applies to most of the *hsiao-shuo* which have come down from that period.

According to the *Records of Chou*, the Western Regions once presented cloth that could withstand fire while Kunwu presented a sword that could cut jade. When this cloth was soiled it needed only to be cleaned in fire, while jade cut by that sword became soft as wax. The same cloth was presented to the court in the Han dynasty, but no such sword was ever heard of.

(Book 2)

Take a turtle, cut it into pieces as large as chessmen and mix these with the juice of amaranth. Wrap them in straw and throw them into a pond in summer. After ten days all the pieces will turn into small turtles.

(Book 4)

Prince Tan of the state of Yen went as a hostage to the state of Chin. . . . When he asked the king's permission to return home, the king would not hear of it and said jokingly: "You may go when the crow's head turns white and the horse grows horns." Prince Tan looked up and sighed, whereupon the crow turned white. He lowered his head and lamented, whereupon the horse grew horns. So the king of Chin was forced to send him back. The king set a man-trap on the bridge, however, hoping to catch the prince. But Tan galloped past too fast for it to trap him. At the pass he found the gate locked, but he crowed like a cock whereupon all the cocks crowed, and so he made good his escape.

(Book 8)

Lao Tzu said: The fate of the myriad people is governed by the Queen Mother of the West. Only kings, sages, saints, fairies and holy men are controlled by the Nine Lords of Heaven.

(Book 9)

Kan Pao or Kan Ling-sheng was a citizen of Hsintsai. After the imperial historians' office was set up in the Tsin dynasty he served as a compiler; but because his family was poor he asked for a provincial post and became magistrate of Shanyin, then governor of Shihan. Subsequently he was promoted to be secretary of the minister of education and later court adviser. (This was in the fourth century.) His *Annals of the Tsin Dynasty* in twenty volumes was highly praised by his contemporaries. He was interested in divination and alchemy and declared that after one of his father's slave-girls and his elder brother came back to life after death, and claimed to have seen the gods, he compiled his *Records of Spirits* in twenty books to prove the existence of supernatural beings. All this is related in his biography in the *Tsin Dynasty History*. The existing *Records of Spirits* in twenty books is not his work. Apart from deities, miracles and transformations, it deals largely with oracles and the search for immortality and shows traces of Buddhist influence.

During the Han dynasty, Chou Shih of Hsiapi was on his way to Tunghai when he met an officer carrying a book, who asked for a lift on his boat. A dozen *li* or so further on, the officer said to Chou: "I have a call to make. I shall leave this book on board, but don't open it!"

After he had left, Chou opened the book and found there the names of men about to die. His own name was in this list. Soon the officer came back and found him reading.

"I told you not to look," he said angrily. "Why didn't you do as I said?"

Chou Shih kowtowed until his head was bleeding.

Presently the officer said: "I am grateful to you for a lift, but I can't take your name off that list. When you get home don't leave the house for three years, then you will escape. Don't say anything about my book."

Upon Chou Shih's return he stayed within doors for more than two years, to the astonishment of his family. Then one of the neighbours died, and Chou's wrathful father insisted that he should go to offer condolences — he had to obey. As he was leaving the door, the same officer appeared.

"I warned you not to leave the house for three years, but you have come out again. What can I do? I want to keep out of trouble and avoid a beating, and now that I have seen you what other course can I take? Three days from now at noon I shall come for you." . . .

Three days later at noon Chou saw the officer coming and gave up the ghost.

(Book 5)

Yuan Chan, whose other name was Chien-li, maintained that there were no ghosts, and no one could convince him otherwise. He insisted that he knew the truth. One day a stranger presented himself, and after exchanging the usual courtesies they fell to discussing philosophy. This stranger showed himself skilled in argument. Yuan Chan talked with him at length, but when they touched on spirits both grew heated. Finally the stranger was defeated in argument and losing his temper said:

"Even sages of old have written of deities and ghosts: how can you deny their existence? Your humble servant is a ghost!"

He changed into a monstrous form and vanished.

Yuan was silent and changed colour. A year after that he died.

(Book 16)

In Chiaohu Temple there was a jade pillow with a small opening in it. Once Yang Lin, a merchant and citizen of Shanfu, came here to pray for good fortune and the priest asked: "Do you want to make a good marriage?"

"I certainly do," said Yang.

Then the priest bade him enter the pillow, and creeping through the opening he saw vermilion pavilions and splendid mansions. A Marshal Chao there married his daughter to him and she bore him six children, all their sons becoming imperial secretaries. Yang stayed there for dozens of years with no thought of return till one day without warning, as if awaking from a dream, he found himself back by the pillow. Long did he grieve.

(Quoted in the *Tai-ping Geographical Record*)

There is a *Sequel to Records of Spirits* in ten books, attributed to Tao Chien the Tsin dynasty poet. This work, which is still available, deals like the last with spirits and miracles. But since Tao Chien was an enlightened and rational man who probably gave little thought to deities and ghosts, it is likely that someone else made use of his name.

Kan Pao, whose other name was Kan Ling-sheng, was a native of Hsintsai. His father Kan Ying had a favourite concubine, but the wife was so jealous that when her husband died she pushed this woman alive into the tomb. Kao Pao and his brother were too young to understand. Ten years later when their mother died and they happened to open the tomb, they found the concubine lying upon the coffin, to all appearances alive. Going closer, they discovered that she was still warm. They carried her home and the next day she came to herself. She informed them that their father had constantly brought her food and drink and slept with her, loving her just as in life. He had told her all the family news, and investigation proved that all of it was true. She survived for several years. Kan Pao's brother often fell ill, losing consciousness for days at a time, though he remained warm and came to himself again. It seems that during these trances he saw spirits and deities of heaven and of earth: all was like a dream and he did not know he had died.

(Book 4)

In the Tsin dynasty there lived a man named Chou Tzu-wen of Chiao Prefecture whose home was in Tsinling. This young man was fond of hunting. One day in a mountain valley he saw a giant fifty to sixty feet tall with a bow and arrows in his hand. The arrow heads were more than two feet across, gleaming like snow. Suddenly the giant called: "Ah Chu!" — this was Chou's childhood name — and without thinking he answered. Then the giant raised his bow and aimed at Chou, who fell under a spell.

(Book 7)

Other Tsin dynasty works were *Hsun's Records of Ghosts and Spirits,* Lu's *Forest of Marvels, Discerning the Marvels* by Tai Tso, *Accounts of Marvels* by Tsu Chung-chih and *Records of Marvels* by Tsu Tai-chih. There were many other books by Kung, Chih, Tsao Pi and others, but nothing is left of these except some quotations. The existing *Accounts of Marvels* attributed to Jen Fang of the Liang dynasty is a Tang or Sung dynasty work, which explains why it is not quoted by Tang dynasty writers.

Liu Ching-shu (circa 390-470) of Pengcheng, who distinguished himself by his brilliance even as a youth, became secretary of Nanping at the end of the Tsin dynasty. In the kingdom of Sung he was a palace steward, but after some years he resigned on account of ill health and returned home to die. His *Garden of Marvels* is well known. Ten books of this are left, but they must have undergone re-editing too.

During the Wei dynasty the great bell in front of the palace tolled without warning by itself, and all men marvelled. They questioned Chang Hua, who said: "There has been a landslide in the copper hills of Shu: the bell simply echoed it." Later, officials of Shu Prefecture reported a landslide just as Chang Hua had foretold.

(Book 2)

During the Yi Hsi period (405-418), a serving-maid named Lan in the Hsu family of Tunghai turned unaccountably pale and wan, yet paid more attention to her appearance than usual. When the family kept a secret watch on her, they saw the broom go from its corner to the maid's bed. Then they burned the broom and the serving-maid recovered.

(Book 8)

In the nineteenth year of the Tai Yuan period (A.D. 394) Huan Shan of Poyang sacrificed a dog to some mountain deity, but the meat was not well cooked and the angry god sent a message through the shaman:

"Huan Shan has offered me uncooked meat. He must be punished by eating such meat himself." That year Huan Shan was transformed into a tiger. Before this change he saw someone threw a spotted skin over him, after which he leaped up and became a man-devouring beast.

(Book 8)

Liu Yung of Tungkuan liked the taste of the scabs which grow over sores and claimed that they resembled some fish like the perch. One day he called on Meng Ling-hsiu who was suffering from mange, and picked up some scabs from his bed to eat. Meng was astounded but pulled off his other scabs to offer Liu. When Liu was Governor of Nankang he had more than two hundred officers under him and it was his habit, whether they did wrong or not, to whip them in turn. He would then eat the scabs which formed over their welts.

(Book 10)

Liu Yi-ching, Prince of Linchuan (403-444), was a man of quiet temperament and a lover of literature. He left many works including *Records of Light and Dark* in thirty books, which was classified with historical anecdotes in the *Sui Dynasty History* but with *hsiao-shuo* in the *Tang Dynasty History*. Though this work is lost, many quotations from it can be found in other books. It is also full of tales of the supernatural, apparently not written by the prince but collected from earlier writings. It was popular in the Tang dynasty, and according to the historian Liu Chih-chi was used as a source book by the compilers of the *Tsin Dynasty History*.

Tungyang Wu-yi, a court officer of the kingdom of Sung, left *Tales of Chi Hsieh* in seven books. The name is recorded in the *Sui Dynasty History*, but the work has disappeared. Wu Chun (469-520) of the Liang period wrote a *Sequel to Tales of Chi Hsieh* which still exists but has been re-edited. Wu Chun or Wu Shu-yang was a native of Kuchang in Wuhsing. At the beginning of the sixth century he was successively secretary of Wuhsing, an officer under the Prince of Chienan and a palace tribune. He was discharged for a fault in the compilation of some annals of the kingdom of Chi, but later recalled to compile a general history. He died before it was finished at the age of fifty-two, and his biography appears in the *Liang Dynasty History*. Since Wu Chun was a well-known poet with a distinctive style, he had many imitators. His tales and anecdotes have a literary flavour and were used as allusions by Tang and Sung dynasty scholars. "The Scholar by the Roadside" is one of his best stories:

> Travelling through the Suian hills, Hsu Yen of Yanghsien came upon a scholar of seventeen or eighteen. The young man, who was lying by the roadside, explained that his feet hurt and asked for a lift in the goose cage which Hsu was carrying. At first Hsu thought he was joking. But the scholar got into the cage, which looked no larger than before while the scholar looked no smaller. He sat down quietly beside the two geese and they appeared not to mind. Hsu picked up the cage again, but found it no heavier. Further on he stopped to rest under a tree and the scholar, coming out of the cage, offered to treat him to a meal. When Hsu accepted with pleasure, the

scholar took from his mouth a copper tray laid with all manner of delicacies: the utensils were of copper, the food rarely flavoured and savoury.

After several cups of wine the scholar told Hsu: "I have a girl with me. May I ask her to join us?"

"Certainly!"

Then from his mouth the scholar produced a girl of not more than sixteen, richly dressed and amazingly lovely, who sat down and feasted with them. Presently, slightly tipsy, the scholar went to lie down.

"Though this is my husband," the girl confided to Hsu, "as a matter of fact I hate him. I have brought my lover with me and shall call him out now that my husband is sleeping. Please don't say anything!"

"Certainly not," agreed Hsu.

Then the girl produced from her mouth an intelligent and charming man in his early twenties, who exchanged polite small talk with Hsu till the scholar started to wake and called her over — she had hidden her lover with a silk screen from her mouth.

The young man now told Hsu: "Though that girl dotes on me, I don't care for her. I have brought another girl with me and would like to have her out. But please keep this to yourself."

"Of course!"

He took from his mouth a young woman of twenty or thereabouts, with whom he drank and amused himself till the scholar could be heard stirring.

"Those two have finished sleeping," said the young man, and popped the young woman back into his mouth.

In a moment the girl came back and said to Hsu: "The scholar is getting up." She swallowed her friend and sat alone with Hsu.

Then the scholar came out and told him: "I am sorry I slept so long. You must have been bored sitting here all by yourself. As it is growing late, I will say goodbye."

With that he swallowed the girl and the utensils, leaving only the large copper tray as a gift for Hsu. This tray was some two feet across, and in parting the scholar said: "I have nothing worth giving you, but keep this as a souvenir."

During the Tai Yuan period (376-396) Hsu served as an adviser in the Imperial Library and showed this tray to Minister Chang San, who discovered from the inscription that it was made in the third year of Yung Ping (A.D. 60).

But these fancies were not Chinese originally. As Tuan Cheng-shih pointed out, they came from India. Thus in the *Yuyang Miscellany* he says: "In a certain Buddhist parable there is a Brahman who conjures up a pot from his mouth, and in this pot are a girl and a screen. When the Brahman falls asleep, the girl takes a pot with a man in it from her own mouth and dallies with the man. When the Brahman wakes, he swallows them one after another and goes off carrying his staff. I fancy Wu Chun read this and found it a good story." The Buddhist parable he had in mind could be found in the *Samyukta-avadana-sutra*, translated by Kang Senghui in the Three Kingdoms period and still extant. Actually this story has other versions too: for example in the *Samadhi-sagara-sutra* there is this description of

Buddha's hair: "There are a myriad rays of light in his hair, which shine with indescribable radiance. Each ray of light contains an image of Buddha practising the Truth, each identical with Buddha himself; yet the Buddhas in these hairs grow no smaller, nor the hairs larger." Here is evidently another version of this story. From the time of the Wei and Tsin dynasties onward, more and more Buddhist scriptures were translated until Indian stories spread throughout China. Since scholars enjoyed these strange tales they adopted them consciously or unconsciously, until these stories became Chinese. For instance, in Hsun's *Records of Ghosts and Spirits* in the Tsin dynasty there is also a story of a priest who enters a cage, which the author admits is a tale from abroad. By Wu Chun's time it has become Chinese.

> In the twelfth year of the Tai Yuan period (387) there came a priest from abroad who could swallow knives, spit fire, and produce jewels, gold and silver from his mouth. His master, so he said, was a Brahman and not a Buddhist. One day on the road he met a man carrying a shoulder-pole from which hung a cage just large enough for a peck or so of grain.
> The priest said to the carrier: "I am tired of walking, will you carry me?"
> The carrier thought the priest must be out of his mind. "As you like," he said. . . .
> The priest got into the cage, yet the cage did not grow larger nor the priest smaller, neither did the carrier find his load any heavier. After several dozen *li*, the carrier stopped to eat under a tree and invited the priest to join him. But the priest said: "I have food," and would not come out. . . .

While taking his meal he told the carrier: "I want to eat with my wife." So he took from his mouth a well-dressed beautiful woman of about twenty, and they had their meal together.

After the meal the priest went to sleep, and the woman said to the carrier: "I have a lover who is coming to eat with me. Don't tell my husband when he wakes."

She produced a young man from her mouth and they ate together. So now there were three people in the cage, yet it was no larger, nor the people smaller. Soon the priest stirred as if about to wake, and the woman put her lover in her mouth. When the priest woke he said to the carrier: "It is time to go." He put first the woman, then the food vessels, into his mouth. . . .

(From the *Tai-ping Imperial Encyclopaedia*)

6. TALES OF THE SUPERNATURAL IN THE SIX DYNASTIES *(Continued)*

The *Sui Dynasty History* mentions nine Buddhist works and classifies them as philosophy and history. The only one left is Yen Chih-tui's *Accounts of Avenging Spirits*, which draws on classical lore and history to prove the doctrine of divine retribution, and already in this we see Buddhism beginning to be blended with Confucianism. All the other titles quoted are lost, but we have fragments of the following four: Liu Yi-ching's *Records of Divine Evidence*, Wang Yen's *Records of Mysterious Manifestations*, Yen Chih-tui's *Collected Tales of Miracles* and Hou Pai's *Stories Exemplifying Marvels*. All these works recorded miracles concerning Buddhist scriptures and images to impress the laity and convert them to Buddhism by convincing them that miracles did take place. But later ages considered these as works of fiction. Wang Yen was a native of Taiyuan in the fifth century, who became a Buddhist as a child in Chiaochih. After witnessing two "miracles," he wrote ten books recording prodigies concerning Buddhist images, scriptures and pagodas, entitling this work *Records of Mysterious Manifestations*. Here he gave detailed accounts of his own experiences. Many of his excellent narratives have been preserved in *Gems of Buddhist Literature* and the *Tai-ping Miscellany*. Here are three examples:

Emperor Ming of the Han dynasty saw in a dream a god nearly twenty feet in height, with a golden body and a circle of light at his neck. He asked his ministers the meaning of this dream and was told: "In the west there is a deity called Buddha which resembles the god of Your Majesty's dream. Perhaps that was the one." So the emperor sent envoys to India to obtain Buddhist scriptures and images.

When these scriptures and images were displayed in China, the emperor, princes and nobles worshipped Buddha, and were amazed to learn that the spirit is immortal. After the return of the envoy Tsai Ying with the monks from the west, Kasyapa Matanga and another monk, who brought an image of Buddha painted by the King of Udhyana, the emperor recognized the god of his dream and ordered painters to make several reproductions which were kept in Chingliang Tower in the South Palace and at the imperial sepulchre by Kaoyang Gate. Moreover, on the walls of the White Horse Monastery they painted horses and carriages circling the pagoda in accordance with the records.

(From *Gems of Buddhist Literature*)

Hsieh Fu of the Tsin dynasty, whose other name was Hsieh Ching-hsu, was a native of Shanyin in Kuaichi. . . . He was a high-minded youth who went to live as a hermit on the Eastern Hill, and believing in the great Buddhist religion he was indefatigable in practising his faith. He made a copy of the *Surangama-sutra* which was kept in the White Horse Monastery. When the monastery caught fire and all other objects and scriptures were destroyed, this sutra was merely singed at the edges so that the text remained complete and undamaged. At Hsieh Fu's death his friends believed that he must have become a saint, and learning about the sutra they were more amazed.

(From *Gems of Buddhist Literature*)

In the Tsin dynasty lived a man named Chao Tai or Chao Wen-ho, a citizen of Peichiu in Chingho. . . . While in his thirty-fifth year he had a sudden pain in the chest and died. His corpse was laid on the ground, and since his heart remained warm and his flesh soft, the body was kept for ten days. Then one morning, with a gurgling in his throat, he revived. He related that when he was newly dead one man approached his heart and two others rode up on yellow horses followed by two attendants. They carried him eastward for some distance to a great city with high, magnificent buildings and dark walls. They took him through the city gate and past two lesser gates. There were thousands of tiled buildings and thousands of men and women ranged in rows. Five or six officers in dark robes were registering the names and announced that their list would be examined by the lord of that place. Chao's name was thirtieth on the list. Soon he and several thousand others went inside. The official, who was sitting facing west, looked through the list of names and sent Chao Tai southward through a black gate. There another official in red was seated before a great hall, calling the roll. He asked Chao:

"What did you do in life? What sins have you committed? What good deeds have you done? I shall weigh your words carefully: see that you speak the truth! I have six messengers constantly in the world of men to record their virtues and sins. Since we have complete records, it is no use for you to lie."

Chao Tai answered: "My father and elder brother were officials of the two thousand picul rank. As I was still young and remained at home to study, I had no post and have committed no sins."

Then Chao was made an official in charge of water conservancy. . . . After this he was promoted to an inspectorate in the Penal Ministry and given troops and horses to inspect Hell. The dungeons he visited used every conceivable torture: there were prisoners whose tongues were pierced with needles so that they were streaming with blood, others with dishevelled hair and no clothes upon them were being driven along by officers brandishing great clubs. There were red-hot beds of iron and pillars of bronze, and men were forced to lie on these beds or grasp these pillars; but when they were burned to death they revived again. . . . Huge sword-trees grew on all sides, their stems and leaves like knives; yet men fought to climb such trees as if in sport, though their limbs and heads were severed or cut to pieces inch by inch. Chao saw his grandfather, grandmother and two brothers in this prison, and at sight of him they wept.

As Chao left the gate of Hell two men with documents approached the warder to inform him that the families of three of the inmates had hung up pennons and burned incense in various temples to redeem their kinsmen's sins, so that now they could leave and go to a happier region. Then Chao saw three prisoners leave Hell: decently dressed they passed through a gate in the south called the Hall of Enlightenment. . . .

Chao, having completed his inspection, went back to the ministry. . . .
The official in charge said: "Because you had done no wrong we made you an inspector. If not for that, you would have been tortured with the rest."
Chao asked: "How must a man live to have happiness after death?"
The official told him: "If you are a zealous disciple of Buddha and observe the rules, you will find happiness after death and be spared all punishment."
Chao asked again: "Suppose a man has sinned before he embraces religion, can his sins be forgiven after he becomes a Buddhist?"
The official answered: "All will be forgiven."
This said, the official opened his casket to look up Chao's age and found that he had another thirty years to live. Accordingly he dismissed him. . . .
This happened on the thirteenth day of the seventh month in the fifth year of the Tai Shih period (A.D. 269).

(From *Gems of Buddhist Literature*)

As Buddhism spread and more scriptures were introduced, there came to be various interpretations of them. Some men embraced religion because life was transient, others were dismayed by the teaching that all is vanity, and to attract these the alchemists invented different scriptures or strange tales about the search for immortality and elixirs. All the *hsiao-shuo* attributed to Han dynasty writers, apart from a few by men of letters, seem to belong to this category. The alchemists who wrote books usually attributed them to famous men of ancient times, thus we find few names belonging to the Six

Dynasties. But the lost *Records of Miracles* which is quoted in later books was written by Wang Fu, a Tsin dynasty Taoist reputed to be a vain and foolish man. During the reign of Emperor Huei Ti, towards the end of the third century, he held disputations with the monk Pai Yuan and was refuted time and again. Then he forged records and invented the legend that Lao Tzu visited the Western Regions and became a Buddha. His work seems to deal entirely with saints and spirits like others of this kind.

During the reign of Sun Hao (264-280), Chen Min was appointed Governor of Chianghsia. He was on his way to his post from Nanking when he heard that men's prayers were often granted at the shrine in Kungting. So thither he went to pray for a peaceful term of office, promising to present a silver staff. Having served his term, he had a staff made of iron plated with silver. When he was transferred to the capital as a court steward, he passed Kungting and presented the staff at the shrine before proceeding on his journey. That evening the witch at the shrine made this pronouncement: "Chen Min promised me a silver staff but has sent me one plated with silver. I shall throw it into the water to return it to him. He is guilty of the unpardonable sin of deceit." When men examined the staff, they found it made of iron and duly threw it into the lake. Then the staff floated on the water and made off as swift as flight to Chen Min's boat, so that the vessel capsized.

(From the *Tai-ping Imperial Encyclopaedia*)

A great tea-plant grows in Tanchiu; people taking it become winged immortals.

(From the *Tai-ping Imperial Encyclopaedia*)

Forgotten Tales in ten books is attributed to Wang Chia of the Tsin dynasty, and was edited by Hsiao Yi of the Liang dynasty. Wang Chia's name appears in the *Tsin Dynasty History*. His other name was Wang Tzu-nien, and he was a native of Anyang in Lunghsi. After living as a hermit in Tungyang Valley he went to Changan, but when King Fu Chien invited him to join the government he declined. He had the gift of prophecy and spoke in riddles. When Yao Chang entered Changan he forced Wang Chia to follow him; but later enraged by one of Wang's answers he had him killed. This was approximately in the year 390. Wang has left some oracles and this *Forgotten Tales*, all ten books of which are still extant and deal largely with marvels. The existing text has a preface by Hsiao Yi stating that there were originally nineteen books with two hundred and twenty items; but this was lost in the general destruction of books at that time, and the work is now incomplete. It was Hsiao Yi who redivided it into ten books. The first nine books of his edition cover all history from the legendary emperor Fu Hsi up to the Eastern Tsin dynasty, while the last deals with the Nine Fairy Mountains. There is a discrepancy between this and the statement in the preface that the book ends with the fall of the Western Tsin dynasty. The language is somewhat ornate and there is no truth in any of the tales, while even Hsiao Yi's preface is based on hearsay. The Ming dynasty scholar Hu Ying-lin suspected that this work was actually written by Hsiao Yi in Wang Chia's name.

Emperor Shao Hao reigned by virtue of the "metal" element. His mother was Huang Ngo who wove at night in the Heavenly Palace and drifted by day in a barge through the boundless waters of Chiungsang. There was then an angel of surpassing beauty, the son of the White Emperor. He was the spirit of the Morning Star, who came to the stream and sported with Huang Ngo, playing haunting melodies and lingering there, forgetting to return. Chiungsang lies on the shore of the Western Ocean. There grows a solitary mulberry tree which rises tens of thousands of feet; its leaves are red, its berries purple, it bears fruit once in ten thousand years, and whoever eats its mulberries will outlive Heaven. . . . The Morning Star and Huang Ngo sat together playing a cithern of cedar wood, and leaning upon it the girl sang:

> How vast the azure sky, how wide earth's range,
> A myriad times all living things must change;
> We gaze upon the water and the sky,
> And sunbeams sparkle as our barge floats by;
> We come at last to Chiungsang's borders sweet,
> Our hearts at peace, our happiness complete.

A lovers' trysting-place is commonly called Sangchung. Thus the *Book of Songs* says: "Meet me at Sangchung." . . .

When Huang Ngo gave birth to Shao Hao, the emperor's clan name was Chiungsang or Sangchiu. In the Warring States Period, Sangchiu Tzu, who wrote works on divination, was descended from this clan.

(Book 1)

At the end of Emperor Cheng Ti's reign (32-7 B.C.) Liu Hsiang laboured hard with singleness of purpose

to edit books in Tienlu Pavilion. One night an old
man in yellow with a green stick came to the pavilion.
Seeing Liu Hsiang reading in the dark he blew on the
top of his stick, which burst into flame. Then he
spoke to Liu Hsiang of things before the creation of
heaven and earth, and Liu Hsiang learned the ancient
texts from him, tearing strips of silk from his gown
to write them down for fear he forget them. The old
man left at dawn. When Liu Hsiang asked his name,
the old man said: "I am the spirit of the star Tai-yi.
The Emperor of Heaven heard that there was a learned
man in the Liu family and sent me down to see you."
He took bamboo tablets from his pocket, saying:
"These are records of heaven and maps of the earth
which I am giving you." Later Liu Hsiang's son, Liu
Hsin, learned all this from his father; but Liu Hsiang
never knew who the old man was.

(Book 6)

Tungting Hill floats on the lake. At its foot are
hundreds of gilded halls where the jade virgins dwell,
and music in every season carries to the crest of the
hill. King Huai of Chu made talented men compose
poems by the lake. . . . Later King Huai gave ear
to evil ministers and all the good men fled. Chu Yuan,
dismissed for his loyalty, lived as a hermit among the
weeds, consorting with birds and beasts and having no
traffic with the world. He ate cypress nuts and mixed
them with cassia oil to cultivate his heart till, hounded
by the king, he drowned himself in the limpid stream.
The people of Chu mourned his loss bitterly and believed he had become a water saint. His spirit wanders

through the Milky Way, descending on occasion to the River Hsiang. The people of Chu set up a shrine for him which was still standing at the end of the Han dynasty.

(Book 10)

世說新語卷下之上

宋 臨川王義慶 撰

梁 劉孝標 注

容止第十四

魏武將見匈奴使自以形陋不足雄遠國使崔季珪代帝自捉刀立牀頭既畢令間諜問曰魏王何如匈奴使答曰魏王雅望非常然牀頭捉刀人此乃英雄也魏武聞之追殺此使

何平叔美姿儀面至白魏明帝疑其傳粉正夏月與

An old edition of the *New Anecdotes of Social Talk* published about 1535

7. *SOCIAL TALK* AND OTHER WORKS

Scholars towards the end of the Han dynasty attached great importance to definitions of character: fame or infamy might depend on a single expression of praise or condemnation. From the third and fourth centuries onwards, much thought was also given to the choice of words in conversation: men's talk was metaphysical and their behaviour unconventional and liberal, differing in these respects from the Han dynasty when absolute moral integrity and rectitude were the ideal. This was due to the spread of Buddhism which advocated otherworldliness, as well as to the popularity of Taoism. Rebels against Buddhism might turn to Taoism, but the escapist tendency was the same; for these two religions which warred against each other also played into each other's hands. And so arose the fashion of "liberal talk." After the house of Tsin moved its capital south of the Yangtse, this fashion became even more pronounced and none but a few men of distinction stood out against it. Since this was the vogue, anecdotes and sayings were compiled from ancient records or contemporary society. Though these works contain nothing but an assortment of *bons mots* and dictums, they reflect the spirit of the age and they developed into a literary genre distinct from the tales of the supernatural.

Accounts of different individuals had an early origin and can be found in *Lieh Tzu* and *Han Fei Tzu*. But Lieh Tzu used them as parables to illustrate his philosophy, Han Fei Tzu to expound political ideas. Anecdotes were not written purely for amusement until the Wei dynasty, attaining their height in the Tsin dynasty. Though recorded sayings which followed the fashion of the time might be held up as models, they were designed more for entertainment than practical use. In the year 362, a Tsin dynasty scholar named Pei Chi of Hotung compiled an anthology of famous sayings from the Han dynasty to his day, calling it the *Forest of Sayings*. This enjoyed considerable popularity until Hsieh An[1] condemned it for quoting him wrongly. Later, however, the work continued to be mentioned from time to time. There were ten books in all but by the Sui dynasty these were lost. Some quotations can still be found in other books.

Lou Hu or Lou Chun-ching was a guest of the five marquises, and every day all five of them sent him food. Growing tired of such rich fare, he tried mixing the fish and meat sent by the five together and the result proved delicious. This was the origin of the "Five Marquises Dish."

(From the *Tai-ping Miscellany*)

Tsao Tsao said: "Let no one come near me when I am sleeping, or I shall cut him down without knowing what I do. Take good care, all of you!" One cold day when he was pretending to be asleep, his favourite page slipped in to cover him and Tsao Tsao struck him dead. After that no one dared go near him.

(From the *Tai-ping Imperial Encyclopaedia*)

---

[1] A famous Tsin dynasty statesman of the fourth century.

Chung Kuai once told people: "I wrote something when I was young which was generally believed to be by Yuan Chi, and men found each word full of meaning. When they knew that I was the author, they said no more."

(From the *Sequel to a Guide to Conversation*)

Tsu Na and Chung Ya used to deride each other.

Chung said to Tsu: "We men from south of the river are as sharp as awls, you from the north are blunt as pestles."

Tsu retorted: "My blunt pestle can smash your sharp awl."

Said Chung: "This is a magic awl which cannot be smashed."

Said Tsu: "If there are magic awls, there must be magic pestles too."

So Chung was silenced.

(From the *Tai-ping Imperial Encyclopaedia*)

Wang Hui-chih once lodged for a short time in someone's empty house and ordered bamboos to be planted there. A man asked why he went to such trouble when he would not be there long. After chanting poems for a while, Wang pointed at the bamboo and asked: "Can one live a single day without this gentleman?"

(From the *Tai-ping Imperial Encyclopaedia*)

The *Sui Dynasty History* mentions another work called *Kuo Tzu* in three books by Kuo Cheng-chih of the Eastern Tsin dynasty, and the *Tang Dynasty History* records that this work had a commentary by Chia Chuan. *Kuo Tzu* is lost, but judging by fragments left it was not unlike the *Forest of Sayings*.

Prince Liu Yi-ching (403-444) of the Sung period wrote *Social Talk* in eight books, and Liu Hsiao-piao added notes to make ten books. Now three books are extant under the title *New Anecdotes of Social Talk*. This text was edited by Yen Shu of the Sung dynasty who cut out some of the notes; but we do not know who changed the title. In the Tang dynasty it was also called *New Sayings*. Probably the name was altered and the words "new anecdotes" added to distinguish it from *Social Talk* listed by Liu Hsiang of the Han dynasty. The present edition of *New Anecdotes of Social Talk* has thirty-eight books dealing with different subjects such as "Virtuous Behaviour," "Personal Enmity" and so forth. It covers the period from the Later Han to the Eastern Tsin dynasty, contains metaphysical and clever sayings, records of noble or eccentric actions, as well as ridiculous errors and strange idiosyncrasies. The full and erudite notes by Liu Hsiao-piao add much to the interest of the whole. These notes are of great value, quoting as they do from more than four hundred works, most of them no longer extant. However, the contents of the *Social Talk* sometimes overlap with the *Forest of Sayings* of Kuo Tzu. Like the tales of marvels, it was probably a compilation of old records rather than an original work. Since the *Sung Dynasty History* tells us that Prince Liu Yi-ching was not a gifted writer himself but that he assembled men of letters from far and near, it is possible that this work was compiled by many hands.

When Yuan Yu was in Yen he had a fine carriage which he never refused to lend. A man wanted to borrow this carriage to bury his mother, but dared not ask for it. Yuan hearing of this sighed and said:

"Though I have a carriage men dare not borrow it. Why should I keep it?" He had the carriage burned.

(From the section "Noble Actions")

Yuan Hsiu had a great reputation, and when Marshal Wang Yen saw him he asked: "What is the difference between the teaching of Lao Tzu and Chuang Tzu and that of Confucius?" Yuan answered: "Chiang-wu-tung (might-not-same)." The marshal, impressed, made him his secretary and he was known as the Three-Word Secretary.

(From the section "Literature")

Tsu Yo amassed money, Yuan Fu collected clogs, and each saw to these things himself, sparing no pains, till it was hard to say which did the better. Someone called on Tsu and found him counting his money. The visitor walked in before Tsu had finished putting it away and two small cases were left out which he thrust behind him, with an air of confusion. Someone else called on Yuan Fu and found him waxing his clogs by the fire, murmuring to himself completely at his ease: "I wonder how many clogs I shall wear in my life?" So Yuan's superiority was established.

(From the section "Cultured Behaviour")

Society's verdict on Li Yuan-li was: "Stern as the swift wind in the pines."

(From the section "Expressions of Praise")

Kungsun Tu made this appraisal of Ping Yuan: "A white stork in the clouds cannot be trapped by a net spread for sparrows."

(From the section "Expressions of Praise")

Liu Ling was often drunk and behaved wildly, sometimes throwing off his clothes to stay naked in his room. When someone saw this and laughed, Liu Ling retorted: "Heaven and earth are my home and these rooms are my breeches. Why should other gentlemen step into my breeches?"

(From the section "Philosophical Outlook")

When Shih Chung asked friends to a feast he would order beautiful maids to serve the wine, and if any guest did not drain his cup Shih would bid his guards kill the maid. Once the chief minister Wang Tao and Marshal Wang Tun called on Shih Chung together. The chief minister had no head for wine, but he forced himself to drink till he was drunk. When it came to the marshal's turn he deliberately refused the wine to see what Shih would do. One after another three maids were killed, yet Wang did not change colour and would not drink. The chief minister remonstrated with him, but the marshal said: "He is killing his own servants: what concern is that of yours?"

(From the section "Luxurious Living")

Popular Talk in three books by Shen Yueh (441-513) of the Liang dynasty must have been rather similar, but this work is lost. Emperor Wu Ti of Liang ordered Secretary Yin Yun (471-529) to compile *Anecdotes* in thirty books, ten books of which still existed during the Sui but disappeared during the Ming dynasty. Now extracts only remain in such works as the *Sequel to a Guide to Conversation* and *Repository of Fiction*. *Anecdotes* also consisted of sayings taken from various sources, first those of emperors and kings, then sayings of different dynasties from the Chou to Southern Chi in chronological order."

In the Hsien Kang period (335-342) of the Tsin dynasty a scholar named Chou Wei died but came back to life. He related that the Heavenly Emperor had summoned him. When he was led up the steps and looked at the emperor, he saw the divinity's face was one foot across.

He asked the attendants: "Is this the Heavenly Emperor named Chang?"

The attendants answered: "The old gods have passed away: this is Emperor Ming Ti of Wei."

(From the *Red Pearl Collection*)

Emperor Hsiao Wu of Tsin (373-396) had never seen a donkey.

Hsieh An asked him: "What do you think it looks like, Your Majesty?"

The emperor put one hand over his mouth to hide a smile and said: "I suppose it must look like a pig."

(From the *Sequel to a Guide to Conversation*)

Once Confucius, travelling through the hills, sent Tzu Lu to fetch water. Tzu Lu met a tiger by the water and killed it, seizing it by the tail. Putting the tiger's tail in his pocket, he carried back the water.

Then he asked Confucius: "How would a superior man kill a tiger?"

Confucius answered: "A superior man would kill a tiger by seizing its head."

"How would an ordinary man kill a tiger?"

"An ordinary man would kill a tiger by seizing its ears."

"How would an inferior man kill a tiger?"

"An inferior man would kill a tiger by grabbing its tail."

Tzu Lu took out the tiger's tail and threw it away, saying resentfully: "The master knew that there was a tiger by the water and sent me there hoping that I would be killed." So he hid a stone in his pocket to kill Confucius.

Then he asked again: "How would a superior man kill a man?"

Confucius answered: "A superior man would kill a man with his pen."

"How would an ordinary man kill a man?"

"An ordinary man would kill a man with his tongue."

"How would an inferior man kill a man?"

"An inferior man would kill a man with a stone."

Tzu Lu went out and threw away the stone, convinced of Confucius' greatness.

(From the *Repository of Fiction*)

Master Kuei Ku wrote to Su Chin and Chang Yi: "Greetings, sirs. You are cutting brilliant figures now, but spring blossoms fade at the approach of autumn. Before long winter will be here. Old age comes on apace. Have you not seen the trees on the river bank? Serfs break off their boughs and water laps at their roots, not because such trees are hated by men but on account of their position. Have you not seen the pines and sandalwood high up in the mountains? Their leaves reach up to the blue sky above while their roots go down to the nether regions below; on top there are monkeys, below red leopards and unicorns; they live on for tens of thousands of years, felled by no axe, nor is this because such trees are dear to men but again on account of their position. Now you are seeking glory which is as fleeting as morning dew, with no thought of lasting achievements; you scorn sainthood and immortality, but prize the vain position of a passing day. The proverb says: Women's love lasts but the space of a feast, men's friendship but the time for a drive. Alas, my friends, I am distressed for you!

(From the *Sequel to a Guide to Conversation*)

The bibliographical section of the *Sui Dynasty History* also mentions the *Forest of Jokes* in three books by Hantan Chun of the Later Han dynasty. Hantan Chun's life is given in the *Later Han Dynasty History* and in the notes of the *History of the Three Kingdoms*. His other names were Hantan Chu and Hantan Tzu-li and he was a native of Yingchuan, a brilliant youth. In the year 151, Magistrate Tu Shang of Shangyu wished to erect a memorial to a girl Tsao Ngo. Hantan Chun, then the magistrate's pupil, wrote the eulogy on the spot, dashing it off without so much as stopping to put in punctuation or change one word. That was how he made his name. In about the year 220, he served as a steward to Emperor Wen Ti of Wei. The *Forest of Jokes* is no longer in existence, and all but about twenty extracts have been lost. Since these jests mock and expose men's weaknesses, they can be considered as belonging to the same category as *Social Talk*. This was the beginning of humorous literature in China.

In the land of Lu, a man with a long pole tried to enter the city gate. Neither holding it erect nor sidewise could he enter, and he was at his wit's end.

Then an old man came up and said: "I may not be a sage, but I have had plenty of experience. Why don't you saw it in half and carry it in that way?"

The man took this advice.

(From the *Tai-ping Miscellany*)

Tao-chiu of Pingyuan married a girl named Mo-tai from Pohai, who was both beautiful and intelligent, and they became attached to each other. After she bore a son Mo-tai went back to her mother's house; and her old mother, Ting, met her son-in-law. Tao-chiu, upon going home, divorced his wife. Before leaving she asked what fault she had committed.

Her husband said: "I saw how old and withered your mother looks and fear you will look the same when you are old. That is my only reason for divorcing you."

(From the *Tai-ping Imperial Encyclopaedia*)

A man whose parents were living went to study in another district for three years. When he came back after that time his uncle asked what he had learned and observed that for long he had not seen his father.

"Yes, I was more distressed than Duke Kang of Chin at Weiyang,"[1] said the youth.

His father reproved him, saying: "What good has your study done you?"

"Unlike the son of Confucius," he replied, "in my youth I received no instruction from my father.[2] That is why I have learned nothing."

(From the *Tai-ping Miscellany*)

---

[1] Both Duke Kang's parents died.
[2] A stock phrase meaning that a man lost his father early.

A fought with B and bit off B's nose. When the case was brought to court, A claimed that B had bitten off his own nose.

The magistrate said: "A man's nose is above his mouth: how could he reach it?"

"He reached it by climbing on the couch," said A.

(From the *Tai-ping Miscellany*)

The *Forest of Jokes* had many successors. The *Sui Dynasty History* mentions a collection of jokes called *Laughter* in two books by Yang Sung-fen, but this is entirely lost. Another work of his, *The Grove of Gossip*, was much quoted, but that was more like the *Social Talk*. The *Tang Dynasty History* refers to the *Records of Jokes* by Hou Pai, whose life is given in the *Sui Dynasty History*. Hou Pai was a native of Wei Prefecture, a good scholar who excelled in quips and repartee. He became a member of the Imperial Academy. His wit made him popular wherever he went, and when Emperor Kao Tsu of Sui heard his reputation he made him a compiler of history of the fifth rank, but Hou died one month later. This was in the second half of the sixth century. Though this work is also lost, many passages from it are quoted in the *Tai-ping Miscellany*. It contained old tales as well as descriptions of Hou's own experience. Rather superficial, it sometimes uses vulgar terms of abuse, and occasionally the jokes go too far and appear in poor taste. Some dealing with events during the Tang dynasty were later interpolations, as was often the case in ancient works, especially in works of fiction.

During the Kai Huang period (581-600), a man named Chu Liu-chin[1] wanted to call on Prime Minister Yang

---

[1] In Chinese these characters can mean "More than six catties."

Su. He met Hou Pai at the gate of the ministry and asked Hou to write his name on the card for him. Hou wrote: Six-Catties-and-a-Half.

After receiving this card, Yang Su summoned the fellow and asked him: "Is your name Six-Catties-and-a-Half?"

"No, my name is Chu Liu-chin."

"Then why did you call yourself Six-Catties-and-a-Half?"

"I asked Mr. Hou Pai to write my name: he must have made a mistake."

Thereupon the minister sent for Hou and asked: "Why did you write his name wrongly?"

Hou answered: "I could not find a balance at the ministry gate to weigh him. Since he told me his name was Chu Liu-chin, I guessed he must be about six catties and a half."

The minister laughed heartily.

(From the *Tai-ping Miscellany*)

The Puchow women who married Shantung men often suffered from goitre. One man's mother-in-law had a badly swollen neck. After this fellow had been married for a few months, his father-in-law suspecting that he was a fool held a great feast to test his wit in front of many kinsmen.

He said: "You who have studied in Shantung must be very intelligent. Will you tell me why storks can cry?"

His son-in-law answered: "It is the will of Heaven."

"Why are pines evergreen?"

"It is the will of Heaven."

"Why do the roadside trees have knots in them?"

"It is the will of Heaven."

The father-in-law said: "You have no sense at all: what use was it your studying in Shantung?" He added bitingly: "The stork can cry because it has a long neck. Pines are evergreen because they are solid. The roadside trees have knots because carts have bumped into them. How can you call these things the will of Heaven?"

His son-in-law answered: "Frogs croak too: is that because they have long necks? Bamboos are evergreen: is that because they are solid inside? Your wife has a big swelling on her neck: was that caused by a cart?"

The father-in-law was put to shame and silenced.

(From the *Tai-ping Miscellany*)

After this appeared the *Forest of Jokes* by Ho Chih-jan of the Tang dynasty, which is also lost. In the Sung dynasty there were similar anthologies by Lu Chu-jen, Shen Chen, Chou Wen-chi and Tien Ho Tzu. There were at least a dozen collections of jokes in the Yuan and Ming dynasties taken from old records or dealing with contemporary events, but displaying few new ideas. The *Miscellany of Ai Tzu*, attributed to Su Tung-po, is rather better than most, but the majority of the tales in this are satires on current abuses, not jokes designed solely for amusement as in the *Forest of Jokes*.

As for later imitations of *Social Talk*, these were legion. The *Tang Dynasty History* mentions that Liu Hsiao-piao wrote a *Sequel to Social Talk* in ten books, but judging by the records in the *Sui Dynasty History*, this was probably identical with the commentary for *Social Talk*. In the Tang dynasty there was another *Sequel to Social*

Talk by Wang Fang-ching. In the Sung dynasty there was the *Forest of Tang Dynasty Sayings* by Wang Tang and *More Social Talk* by Kung Ping-chung. In the Ming dynasty there was Ho Liang-chun's *Forest of Sayings*, Li Shao-wen's *Ming Dynasty Social Talk*, Chiao Hung's *Miscellany of the Jade Hall*, Chang Yung's *Anecdotes from Past History* and Cheng Chung-kuei's *Idle Talk*. These were either gleaned from past records, introducing nothing new, or artificial descriptions of contemporaries; yet men went on writing such books. In the Ching dynasty there was Liang Wei-shu's *Jade-Sword Anecdotes*, Wu Su-kung's *Sayings of the Ming Dynasty*, Chang Fu-kung's *Sayings of the Han Dynasty*, Li Ching's *Sayings of Women*, Yen Tsung-chiao's *Sayings of Monks*, Wang Cho's *Contemporary Sayings* and Wang Wan's *Bell of Anecdotes* with Huei Tung's notes. In this century we have Yi Tsung-kuei's *New Sayings*.

8. THE TANG DYNASTY PROSE ROMANCES

Fiction, like poetry, underwent radical changes in the Tang dynasty. Though tales were still written about marvels and strange phenomena, the plots became more elaborate and the language more polished. Compared with the tales of the Six Dynasties, which give the bare outlines of stories, there was a marked advance. Another and more significant fact was that by this time writers were consciously writing fiction. Thus Hu Ying-lin of the Ming dynasty said: "Tales of miracles and the other world were popular during the Six Dynasties, but these were not entirely imaginary: most of them were based on hearsay and false reports. The Tang dynasty scholars, on the other hand, deliberately invented strange adventures and wrote them as fiction." In fact, Tang writers were consciously romancing. Their prose romances appeared singly or in collections; they were usually fairly long with a complex plot, and sometimes had jests thrown in too. The conventional critics thought them a low form of literature and dubbed them *chuanchi* (romances) to distinguish them from the work of Han Yu and Liu Tsung-yuan.[1] But these stories became popular among the people, and men of letters would write them for use as introductions when they sought the patronage of high officials. Many such prose romances

---

[1] The two most famous Tang dynasty prose writers of the early ninth century.

were preserved in the Sung dynasty *Tai-ping Miscellany* (in later collections mistakes are often made regarding the date and authorship). Indeed, they formed an important part of Tang dynasty literature. These stories had no worthy successors, however, though some were retold or imitated in later dynasties. But they made their influence felt in later drama, for Yuan and Ming dramatists often drew their plots from these stories.

Of course, in the Tsin dynasty there was already fiction deliberately written as such. Some examples are Yuan Chi's "Story of a Great Man," Liu Ling's "The Virtue of Wine," Tao Chien's "Peach Blossom Stream" and "The Master of Five Willows." But these were allegories rather than pure entertainment, and we can see this tradition carried forward in the Tang dynasty in Wang Chi's "The Land of Drunkenness," Han Yu's "The Mason Wang Cheng-fu" and Liu Tsung-yuan's "Hunchback Kuo," which are different from the prose romances. The Tang prose romances had their origin in the tales of marvels of the Six Dynasties, but with their more distinguished style and more complex plots they constituted a distinctive literary form. Occasionally, it is true, the prose romances also use parables to convey a mood or speak of divine retribution, yet on the whole the aim is to write tales of imagination, whereas the earlier tales recorded supernatural happenings as warnings to men.

In the first part of the seventh century Wang Tu wrote a story entitled *The Ancient Mirror*. It relates that he acquired a wonderful mirror from a man named Hou which could control spirits. Later his brother Wang Chi went on a long journey, taking the mirror with him, and it killed several monsters before finally vanishing. This is a fairly long narrative made up of various miraculous events connected with the mirror, bearing some resemblance to those Six Dynasties tales. Wang Tu (circa 585-625), a native of Chi in Taiyuan, was the brother of Wang Tung and Wang Chi, both of whom wrote on philosophy. He was born in 584, and during the Ta Yeh period of the Sui dynasty served for a time as a censor. In the Tang dynasty he worked as a compiler of the official history and then became magistrate of Juicheng. He died during the Wu Teh period before the history was completed. This story is the only piece of literature he left. Since it is nowhere recorded that his brother Wang Chi undertook a long journey after his retirement from official life, this story must be entirely imaginary.

Another early Tang prose romance, *The White Monkey*, is by an unknown author and did not figure in any collection of tales until the Sung dynasty when it was included in the *Tai-ping Miscellany*. The story takes place in the Liang dynasty when an officer named Ouyang Heh goes on an expedition to the south and reaches Changlo, penetrating deep into the region of cave-dwellers. There his wife is carried off by a white monkey; by the time he rescues her she is pregnant, and a year later she gives birth to a son who looks like a monkey. When Ouyang Heh is executed by Emperor Wu Ti of Chen, his friend Chiang Tsung adopts the child. Later in the Tang dynasty this son wins fame, but he still resembles a monkey. Obviously some enemy of the Ouyang family wrote this story. Evidently the tradition of inventing stories to slander people goes back to early times in Chinese fiction.

Chang Tsu of Luhun in Shenchow lived during the reign of Empress Wu. He passed the imperial examination in 679 and served as staff officer to the Prince of Chi. By successfully passing the official examinations he won a reputation for literary accomplishment and was made a tribune in the capital. But he was somewhat flippant and unsteady in character, and the prime minister Yao Chung took a dislike to him. At the beginning of the Kai Yuan period (713-741) the censor Li Chuan-chiao accused him of slandering the government and he was banished to the south. He was recalled to serve for the rest of his life as an officer in charge of the city gates in the capital. He lived from about 660 to 740. In Japan they have a work called *The Fairies' Cavern* written by him when he was a junior officer in Hsianglo County, Ningchow. According to Mo Hsiu-fu's *A Record of Kweilin*.[1] Chang Tsu when young distinguished himself so brilliantly in the examinations that he was appointed junior officer in Hsianglo County by the imperial secretary Hsueh Yuan-chao; so this is a work he wrote in his youth. The romance tells how he sets out on an official mission to the northwest. On his way he puts up at a great mansion where he meets two girls, Tenth Sister and Fifth Sister. They feast, amuse themselves together and write naughty verses, but he leaves the next day after spending the night with them. The language is a mixture of euphuisms and colloquialisms, and the general tone is not unlike that of his *Notes on Court and Country* and *Sinews and Marrows of the Dragon and Phoenix*. Thus the *Tang Dynasty History* comments: "He was an extremely fast writer, but showy and superficial, not given to deep reflection. His works, though slovenly and full of abuse, were exceedingly popular at the time and young scholars would make copies of them. . . . Envoys from the king-

---

[1] Written at the end of the Tang dynasty.

doms of Silla[1] and Japan would pay gold for his writings." *The Fairies' Cavern* was long lost in China and later writers did not imitate Chang Tsu's style. Here is a passage describing a feast.

Tenth Sister bade Hsiang-erh make music to entertain the guest: there were bronze and stone instruments, flutes and pipes, and it seemed that fairies were playing the lute and trumpet, angels the cithern and the pipe-organ, so that even dark storks must bend their heads to hear and white fish leap in the waves in time to the beat. Those liquid notes sent dust rising from the rafters, those charming melodies brought snow fluttering from the sky; even the sage Confucius would have lost all thought of food in his enchantment,[2] for like the songs of the peerless singer Han Ngo[3] this music lingered for three days in the house. . . .

The two damsels rose to dance and pressed me to drink. . . .

While dancing I made this song:

> I have travelled inspecting the borders,
> Now before two bright angels I stand;
> Their dark eyebrows are willows in winter,
> Their soft cheeks lotus blooming on land;
> At the sight I am thrown into raptures,
> Sinking willingly under their spell;
> And tonight, if I cannot possess them,
> I shall feel I am banished to Hell!

This sent the maidens into peals of laughter. After the dance I thanked them, saying: "I am a man of no

---
[1] An ancient Korean state.
[2] It is recorded in *The Analects* that after listening to the *Shao* music Confucius forgot the taste of food.
[3] A legendary figure in *Lieh Tzu*.

talents, most fortunate to have enjoyed your company. I am overwhelmed and do not know how to thank you for such music and entertainment."

Then Tenth Sister made this poem:

> Today we sport like duck and drake,
> Tomorrow we may weep;
> Unless we nestle by your side,
> Where else, sir, should we sleep?

She said: "There is nothing commendable about us; you must have been teasing to talk of the willow and the lotus. . . ."

But it was after the reign of Emperor Ming Huang (713-756) that more writers of prose romances appeared. Shen Chi-chi of Soochow, who lived from approximately 750 to 800, was a good classical scholar who was recommended by Yang Yen the prime minister to be a compiler of the official history. When Yang Yen was killed in 781, Shen was demoted to the post of an officer of civil affairs in Chuchow, later returning to the capital to serve as a junior secretary in the Ministry of Ceremony till his death. His *Annals of the Chien Chung Period* (780-783) was considered good historical writing, and his life appears in the *Tang Dynasty History*. One of his prose romances, *The Story of the Pillow,* was included in two Sung dynasty collections: *Choice Blossoms from the Garden of Literature* and the *Tai-ping Miscellany.* The tale takes place in the year 719 when an old Taoist puts up in an inn on his way to Hantan, notices that another young traveller is in low spirits and lends him a pillow. Then the young man dreams that he marries a daughter of the aristocratic Tsui family of Chingho, passes the imperial examination, becomes prefect of Shenchow and governor of the metropolitan area; after that he defeats the northern tribes and is appointed Vice-Minister of Civil Affairs, Minister of Finance and Imperial Secretary. Because envious ministers slander him, he is demoted to the prefectship of Tuanchow. Three years later he is recalled to court and before long made chief minister again.

He was consulted by the emperor as often as three times a day on affairs of state, and his experience and statecraft earned him the reputation of a brilliant premier. But once more his colleagues intrigued against him, charging him with being in secret collusion with frontier generals who were plotting treason; he was condemned to imprisonment and speedily arrested by officers sent to his house. Apprehensive that his life might be forfeited, he told his wife:

"In my old home in Shantung I had enough good land to keep me from cold and hunger. What possessed me to become an official? See where it has landed me! If only I could put on my short jacket again, and canter on my black colt down the road to Hantan!"

He drew his sword to kill himself, but his wife stopped him. Though all the others involved in this case were executed, his life was spared through the intervention of some palace eunuchs, and he was banished to Huanchow. A few years later the emperor, realizing that he had been wrongly accused, recalled him as chief minister of state with the title of the Duke of Yen, showering him with exceptional honours. He had five sons . . . all his kinsmen by marriage belonged to the greatest families in the empire, and he had over ten grandsons. . . . When he grew old and begged repeatedly for permission to retire, the emperor would not hear of it. When he fell ill, men came one after another from the palace to inquire after him, and he had the best doctors and the rarest medicines . . . but he died. Then the young man yawned and woke up to find himself lying in the inn with the Taoist seated beside him. The innkeeper had not finished cooking the millet and all was exactly as before.

The young man started and said: "Was it all a dream?"

The old Taoist told the innkeeper: "This is the way of all flesh."

After musing sadly for a while, the young man thanked the Taoist. "Now I understand the cycle of honour and disgrace, of success and failure, the principle of apparent loss and gain, and the meaning of life and death. You did this, master, to check my ambition. I shall take due warning!" So he bowed and left.

Though this imaginary tale is of considerable interest and had a moral lesson for an age like the Tang dynasty when men were contending for official honours, it was not entirely original. In Kan Pao's *Records of Spirits* we read the story of the priest of Chiaohu Temple who made Yang Lin sleep with the jade pillow (see Chapter 5), where the general plot is the same, so the *Story of the Pillow* must be based on that earlier story. In the Ming dynasty, Tang Hsien-tsu's poetic drama *Dream of Hantan* was based on this romance. Since Shen Chi-chi wrote good prose and pointed a moral, though this was a romance it was highly regarded by his contemporaries and even compared to Han Yu's "Story of Mao-ying."[1] There were also critics, however, who thought it flippant because Shen was an official historian and they judged the tale as history rather than fiction. Shen also wrote a story called *Jen the Fox Fairy* about a fairy who changes into a woman but remains faithful to her husband till her death. "Few women nowadays are equal to this!" This remark shows the satirical touch in Shen's writing.

Another writer was Shen Ya-chih, described by the poet Li Ho as "the gifted scholar of Wuhsing." His other name was Shen Hsia-hsien and he lived from the end of the eighth to the middle of the ninth century. He passed the imperial examination in 815, and a dozen or so years later served as law officer under Commissioner Po Chi of Tehchow. When Po Chi was disgraced, Shen was demoted to the rank of subordinate officer in Nanking, ending his career as secretary of Yingchow. He left twelve books which are still extant, and was noted for his fine writing and rich imagination. His works include three prose romances, all of which describe imaginary incidents in poetic language, deviating from the normal practice of those days by making fairies and spirits die like mortals. *A Sad Tale of the Hsiang River* tells how a man named Cheng meets a lonely maid and they spend several years together till she tells him that she comes from the Dragon King's palace and now that her term of banishment has expired she must leave him. About a dozen years later Cheng sees her again in the distance on a painted barge, singing a plaintive song; but a great storm rises and she vanishes. *Strange Dreams* relates how Hsing Feng meets a beautiful woman in a dream who performs the Dance

---

[1] An allegory about the brush used for writing.

of the Bending Bow for him, and how Wang Yen in a dream serves under the king of Wu[1] and is praised for the dirge he writes at the king's command on the death of the celebrated beauty Hsi Shih. *A Dream of the Princess of Chin* is written in the first person. The author on his way to Changan puts up at an inn at Tochuan, where he dreams that he is an officer in the ancient kingdom of Chin and distinguishes himself. Since Princess Nung-yu's[2] consort has died, he marries the princess and his mansion is called Tsuiwei Palace. The duke treats him handsomely until one day the princess dies suddenly, though not of illness; then the duke dismisses him.

The duke gave a great farewell feast for me, at which the music of Chin was played and the dances of Chin were performed: the dancers swung their arms, stamped their feet and sang a melancholy air. . . . This over, I bowed and took my leave, and the duke bade me return to the palace to bid farewell to the princess' maids. Entering, I saw trinkets dropped and broken by the steps, but the gauze windows were unchanged and the maids wept at the sight of me. Nearly prostrated with grief, I wrote this poem on the gate:

> The mourning prince has sent me to the east,
> Nor shall I see Chin's palaces again;
> I grieve in springtime for my lady's death,
> While drifting petals fall like crimson rain.

So I left . . . and awoke to find myself lying in the inn. The next day I related this story in full to my

---

[1] King Fu Chai (495-443 B.C.).
[2] Duke Mu's daughter, according to legend, who became immortal with her husband. Duke Mu reigned from 659 to 621 B.C.

friend Tsui Chiu-wan, an antiquarian from Poling, who said: "According to the records, Duke Mu of Chin was buried in Chi-nien Palace at Tochuan: it was surely his spirit that came to you in a dream." I looked up the old local records and it was just as he said. Alas! if the princess was a fairy, how came she to die again?

Then there was Chen Hung who wrote with strong feeling, loved to dwell on the past, and made stirring scenes from history live again. He became a historian early in his career and in 805 was appointed an officer of ceremony. Since this post left him with ample leisure, he compiled thirty books of annals in the next seven years. While in Changan he was on friendly terms with the poet Pai Chu-yi and wrote the story for his long poem *The Eternal Grief*. The *Tang Dynasty History* ascribes *The Peaceful Days of the Kai Yuan Era* to Chen Hung, while the commentary to this work says that Chen Hung was an officer in charge of foreign tributes in the Chen Yuan period. This was probably the same man, for Chen Hung lived from the later half of the eighth to the middle of the ninth century. Another of his prose romances *The Old Man of the East City* is written in a melancholy vein, describing how old Chia Chang recalls the good old days before An Lu-shan's revolt[1] and contrasts past splendour with the more recent decline. *The Story of Eternal Grief*, written early in the Yuan Ho period in the same style as the other, also recalls the past: Lady Yang's entry into the palace and her death later on the way to Chengtu. The romantic story of Lady Yang was extremely popular in the Tang dynasty, but no other account is as complete

---

[1] 755-761.

as this version, which gained wider currency through Pai Chu-yi's famous poem. Hung Sheng's poetic drama *The Palace of Eternal Youth*,[1] written at the beginning of the Ching dynasty, was based mainly on Pai Chu-yi's poem and this prose romance. There are several versions of Chen Hung's story. Already certain discrepancies can be seen in the texts in the *Tai-ping Miscellany* and in *Choice Blossoms from the Garden of Literature*, while the Ming dynasty versions diverge even more. Apparently one Ming compiler, Chang Chun-fang, tried to improve on the tale.

At the end of the Tien Pao period, the lady's brother, Yang Kuo-chung, seized the position of prime minister and abused the state power till An Lu-shan led his troops against the capital on the pretext of overthrowing the Yang family. Tungkuan Pass fell and the imperial retinue set out for the south past Hsienyang to Mawei Station, where the troops wavered, the halberdiers would not advance, and the attending officers knelt before their horses begging for the execution of the evil minister to pacify the empire. Yang Kuo-chung met his death on the road. But still the attending officers were not satisfied. When the emperor questioned them, the bolder among them asked for Lady Yang's death to end the unrest. The emperor knew he could not save her, but could not bear to see her die; so hiding his face in his sleeve he bade them take her away. So she was strangled with a length of silk.

(From *Choice Blossoms from the Garden of Literature*)

---

[1] Translated and published in English by Foreign Languages Press, Peking, 1955.

The Story of Eternal Grief. An illustration from the play *Sterculia Rain* written by Pai Pu (1226-?) of the Yuan dynasty, 1592 edition

At the end of the Tien Pao period the lady's brother, Yang Kuo-chung, seized the position of prime minister and usurped state authority till Tartar tribes rebelled in the northeast and the two capitals fell one after the other. The imperial retinue set out for the south but more than a hundred *li* outside the capital the troops wavered, the halberdiers would not advance, and the attending officers kneeled before their horses begging for the execution of the evil minister to appease them. Yang Kuo-chung met his death on the road. Still the attending officers were not satisfied, and the bolder among them asked for Lady Yang's death to end the people's anger. The emperor turned pale, but he could not bear to see her die. Covering his face with his sleeve, he told them to drag her away. As she bowed before the emperor, tears of blood gushed from her eyes and she dropped her gold and emerald trinkets to the ground, which were kept by the emperor. Alas, that such a charming beauty, the favourite of so great a sovereign, should yet perish by a length of silk! Thus Shu-hsiang's mother said, "What is most loved must be most hated too,"[1] and Li Yen-nien[2] wrote in his song, "Beauty overthrows states and cities."

(The Ming dynasty version)

Pai Hsing-chien or Pai Chih-tui was a native of Taiyuan, whose family moved to Hancheng and thence to Hsiakuei. He was the younger brother of Pai Chu-yi. At the beginning of the ninth century he passed the imperial examination and served in the capital as an officer in charge of the city gates and officer in charge of foreign

---

[1] A quotation from the *Tso Chuan*.
[2] A famous Han dynasty musician.

tributes, dying of illness in the winter of 826 when just over fifty. His life is found in the *Tang Dynasty History* appended to that of Pai Chu-yi. He left twenty books, now lost. The *Tai-ping Miscellany* has one of his prose romances, *Story of a Singsong Girl*. This tells how the son of a noble family in Yingyang becomes enamoured of a singsong girl named Li in Changan. Owing to poverty and illness, he is forced to turn professional mourner; but Li comes to his rescue and encourages him to study so that he passes the examination and is appointed a staff officer at Chengtu. This is a delightful romance owing to its skilful descriptions and the many human and interesting touches. During the Yuan dynasty this story was made into a drama called *Chuchiang Pool*, and in the Ming dynasty Hsueh Chin-yen wrote another drama on this theme called the *Embroidered Jacket*. Pai Hsing-chien also wrote a prose romance entitled *Three Dreams*, which consists of three stories: men visit a place and meet others there in dreams, men see the actions of others in dreams, two people communicate through dreams. The narrative style is simple and the plot original. The first of these three stories is the best.

During the reign of Empress Wu, Liu Yu-chiu, a subordinate officer of Chaoyi, was on his way home one night after a mission when, ten *li* or so from his house, the road took him past a Buddhist monastery from whence he heard singing and laughter. Since the monastery's walls were low and broken in places, he was able to see inside. Stooping, he saw a small company gathered there, of about a dozen men and women, feasting together around a table laden with food; but imagine his astonishment and bewilderment when he saw his own wife chatting and laughing there! After some thought he was convinced that this could not be his wife, yet he did not like to leave. He watched her expression and gestures carefully till he knew that this was she; but when he decided to go in and investigate, he found the monastery gate shut. He threw a tile which hit and smashed a pot, whereupon the feasters scattered and disappeared. Liu climbed in over the wall to examine the rooms with his attendants, but there was no one there and the gate was still closed. Even more puzzled now, he galloped home and discovered his wife in bed. Hearing of his arrival she came out to greet him, and told him with a laugh: "Just now I dreamed I was in a monastery with about a dozen strangers whom I had never met, having a meal in the courtyard. Then someone threw in a tile which upset the dishes, and I woke up."

At that Liu told her what he had seen. This is an example of a visit to a place and a meeting with others in a dream.

9. THE TANG DYNASTY PROSE ROMANCES
(Continued)

Two noteworthy Tang authors of prose romances were Yuan Chen, who wrote little but was extremely well-known and influential, and Li Kung-tso, who wrote more and was equally influential although less famous.

Yuan Chen (779-831) of Honei in Honan Prefecture was a government scholar who was appointed an imperial compiler. Early in the ninth century he came first in the government essay test and was made an adviser, later a censor; subsequently he was demoted and sent to Chiangling, became secretary of Kuochow, was recalled to court as secretary to the privy councillor, later made senior academician, then was appointed vice-minister of works and deputy prime minister, then sent to be prefect of Tungchow and Yuehchow and intendant of Chetung; in the beginning of the Tai Ho period (827-835) he became prime minister and military governor of Wuchang, as well as prefect of Ngochow. In 831 he died suddenly of illness at his post at the age of fifty-three. His life is recorded in the *Tang Dynasty History*. As a young man he wrote poems with Pai Chu-yi and they were spoken of as the Yuan-Pai School, but one only of his romances is left: *The Story of Ying-ying*.

This romance is also known as *Encounter with a Fairy*. The story is as follows: Towards the end of the eighth century there is a young scholar named Chang, gentle, refined and exceedingly handsome, but abiding so strictly by moral conventions that he reaches the age of twenty-three without having had any love affairs. Chang goes to Puchow and puts up in Puchiu Monastery, where a certain Widow Tsui happens to be staying on her way back to Changan. This lady is distantly related to Chang. While they are at the monastery General Hun Chen dies at Puchow and during his funeral the soldiers mutiny and loot the town, to the great dismay of Widow Tsui. Since Chang has friends among the colleagues of the Puchow general, a guard is sent to the monastery, and some days later Civil Commissioner Tu Chueh comes to take over the command and suppresses the mutiny. To express her gratitude to Chang for his protection, Widow Tsui invites him to a meal, Chang falls in love with her beautiful daughter Ying-ying and asks the maid Hung-niang to take Ying-ying two poems on spring. That same evening he receives a reply written on coloured paper with the title "The Bright Moon of the Fifteenth Night." The verse runs:

> To await the moon I sit in the west chamber;
> To greet the wind I have left the door ajar,
> When a flower's shadow stirs against the wall,
> I fancy my lover has come.

Chang is amazed and overjoyed. But when Ying-ying comes to him her dress is sober, her face stern, and after rebuking him she leaves, casting Chang into despair. A few nights later she comes again, but leaves at dawn without having uttered a word.

Chang rose when it was still dark, wondering if after all it had been a dream. But when dawn broke her powder was on his arms, her perfume in his clothes, while a tear she had shed still glittered on the matting.

For more than ten days he did not see her again. He started writing a poem called "Encounter with a Fairy," which consisted of thirty couplets; but before he had finished Hung-niang chanced to pass by and he gave her the poem to take to her young mistress. After this Ying-ying let him come to her, and for nearly a month he slipped out of her room at dawn and in at dark, the two of them sleeping in that west chamber of which I spoke before. Chang often asked his mistress what her mother thought of him, and Ying-ying said: "I know she would never cross me." She wanted to marry at once, but Chang had to go to the capital and he took a tender leave of her. She did not reproach him but great distress showed on her face. On the eve of his departure he could not see her. . . .

The next year Chang fails in his examination and stays on in the capital, corresponding with Ying-ying who writes in return. Chang shows her letters to his friends, till their story is widely known. Yang Chu-yuan writes a poem on Mistress Tsui and Yuan Chen writes another thirty stanzas to complete Chang's "Encounter with a Fairy." All who hear the tale are amazed, but Chang decides to break with Ying-ying. When his good friend Yuan Chen asks the reason, Chang replies:

"When Nature has created something of remarkable beauty, it must destroy itself or others. If Ying-ying were to marry some rich nobleman and become his darling, she might turn into a dragon or a serpent and cause unthinkable chaos. In olden times King Chou-hsin of Shang and King Yu of Chou ruled countries of ten thousand chariots and wielded great power, yet a single woman caused their ruin, scattering their hosts and bringing destruction upon them, so that to this day they are held up to derision as a warning to all men. My virtue, I know, is not sufficent to withstand such magic and this is why I am repressing my feelings."

More than a year later Ying-ying marries another man, and Chang takes a wife too. He goes to Ying-ying's house and sends in the message that her cousin wishes to see her, but she will not come out. A few days later when he is about to leave, she writes him this poem in farewell.

> Do you, who though you spurn me now
> Once loved me as your life,
> Transform that love you had for me
> To pity for your wife!

From this time on no further word passes between them, and many of Chang's contemporaries praise him for the skill with which he has extricated himself from this entanglement.

Chang in this story is Yuan Chen himself, who actually had an affair of this kind. Though the language is not outstanding, the story possesses genuine feeling and is thoroughly readable; but in the end the author tries too hard to justify himself, leaving a rather bad taste. Since such poets as Li Shen and Yang Chu-yuan wrote poems on this tale, however, while Yuan Chen himself was a noted poet who later became a high-ranking official, this romance caught the public fancy. Chao Teh-ling of the Sung dynasty wrote a ballad in ten stanzas based on it; in the Golden Tartar period there was the chantefable *The West Chamber* by a scholar named Tung; in the Yuan dynasty Wang Shih-fu wrote his famous play *The West Chamber*, to which Kuan Hanching produced a sequel; in the Ming dynasty Li Jih-hua and Lu Tsai wrote *The West Chamber, a Southern Drama*. Many other operas were based on this story, which is talked of even today. Of all the Tang prose romances still extant, only this and *The Dragon King's Daughter*[1] by Li Chao-wei have enjoyed comparable fame.

Li Kung-tso of Lunghsi was an imperial scholar who served early in the ninth century as subordinate officer of Chianghuai, later returning to Changan. More than thirty years afterwards he was secretary of the Yangchow prefectural government, but in 843 he was demoted two ranks. Born in the reign of Emperor Tai Tsung (763-779), he was still living in the time of Hsuan Tsung (847-859), but his exact dates are unknown. The names of men related to the imperial house listed in the *Tang Dynasty History* include that of Li Kung-tso, but this was another man. Four of Li's romances have come down to us, the most famous being *The Governor of the Southern Tributary State*. This tells of a man of Tungping named Chunyu Fen who has a house ten *li* east of Kuangling with a great ash tree growing in front of it. In the autumn of the year 792 he is carried home drunk by two friends, who lay him down in the east room while they stable the horses and wash their feet. Chunyu Fen rests his head on the pillow and falls asleep. Presently two messengers in purple arrive to announce that their king has sent to fetch him. He walks out of the gate, mounts the carriage and drives towards an opening in the old ash tree. The carriage drives through the tree

---

[1] Translated and published in English by Foreign Languages Press, Peking, 1954.

and after passing hills and streams they enter a great city. On the citadel is written in letters of gold "The Great Kingdom of Ashendon." Chunyu marries the king's daughter and becomes prince consort, after which he is appointed governor of the southern tributary state. He governs for thirty years and "the people benefiting from his good rule sang his praises, set up tablets extolling his virtue and built temples to him." The king loads him with honours, he is highly exalted and has five sons and two daughters. He leads an army against the kingdom of Sandalvine, but is defeated, and when the princess dies he leaves the province; nevertheless his power increases till the king begins to fear him, forbids him all further contact with his associates and orders him to live in retirement. Finally he is sent home. He awakes to find his servants sweeping the courtyard, his two guests still washing their feet by the couch, the slanting sun still setting behind the west wall, his unfinished wine still by the east window — yet he has lived through a whole generation in his dream! The theme of this romance reminds us of *The Story of the Pillow,* but here there is far more descriptive detail. Tang Hsientsu in the Ming dynasty based his drama *The Governor of the Southern Tributary State* on this tale. At the end of the story Chunyu bids his servants dig at the foot of the tree, and there he finds ant-heaps in the same position as the cities of his dream. Though the story has certain imperfections, its charming blend of reality and fantasy makes it infinitely superior to *The Story of the Pillow.*

It was some ten feet long, terminating in a cavity lit by the sun and large enough to hold a couch. In this were mounds of earth which resembled city walls, pavilions and courts, and swarms of ants were gathered there. From the ant-hill rose a small, reddish tower occupied by two huge ants, three inches long, with white wings and red heads. These were surrounded by a few dozen large ants, whom the smaller ones dared not approach. The two huge ants were the king and queen and this was the capital of Ashendon. Then the men followed up another hole which lay under the southern branch of the tree and was at least forty feet long. In this tunnel there was another ant-hill with small towers, swarming with ants. This was the southern tributary state which Chunyu had governed. . . . As he thought back, Chunyu was very shaken, for all that they had discovered coincided with his dream. He would not let his friends destroy these ant-hills, but ordered the tunnels to be covered up as before. . . .

Then he thought of the invasion by the kingdom of Sandalvine, and asked his two friends to trace it. They found that some six hundred yards east of the house was a river-bed long since dry, and next to that grew a large sandal-tree so thickly covered with vines that the sun could not shine through. A small hole beside it, where a swarm of ants had gathered, must be the kingdom of Sandalvine. If even the mysteries of ants are so unfathomable, what then of the changes caused by great beasts in the hills and woods?

The Story of Hsieh Hsiao-ngo is about a girl from Yuchang whose mother dies when she is eight and who marries a gallant citizen of Liyang. Her father and husband are merchants and on one of their business trips they are killed by brigands; then Hsiao-ngo breaks her leg and falls into the river, but is saved by a passing boat. She reaches Shangyuan County and takes refuge in Miaokuo Nunnery. In a dream her father tells her that his murderer's name is "Monkey in a carriage, grass at the east gate," while her husband tells her that his murderer's name is "Walk among the grain, a man for a day."[1] She consults various wise men, but none can solve this puzzle till the writer Li Kung-tso explains to her that the first murderer is called Shen Lan, the second Shen Chun. So Hsiao-ngo disguises herself as a manservant and meeting these two brigands at Hsunyang she kills them. When this case is reported to the court the rest of the brigands are captured and Hsiao-ngo is pardoned. This rather pointless story, which hinges upon guessing a riddle to solve a murder case, also enjoyed great popularity. Li Fu-yen rewrote it for his collection of tales *More About Mysteries and Monsters,* while in the Ming dynasty it was once more rewritten as a story in the vernacular included in Ling Meng-chu's *Amazing Stories.*

Another of Li Kung-tso's romances was *Old Woman Feng of Luchiang.* After Tung Chiang's wife dies he marries again, and the old woman sees a young woman weeping in a room by the roadside, which she finds is the dead wife's tomb. When she tells Tung Chiang, he angrily accuses her of lying and drives her away. The plot is simple in the extreme and the language undistinguished. The fourth romance, *Li Tang,* narrates that Prefect Li Tang of Chuchow in the year 765 hears from some fishermen that there is a great iron chain in the

---

[1] These are clues to the component parts of the Chinese characters.

lake at the foot of Tortoise Mountain. When he gets a team of oxen to pull it out, a sudden storm arises.

A beast like a monkey with white head and shaggy mane, teeth white as snow and golden claws rushed ashore. It towered some fifty feet though it crouched like an ape, but its eyes were closed and it seemed half asleep. . . . Presently it craned its neck and its eyes flashed open. These eyes, bright as lightning, glared at them wild with rage. As the onlookers took to their heels, the beast slowly dragged its chain with the oxen attached down into the water, never to emerge again.

Li Tang and other notables of Chuchow are amazed and utterly bewildered. Later Li Kung-tso, the writer, goes to the ancient land of Wu, sails on Tungting Lake, climbs Pao Mountain and finds a holy document in a cave — the eighth volume of the ancient *Yotu Canon*. From this he learns the identity of the monster. The manuscript is in archaic writing, half destroyed by worms and barely legible, but Li and a Taoist priest succeed in deciphering the following account:

When Yu pacified the flood, he went thrice to Tungpo Mountain. The wind howled, thunder rumbled, rocks crashed and forests wailed. The Lord of Earth curbed the rivers, the Elder of Heaven disciplined the troops, yet they could not control the waters. Then Yu in wrath summoned the hundred deities and gave orders to Kuei and Lung so that all the lords of mountains bowed down in awe. Yu took captive Hungmeng, Changshang, Toulu and Lilou. He searched out the spirit of the Huai River, Wu-chih-chi, who was quick in speech and knew the depth of water and the extent of land. In appearance it was most like an ape, with a blunt nose, craggy brows, green body, white head, gold eyes and teeth as white as snow. Its neck was a hundred feet long, it was stronger than nine elephants when it attacked, and could leap great heights or gallop like the wind, appearing in a flash to be gone immediately. Yu sent Tunglu out, but he could not trap it. He sent Wu-Mu-Yu out, but neither could he catch it. He sent Keng-chen out, and this time the monster was captured. For thousands of years all the spirits and demons of water, wood, mountain and stone, raged up and down, howling and wailing, till Keng-chen pursued the monster with his spear, fastened a great chain to its neck, a gold bell to its snout, and banished it to the foot of Tortoise Mountain south of the Huai River, that the Huai might for ever flow safely into the sea. After this, men made pictures of the monster and suffered no more from the stormy waves of the Huai.

Chu Hsi of the Sung dynasty in his *Studies on the Poems of Chu* refuted the popular legend that Wu-chih-chi had been conquered by the god Seng-chia; Lo Mi's *Unauthorized History* had a note on Wu-chih-chi; the Yuan dynasty playwright Wu Chang-ling made Wu-chih-chi Monkey's sister; in the Ming dynasty the writer Sung Lien also referred to this monster. Hence we can see that from the Sung dynasty onwards this legend was so widespread that scholars thought it necessary to refute it. In fact, the whole story originated in Li Kung-tso's mind, but the sage king Yu of his story later changed into the god Seng-chia or the God of Ssuchow, and when Wu Cheng-en of the Ming dynasty wrote his *Pilgrimage* to the West, this obstreperous monster, capable of such rapid transformations, turned into Monkey Sun Wu-kung. After that the earlier legend was forgotten.

There are many other prose romances worth our attention. *The Dragon King's Daughter* by Li Chao-wei of Lunghsi tells of the scholar Liu Yi who, on his way back to the Hsiang River Valley after failing to pass the civil service examination, meets a girl in Chingyang tending sheep. She tells him she is the dragon king's daughter, banished here by her husband and his parents, and she begs Liu Yi to take a letter to her father, the Lord of Tungting. The dragon king's hot-tempered brother, the Lord of Chientang, kills the girl's husband, brings her home and urges Liu Yi to marry her; but the scholar refuses. After Liu Yi's wife dies he moves to Nanking where he marries a daughter of the Lu family from Fanyang, who proves to be the dragon king's daughter. Later he goes to Nanhai, then returns to Tungting. His cousin Hsueh Ku meets him once on the lake and is given fifty pills of elixir; but after this no more is heard of Liu. In the Golden Tartar period this story was dramatized; Shang Chung-hsien of the Yuan dynasty wrote another drama *The Story of Liu Yi;* later the plot was altered to make the drama *Boiling the Sea,* and Li Yu of the Ching dynasty combined both versions into one drama *The Mirage.*

Prince Huo's Daughter, by Chiang Fang, narrates that Li Yi passes the examination at twenty and goes to Changan. Eager to make the acquaintance of some famous courtesan, he meets Prince Huo's daughter, Jade, and lives with her for two years; but when he is appointed chief clerk of Cheng County he leaves her, promising to marry her later. His mother has arranged a match for him with a cousin, however, and he dares not incur her anger by declining it. So he abandons Jade. The girl, not hearing from him for so long, falls ill. She traces him and begs him to visit her, but he refuses. One day when he is at Chungching Temple, a young gallant in a yellow shirt carries him off by main force to Jade's house; and though the girl is mortally ill she rises from her bed to upbraid him for his heartlessness, then dies of grief. Li Yi puts on mourning and weeps bitterly. He marries his cousin, but is haunted by a ghost which makes him suspect his wife of unfaithfulness and divorce her. He marries three times, but always the same thing happens. Tu Fu[1] in a poem "The Youth" mentions the young man in a yellow shirt, referring to this story.

Another prose romance, *Mistress Liu* by Hsu Yao-tso, relates that the poet Han Hung obtains possession of beautiful Mistress Liu, but when An Lu-shan's rebellion breaks out he leaves her in Faling Nunnery while he goes to serve the military governor of Tzuching. After the rebellion is suppressed, he finds she has been carried off by the Tartar general Sachari; but a gallant officer named Hsu succeeds in stealing her away for him. This tale, which is also found in Meng Chi's poems, must be based on a true story.

Other interesting prose romances are Liu Cheng's *Story of Shang-ching*, Hsueh Tiao's *Wu-shuang the Peerless*, Huangfu Mei's *Story of Fei-yen* and Fang Chien-li's *The Courtesan Named Yang*. Then there was Tu Kuangting's *The Man with the Curly Beard* which was extremely popular. Tu was a Taoist priest in Chengtu who served under Wang Yen and left many works, mostly

---
[1] 712-770.

dealing with magic and alchemy. This story describes how Yang Su's[1] maid, a girl with a red whisk, recognizes Li Ching's[2] worth while he is still a common citizen and they elope together. During their journey they come across a man with a curly beard who predicts greatness for Li, giving him wealth and teaching him military arts so that he can assist the first emperor of Tang to found a new dynasty. The man with the curly beard goes to sea with pirates and kills the king of Fuyu,[3] making himself king there instead. This story was a favourite in later ages, and pictures were painted of the three gallants in it; in the Ming dynasty Ling Meng-chu wrote a play entitled *The Man with the Curly Beard,* while both Chang Feng-yi and Chang Tai-ho wrote plays called *The Girl with the Red Whisk.*

In addition to these, there were *The Story of Li Ching, Duke of Wei* by an anonymous author, *The Story of Li Lin-fu,*[4] author also anonymous, *The Story of Eunuch Kao*[5] by Kuo Chih and *The Story of An Lu-shan* by Yao Ju-neng. These works were probably intended as biographies, but since they deal with trivial incidents and are casually written, they were later considered as fiction.

---

[1]Duke of Yueh in the Sui dynasty.

[2]A famous commander at the beginning of the Tang dynasty and later Duke of Wei, he won important victories against the Turks and other foes.

[3]A legendary island kingdom, the location of which is unknown.

[4]Prime minister from 734 to 752. The troubles in Emperor Ming Huang's reign were attributed to his bad government.

[5]Emperor Ming Huang's favourite.

The Man with the Curly Beard. From the prose romance *The Girl with the Red Whisk* written by Chang Feng-yi (1527-1613), 1625 edition

10. COLLECTIONS OF TANG DYNASTY TALES

The best known of the many collections of prose romances in the Tang dynasty was Niu Sheng-ju's *Accounts of Mysteries and Monsters*. Niu Sheng-ju or Niu Ssu-an (780-848) was a native of Titao, Lunghsi, who moved to Honan. Early in the ninth century he came first in a court test. He pointed out faults in the government frankly, going so far as to criticize the prime minister, and was appointed subordinate officer in Yichueh. When Emperor Mu Tsung came to the throne, he was gradually promoted to the position of censor, vice-minister of finance and deputy prime minister; under Emperor Wu Tsung he was demoted to a minor post in Hsunchow; but in the reign of Emperor Hsuan Tsung he was recalled to court as junior tutor to the crown prince. He died at the age of sixty-nine, receiving the title of high marshal and the posthumous title Wen-chien. His life appears in the *Tang Dynasty History*. Niu Sheng-ju was a stubborn character but fond of supernatural tales. His *Accounts of Mysteries and Monsters* in ten books is lost, but we know something of the contents from thirty-one of these tales included in the *T'ai-ping Miscellany*. While these are rather similar to other prose romances of the time, Niu made it quite clear that this was fiction and that readers should not take it as fact. Writers like Li Kung-tso and Li Chaowei displayed their brilliance in descriptive passages but were loath to admit that these accounts were imaginary, whereas Niu was proud if he could invent plots too, and would explain how he came to write a story. The following tale is an example.

At the end of the second month of the year 762, Yuan Wu-yu was travelling alone through the suburbs of Yangchow. When dusk fell a great storm blew up; and since there had been fighting in these parts and most of the inhabitants had fled, he sought shelter in an empty cottage by the roadside. Soon the rain stopped and a crescent moon appeared. He was sitting by the north window when he heard footsteps in the west corridor and saw four men in the moonlight, all dressed in some antique fashion, who were chatting and jesting to their hearts' content as they composed poems together.

One of them said: "Tonight there is something of autumn in the air with this fine breeze and moonlight. We must write poems to express our feelings." . . .

Since they chanted aloud, Yuan could hear them distinctly.

The tall man started:

> "The songs I sing are loud and clear;
> My silks washed snowy white."

Then the stocky fellow in black chanted:

> "The company at night is good,
> I hold the torches bright."

A third man, also short and in shabby light brown clothes, continued:

> "At dawn cool water from the well
> With rope of straw I draw."

The fourth man in black chanted:

"I heat the water till it boils,
And ever crave for more."

Yuan felt no fear of these four men, nor did they notice the presence of a stranger. The praise they lavished on each other outdid even Yuan Chi's[1] self-laudatory poems. Just before dawn they retired, and when Yuan looked for them he found in the hall an old pestle for pounding clothes, a lampstand, a wooden bucket and a cracked pot. These, he realized, were the four men.

When Niu Sheng-ju was at court he had a rival in Li Teh-yu, and the factions of these two ministers warred against each other. Since Niu was fond of writing, Wei Kuan, one of Li's protégés, wrote *A Tale of Chou and Chin*, attributing it to Niu to involve him in trouble. In this story the writer fails in the examination and is on his way back to Honan when night overtakes him at the foot of Mingkao Mountain, and he loses his way. He spends the night in the temple of a Han empress, feasting with empresses and imperial concubines of the Han and Tang dynasties. The Han empress asks who the present ruler is, and he tells her: "The eldest son of the last emperor."

Lady Yang says with a laugh: "So the son of that woman Shen is emperor? Fantastic!"

After composing poems, he shares the couch of Lady Chao-chun of the Han court, leaving at dawn the next day. "And what happened after that we do not know."

---

[1] 210-263. Famed for eighty-two poems which he wrote to express his thoughts.

Li Teh-yu then spread the rumour that Niu's name had appeared in certain oracles and his tales of marvels were written to overawe people, while this romance in which he mixed with imperial concubines and empresses was meant to prove that he was no ordinary man. "He dares even deride the emperor by calling him 'the son of that woman Shen,' referring to the last empress as 'woman'! This outrageous insult to His Majesty sends shivers down our spines!" Li asserted that either Niu would turn traitor himself or his descendants would do so. "The whole clan, young and old, must be wiped out to uphold justice and make the state secure." This is the most extraordinary instance of attacking an enemy through fiction; but Li's scheme fell through.

Since Niu was a competent writer and high official, his work was well known and widely imitated. Li Fu-yen wrote *More About Mysteries and Monsters* in ten books divided into two parts: one on magic, the other on divine retribution. Hsueh Yu-ssu wrote *Tales of Hotung* in three books, also concerning miracles and supernatural happenings, and claiming in its preface to be a sequel to Niu's work. *Records of a Palace Chamber* in ten books, dealing with fairies and ghosts, was by Chang Tu, a relative of Chang Tsu and one of Niu's grandsons, who carried on his grandfather's tradition.

The *Tuyang Miscellany* by Su Ngo of Wukung relates happenings in the Tang dynasty, with the emphasis on strange and rare objects from distant lands. Kao Yen-hsiu, whose pseudonym was Tsan-liao-tzu, wrote the *Forgotten History of the Tang Dynasty*, which should be considered as fiction of a slightly different type, for though it has some tales based on fact it deals mostly with dreams and fairies. Kang Pien's *Free Talk* was more concerned with worldly affairs, Sun Chi's *Record of the Courtesans' Quarters* was devoted to singsong girls, Fan Shu's *Yunhsi Miscellany* consisted mainly of poems. Though these collections deal more with human beings than with the supernatural, the authors were auxious to tell good stories and wrote carefully in the tradition of the Tang prose romances. Pei Hsing's *Strange Tales* is a work on fairies and miracles in somewhat flowery language. Pei Hsing served as a secretary under Kao Pien the vice-military governor of Huainan, who consoled himself with magic and alchemy when his ambitions were thwarted and died in a local rebellion. This work may have been written at Kao's instigation. The well-known story of Nieh Ying-niang's defeat of the assassin Kung-kung-erh comes from this collection. After this tale was included in *Stories of Famous Swordsmen* of the Ming dynasty, a work attributed to Tuan Cheng-shih, it became widely known and even now writers still refer to it.

Tuan Cheng-shih, a native of Lintzu in Chichow, was the son of the prime minister Tuan Wen-chang. Thanks to his father's position he became an imperial editor, then prefect of Chichow. In the middle of the ninth century he returned to the capital to take up the post of Junior Master of Ceremony, dying in 863. His family had a library of rare books and he was widely read, erudite, well-versed in Buddhist lore. As a youth he loved hunting and enjoyed literary fame. His writings, both profound and versatile, were highly regarded. His *Record During Office at Luling* in two books is lost, but his *Yuyang Miscellany* in twenty books divided into thirty sections is still extant. There is also a sequel to this in ten books. The contents include anecdotes from rare books or tales of miracles, and there are different headings in the manner of an encyclopaedia for fairies, Buddhist lore, spirits, animals, plants and so forth. This form probably originated with Chang Hua's *Records of Strange Things*, but this was the first use of it in the Tang dynasty. The different sections have separate titles which are somewhat archaic and obscure. Thus the section on magic is called "The Pitcher Man," that on Buddhist lore "The Pattra," that on burials "The Necropolis," and that on the supernatural "The Nokao."[1] The tales are as bizarre and archaic as the titles.

Chi of Hsia was the Bright Lord of the East, King Wen the Bright Lord of the West, the Duke of Shao the Bright Lord of the South, Chi Cha the Bright Lord of the North; these in the four seasons ruled over the ghosts of the four quarters. Those most loyal and pious become lords underground after death; after one hundred and forty years they learn how to become immortals, apprehending the Great Truth. Those with the highest virtue receive after death a mandate from the Three Offices to rule underground; after a thousand years they turn into the Five Divine Emperors, after another one thousand and four hundred years they may wander in heaven as immortals in the Nine Palaces.

(Book 2)

Five signs presage the birth into Heaven: first, light which clothes the body without any garment; secondly, a strange desire engendered by the sight of things; thirdly, frailty; fourthly, doubt; fifthly, fear.

(Book 3)

---

[1] A summons to the spirits of the dead.

At the beginning of our dynasty the monk Hsuan Tsang journeyed to India to seek Buddhist sutras and was held in high esteem by the men of the Western Regions. I once encountered a Japanese monk, Chinkang-san-mei, who told me that he had made the pilgrimage to central India and in the monasteries there seen paintings of Hsuan Tsang with his hempen sandals, his spoon and chopsticks; and these were mounted on coloured clouds inasmuch as they were unknown in the west. On feast days men worshipped these.

(Book 3)

The Holy Master Chang, whose name was Chang Chien or Tzu-ko, was a native of Yuyang. He was a disreputable vagabond in his youth. Once he caught a white sparrow with his net and taking a fancy to the bird he kept it till in a dream he saw that Holy Master Liu was angry, threatening to kill him. But the white sparrow always gave him warning, so that Chang was prepared beforehand and came to no harm. Then Holy Master Liu came down from heaven to see him and Chang entertained him to a great feast during which he secretly rode off in Liu's carriage with white dragons, brandishing the whip as he went up to heaven. Liu mounted another dragon to give chase but he could not overtake him. When Holy Master Chang reached the heavenly palace, he changed all the officers, closed the North Gate, made the white sparrow a high minister and noble, and put an end to the breed of sparrows on earth. Holy Master Liu, having lost his place, wandered through the Five Holy Mountains wreaking destruction, until in dismay Chang appointed him governor of Taishan, in charge of the records of men's life and death.

(Book 14)

During the Ta Li period (766-779) a scholar whose cottage was at Weinan died of disease in the capital, and his wife Liu lived on in the cottage. . . . By the time she had sacrificed to her husband dusk fell, and Liu was sitting outside to enjoy the cool of the evening when a wasp began to circle her head. As she struck it with her fan, it fell to the ground and turned into a walnut. She picked it up and played with it till it began to grow: first it was as large as her fist, then the size of a bowl. She watched, startled, while it became as big as a plate; but then with a crash it broke into two parts which whirled in the air with a noise like a swarm of bees. Suddenly the two halves clapped together on her head. Her skull was crushed, her teeth were imbedded in a tree. The thing flew away, and none knows what it was.

(Book 14)

A section relating to disfigurement is called "The Tattoo" another on keeping falcons is headed "The Vulture." A section in the sequel entitled "Criticisms" contains some researches, while "Pagodas" deals with monasteries. Since Tuan touched on so many topics, there is much that is unusual and interesting in his work, which was not only well regarded by scholars but enjoyed the same popularity as other prose romances.

Tuan Cheng-shih was a good poet too, but his poems are abstruse and mannered like his prose. He was one of the three leaders of a school of poetry, known as the

"Three Sixteens Style,"[1] the other two being Wen Tingyun of Chi and Li Shang-yin, alias Li Yi-shan, of Honei. Wen Ting-yun also left three books of fiction called *Kan Sun Tzu*, some quotations from which can be found in the *Tai-ping Miscellany*: but these are brief anecdotes, sketchily written and lacking in interest, quite unlike his highly ornate and colourful poetry. We do not know whether Li Shang-yin wrote any fiction or not. The *Miscellany of Yi-shan*, which is not listed in the bibliographical section of the *Tang Dynasty History*, was thought by Chen Chen-sun of the Sung dynasty to be the work of Li Shang-yin. This contains topical sayings and colloquial jests arranged under different headings. Though the contents are trivial they shed a certain light on Tang society; thus the book serves for more than entertainment.

Desecration:

    The announcement of an official's approach
      under the pines
    Tears shed while watching flowers
    Mats spread on moss
    Willows cut down
    Breeches sunned under blossoming trees
    Heavy loads carried on spring excursions
    Horses tethered in a rock garden
    Bonfires lit by moonlight
    A general on foot
    Storeyed pavilions by a hill
    Vegetables in an orchard
    Poultry in a garden

---

[1] Tuan Cheng-shih, Wen Ting-yun, and Li Shang-yin, poets of the late Tang dynasty, were all sixteenth in sequence among the sons in their family, hence the name of the school.

Bad Form:

> To wrangle with fellow guests
> To upset the table when a guest
> To sing love-songs in the presence of one's
>   mother-in-law
> To spit chewed meat out on a plate
> To point one's feet at others while lying down
> To lay chopsticks across a bowl

Prohibitions:

> Don't get drunk
> Don't frighten people in the dark
> Don't harm men in secret
> Don't enter a widow's house alone
> Don't open another's letter
> Don't borrow without the owner's permission
> Don't walk alone in the dark
> Don't keep bad company
> Don't borrow things and keep them for weeks

Towards the end of the ninth century Li Chiu-chin, magistrate of Lingchin, who was also called Yi-shan, was writing poems too. As a young scholar he had enjoyed the company of singsong girls and his name appears in Sun Chi's *Record of the Courtesans' Quarters*. He may therefore be the author and not Li Shang-yin. No further proof of this can be found, however. Later scholars imitated this style of writing: in the Sung dynasty there were works of this kind by Wang Chun-yu and Su Tung-po, and in the Ming dynasty another sequel by Huang Yun-chiao.

11. SUPERNATURAL TALES AND PROSE ROMANCES IN THE SUNG DYNASTY

After China was united again under the Sung dynasty, the libraries of different kingdoms were collected together, and to allay discontent among the prominent scholars of the former states the government summoned them to court as highly paid compilers. They produced the *Tai-ping Imperial Encyclopaedia* and *Choice Blossoms from the Garden of Literature*, each in a thousand books, as well as the five-hundred-book *Tai-ping Miscellany* compiled from past works of fiction, anecdotes and unofficial histories. The compilation of this work started in the spring of 977 and was completed by the following summer, the manuscript was then sent to the Imperial Bureau of History and early in 981 was printed; but because certain ministers argued that this work was not urgently needed, the printed blocks were kept in Taiching Pavilion and few Sung dynasty scholars had access to the book. The *Tai-ping Miscellany* drew on extensive sources, making use of 344 past works; thus many lost volumes of fiction from the Han and Tsin dynasties down to the Five Dynasties are represented there. The work was divided into fifty-five sections, some long and some short, giving us an over-all picture of the types of writing popular in the Tsin and Tang dynasties. It is therefore not merely a treasure-house of stories but an assessment of literary trends also. Here are some of the main sections (at the end are nine books of miscellaneous writing which include Tang prose romances):

Immortals (55 books)
Fairies (15 books)
Monks (12 books)
Divine Retribution (33 books)
Omens (11 books)
Fate (15 books)
Dreams (7 books)
Gods (25 books)
Ghosts (40 books)
Monsters (9 books)
Spirits (6 books)
Incarnations (12 books)
Dragons (8 books)
Tigers (8 books)
Foxes (9 books)

The chief compiler of the *Tai-ping Miscellany* was Li Fang. Among the twelve others who worked under him were Hsu Hsuan and Wu Shu, both of whom wrote tales which have come down to us. Hsu Hsuan (916-991) from Kuangling in Yangchow was a scholar of the Imperial Academy in the Southern Tang Kingdom, who went to the new capital when his state surrendered to the house of Sung. He served as secretary of the imperial academy and court officer, but in 991 he was demoted to the post of sub-prefect of Chingnan, where he fell ill and died of a chill at the age of seventy-six. His life is recorded in the *Sung Dynasty History*. Before taking up residence in the Sung capital he had already started writing stories about marvels. Over a period of twenty years he wrote his *Investigation of Spirits* in six books, containing no more than 150 tales. When helping to compile the *Taiping Miscellany,* he wanted to include his own tales but dared not take this decision himself. He asked Sung Po to sound out Li Fang, who said: "Of course any tales by Mr. Hsu must be well worth using." So his writings were included. They are rather colourless and flat, however, lacking the old simplicity of the Six Dynasties tales or the romantic colour of the Tang stories. Early Sung writers tried to make tales of the miraculous "convincing," and so the decline in this tradition set in.

An old woman Wang of Kuangling had lain ill for several days when she suddenly told her son: "After my death I shall become a cow in the Hao family at Hsihsi, and you had better buy it. You will know it by the character 'Wang' on its belly."

Soon she died.

Hsihsi was a place west of Hailing. There a man named Hao had a cow with white hair forming the character "Wang" on its belly. The son sought and found it, bought it for a roll of silk and took it home.

(Book 2)

In Kuachun a fisherman's wife fell ill of the wasting disease, and as this consumption spread several people died. One man declared that if a sick person was nailed up alive in a coffin and abandoned, this epidemic would end. Before long, his own daughter falling ill, he nailed her alive in the coffin and put it in the river. The coffin floated to Chinshan where a fisherman saw it, wondered what could be in it, and dragged it ashore. When he opened the coffin, he found the girl still alive. He kept her in his cottage, feeding her with fish and eels till she was cured.

After that she married the fisherman and is alive to this day.

(Book 3)

Wu Shu (947-1002) was Hsu Hsuan's son-in-law and a native of Tanyang in Junchow. A brilliant youth who was a rapid writer, he was a government scholar and compiler of the Southern Tang Kingdom. He went to the Sung capital when his kingdom fell, became a secretary in the war ministry and died at the age of fifty-six. His life also appears in the *Sung Dynasty History*. He wrote the *Record of Strange Men in the Yangtse and Huai River Valleys* in three books. Twenty-five of these tales have been collected from the Ming dynasty *Yung Lo Encyclopaedia*. They deal with gallant men, magicians and priests, and are filled with descriptions of supernatural events. Tuan Cheng-shih's *Yuyang Miscellany* written in the Tang dynasty included a tale about nine gallant brigands and their strange adventures; but Wu Shu was the first to write a book about such strange men; later some Ming dynasty scholars took material from the *Tai-ping Miscellany* to make *Stories of Famous Swordsmen* — passing it off as an original work — which so encouraged this fashion that from that time to the present day there has been a spate of stories about swordsmen and their miraculous feats.

When Cheng Yu-wen served as a staff officer in Hungchow, the window of his house overlooked the main street. One day he was sitting at the window just after rain had left the road greasy with mud, when along came a tattered urchin selling shoes, and a young rogue bumping into him knocked his shoes into the mire. The small boy begged with tears for some compensation, but the scoundrel refused with an oath.

The boy said: "We have nothing to eat at home and I was going to sell these shoes for food, but now you have dirtied them."

A scholar passing by took pity on the lad and gave him some money.

The young bully cried angrily: "This boy was begging from me! Can't you mind your own business?"

He swore at the scholar, who looked thoroughly incensed. Admiring the scholar's sense of justice, Cheng invited him in and, much impressed by his conversation, kept him there for the night. They went on talking that night until Cheng had to go for a while to the inner apartments; but when he came out the scholar had disappeared. Though the outer gate was still shut there was no trace of him.

Soon the scholar returned and said: "I could not stomach that bully today. I have cut off his head." He tossed it to the ground.

Cheng was shocked and protested: "The fellow was offensive, true, but won't you get me into trouble if you go around cutting off heads and spilling blood?"

"Don't worry," said the scholar. He took out a small quantity of some drug and smeared it on the severed head, which he had grasped by the hair. Then the head changed into water, and he told Cheng: "I have no way of repaying your hospitality, unless you care to learn this trick?"

But Cheng said: "With my social position I really dare not."

Thereupon the scholar made a deep bow and left, vanishing though all the doors were still closed and locked.

Though the Sung dynasty is commonly spoken of as an age in which Confucianism was respected while Buddhism and Taoism were tolerated, the underlying popular belief was still shamanism. The works of Hsu Hsuan and Wu Shu were followed by much mystical writing about miracles and oracles, books such as Chang Chun-fang's *A Carriage-Load of Marvels*, Chang Shih-cheng's *Collection of Marvels*, Nieh Tien's *Tracing Marvels*, Chin Chai-ssu's *Marvels in Loyang* and Pi Chung-hsun's *Leisure Hours of a Secretary*. After Emperor Hui Tsung (1101-1125) under the influence of the Taoist priest Lin Ling-su set his heart on alchemy and styled himself the True Lord, the whole empire went in for Taoism, which remained fashionable even after the capital moved south. Indeed, when Emperor Kao Tsung (1127-1162) abdicated in favour of his son, he also took pleasure in tales of marvels and saints. *A Cart-Load of Ghosts* in five books by Kuo Tuan of Liyang, prefect of Hsinkuo, and *Tales of Yi Chien* in 420 books by Hung Mai of Poyang, an imperial academician, were evidently presented to the court. All such works lay stress on specific incidents with little descriptive embellishment, much in the style of Hsu Hsuan. *Tales of Yi Chien* enjoyed a certain fame, however, on account of the author's prominence and the size of the book.

Hung Mai (1096-1175) was a learned and widely read youth but he kept failing in the government examination though his brothers passed, not succeeding till he was fifty. When his father Hung Hao offended the prime minister, Hung Mai suffered the consequences too, becoming a government tutor in Foochow and later serving in the ministries of civil office and ceremony. After carrying out successful negotiations with envoys from the Golden Tartars, he went as an emissary to the Tartars; but his insistence on etiquette nearly resulted in his detention in the north, and upon his return to court he was reprimanded for failing in his mission. He became prefect of Chuanchow, Chichow, Kanchow, Wuchow, Chienning and Shaohsing successively. In 1175 he was appointed imperial academician of Tuanming Palace, and he died that same year at the age of eighty, receiving the posthumous title of Wen-min (Cultured and Intelligent). His life appears in the *Sung Dynasty History*. Hung Mai was courageous and often spoke out boldly at court; he had wide knowledge, left many writings, and proved the best scholar of his generation. He compiled *Tales of Yi Chien* in his old age for personal pleasure, starting it in the early sixties of the twelfth century and completing it about a dozen years later. He first wrote two hundred books, then a sequel of a hundred, yet another sequel of a hundred, and finally twenty books of a third sequel. So in bulk this work rivals the *Tai-ping Miscellany*. Now only the following portions are extant: eighty books of the first part, fifty of the second, a few of the third series, and two abridged editions in fifty and twenty books. Strange tales should be rare and distinctive, but according to the author's preface he took a certain pride in quantity and was in such a hurry to finish the work before he died that he sometimes wrote as many as ten books in fifty days. And when he was sent tales from old tomes with some slight modifications — occasionally he received several volumes of these — he included them as they were without further editing. Since he aimed at quantity he could not do justice to these tales of marvels. He wrote thirty-one short prefaces, however, none of them repetitious but all containing original ideas. Chao Yu-shih[1] made a summary of these in his *Notes After Entertaining Guests*, describing them as "unsurpassed"; thus he was one who appreciated Hung Mai's worth.

There were imitations of Tang dynasty prose romances too. *The Story of Green Pearl,* wrongly attributed to a Tang dynasty writer, and *The Private History of Lady Yang* in two books, were both by Lo Shih of the Sung dynasty. The bibliographical section in the *Sung Dynasty History* also mentions three other tales by this author: *The Story of the Prince of Teng, The Story of Li Po* and *The Story of Hsu Mai,* all of which are lost. Lo Shih (930-1007) was a native of Yihuang in Fuchow who went to the Sung court from the kingdom of Southern Tang and served as an assistant imperial editor, before becoming prefect of Lingchow. After presenting a poem to the court he was appointed an imperial compiler. In all he presented 420 books to the court dealing with examinations, acts of piety and tales of the supernatural. His appointments included the posts of imperial editor, compiler of official history, master of ceremony, prefect of Chuchow, Huangchow and Shangchow, and finally a chief editor with honorary titles. He died at the age of seventy-eight. His life is recorded in the *Sung Dynasty History*. Lo Shih was a good geographer also and he wrote the *Tai-ping Geographical Record* in two hundred books, quoting from over a hundred sources, including occasional works of

---

[1] A scholar of the first half of the thirteenth century.

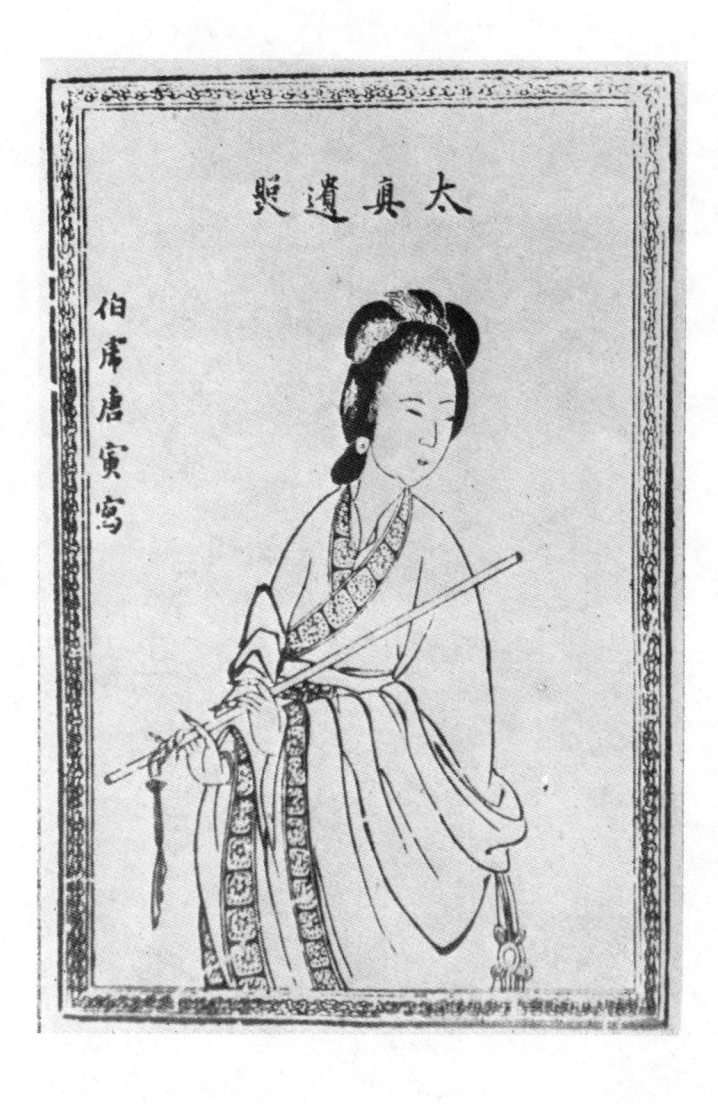

Portrait of Yang Kuei Fei. Drawn from imagination by Tang Yin (1470-1523)

fiction. *The Story of Green Pearl* and *The Private History of Lady Yang* are based on material from historical legends as well as from certain geographical records. These stories end with a moral like the Tang romances, but the tone is more strait-laced and solemn, as was characteristic of Sung scholars. This is most clearly seen in *The Story of Green Pearl*.

When the Prince of Chao seized power unlawfully, Sun Hsiu sent men to Shih Chung to ask for Green Pearl. . . .

Shih returned the wrathful answer: "Anything else you could have, but not Green Pearl."

Then Sun slandered Shih so that his whole family would be wiped out.

When guards came to arrest him, Shih said to Green Pearl: "This is on account of you."

In tears, Green Pearl replied: "I will show my loyalty by dying before you."

She threw herself from the pavilion and was killed. Shih Chung was taken to the east market and executed. Later generations called this pavilion Green Pearl Pavilion; it stands in Pukeng Lane near the Ti Fountain, east of Loyang. Green Pearl had a pupil, Sung Wei, a dazzling beauty skilled in playing the flute, who was later taken to Emperor Ming Ti's palace. In Paichow now is a stream flowing from Shuangchio Mountain to meet the Yungchow River which is known as Green Pearl River, just as in Kueichow there are Chao-chun Village and Chao-chun Fair, and in Soochow there are Hsi Shih Valley and Rouge Pool, all named after famous beauties. At the foot of Shuangchio Mountain there is also a Green Pearl Well. According to the local elders, those who drink from this well will have beautiful daughters; but some wise men in the villages who believed that no good could come of beauty, filled it up with big boulders, since when the girls born are beautiful but deformed. Strange indeed is the effect of natural scenery!. . .

Later poets writing of girls skilled in singing or dancing would allude to Green Pearl. . . . What, pray, is the reason for this? It is because though she was nothing but an illiterate serving-maid, yet such was her gratitude to her lord that she cared not for her own life; such was her chastity that she won admiration and praise from posterity. The men who enjoy high emoluments and high positions with no sense of humanity or righteousness, becoming turncoats and changing masters daily, blind to all but their own interest — these men, I say, are inferior in integrity to such a woman. Is this not shameful? I have therefore written this story, not simply because of her beauty or as a warning, but to criticize those who have no sense of gratitude and justice.

Later Chin Chun from Chiao County in Pochow also wrote romances, four of which can be found in *Notes from the Green Latticed Window* compiled by Liu Fu of the Northern Sung dynasty. Chin Chun attempted to imitate the Tang dynasty style, but both his manner and his subject matter are inferior, though occasionally one comes upon some fine phrase. Most of his stories deal with the past, and he shows great reluctance to touch on recent events. This was also due to the bigotry of the literati of the time — Lo Shih was just the same. One of Chin Chun's stories is the *Tale of Lady Swallow*, which has a preface saying that the manuscript was discovered in a broken basket hidden away in a corner of the house of a family named Li. It tells how Lady Swallow enters the Han palace, all that happens till she hangs herself and how through divine retribution she is changed into a giant tortoise. Ming scholars admired this work and believed it dated from the Han dynasty on account of such passages as the following: "The orchid-scented bath was full, and the lady seated in it seemed like translucent jade immersed in a cool spring three feet deep." In the same way, today, some men take the spurious *Secret Tales of the Han Palace* by Yang Shen of the Ming dynasty for an ancient text. *The Private Life of Lady Swallow* attributed to Ling Hsuan of the Han dynasty tells the same story but in better language. Two other stories by Chin Chun are *Tale of Li Mountain* and *Tale of the Hot Spring*, which deal with the scholar Chang Yu who is on his way back to Chengtu having failed in the examinations when at the foot of Li Mountain he hears legends about Lady Yang from the country people. Some days later he passes Li Mountain again and dreams that Lady Yang has summoned him to question him about recent events; she gives him a bath and dismisses him the next day. Awaking from this dream he writes some poems in the stationhouse. After this he is walking in the country when a shepherd hands him a poem given him by a lady the previous day, and this is Lady Yang's reply to Chang's poems. *The Singsong Girl Tan Yi-ko* is a story of the author's own time. Tan Yi-ko, a girl from a good family which has met with misfortune, goes to Changsha and becomes a singsong girl. She falls in love with Chang Chen-tzu of Juchow, who promises to marry her; but his mother forces him to marry another. Three years later his wife dies, and since by this time a visitor from Changsha has reproached Chang for breaking faith and praised Yi-ko's virtue, he marries the singsong girl. Later their son passes the imperial examinations, Yi-ko becomes a noble lady and they live happily till old age, blessed with many descendants. This story plagiarizes *Prince Huo's Daughter* by Chiang Fang, giving it a happy ending.

The author of *Forgotten Tales of the Ta Yeh Period* (605-617) is unknown, but the work has been attributed to Yen Shih-ku of the Tang dynasty. Another name for it is *Forgotten Tales of the Sui Dynasty*. A postscript says that it was discovered towards the middle of the ninth century in a pavilion of Wakuan Monastery in Shangyuan under the title *Records of Southern Beauties*, and it consisted of certain records left out of the *Sui Dynasty History*; but since the manuscript was unfortunately mutilated, the editor had to revise it before publication. No name is appended to this postscript, which is in fact by the author of the book. The story starts when Emperor Yang Ti of Sui decides to visit Yangchow and orders General Ma Shu-mo to build the Grand Canal. It goes on to describe the scenes of dissipation during the journey, the building of the labyrinth and the emperor's orgies there, which make his subjects begin to set their hopes on the Prince of Tang. Later Yuwen Hua-chi plots revolt and obtains the emperor's permission to give the government slaves freedom. So the revolt breaks out. The narrative is somewhat involved and much of it is not authentic history, but the style is pleasing and a number of the episodes quite charming.

Then another attendant was sent from Changan for the imperial retinue. This was Yuan Pao-erh, a slender girl of fifteen with delicate features, to whom the emperor grew much attached. One day a rare flower was presented from Loyang called Welcome-the-Imperial-Carriage, for, coming from some valley of Mount Sung it originally had no name. This, then, was presented to the emperor. . . .

The emperor bade Pao-erh take this flower in her hand and styled her the "Mistress of Flowers." Yu Shih-nan was beside the emperor at the time, drafting an edict for the northeast expedition, and Pao-erh stared hard at him for many minutes together. The emperor said to Yu:

"When I read in old records that Lady Swallow was so light that she could dance on a man's palm, I thought you writers must be guilty of exaggeration, for such a thing was impossible. But since getting Pao-erh, I know that it is quite true. What an odd child she is — look at the way she is watching you now! You are quick with your pen: write something to tease her!"

Obeying the royal command, Yu wrote:

> Learning to paint, she mixes the wrong colours,
> Sweet fool with her drooping sleeves!
> The emperor is touched by her artlessness;
> May she always, flower in hand, attend his carriage!

The emperor was delighted. . . .

As a result of the dissipated life he led, the emperor suffered from strange hallucinations. Once at Cock Tower on Lord Wu's estate he thought he saw the last king of Chen. . . . There were several dozen dancing girls in attendance, one of them more beautiful than the rest, and the emperor could not take his eyes off her.

The last king of Chen said: "Don't you know this girl, Your Majesty? This is Li-hua. I remember sailing north with her in my battleship past Peach Leaf Mountain. She is still unhappy to recall how she was trying out a pen at Lingchun Pavilion, in the middle of writing a reply on red silk to Chiang Chung's poem, when General Han Chin-hu galloped up on his black charger at the head of thousands of men in armour and gave us no quarter. So all our misfortunes came about."

Li-hua offered the emperor newly brewed wine in a green conch, and the emperor was very merry. But when he asked her to perform her famous Dance of Flowers in the Backyard, she told him she was out of practice and that since wrenching her back by throwing herself into the well she could no longer sway as in the old days. When the emperor insisted, however, she slowly rose and danced one measure.

The last king of Chen asked: "How does your Lady Hsiao compare with this girl of mine?"

The emperor said: "They are like the orchid in spring and the chrysanthemum in autumn — both fine blossoms in their season."

The Opening of the Canal also relates how General Ma Shu-mo is ordered by Emperor Yang Ti to build the Grand Canal, how he brings sufferings upon the people by digging up graves, accepting bribes and devouring infants, till finally his cruelty is exposed and he is executed. The *Story of the Labyrinth* tells of Emperor Yang Ti's dissipation in his later years. Wang Yi advises him earnestly against this life, and he keeps away from his harem for two days, but finding time drag he goes back;

then he hears the omen and knows that his dynasty is doomed. *Tales of Seas and Mountains* also deals with Emperor Yang Ti, describing his birth, the palaces he builds, the ghosts he sees, his journey to Yangchow, the advice Wang Yi gives him and so on till his murder. These three tales resemble the *Forgotten Tales of the Sui Dynasty*, except for a greater wealth of detail, but the language, interspersed with colloquialisms, is less distinguished. Since the last tale was included in Liu Fu's *Notes from the Green Latticed Window*, it must obviously date from the Northern Sung period, and no doubt this is true of the two others. In the present text the author's name is given as Han Wo of the Tang dynasty, but this attribution was made by Ming scholars. Men do not like to live under a dissipated and extravagant ruler, but they like to talk about him; so the Tang dynasty people enjoyed discussing Emperor Ming Huang and the Sung dynasty people Emperor Yang Ti. Later Lo Kuan-chung of the Ming dynasty combined these stories to make the *Romance of the Sui and Tang Dynasties*, which was rewritten by Chu Jen-hu of the Ching dynasty.

The *Story of Lady Mei* is by an unknown author. I suspect it originated because someone saw a painting of a beautiful lady holding a spray of plum blossom and attributed it to the reign of Emperor Ming Huang. It relates that a girl called Tsai-ping is chosen for the imperial palace, but Lady Yang grows jealous and has her dismissed. Then An Lu-shan's rebellion breaks out and she is killed in the fighting. A postscript to this work says that the manuscript was written in 848 and preserved in the collection of Chu Tsan-tu till the editor and

Yeh Meng-teh[1] discovered it. The author of the postscript is nameless, but he was the forger of this manuscript. Since he claimed to live at the same time as Yeh Meng-teh, this work must date from near the end of the Northern Sung dynasty. In certain modern editions the author's name is given as Tsao Yeh of the Tang dynasty, but this again was inserted by some Ming dynasty man.

---

[1] A noted scholar and high official at the beginning of the twelfth century.

12. STORY-TELLERS' PROMPT-BOOKS OF THE SUNG DYNASTY

The tales of the supernatural by Sung dynasty scholars were flat and insipid, while their longer prose romances usually avoided contemporary topics and dealt with the past; they were neither good imitations of earlier works nor yet original tales. Among the townsfolk, however, a new form of literature appeared: stories written in the vernacular which are close to modern short stories.

Stories written in the vernacular did not originate in the Sung dynasty. During the reign of Kuang Hsu (1875-1908) in the Ching dynasty, some old scrolls were discovered in the Thousand-Buddha Caves at Tunhuang, most of which were taken to England or France, the remainder going to the Peking Library. These scrolls, stored at the beginning of the Sung dynasty, were mostly Buddhist canons, though some were tales in the vernacular which had been transcribed at the end of the Tang dynasty or during the period of the Five Dynasties. *The Tang Emperor's Visit to the Nether Regions, The Filial Son Tung Yung* and *The Story of Chiu Hu* are now in the British Museum; *Wu Tzu-hsu Goes to the State of Wu* is in the possession of a collector in China. Not having seen these myself, I cannot compare them with the later stories. My guess is that this literary genre arose for two purposes: entertainment and religious teaching, especially the latter. Thus all those tales just mentioned include religious admonitions, and in the Peking Library we find popular versions of such Buddhist sutras as the *Vimalakirti-nirdesa* and the *Saddharma-pundarika* as well as stories of *Sakyamuni's Attainment of Buddhahood* and *Maudgalyayana's Descent to Hell*.

The beginning and the end of *The Tang Emperor's Visit to the Nether Regions* have been lost; only the middle of the story remains. This tells how Emperor Tai Tsung's spirit was haled before the judge of Hell for fratricide.[1] Hushing up the mistakes of the reigning house was not common before the Sung dynasty, yet this legend, which casts aspersions upon a Tang dynasty emperor, must have been written during the Tang dynasty. Here is an extract:

> The officer was too embarrassed to give his name.
> "Come closer!" ordered the emperor.
> Then he muttered in a low voice that his name was Tsui Tzu-yu.
> "I'll remember that," said the emperor.
> The officer sent an attendant to take the emperor to the gate of the court, and the attendant said: "Wait here, Your Majesty, while I go in and tell the judge to come." He went inside and bowed. "Your Honour, the King of Hell ordered me to bring the emperor's living spirit here for judgement. He is outside now: I have not brought him in yet."
> The judge hastily stood up.

Another Sung dynasty tale in the vernacular, *The Nine Admonitions of the Duke of Liang,* is couched in language as crude and simple as the last. It tells how Empress Wu (684-704) deposed the crown prince, making him the

---

[1] Before coming to the throne, he had quarrelled with his brothers and killed them.

Prince of Luling, in order to give the throne to her nephew Wu San-ssu. The prime minister Ti Jen-chieh advised her against this nine times, till finally the empress changed her mind and recalled the crown prince. Since this tale begins with an inscription on a stone tablet erected in commemoration of Ti Jen-chieh, Duke of Liang, written by Fan Chung-yen when he was sent to Poyang in 1033, it must date from after that year.

At midnight Empress Wu had another dream: She was playing chess with the Heavenly Maid and her king kept being checkmated so that she was beaten again and again. She woke up much afraid. The next morning when she held court she asked her ministers the meaning of this dream. Ti Jen-chieh said: "This dream bodes no good for our empire. Your Majesty dreamed that you were playing chess with the Heavenly Maid and that you kept being checkmated and lost the game. If the king is checkmated, it means he is not in his rightful place. Now the crown prince has been banished to Fangchow, hundreds of miles away. This is what the chess game meant. This is why you had this dream. I beg Your Majesty to make the prince your heir. To choose Wu San-ssu is not right."

("The Sixth Admonition")

But when we look at the vernacular tales that have come down to us from the Sung dynasty, they differ from the sermons and moral tales of the late Tang dynasty; in fact they developed from the story-tellers' scripts used in the amusement parks, for strange tales old and new were told in the Tang dynasty too. Tuan Cheng-shih says in his *Yuyang Miscellany*: "At the end of the Tai

Ho period (827-835) I went to a place of entertainment on my brother's birthday, and there was a story-teller. . . ." Li Shang-yin also writes in one of his poems:

> Some joke about Chang Fei's beard,
> Some about Teng Ai's stammer.[1]

Quite likely stories about the history of the Three Kingdoms were already being told, but further details are unknown to us. When the Sung capital was Pienliang[2] and there was abundance and general prosperity, many forms of popular entertainment were known, including variety shows in the market-places where story-telling figured. Story-tellers specialized in different types of tales. According to Meng Yuan-lao's *Reminiscences of the Eastern Capital*,[3] there were *hsiao-shuo*, *ho-sheng*, jokes, stories of the Three Kingdoms and stories of the Five Dynasties. After the Sung capital moved south to Hangchow the same fashion persisted. Wu Tzu-mu in his *Reminiscences of Hangchow*[4] says that stories were divided into four groups: "Story-tellers rely on their eloquence. There are four schools, each with its own traditions: *hsiao-shuo* or *yin-tzu-erh* are stories of romantic love, tales of the supernatural, historical legends, accounts of law-courts and detection, of sword-fights, contests with clubs or of the vicissitudes of fortune. . . . Stories old and new flow from the story-tellers' lips as smoothly as running water. Then there are Buddhist tales, and reli-

---

[1] Chang Fei and Teng Ai were famous generals in the *Romance of the Three Kingdoms*.
[2] Present-day Kaifeng.
[3] Written in 1147.
[4] Written in the second half of the thirteenth century.

gious dialogues . . . as well as popular Buddhist sermons. Historical romances tell of the rise and fall of dynasties, of battles or events in the Han or Tang dynasties. The *ho-sheng* deal with particular persons or things. Nai-teh-weng in his *Notes of the Chief Sights in the Capital*[1] describing Hangchow in its heyday, also spoke of four groups of stories: *hsiao-shuo*, Buddhist lore, historical romances and *ho-sheng*. He divided *hsiao-shuo* into tales of romantic love and the supernatural, stories of law-courts, detection, athletic contests and changes of fortune, and accounts of battles and wars. The four categories of stories mentioned by Chou Mi in his *Tales of the Old Capital*[2] are slightly different again. He speaks of historical tales, Buddhist legends, romances and jokes, but not of *ho-sheng*. He also mentions that the story-tellers had their own guild. From this we can see that story-tellers were divided into different categories and that they had an organization to help them to improve their craft.

Though story-tellers had to rely on their ingenuity and ready wit, they also had prompt-books known as *hua pen* to fall back on. Wu Tzu-mu describes the scripts of historical romances as "a medley of fact and fiction. . . . These stories relate events of past dynasties and in no time at all convey the main theme to their hearers." Nai-teh-weng says more or less the same. We know from this that the historical romances were half true and half imaginary, besides being compact and swift-moving. *Popular Tales of the Five Dynasties* and

---

[1] Written in 1235.
[2] Written towards the end of the thirteenth century, when the Sung dynasty had fallen.

Popular Stories of the Capital follow this tradition and have a similar style.

Popular Tales of the Five Dynasties are historical romances which must belong to the category "Stories of the Five Dynasties" mentioned by Meng Yuan-lao. This work devotes two books to each of the Five Dynasties: Liang, Tang, Tsin, Han and Chou. Each tale opens with a poem, the story follows and another verse ends the whole. The first tale about the Later Liang dynasty (907-923) is rather unusual. It opens with a summary of history from the earliest times, relating the rise and fall of different dynasties. It also contains the idea of divine retribution.

> Long years the dragons and tigers fought,
> In the Five Dynasties: Liang, Tang, Tsin, Han and Chou;
> States rose and fell as candles gutter out in the wind,
> In swift succession sovereigns lost their thrones.

After the primeval chaos was first divided and knowledge spread, Fu Hsi made the trigrams and invented writing, the Yellow Emperor ruled with little effort and the world became civilized. . . . Then all the barons obeyed him save only Chih Yu and the Fiery Emperor who harried the barons. So the Yellow Emperor led the barons and raised a great army. . . . He slew the Fiery Emperor, captured Chih Yu, and pacified all nations. Thus the Yellow Emperor was the first to slaughter men and to teach the use of arms. . . .

Then King Tang set upon King Chieh,[1] King Wu upon King Chou.[2] These were subjects who killed their liege lords and usurped their realm, and in this they

---
[1] The last king of the Hsia dynasty.
[2] The last king of the Shang dynasty.

were guilty of a crime. Later, when the Chou dynasty was in decline, the barons grew powerful; and in the two hundred and forty years of the Spring and Autumn Period[1] many subjects killed their masters, many sons their fathers. Then seeing that morality and law were forgotten, the sage Confucius wrote without reserve the book called the *Spring and Autumn Annals*, praising the good and condemning evil men. Thus Mencius said that after Confucius wrote the *Annals*, all traitors and villains trembled. Then there came Liu Chi, the First Emperor of Han, who took the realm from the Emperor of Chin by no act of treason:

>Grasping three feet of gleaming steel,
>He conquered all the land!

After Liu Chi killed his rival Hsiang Yu and founded the empire of Han, he grew suspicious of his three best supporters, Han Hsin, Peng Yueh and Chen Hsi, and had them killed. Then, wrongly slain, they appealed to the Heavenly Emperor, and Heaven took pity on them because they had been slaughtered though innocent, and decreed that their spirits should be born again as three heroes. Han Hsin's spirit went to the family of Tsao and became Tsao Tsao, Peng Yueh's spirit went to the family of Sun and became Sun Chuan, while Chen Hsi's spirit went to the imperial house and became Liu Pei. These three carved up the Han empire between them . . . and the story of their three states was known as the *History of Three Kingdoms*. . . .

The story-teller proceeds from the Tsin to the Tang dynasty, then to the rebellion of Huang Chao (875-884)

---

[1] 722-481 B.C.

and Chu Wen's establishment of the Later Liang dynasty. The second part is missing, but the story should conclude with the end of that dynasty. Certain parts of the narrative are longer and more detailed than others. The narrator's treatment of important historical events is rather summary, but minor incidents are elaborated. For the reader's entertainment, he introduces parallel cases, short verses and jokes. Here is the passage describing how Huang Chao, having failed in the examination, joins Chu Wen and some other brigands and goes to rob the Ma family in Hou Family Village:

Huang Chao said: "When we go to rob them, you need do nothing. I have a sword called Sangmen which was given me by Heaven: when I draw it, no one can resist me." So they left. On their way was a great peak known as Hanging Sword Peak, which took half a day to climb — a towering mountain! Its foothills stretched out to the corners of the earth and its top reached up to heaven! Old grey elms brushed the infinite sky, one lonely pine rose sheer to pierce the azure; the mountain pheasant contended with the cock of the sun, the Milky Way flowed into the mountain brook, the spray of the waterfall mingled with the rain and rugged crags jostled the clouds. You want to know how high it was?

> Some years ago a woodcutter
> Was climbing there and fell;
> He hasn't reached the bottom yet,
> As far as I can tell!

When Huang Chao and his three brothers had crossed this high mountain, they saw Hou Family Village in the distance. What a fine village that was! The rocks reached up to the clouds and the hills came down to the streams, weeping willows by the dyke swept over the bridge in the breeze and wild flowers by the roadside gleamed in the sun above the lonely ford! When the four brothers saw that the village was little more than a mile away and it was barely noon, they went into the woods to rest, meaning to go to Ma's house that evening.

We do not know how many volumes *Popular Stories of the Capital* originally had, for today only Book 10 to Book 16 are available. Each book contains one story, and these are *The Jade Bodhisattva, The Monk's Poem, Ghosts of the Western Hill, The Honest Clerk, The Dismissed Prime Minister, Fifteen Strings of Cash*[1] and *The Double Mirror*. Each is a complete story with a beginning and an end which can be read at one sitting, just as described in Wu Tzu-mu's *Reminiscences*. Most of the stories were based on recent events or earlier tales, and though their main purpose was to entertain they pointed a moral too. They usually start with a preamble or short tale before embarking on the main story. In *The Jade Bodhisattva*, for example, to lead up to the Prince of Hsienan's excursion to see the spring sights, the story-teller quotes about a dozen verses:

> The sunny hills are pleasing to the eye,
> From sandy shores the homing geese take flight;
> Outside the Eastern Gate the flowers spring,
> The southern fields turn emerald overnight.
> Before crows nest on poplars by the dyke,
> To feast my eyes on hills in spring I come;

---

[1] Translated and published in English by Foreign Languages Press, Peking, 1957.

> The apricots are not in blossom yet,
> But crimson petals flutter from the plum.

This poem on the countryside in early spring is not as good as this verse on mid-spring. . . . Still, none of these three can compare with the lines written by Wang An-shih[1] when he saw petals blown off and knew that it was the wind that drove spring away:

> The wind in spring may chuckle,
> The wind in spring may frown;
> It coaxes buds to open,
> And then it blows them down.

But Su Tung-po denied that the wind was to blame: it was the spring rain that drove the spring away.

> Before the shower the trees were bright with flowers,
> The shower has passed, but now no flowers abide;
> Across the wall flit butterflies and bees —
> Can spring be hiding on the other side?

Chin Shao-yu blamed neither the wind nor the rain, but said spring slips away with the willow catkins:

> When April comes the spring must go,
> Off catkins float or sink to rest;
> The fickle catkins will not grieve,
> One flutters east, another west.

According to Wang Yen-sou, though it was not the fault of the wind or the rain, nor of the willow catkins, the butterflies, the orioles, the cuckoos or the swallows; for as soon as ninety days were up it was time for spring to depart.

---

[1] Prime minister during the reign of Emperor Shen Tsung (1068-1085). He enforced a number of reforms to strengthen the government's authority, but these ended in failure.

> It would be wrong to blame the wind or rain,
> For spring must vanish though we know not why;
> Now fade the red cheeks of the tiny plum,
> Their small beaks gold no more, young swallows fly;
> Now cuckoos cry and blossoms drift away,
> While silkworms glut themselves on mulberry leaves;
> And as spring vanishes, no man knows where,
> Beside the lonely stream the poet grieves.

Why do I quote this poem about spring's departure? During the Shao Hsing period there lived in Hangchow, the southern capital, a certain Prince of Hsienan, a native of Yenan and the military governor of three garrison areas. One day, observing that spring was nearly over, he took his womenfolk out to enjoy the scenery. . . .

Such prefaces, using poems or anecdotes, are different from those of the historical romances which start with the beginning of history; but whether these introductions resemble the main story or are entirely dissimilar, they usually deal with contemporary events. Those that differ from the main story afford a contrast, while those that are similar give a foretaste of what is to come, leading suddenly to the main narrative and making the general purport clear from the start. This is probably what Nai-teh-weng and Wu Tzu-mu referred to in their accounts. These preambles were known as "triumphant beginnings," the word "triumphant" being used because most of the audience were soldiers: the stories were not told to members of the court. The form resembles that of the *Popular Tales of the Five Dynasties* in so far as minor episodes are elaborated, but greater detail is given. *Ghosts of the Western Hill* describes how a scholar named Wu is deceived by ghosts and everyone he meets is a ghost. This is based on a tale in an earlier collection of ghost stories, *An Assembly of Ghosts*, but it is told with a greater wealth of minute particulars than even the later romances of the Ming and Ching dynasties. Here is one example:

Fortunately, after he had kept school for a year, all the families in that street sent their children to him and he made quite a comfortable living. One day as he was teaching he heard the bell above his black door-curtain ring and someone walked in. It was no other than his old neighbour Mrs. Wang, who had moved away ten years ago. The woman was a go-between, living by that profession.

Wu greeted her, saying: "I haven't seen you for a long time, ma'am. Where are you living now?"

Mrs. Wang replied: "I thought you might have forgotten me. I am living by the city wall just inside Chientang Gate."

"How old are you this year, ma'am?"

"Seventy-five. And you?"

"I am twenty-two."

"What, only twenty-two! You look more than thirty. I dare say your work is very tiring. In my humble opinion, you need a wife to keep you company."

Wu said: "I have asked friends several times to help, but there was no one suitable."

"Well, this is a lucky coincidence, I can tell you! I know just the girl for you. She has property worth one thousand strings of cash as well as a maid-servant. And not only is she a beauty but she can play all sorts of musical instruments, she can write and keep accounts, and she comes from a rich official family. She refuses to marry anyone but a scholar. Are you interested?"

When Wu heard this he was overjoyed. Beaming all over his face, he said: "If I could find such a wife that would be wonderful! Where is she now? . . ."

After the fall of the Southern Sung dynasty, variety shows died out and story-telling became less popular too. But the scripts were left, and later writers who were attracted by them copied their style; so though the later imitations were not genuine prompt-books, this form of literature persisted. The later collections include *Amazing Stories, Making the Drunkard Sober* and historical romances like the *Romance of the States of Eastern Chou* and the *Romance of the Sui and Tang Dynasties*. There was no longer a strict division between different forms, however, but all were known as *hsiao-shuo*.

13. IMITATIONS OF PROMPT-BOOKS IN THE SUNG AND YUAN DYNASTIES

The popularity of the stories in the vernacular induced many writers of that time to imitate them. During the Northern Sung dynasty Liu Fu compiled two collections of tales: *Notes from the Green Latticed Window* and its sequel. Though the language is crude these are not prompt-books; but each tale has a sub-title in the form of a verse like those at the end of Yuan dynasty dramas, and I suspect that this custom originated with the prompt-books in the Sung capital. Some written stories in the Sung dynasty took over the form of the prompt-books, and two of these are still extant: *Tripitaka's Search for Buddhist Sutras* and *Tales of the Hsuan Ho Period* (1119-1125). Both begin and end with verses, the narrative is interspersed with verses, and the language is largely colloquial. These are not entirely the same as the prompt-books, however: unlike the historical romances and tales in the vernacular, these are written as books and have no story-teller's preamble. Chien Tseng[1] in his catalogue of books classed *Tales of the Hsuan Ho Period* with such prompt-books as *Mother Lamp-Wick*, calling them all chantefables since they combine verse and prose. But *Tales of the Hsuan Ho Period* cannot compare with stories like *Fifteen Strings of Cash* or *The Double Mirror* in *Popular Stories of the Capital*, which are the work of highly skilled profes-

---
[1] A bibliographer of the Ching dynasty.

sional story-tellers. Though *Tales of the Hsuan Ho Period* has verse and prose intermingled, it was not told by a professional story-teller but compiled by patching up old stories based on earlier records and popular legends; the form is similar, but this collection lacks spirit and the language is flat and insipid. *Tripitaka's Search for Buddhist Sutras* is even more crudely written. Nevertheless, during this period when the art of story-telling had declined and prompt-books were gradually turning into written tales, these works at least provided a link with the past.

An old three-volume edition of *Tripitaka's Search for Buddhist Sutras* has been preserved in Japan; another small edition is described in the title as a chantefable, but the contents are the same. A postscript to this book says that it was printed by the Chang Family Shop in Chung-wa-tzu, and since this was a Hangchow publisher in the Sung dynasty the book was considered a Sung dynasty edition. It is quite possible, however, that the Chang Family Shop carried on into the Yuan dynasty and that this book was printed then. There are seventeen chapters in it — the earliest known example of fiction divided into chapters — and each contains a number of verses. This is why the work was described as a chantefable. In both existing editions the first chapter is missing. The second chapter tells how Tripitaka met Monkey.

> The six men set off together. . . . At noon one day they met a scholar in white coming from the east. This scholar bowed to the monk and said: "Greetings! Where are you going? Are you on your way to the Western Paradise to find Buddhist sutras?"

The master joined his hands together as he answered: "The people of this eastern land have no Buddhist scriptures. Thus I have been ordered to fetch sutras."

The scholar said: "You have already set off twice to find sutras and met with trouble half way. If you go again, you will risk a thousand deaths."

"How do you know?" asked the master.

"I am no other than the king of eighty-four thousand monkeys with bronze heads and iron brows who live in Purple Cloud Cavern on the Mountain of Flowers and Fruit. I have come to help you get these sutras. There are a million stages on this journey and you must pass thirty-six kingdoms, all beset with danger."

"This is a most fortunate encounter," said the master. "All the men of the eastern land will benefit greatly." Forthwith he changed the scholar's name to Friar Monkey, and all seven of them went on the following day. Monkey made this verse to mark the occasion:

> Millions of stages I have passed,
> Coming here to assist the great master;
> My whole heart is set on the faith,
> I shall go with him to Western Cock-Claw Mountain.

The master answered with another verse:

> Today I was predestined
> To encounter a great saint;
> If we meet with devils on our way,
> You must use your holy power to protect the faith!

Thanks to Monkey's magic power they reach the palace of the god Brahma. There, when Tripitaka has delivered his sermon, he is given a cap that can make its wearer invisible, a holy wand with a golden ring and an alms bowl. Then they go back to earth. They pass

Fragrant Wood Monastery and the perils of Great Serpent Mountain and Nine-Dragon Pool; but Monkey's magic enables them to proceed safely. Then the deity Sandy transforms himself into a golden bridge, they cross a great river, pass through the Land of the Devil's Mother and the Land of Women and come to the Pool of the Heavenly Mother. There Tripitaka wants some fairy peaches and asks Monkey to steal them.

The master said: "Today the fairy peaches are ripe. Let us take a few."

Monkey said: "When I was eight hundred years old I stole ten peaches and was caught by the Heavenly Mother. For that I was given eight hundred strokes with an iron rod on the left side and three thousand strokes on the right, then sent to live in Purple Cloud Cavern on the Mountain of Flowers and Fruit. Even now my sides are aching: I certainly won't steal again. . . ."

Further on they saw a precipice a hundred thousand feet high, with a cavern in the rock four or five *li* wide and two unfathomable lakes which stretched for several dozen *li* — no bird would fly over them. The seven of them, sitting down to rest, raised their heads to look at the distant precipice where peach trees with luxuriant leaves had grown to touch the sky, looking down on the lake. . . .

Monkey said: "There must be a dozen peaches there but they are guarded by local deities: there is no way to steal them."

The master said: "You have great magic power, you are bound to succeed."

While he was still speaking three peaches dropped into the lake, and he cried out in alarm. Monkey said: "Master, don't be afraid! These are just ripe peaches that have fallen into the water."

Then the master said: "Fetch them here for me to eat. . . ."

Monkey struck the rock with his wand and two young boys appeared, one of whom said he was three thousand years old, the other five thousand. . . . He struck a few times more till another boy came out.

"How old are you?" asked Monkey.

The boy answered: "Seven thousand."

Then Monkey put down the wand and told the boy to come and sit on his hand, and he asked the monk to eat him. The master took fright and wanted to run away. But Monkey rolled the boy in his hand and changed him into a date, and this he swallowed. Upon his return later to the Tang empire, he spat it out in western Szechuan. A ginseng plant grows there to this very day. Then a figure appeared in the sky who chanted aloud:

> Rogue from the Flower and Fruit Mountain,
> You played your tricks here when young;
> Now I see you again from the sky —
> The thief who stole the peaches has returned.

They finally reach India where they obtain 5,400 volumes of Buddhist sutras but fail to get the *Prajna-paramitra-hridaya-sutra*, which is given them by a bodhisattva after their return to Fragrant Wood Monastery. When these seven pilgrims reach China again, the emperor welcomes them outside the city gate and Buddhism spread through all the country. On the fifteenth of the seventh month at noon, a lotus barge descends from the Heavenly Palace and Tripitaka rides on it to the Western Paradise. The emperor gives Monkey the title of Great Saint of Bronze Sinews and Iron Bones.

Tales of the Hsuan Ho Period used to be attributed to the Sung dynasty, but in it are quotations from scholars whose names seem those of Yuan dynasty men. This work must either date from the Yuan dynasty or have been written in the Sung with interpolations added in the Yuan. If certain of the expressions appear to belong to the Sung dynasty, this may be due to the fact that much of the work was copied from earlier records and not written in the author's own words. This book is divided into two parts, starting with the sage kings Yao and Shun and ending with Emperor Kao Tsung's establishment of the Southern Sung capital at Linan, present-day Hangchow. The narrative follows a chronological order like the popular histories, but sections of other records are embodied verbatim instead of being rewritten; thus the style — it is only too apparent — is not consistent. There are ten sections in all. The first speaks of the faults of past rulers caused by profligacy, and serves as a sort of preamble in the style of the Sung dynasty story-tellers. The second describes the troubles caused by Wang An-shih's reforms,[1] and is typical of the political diatribes of scholars towards the end of the Northern Sung dynasty. The third tells how Wang An-shih introduced Tsai Ching[2] into the government, and how Tung Kuan[3] and Tsai Yu[4] inspected the frontier. The

---

[1] See note on p. 148.
[2] He became prime minister under Emperor Hui Tsung (1101-1125).
[3] A powerful eunuch in the reign of Emperor Hui Tsung.
[4] Tsai Ching's son.

first section is written in the vernacular, the second and third in classical language interspersed with verses. The fourth section deals with the rebels of the Liangshan Marshes,[1] beginning with how Yang Chih tries to sell his sword and kills a man, and going on to how Chao Kai steals the presents and persuades twenty men to go with him to Liangshan to turn rebel, how Sung Chiang kills Yen Po-hsi and flees to the temple of the goddess, coming out when the soldiers have left to thank the deity.

With a sudden sound a scroll appeared on the altar. Sung Chiang unrolling this discovered a Heavenly Writ containing thirty-six names and a four-line verse:

> Conquest by Mountain Wood;
> Arms wielded by Water Workers;[2]
> Some day he will become a leader of men;
> His fame will spread through the land.

Sung Chiang read this in silence, but thought to himself: "This obviously refers to my name." Unrolling the scroll further and reading carefully, he saw the names of thirty-six commanders. What were they? Wu Chia-liang the Star of Wisdom, Li Chin-yi the Jade Unicorn, Yang Chih the Green-Faced Beast, Li Hai the River-Churning Dragon, Shih Chin the Nine-Coloured Dragon, Kungsun Sheng the Cloud-Piercing Dragon, Chang Shun the White Strip in the Waves, Chin Ming the Thunderbolt, Yuan Hsiao-chi the Living King of Hell, Yuan Hsiao-wu the Year God, Yuan Chin the

---

[1] This refers to the famous peasant revolt suppressed in 1121. Its story forms the basis of the novel *Shui Hu Chuan*.

[2] Mountain 山 and Wood 木 together approximate to Sung 宋, while Water 水 and Workers 工 make Chiang 江.

Killer, Kuan Pi-sheng the Big Sword, Lin Chung the Leopard Head, Li Kuei the Black Whirlwind, Chai Chin the Small Whirlwind, Hsu Ning the Golden Lance, Li Ying the Heaven-Smiting Eagle, Liu Tang the Red-Headed Devil, Tung Ping the Impetuous, Lei Heng the Winged Tiger, Chu Tung the Fine Beard, Tai Tsung the Fast Walker, Wang Hsiung the Young Hero, Sun Li the Sick Hero, Hua Yung the Archer, Chang Ching the Featherless Arrow, Mu Heng the Irresistible, Yen Ching the Debonair, Lu Chih-shen the Rough Monk, Wu Sung the Friar, Huyen Cho the Iron Mace, So Chao the Spearhead, Shih Hsiu the Reckless, Chang Chen the Fiery Boatman, Tu Chien the Sky-Reacher and Chao Kai the Heavenly Prince.

At the end of this list Sung Chiang read: "This Heavenly Writ is sent down to the thirty-six brave generals to be commanded by Sung Chiang, Defender of Justice. Let him spread the virtues of loyalty and justice and wipe out evil-doers and wicked men!"

Then Sung Chiang goes with Chu Tung and eight others to Liangshan. By then Chao Kai has died and Sung Chiang is chosen as leader of the rebels.

Each general led his brave men to attack different districts and counties, burning and killing. They took twenty-four sub-prefectures and more than eighty counties as they advanced in Huaiyang, Chinghsi and Hopei, robbing and holding men for ransom, and amassing much loot.

Finally Lu Chih-shen and the others join Sung Chiang, making up the required number of thirty-six generals.

One day Sung Chiang proposed to Wu Chia-liang: "We have now our full complement of thirty-six generals. Let us not forget how the God of the Eastern Mountain has protected us, but go and burn incense there as we pledged." They chose a day on which to set out, and Sung Chiang wrote these four lines for his flag:

> Thirty-six we came,
> As twice eighteen we leave;
> If one is missing,
> We shall not return.

So Sung Chiang led his thirty-six generals to present a gold incense-burner to the God of the Eastern Mountain, fulfilling his pledge. The court was powerless against him, and had to issue an edict inviting Sung Chiang and his band to come over. Commander-in-chief Chang Shu-yeh, who came of a long line of generals, came to persuade Sung Chiang and his thirty-six generals to declare their allegiance to the house of Sung. Then all of them were given honorary titles and posted as inspectors of different provinces. So the rebellions in the north, east and west were pacified. Later Sung Chiang distinguished himself in the capture of Fang La and was made a governor.

The fifth section tells how Emperor Hui Tsung visits the courtesan Li Shih-shih, how Tsao Fu advises against this, and how Chang Tien-chueh retires. The sixth section deals with the coming of the Taoist priest Lin Ling-su and the miracles which occur after his death. The seventh section describes the magnificent display in winter during the Lantern Festival celebrations. Here is an example of these sections, all of which are written in the vernacular:

On the eve of the Lantern Festival in the sixth year of the Hsuan Ho period, from a red cord fastened to the palace gate a stork flew down with an edict in its beak. An officer took this and unfolded it to announce the decree to the populace. Then guards holding gilded placards raised a shout and the citizens of the capital surged forward like clouds or billows, wearing sprigs of plum and willow on their heads. So they came to Sea-Monster Mountain to see the lanterns. Three or four officials of noble rank who were above Hsuanteh Gate . . . were ordered by the emperor to scatter gold and silver coins for the citizens. Yuan Tao, the officer in charge of singsong girls, wrote these verses about this distribution of largesse:

> The citizens enjoy the spectacle,
> Glad of this peaceful reign and the Lantern Festival;
> The green Sea-Monster Mountain towers high,
> The palace gate is decked with pearls,
> Surely the goddess of the moon has left paradise
> And come down to the world of men.
> The rain of mercy descends,
> The emperor looks down from his balcony,
> Golden coins are scattered wide.
> Today the people may jostle and push at will
> And the officers will pardon
> Their lack of politeness.

After the scattering of coins the citizens strolled through the city which was indeed a splendid sight.

> Bright lanterns turn the night to day,
> While songs and flutes make an eternal spring.

The eighth section in the later half of this work relates how the Golden Tartars transport grain and how the capital is taken by storm. The ninth and tenth sections deal with the invasion of the Golden Tartars: how they enter the capital, take the emperor and empress to the north and humiliate them, and then how Emperor Kao Tsung makes Hangchow his capital. These episodes are taken from *After the Invasion, Records of Grievances* and its sequel. These works, which are still extant, were attributed to Hsin Chi-chi,[1] though as early as the Southern Sung dynasty scholars had pointed out that they could not be written by this poet. The book concludes as follows:

Now learned men say that Emperor Kao Tsung lost two opportunities to regain the northern territory. In the early part of his reign he lost an opportunity because his ministers Huang Chien-shan and Wang Po-yen were anxious to keep peace, while during the Shao Hsing period he lost another opportunity because the prime minister Chin Kuei was working for the enemy. Because of these two lost opportunities, the northern territory was not recovered, the death of the former emperor was not avenged, the national disgrace was not wiped out! This makes all loyal and just men gnash their teeth and long to tear those traitors limb from limb!

This comment is typical of scholars during the Southern Sung dynasty after Chin Kuei lost power.

---

[1] 1140-1207.

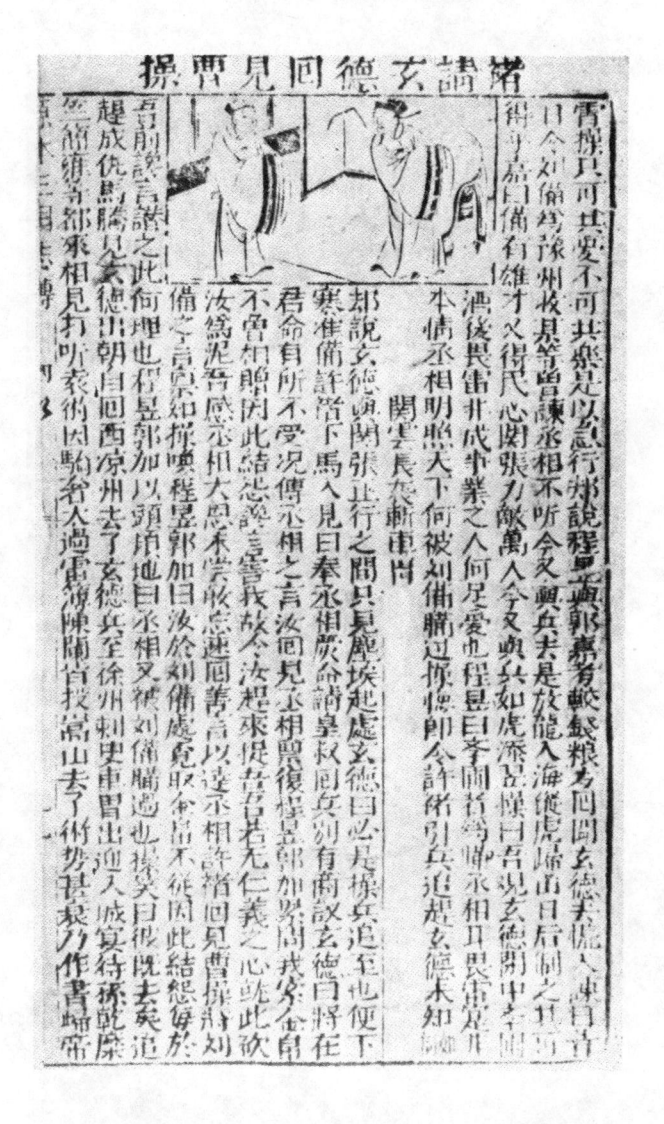

Text and illustration from an old edition of the
Romance of the Three Kingdoms published about 1610

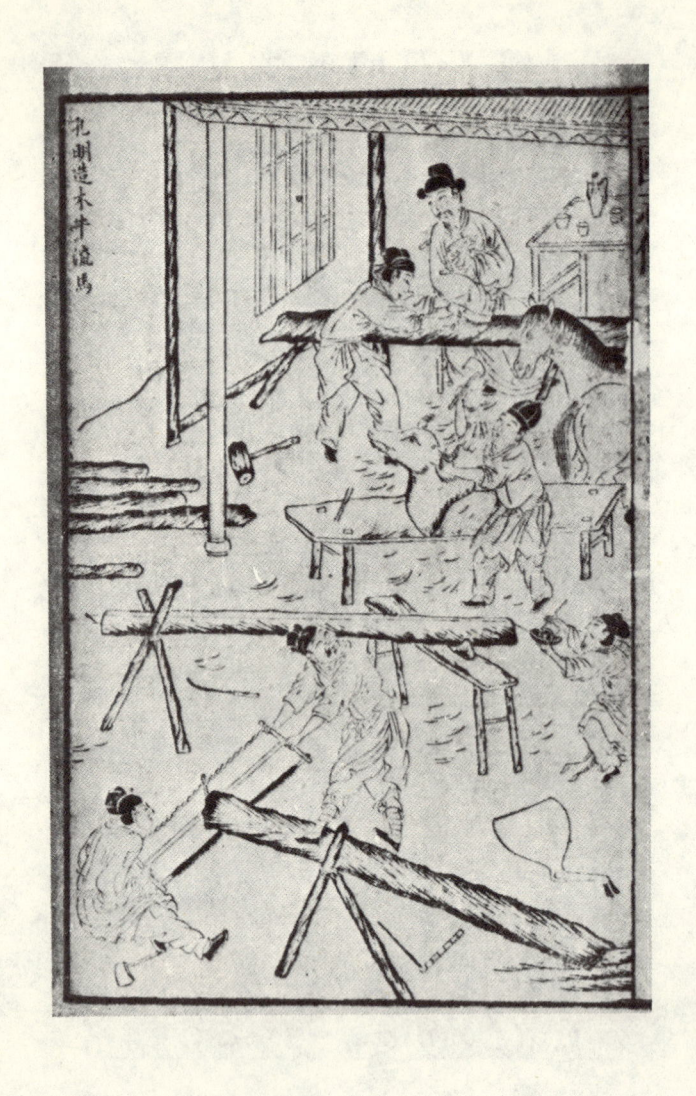

Illustration from an old edition of the *Romance of the Three Kingdoms* published about 1625

14. HISTORICAL ROMANCES OF THE YUAN AND MING DYNASTIES

In the Sung dynasty there were many talented storytellers who narrated both short stories and popular histories, but as far as we know there were no written works of this kind. The Yuan dynasty, when times were troubled and culture at a low ebb, had even less literature. The Japanese Government Library has five popular works of fiction with illustrations published by the Yu Family of Hsinan during the Tzu Chih period (1321-1323) of the Yuan dynasty. These are *King Wu's Conquest of the Shangs, Annals of the Seven States (II)* or *Yueh Yi's Victory Over the State of Chi, The Annexation of the Six States by the Emperor of Chin, Han Hsin's Death at the Hands of Empress Lu* and *The Story of the Three Kingdoms.* Of these five only the last has been reprinted, and I have not read the other four. *The Story of the Three Kingdoms,* fully illustrated, was printed with woodcuts at the top of each page. The story starts with the pledge made by Liu Pei[1] and his two sworn brothers in the Peach Garden and ends with the death of Chuke Liang.[2] The preamble tells how the First Emperor of Han killed his ministers unjustly and the Jade Emperor passes judgement on him, ordering Han Hsin's

---

[1] Later king of Shu from 221 to 223.

[2] Liu Pei's prime minister, later a legendary figure on account of his wisdom.

spirit to return to earth as Tsao Tsao,[1] Peng Yueh's spirit to become Sun Chuan,[2] and the First Emperor's spirit to become the last emperor of Han. The idea is the same as in the *Popular Tales of the Five Dynasties*, but this is less well written than the earlier work: the language is crude and disjointed. Here is the account of the Battle of the Red Cliff:

> When Chuke Liang crossed the river and came to Hsiakou, Tsao Tsao on his boat groaned: "I am doomed!"
>
> His officers said: "It is all the fault of Chiang Kan." They drew their swords and cut Chiang Kan to pieces. Then Tsao Tsao boarded his boat and hastily tried to escape. When he came to the mouth of the river he saw that the vessels on all sides were in flames. Some dozen boats came alongside and from one of them Huang Kai cried: "Let Tsao Tsao be killed and the world will be at peace and secure!"
>
> Because Tsao Tsao's officers were unused to naval battles, the arrows they let fly shot down their own men. Now Tsao Tsao was taken by surprise, there was fire on all sides and arrows were raining down. He wanted to escape, but on the north there was Chou Yu, on the south Lu Su, on the west Ling Tung and Kan Ning, on the east Chang Chao and Wu Pao. They were closing in from all sides.
>
> The chronicler says: "Had not Tsao Tsao been destined to become emperor, he could never have escaped."

---

[1] Father of the founder of the Wei dynasty (220-265).
[2] King of Wu (222-252).

So Tsao Tsao succeeded in flying to the northwest, where a horse was found for him when he went ashore. The fire had started in the evening, but not till the next day did he break through. When Tsao Tsao looked back he could see smoke and flames covering the sky over the boats at Hsiakou, and less than ten thousand of his troops were left. Tsao Tsao went northwest. He had gone little more than a mile when five thousand troops on the bank led by General Chao Yun barred the way. The officers fought hard and Tsao Tsao broke through. . . . At night he reached a great forest. . . . Tsao Tsao made for Huajung, but he had not gone five miles when Lord Kuan barred his way with five hundred swordsmen. Tsao Tsao begged Lord Kuan to remember his former kindness, but Lord Kuan said that Chuke Liang had given strict orders to stop him. Tsao Tsao broke through the formation, and such a cloud of dust arose that he was able to escape. Lord Kuan pursued him a short way and then turned back. Going east for three or four miles, he found Liu Pei and Chuke Liang. . . .

Chuke Liang said: "Lord Kuan is a warm-hearted man and Tsao Tsao was good to him, so he let him escape."

When Lord Kuan heard this he remounted his horse in anger, asking leave to go after Tsao Tsao once more.

Liu Pei said: "Are you not worn out?"

Chuke Liang said: "I will go with him. All will be well. . . ."

The brevity and crudeness of the language are reminiscent of a prompt-book, for the story-teller would fill in the bare outline with dramatic details to entertain the audience. But the fact that this book has illustrations shows that it must have been printed as reading material. The other four works are probably of the same kind.

Even in the Sung dynasty, stories about the Three Kingdoms were popular. During the Three Kingdoms period there were many gallant men of great courage and wisdom who had countless stirring adventures; moreover the history of that period was more colourful than at the founding of the Han dynasty and less confusing than during the Warring States Period, making this a suitable subject for romances. So the poet Su Tung-po said: "Wang Peng once told me that when children are naughty and their families cannot stand them, they would toss them some money and make them sit in a flock to listen to old stories. When tales of the Three Kingdoms are told and the children heard of Liu Pei's defeat they frown or even snivel, while when they hear of Tsao Tsao's defeat they cry out for joy. This shows that good and evil men leave their mark in history for hundreds of generations."

In the Sung dynasty amusement park stories about the Three Kingdoms formed one special category, as did stories about the Five Dynasties. Playwrights of the Golden Tartar and Mongol periods often borrowed themes from the history of the Three Kingdoms: the Battle of the Red Cliff, the Death of Chuke Liang or the Battle of Wits. There are even more in present-day opera, all testifying to the popularity of these tales. Stories about the Three Kingdoms are particularly well known thanks to the popular romance by Lo Kuan-chung.

Lo Kuan-chung or Lo Pen was a citizen of Chientang, whose name has also been given as Lo Kuan. According to one account, he lived at the beginning of the Ming dynasty: at all events he was alive during the later half of the fourteenth century. He wrote several prose romances, and one Ming dynasty account attributes several dozen works to him. Those still in existence, apart from *The Romance of the Three Kingdoms*, are *The Romance of the Sui and Tang Dynasties, The Romance of the Five Dynasties, The Sorcerer's Revolt and Its Suppression by the Three Suis* and *Shui Hu Chuan*. Lo Kuan-chung was also the author of a play, i.e. *The Meeting of the Dragon and the Tiger*. All his romances, however, have been re-edited, cut or amplified by later writers: the originals no longer exist.

The earliest edition known to us of *The Romance of the Three Kingdoms* is that of 1494, which is divided into twenty-four books and two hundred and forty chapters. This professes to be based on the history of the Three Kingdoms by Chen Shou of the Tsin dynasty. It covers ninety-seven years of history in all, from the Peach Garden pledge of friendship in A.D. 184 to the capture of Nanking by Wang Chun in 280. The events are taken from Chen Shou's history and Pei Sung-chih's commentary, elaborated and narrated in the story-tellers' style. Most of the views on history conform to those of Chen Shou, Pei Sung-chih, Hsi Tso-chih and Sun Sheng,[1] and many verses by past "chroniclers" are quoted. The narrative is restricted by being based on history, and when the author inserts imaginary details, fact and fiction are intermixed. Thus Hsieh Chao-chih[2] of the Ming dynasty complains that the work is pedantic because it sticks too close to historical facts, while Chang Hsueh-

---

[1] Tsin dynasty historians.
[2] A seventeenth century scholar.

cheng[1] of the Ching dynasty comments that it is rather confusing to have three-tenths of fiction mixed with seven-tenths of fact. There are shortcomings in the characterization too. Lo Kuan-chung wished to make Liu Pei a kindly man, but draws a character who seems a hypocrite. Wanting to depict Chuke Liang's wisdom, he makes him appear a sorcerer. His only success is in the portrayal of Lord Kuan Yu, who is a gallant general to the life. Here is one description of Kuan Yu's appearance and courage:

> Below the steps someone came forward with a great shout. "Let me go! I shall cut off Hua Hsiung's head and bring it back to the camp!"
>
> They turned and saw standing before the tent a man of gigantic stature with a long beard, eyes like those of a phoenix and eyebrows like recumbent silkworms; his face was ruddy as ripe dates, his voice deep as a bell. Yuan Shao inquired who this officer might be and Kungsun Tsan told him it was Liu Pei's sworn brother Kuan Yu. Yuan Shao asked his rank, and Kungsun replied that he was a knight archer under Liu Pei.
>
> Yuan Shu roared: "Are you trying to make fools of us? Do you think we have no generals to send out? How dare an archer boast so wildly? Drive the fellow out with clubs!"
>
> But Tsao Tsao hastily stopped him, saying: "Don't be angry! A man who talks so big must have some ability. Let him enter the lists: you can punish him if he fails.". . .

---

[1] An eighteenth century historian.

Kuan said: "If I fail, you can cut off my head!" Tsao Tsao ordered a cup of hot wine to be brought for him before he rode out.

Kuan said: "You can pour it out; I shall soon be back."

Leaving the camp he drew his sword and leaped into his saddle. The barons heard a great drumming outside the palisade and a deafening shout, as if heaven and earth had crashed and mountains had crumbled. They were all amazed. Before they could send a man to bring them news, a horse's bells were heard tinkling and Kuan rode back. When he tossed Hua Hsiung's head to the ground, the wine was still warm. . . .

Again, when Tsao Tsao is defeated at the Red Cliff, but Chuke Liang realizes that their enemy is not fated to perish there, he sends Lord Kuan to defend Huajung in order that Tsao Tsao may escape; but he deliberately lays stress on military discipline and exacts a pledge from Lord Kuan before he sets out. In this passage Chuke Liang is described as a crafty strategist, but Lord Kuan is shown to have great dignity. This presentation is quite different from the Yuan dynasty story-teller's prompt-book.

On the road to Huajung were three bodies of troops: one remained behind, one filled up the moats, and one followed Tsao Tsao over the steep mountains till they came to easier terrain. When Tsao Tsao looked back he had little more than three hundred horsemen behind him, and not one had his full accoutrement. A little further on, whipping his horse, Tsao Tsao laughed long and loud. His men asked him why he was laughing.

He said: "Chuke Liang and Chou Yu are always said to be crafty, but to my mind they are fools. I brought this defeat on myself by belittling the enemy. Had they had an army ambushed here, we could have been captured easily."

The words were hardly out of his mouth when a signal was heard and five hundred swordsmen in formation appeared on both sides, with Lord Kuan in the middle barring their way, wielding his green-dragon sword and astride his roan horse. At this sight, Tsao Tsao's men were frightened out of their wits and gazed at each other in silent consternation.

Tsao Tsao in their midst said: "Since it has come to this, let us fight to the death."

His officers said: "Our men are no cowards but our horses are utterly spent. To fight means certain death."

Cheng Yi said: "I know Lord Kuan. He swaggers in front of his superiors but is kind to his inferiors. He will bully the strong but take no advantage of the weak. He must rescue those in distress; his kindness and gallantry are known throughout the world. He owes you gratitude from the past, so why not appeal to him? Then we shall certainly escape with our lives."

Tsao Tsao followed his advice. Riding up to Lord Kuan forthwith, he bowed from the saddle and said: "How are you, sir? It is a long time since we met."

Lord Kuan bowed back from his saddle and replied: "I am here under orders from our commander Chuke Liang. I have waited for Your Lordship for many hours."

Tsao Tsao said: "My army is routed, my position is desperate — I have no way out. I hope you will remember what passed between us in the old days."

Lord Kuan answered: "Though in the old days I received many favours at Your Lordship's hands, I repaid my debt of gratitude by helping you in the Battle of Paima. I am here today under orders and not free to do as I like."

Tsao Tsao said: "Can you remember how you went through the Five Passes, killing the defending generals on the way? A gentleman of the old school would think justice and gallantry the chief things in life. You have made a careful study of the *Annals* of Confucius, have you forgotten the story of how Lord Yu pursued Tzu-cho?"

When Lord Kuan heard this he hung his head and was silent. For Lord Kuan was a man who loved justice as his life. How could he remain unmoved when he saw Tsao Tsao's troops nearly bursting into tears of terror, and remembered the occasion when Tsao Tsao had let him escape at the Five Passes? He wheeled round on his horse and ordered his men: "Fan out!" This was to let Tsao Tsao break through.

The moment that Lord Kuan moved away, Tsao Tsao and his officers galloped ahead, and by the time Lord Kuan turned back Tsao Tsao's men had already escorted him through the cordon. Lord Kuan raised a loud shout, whereat Tsao Tsao's officers dismounted and kowtowed, begging him with tears to spare them. He had no desire to kill them all, and as he hesitated Chang Liao galloped over to help Tsao Tsao escape. Lord Kuan saw that this was another old friend of his.

So heaving a long sigh he let them all go. A later chronicler wrote a poem on this:

> This hero, this champion of justice,
> Never forgot a favour in his life;
> His prowess was splendid as the sun and moon,
> His fame shook earth and heaven,
> His loyalty and courage were peerless in the
>   Three Kingdoms;
> His strategy to trap the enemy with flood
>   was superb;
> Even today, more than ten centuries later,
> The soldiers worship this heroic spirit.

After the Hung Chih period (1488-1505) many versions of this novel appeared: it is still impossible to say how many editions were published in the Ming dynasty. During the reign of Kang Hsi (1662-1722) in the Ching dynasty, Mao Tsung-kang, following the example of Chin Sheng-tan[1] who abridged *Shui Hu Chuan* and *The West Chamber,* made drastic changes in the text and claimed that he had found an older version, printing his revised edition with a commentary. After that all the old editions were forgotten. From his preface we can see the nature of his revisions. First, there were certain changes in the text. Thus in Chapter 159 of the earlier editions the empress helps her brother Tsao Pei against the dethroned emperor, while in Mao's text she helps the emperor against her brother. Secondly, there were some additions. Thus Chapter 167 of the original makes no mention of Liu Pei's wife Lady Sun, but in Mao's version we read: "When Lady Sun in the land of Wu heard that Liu Pei's army had been defeated and it was rumoured

---
[1] Circa 1610-1661. A Ching dynasty scholar condemned to death in 1661 as a warning to other refractory men of letters.

that he had died in battle, she led troops to the river bank and bewailed his death, looking towards the west. Then she threw herself into the river and drowned herself." Thirdly, there were cuts. For example, in Chapter 205 of the older text when Chuke Liang destroys Ssuma Yi's troops by fire in Shangfang Valley, he wants Wei Yen to be killed as well; and in Chapter 234 when Teng Ai calls upon Chuke Chan to surrender, Chuke Chan hesitates till his son Chuke Shang reproaches him, whereupon he determines to fight to the death. Neither of these episodes appears in Mao's version. There are other minor alterations, such as a rearrangement of certain chapters, stylistic changes, the removal of certain of the author's comments, the modification of minor details or of poems.

The original text of *The Romance of the Sui and Tang Dynasties* is lost, but we have a revised version by Chu Jen-hu published in 1675. The preface says: *"The Romance of the Sui and Tang Dynasties* was written by Lo Kuan-chung and revised by Lin, and it was a good novel. The story did not begin, however, till the episode of cutting silk in the Sui Palace; hence there were many things missing in it from the start. Later there were a couple of Tang dynasty stories, unconnected with the rest, making readers conscious of the book's shortcomings." From this we can see how the revised edition was made.

The revised *Romance of the Sui and Tang Dynasties* is divided into a hundred chapters. The book starts with the conquest of the kingdom of Chen by the emperor of Sui and proceeds to tell how the king of Northern Chou abdicates, then the Sui dynasty is overthrown by the first emperor of Tang, Empress Wu rules the country, Emperor Ming Huang goes to Chengtu and Lady Yang is strangled at Mawei, but after the recovery of the two capitals, Changan and Loyang, Emperor Ming Huang abdicates and sends a priest to find Lady Yang's spirit. The book ends with the disclosure by a saint that Emperor Ming Huang and Lady Yang are reincarnations of the Sui emperor and his concubine Chu Kuei-erh. The first seventy chapters deal with the exploits of gallant men at the end of the Sui and beginning of the Tang dynasty: Chin Chiung, Tou Chien-teh, Shan Hsiung-hsin, Wang Po-tang, Hua Mu-lan and others. According to the preface, the episode in which Emperor Ming Huang and his lady-love are described as reincarnations of earlier imperial lovers was taken from Yuan Yu-ling's *Lost Records* and included because the author found this an interesting theory. Most of the other episodes were based on historical records or legends written during the Tang and Sung dynasties such as *Forgotten Tales of the Ta Yeh Period, The Tales of Seas and Mountains, Story of the Labyrinth, The Opening of the Canal, Anecdotes of the Sui and Tang Dynasties, Accounts of Emperor Ming Huang, Accounts of a Courtier, True Tales of the Kai Yuan and Tien Pao Periods, Liu's Anecdotes, The Story of Eternal Grief, Forgotten Tales of the Kai Yuan and Tien Pao Periods, Story of Lady Mei* and *The Private History of Lady Yang*. So all the stories in this work were based on historical anecdotes just as in *The Romance of the Three Kingdoms*. The language, however, is that of the late Ming dynasty: superficially elegant and showy. There is probably little of the original style left. The book contains jests too, but these lack spirit. Here is an example:

One day, when Emperor Ming Huang was sitting at his ease in Chaoching Palace, attended by An Lu-shan, he observed that An's stomach jutted out over his knee and pointing at it he said: "This boy has a belly like a pot: I wonder what's in it?"

With a bow, An replied: "Nothing but a loyal heart. With this loyal heart I serve Your Majesty." The emperor was pleased by this reply.

But the heart hidden in the human breast is unfathomable. Though An protested that he had a loyal heart, it was in truth full of sin. For the emperor treated An as his trusted right hand, but An's heart was that of a thief, a wolf or a cur. Indeed he was heartless! A man of understanding should suffer pain at the very thought of this scoundrel and long to carve up his wicked heart, yet An declared he was loyal. The emperor failed to perceive the reprobate's ambition and believed him to be sincere: the very height of folly! However, enough of idle comments.

When Emperor Ming Huang had sat with An for a while, he turned to his attendants and asked for Lady Yang. It was late spring and the weather was growing warm. In the inner palace the lady was bathing in her scented bath. Her maids reported to the emperor: "Her Ladyship has just finished her bath."

The emperor said with a smile: "A beautiful lady coming out of her bath is like the lotus emerging from the water."

He ordered the maids to bring Lady Yang to him without completing her toilet, and in no time she arrived. What was Lady Yang's appearance after her bath? Here is a verse describing her:

> Pure as white jade, but soft and luminous,
> Her sweet body more fragrant than ever,
> She is charming with her cloudy hair dishevelled,

> In a trailing skirt of silk,
> Cool gauzy jacket.
> So alluring she stands in the breeze
> That even a lotus flower above the water
> Is utterly eclipsed by her beauty.

I have never seen *The Romance of the Five Dynasties*. According to a catalogue in the Japanese Government Library, this novel is in two volumes and sixty chapters; the author's name was Lo Pen and there is a commentary by Tang Hsien-tsu.[1]

The original text of *The Sorcerer's Revolt and Its Suppression by the Three Suis* has also disappeared. A comparatively early version is the twenty-chapter edition revised, according to the preface, by Wang Shen-hsiu. This novel describes how Wang Tse of Peichow raised a revolt by means of sorcery and magic. According to the official *Sung Dynasty History*, Wang Tse was a native of Chochow who moved during a famine to Peichow. In 1047 he assumed the title of Prince of Tungping and inaugurated the Teh Sheng Era, but after sixty-six days his rebellion was crushed. The novel is based on these happenings. It opens with a native of Pienchow named Hu Hao who possesses a magic painting. His wife burns the painting but the ashes whirl around her and she becomes pregnant, later giving birth to a daughter whom they call Yung-erh. A fox fairy teaches this girl magic so that she can conjure up men and horses out of paper and peas. Wang Tse is a sergeant in Peichow who marries Yung-erh and is then joined by sorcerers like Monk Tan-tzu, Chang Luan and Pu Chi, who predict that he

---

[1] Famous Ming dynasty playwright (1550-1616), author of *The Peony Pavilion*.

will become king. Because the local prefect is grasping and cruel, they use magic means to get money and grain from the government storehouses in order to raise an army and start a rebellion. Wen Yen-pu leads troops to suppress them, and when Chang Luan, Pu Chi and the monk see that Wang is not ruling well, they leave him. Even so, Wen cannot defeat Wang's magic. Then Monk Tan-tzu transforms himself into Chuke Sui to help the general, Ma Sui contrives to split Wang Tse's lips so that he can no longer utter incantations, and Li Sui and his troops dig an underground tunnel by which they enter the city. So Wang Tse and Yung-erh are captured. Since the three men are all named Sui, this novel was called *The Sorcerer's Revolt and Its Suppession by the Three Suis*.

The popular edition of this novel has forty chapters with a preface by Chang Wu-chiu which says that this book was revised by Feng Meng-lung.[1] This edition was made in 1620 and has fifteen additional chapters inserted at the beginning, describing how a monkey learns magic from a goddess, how this magic is stolen by Monk Tan-tzu, and how the fox fairy learns her magic. There are five other additional chapters describing sorcery, and in addition to some purely imaginary episodes certain older legends have been incorporated. For instance, in Chapter 29 Tu Chi-sheng sells charms and uses his magic to cut off his son's head, covers it with a quilt and joins the head to the body again; but because he boasts of his skill, Monk Tan-tzu steals away the child's soul and covers it with a dish in a noodle shop. Though Tu utters incantations time and again, the child will not come back to life.

---
[1] The well-known compiler of stories. See Chapter 21.

Staring, panic-stricken, at the spectators Tu pleaded: "Gentlemen, though we have different lines we all work for our living. If I spoke carelessly just now, forgive me! Please let me join the head up: then you can all come and have a drink with me. Within the four seas all men are brothers." After this apology he said: "Now I've admitted my fault, I'll join it up." But when he uncovered the body after chanting his incantations, the head was still severed. At his wit's end, Tu cried: "You are making it impossible for me though I've apologized again and again. I've admitted being in the wrong and begged you to overlook it. How can you be so harsh!" Opening a paper packet in a cage behind him, from this he took a gourd seed. He dug up some earth and buried the seed, then chanted incantations, spat on it and shouted: "Now!" Lo and behold, a vine sprouted from the ground and put forth branches and leaves; the next instant it blossomed, the flowers faded, and a small gourd appeared! All the onlookers cheered. Tu plucked the small gourd with his left hand and brandished a sword in his right. "Since you were cruel enough to take away my son's soul so that I can't join his head to his body, you shan't live either!" He struck the gourd with his sword, slicing it in two.

The monk upstairs in the shop was just going to eat his noodles when his head rolled from his shoulders, horrifying all the customers in the shop. The more timid among them left their noodles and rushed downstairs, while the bolder stayed to look. The monk hastily put down his bowl and chopsticks and got up to grope on the floor. He found the head and holding it by both ears put it back on his neck. When he had fixed it straight and felt it with his hands, he exclaimed: "I was so busy thinking of my noodles that I forgot to return his son's spirit to him!" He reached out to lift up the dish. At once Tu's child jumped up from the ground alive and the crowd cheered.

Tu said: "Today for the first time in my life I've come across a true master."

This story was based on an old legend. According to Yuchih Wo,[1] this miracle happened during the ninth century while according to Hsieh Chao-chih of the Ming dynasty it happened in the sixteenth century; but the sorcerer's name was not given and the monk was killed by his magic in the legend; thus this version is slightly different. That a man named Ma Sui attacked Wang Tse and was killed is recorded in history, for Cheng Hsieh[2] in the Sung dynasty wrote an account of Ma Sui.

---

[1] A writer of historical anecdotes during the Five Dynasties period.
[2] Imperial academician and prefect of Kaifeng in the reign of Emperor Shen Tsung (1068-1085).

15. HISTORICAL ROMANCES OF THE YUAN AND MING DYNASTIES *(Continued)*

Also popular from the Southern Sung dynasty onwards were legends about the brigands of Liangshan, whose leader Sung Chiang was a historical figure. The official *Sung Dynasty History* records that in 1121 troops were sent against the "brigands" south of the Huai River who, led by Sung Chiang, had attacked Huaiyang Garrison Area. When they had advanced to east of the capital and north of the Yangtse River, thence to the Haichow Area, Prefect Chang Shu-yeh was sent to persuade them to surrender. The official history makes no mention of what happened to the "brigands" after their surrender, but tradition has it that Sung Chiang helped to suppress the revolt of Fang La (1120-1121) and was appointed a military governor. Actually Fang La's revolt was put down by Han Shih-chung, and Sung Chiang had nothing to do with it. Only in the biography of Hou Meng in the official history is it stated that, when Sung Chiang was advancing on the capital, Hou Meng memorialized the throne to suggest that since Sung Chiang and his men had time and again defeated tens of thousands of government troops, it would be expedient to grant them an amnesty and order them to suppress Fang La's revolt to expiate their crime. No doubt this is the basis for the legend. But in fact this proposal was never carried out: Sung Chiang and the others were killed. According to Hung Mai's *Tales of Yi Chien*: "In the seventh year of Hsuan

第五十二回

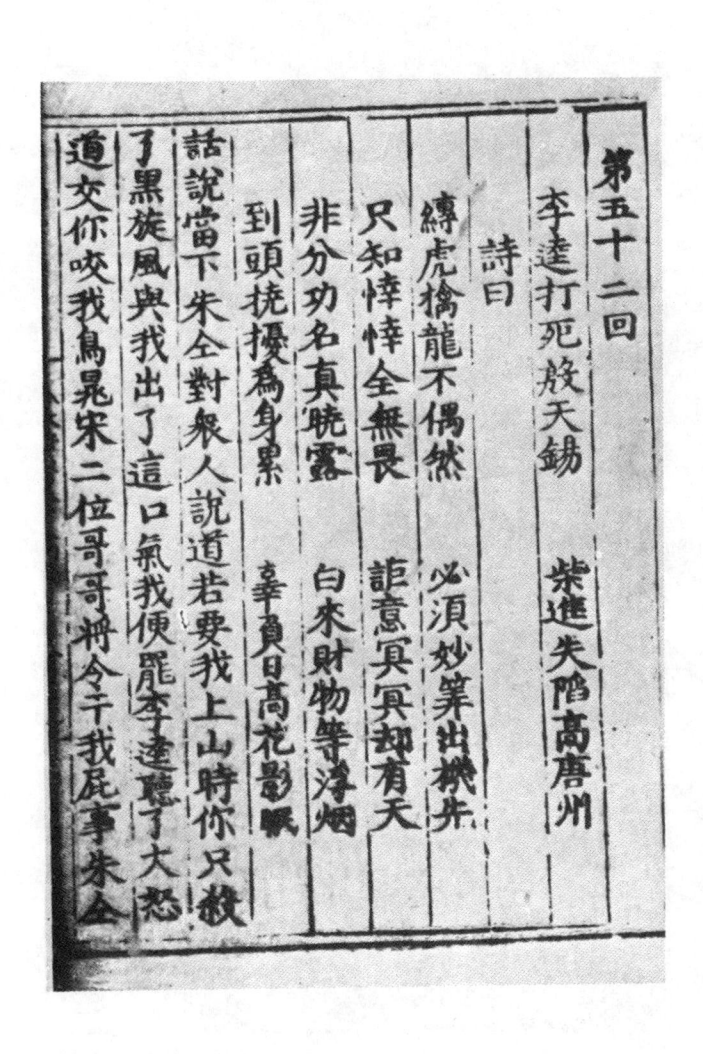

李逵打死殷天錫　　柴進失陷高唐州

詩曰

縛虎擒龍不偶然
只知悻悻全無畏
非分功名真曉露
到頭撓擾爲身累

必須妙筆出桃井
詭意冥冥却有天
白來財物等浮烟
辜負日高花影眠

話說當下朱仝對衆人說道若要我上山時你只教了黑旋風與我出了這口氣我便罷李逵慌了大怒道交你咬我鳥晁宋二位哥哥卻令干我屁事朱仝

An old edition of *Shui Hu Chuan* published about 1550

Illustration from an old edition of *Shui Hu Chuan* published about 1600

Ho (1125), the Vice-Minister of Civil Affairs Tsai Chu-hou was appointed governor of Chingchow, but because of illness he did not go to his post. Instead he went home to Nanking where he died. Soon afterwards a good friend of his named Wang also died but returned to life to announce that he had seen Tsai suffering torment in Hell and had been ordered to come back and tell Tsai's wife that it was on account of the affair in Yunchow. Tsai's wife, weeping bitterly, said that the previous year when Tsai was in command of troops in Yunchow, five hundred of the 'brigands' of Liangshan had surrendered but he put them all to the sword. Though she advised repeatedly against it, he would not listen to her. . . ." This book of anecdotes was written in 1166, not more than forty-odd years after the event, and should therefore be fairly reliable. The reference to Hell was of course purely legendary, but the execution of the "brigands" could hardly be fictitious. So ended the brave men of Liangshan.

While Sung Chiang and his men were in Liangshan they had considerable strength. The Sung history reveals that they invaded ten prefectures and the government troops were powerless against them. By degrees tales of their daring spread, gradually assuming the character of legends, and when scholars took these and improved on them the written accounts appeared. At the end of the Sung dynasty, Kung Kai[1] wrote an encomium on the thirty-six men of Liangshan, stating in a prefatory note: "Stories of Sung Chiang are told in popular legends but these are not worth our attention, though such men as Kao Ju and Li Sung recorded them and scholars did

---

[1] A scholar and artist at the end of the Sung dynasty.

not disapprove." Though the records of Kao Ju and Li Sung[1] can no longer be found, this shows that by the end of the Sung dynasty written accounts already existed. The *Tales of the Hsuan Ho Period* is a compilation of various old records, and the section dealing with the gathering together of the Liangshan rebels is probably one of the earliest written accounts. The episodes here are as follows: (1) Yang Chih, escorting the imperial tribute, is held up by the snow and fails to complete his mission on time; (2) Yang Chih is driven by poverty to sell his sword and kill a man, for which he is exiled to Weichow; (3) Sun Li takes Yang Chih to the Taihang Mountains to become a rebel; (4) Chao Kai and others rob the bearers of imperial tribute; (5) Sung Chiang sends a message so that Chao Kai may escape; (6) Sung Chiang kills a woman and leaves a poem; (7) Sung Chiang receives a message from heaven; (8) Sung Chiang goes to Liangshan to seek Chao Kai; (9) Sung Chiang and the others rise in revolt; (10) Sung Chiang goes to thank the god of the East Mountain; (11) Chang Shu-yeh persuades the rebel leaders to surrender; (12) Sung Chiang achieves distinction by defeating Fang La and is made a governor.

But this account in the *Tales of the Hsuan Ho Period* already differs considerably from the encomium of Kung Kai. According to Kung, Sung Chiang was one of the thirty-six rebel leaders, while in the tales he is set apart from the others. Certain names like Wu Chia-liang, Li

---

[1] Here Lu Hsun was led astray by a mistake made by Hu Shih. There was no such man as Kao Ju. Li Sung was a famous court painter of the Sung dynasty. There were probably portraits by him, but no written records.

Chin-yi, Li Hai, Yuan Chin, Kuan Pi-sheng, Wang Hsiung, Chang Ching and Chang Chen occur in the tales and in the encomium with slight differences, and not all the epithets are identical either. The Yuan dynasty playwrights often wrote about the Liangshan rebels, especially Sung Chiang, Yen Ching and Li Kuei; but their characters appear rather different from the later versions, though Sung Chiang is described by them too as a kindly and generous character. Chen Tai[1] of the Yuan dynasty, however, left some anecdotes recording the words of a boatman who told him that Sung Chiang had a wild, impulsive nature — this is quite unlike the other versions. No doubt at that time many such legends were current, and though written accounts existed they were brief and contradictory. Then men started selecting certain of the legends and compiled them into one great novel, making the story more consistent and readable. This is how we come to have the later *Shui Hu Chuan*. The writer or compiler was believed to be Lo Kuan-chung or Shih Nai-an. Perhaps Shih Nai-an wrote the book and Lo Kuan-chung revised it, or Shih started the book and Lo completed it.

The earliest version of *Shui Hu Chuan* no longer exists. Chou Liang-kung[2] said that it was generally believed that Lo Kuan-chung wrote this novel in one hundred chapters, beginning each with some preamble; then in the Chia Ching period (1522-1566) Kuo Hsun[3] reprinted the work, cutting out the preambles and leaving the main text only. He omitted stories like that about the Mother

---

[1] A scholar of the early fourteenth century.
[2] 1612-1672.
[3] Marquis of Wu-ting, an author and publisher.

Lamp-Wick, for instance, which were originally separate story-teller's tales inserted into this novel by Lo Kuan-chung. Other details about the first version are not known.

There are six existing editions, four of them important.

One edition has one hundred and fifteen chapters and the name of Lo Kuan-chung as the compiler. At the end of the Ming dynasty this was printed in one volume with *The Romance of the Three Kingdoms*. Separate editions are not known. This version starts when Marshal Hung sets free the monsters by mistake, then the hundred and eight rebels assemble at Liangshan, they surrender, defeat the Kitai Tartars and suppress the revolts of Tien Hu, Wang Ching and Fang La; after that Lu Chih-shen dies in Liuho and Sung Chiang is poisoned; miracles take place and the rebels become gods. The language of this version is rough and uneven, and most of the poems interspersed in it are vulgar; thus it seems to be an early unpolished version. Though not the original text, it is close to it. Here is a passage describing how Lin Chung is exiled to Changchow for offending Kao Chiu. There he is put in charge of the army fodder, and during a snowstorm leaves his tumbledown hut to buy wine.

After Lin Chung had put down his baggage he saw that the building was in ruins and thought: "How can I pass the winter in this hut? As soon as the snow stops I must find a mason to repair it." He warmed himself at the fire by the earthen bed but still feeling cold he thought: "Just now the old guard said there is a market-place five *li* away: why not go and buy some wine there?" So he left, slinging the wine gourd over his lance and heading east. After going a few hundred yards he saw an old temple. Lin Chung bowed before the shrine and said: "May the gods protect me! I shall come later to make offerings." Then he went another *li* and saw an inn. He marched straight inside and the innkeeper asked: "Where do you come from, sir?"

Lin Chung said: "Don't you recognize this winegourd?"

The innkeeper said: "That belongs to the old guard at the fodder depot. Since you are one of us, please be seated and let me treat you to a meal to show my welcome."

When Lin Chung had finished his meal, he bought a leg of beef and a gourdful of wine, and with these hanging from his spear he started back. It was growing late. When he hurried back to his lodgings he cried out in horror. It seems that all-seeing Heaven protects loyal and gallant men: this snowstorm had evidently saved his life. For his two-roomed thatched hut had collapsed under the weight of the snow.

An edition with a hundred and ten chapters has similar contents, and a version with a hundred and twenty-four chapters, written in broken, often unintelligible language, also belongs to the same category.

Then there is the 100-chapter edition which states in the preface that the author was Shih Nai-an but the novel was edited by Lo Kuan-chung. This version was produced by Kuo Hsun's family during the Chia Ching period, with a preface by Wang Tai-han who used the pen-name Tien-tu-wai-cheng. I have not seen this book. Another 100-chapter edition with a preface and commentary by

Li Chih[1] was probably based on Kuo Hsun's edition, and this also states that the work was compiled by Shih Nai-an and revised by Lo Kuan-chung. This edition, too, is rare. In Japan the first ten chapters were reprinted in 1728, the eleventh to the twentieth in 1759. This text also starts with the escape of the monsters and goes on to the stories of Lu Chih-shen and Lin Chung just as in the 115-chapter edition. The fifth chapter has this remark about Lu Chih-shen: "Thus his fame spread for thousands of *li* in the north, and he attained Buddhahood in the foremost city of the Yangtse Valley." Since this refers to Lu Chih-shen's death at Liuho Pagoda in Hangchow, the conclusion of this version must have been the same. But great differences are apparent in the language, so much so that this is virtually a new version. The weak poems are cut, many euphuisms are inserted, and the descriptions are more detailed. For example, the account of how Lin Chung bought wine in the snow is more than twice the length of that in the other version:

> Lin Chung put his clothes and bedding on the bed, then set about lighting a fire. There was a pile of charcoal by the house and he went to fetch a few sticks to light the stove. Looking up, he saw that all four walls of the building were crumbling and the whole structure was shaking in the north wind. Lin Chung wondered: "How can I pass the winter in this hut? As soon as the snow stops I'll go to town and find a mason to repair it." After warming himself for a while by the fire he still felt bitterly cold and thought: "Just

---

[1] 1527-1602. A Ming dynasty philosopher to whom many commentaries on popular novels were attributed.

now the old guard said there is a market-place five *li* away: why not go and buy some wine there?" Forthwith he took some loose silver from his bundle, slung the wine gourd over his lance and banked the fire. Then he put on a felt cap, took the key and went out, pulling the door to after him. He walked to the gate, closed it behind him and locked it, then pocketing his key he sauntered eastwards, crunching on ice like splintered jade in the snow, while the north wind howled behind him. It was snowing hard and after walking a few hundred yards he came to an old temple. Lin Chung bowed towards it and said: "May the gods protect me! I'll come back another time to burn offerings." He walked on till he saw some houses and stopping to look he observed a broom sticking out from one bamboo fence. So he marched straight into this inn.

"Where are you from, sir?" asked the innkeeper.

Lin Chung said: "Don't you recognize this gourd?"

The innkeeper looked at it and answered: "That's the gourd belonging to the old guard at the fodder depot."

"Well, I see you know it all right," said Lin Chung.

"Since you're a friend in charge of the fodder, please take a seat," invited the innkeeper. "This is bitter weather. I'll stand you three cups of wine to serve as a welcome."

The innkeeper cut a plate of cooked beef and warmed a pot of wine. Lin Chung bought some beef himself too, and after drinking a few cups bought another gourdful of wine. He wrapped up his two lots of beef, left some loose silver, slung the gourd over his lance and pocketed the meat; then he said goodbye to the innkeeper, left the wicker gate and walked back in the teeth of the north wind. Dusk was falling and the snow was coming down now thick and fast. A scholar in the old days wrote this poem to describe a poor man's sensations on seeing the snow:

> A bitter blast sweeps all the earth
> While thick and fast descends the snow —
> Great flakes like wisps of cotton fluff —
> Thatched huts are crushed and totter low.
> The rich man by his glowing fire
> Hopes snow may cover all the land.
> He sits at ease in padded clothes,
> A spray of blossom in his hand.
> "A happy omen!" he predicts,
> And wastes no pity on the poor;
> While hermits and recluses gloat
> And to the snow write poems galore.

Trudging through the snow in the teeth of the north wind, Lin Chung made his way quickly to the fodder depot. He unlocked the gate, looked in and cried out in horror. It seems that all-seeing Heaven protects the good and just: Lin Chung's life was saved by this snowstorm, for those two thatched rooms had given way under the weight of the snow.

Then there is a 120-chapter edition which also names Shih Nai-an as the compiler and Lo Kuan-chung as the editor, just as in the 100-chapter edition with a preface by Li Chih. This edition has a preface by Yang Tingchien, who says he was a pupil of Li Chih and compiled this edition at the request of Yuan Wu-yai.[1] Some editor's notes are followed by an account of the Liangshan

---

[1] A Soochow publisher.

outlaws based on the *Tales of the Hsuan Ho Period* and a list of the hundred and eight brigand leaders. The whole narrative down to the outlaws' surrender is the same as in the 115-chapter edition, but the defeat of the Kitai Tartars is somewhat different, the poems are omitted, and the account of the suppression of Tien Hu and Wang Ching is entirely dissimilar, though the quelling of Fang La's revolt is the same. The language of this edition is virtually identical with that of the 100-chapter edition, apart from minor changes in certain phrases. Thus in the other edition Lin Chung says: "Well, I see you know it all right." This edition has: "That's it." New poems are added by the editor and this is explained in the notes as follows: "The old edition omitted the poems in order not to break the continuity or confuse readers, and the result was clear and direct. But certain verses describe the characters and afford necessary pauses in the narrative, and not all these should be cut. We have therefore put them back, either using the verses in the old edition or adding new ones in order to point the moral and afford entertainment." This edition also has a commentary ascribed to Li Chih but with different contents from that in the 100-chapter edition. Both these commentaries are poor, and were in fact written by others under Li Chih's name.

According to the editor's notes: "The oldest edition had preambles by Lo Kuan-chung in the form of popular tales like that about Mother Lamp-Wick; but that edition no longer exists. Some later versions introduced changes in the suppression of the 'four big revolts,' and some editors shortened the 120-chapter edition believing it was too long; but this was not skilfully done. Kuo Hsun did well in changing the position of the episode regarding Sung

Chiang and Yen Po-hsi; but when he came to the revolts, he cut out the passages dealing with Wang Ching and Tien Hu and added others about the Kitai Tartars in an attempt to balance and tighten the plot. Actually a great work should not be handled in this way." From this we can see that the old edition of a hundred chapters no longer existed at that time. Another edition, probably with one hundred and twenty chapters, included the "four big revolts" of Sung Chiang, Wang Ching, Tien Hu and Fang La, whose names were seen by Chai Chin on a white screen in the emperor's writing. Kuo Hsun ignored the tradition of "four big revolts," omitted the episodes of Wang Ching and Tien Hu and added material on the Kitai Tartars, making a novel of a hundred chapters. Later the sections on Wang Ching and Tien Hu were restored to make a new 120-chapter edition which kept the Kitai Tartars and did not count Sung Chiang's revolt as one of the "four big revolts." In point of fact, when the *Tales of the Hsuan Ho Period* spoke of "rebels from three sides," this referred to Sung Chiang's men attacking Huaiyang, Chinghsi and Hopei; but some editor misunderstood this and introduced Wang Ching and Tien Hu. I fancy the story about the defeat of the Kitai Tartars may have started earlier than the Ming dynasty. In the Sung dynasty frequent foreign invasions and bad government naturally made men set their hopes on brigand heroes, and they created legends of this sort to comfort themselves. A variety of versions appeared which were not consistent. The novels written later varied because different episodes were chosen, and because there were different story-teller's prompt-books. This probably accounts for the fact that both the 100-chapter edition and the 115-chapter edition include the

Tien Hu and Wang Ching stories, though the language is quite different. The final episode about the suppression of Fang La appears in all versions. This can be explained only if an older version than the one on which Kuo Hsun based his edition had the story of Fang La immediately following the surrender, as in the *Tales of the Hsuan Ho Period*. However, we have no evidence of this.

From the foregoing, it is apparent that the existing editions can roughly be divided into two groups: one brief, the other more detailed. Hu Ying-lin said in his anecdotes: "The novel I read about the Liangshan outlaws twenty years ago was well worth poring over. For the last ten years or so the Fukien book-sellers have been printing abridged versions, retaining the main episodes only and omitting all the incidental comments and delightful descriptions in such a way as to make the book completely worthless. In a few more decades, if no old edition is left for comparison, this novel will be lost for ever." We do not know which old edition he saw, but the relatively condensed 115-chapter edition should be earlier than the more detailed version, for its language is rather different, and if it were merely an abridged text there would not be so many discrepancies. The writer of the shorter version was said to be Lo Kuan-chung, and this confirms what Chou Liang-kung heard from his elders. Not till Kuo Hsun's edition came out was this novel attributed to Shih Nai-an. My theory is that Shih Nai-an was a fictitious name which did not previously exist and was invented by the author of the more detailed version. Later readers, seeing this and not realizing that it was fictitious, embroidered on it and made him Lo Kuan-chung's teacher and fellow countryman. Hu Ying-lin also believed the preface and said that Shih Nai-an used to browse on old volumes in bookshops till in a pile of waste paper he found Chang Shu-yeh's order to the brigands to surrender, and having learned about the one hundred and eight brigand leaders he wrote this novel. Hu stated further that there was an account of Shih Nai-an in Tien Shu-ho's *Notes on the West Lake*. Here he was mistaken, however: there is no such account. Recently Wu Mei[1] in his *Anecdotes on Drama* claimed that *The Girl's Chamber* was written by Shih Hui, who was none other than Shih Nai-an. It is true that Shih Hui was a native of Hangchow, but we do not know how Wu Mei came to the conclusion that his other name was Nai-an. This seems hardly conclusive.

Then there is the 70-chapter edition, with an extra introductory chapter by way of preface, attributed to Shih Nai-an. This abridged edition was by Chin Sheng-tan, who claimed that he had found an early version with seventy chapters only. After the episode in which Sung Chiang receives the oracle from heaven, the book ends with Lu Chun-yi's dream that all the brigands have been caught by General Chang Shu-yeh. Chin claims that all the chapters after the surrender were written by Lo Kuan-chung and that they are inferior. This edition differs little from the first seventy chapters of the 120-chapter edition, though many verses have been cut. Since the 120-chapter edition mentions that there was an old version without many verses, it is possible that Chin procured an earlier text; but since there are places where the narrative is disjointed owing to verses omitted, he prob-

---

[1] Late authority on traditional Chinese theatre.

ably still based it on the 100-chapter edition. Chou Liang-kung wrote in his *Anecdotes on Books*: "Not long ago Chin Sheng-tan took it into his head that all the chapters after the seventieth were by Lo Kuan-chung and did his best to condemn them, even forging a preface to his edition. This is how the novel came to be attributed to Shih Nai-an." Since Chou Liang-kung was contemporary with Chin, his words should carry weight. But Chin's edition is outstanding for its style. Thus in Chapter 5, when Lu Chih-shen questions the monk of Wakuan Monastery:

> The monk was startled when Lu Chih-shen came up. Jumping to his feet he said, "Please take a seat, brother! Have a cup with me."
> Grasping his wand, Lu demanded: "Why did you give up the monastery?"
> The monk said: "Sit down, brother, and let me. . . ."
> "Out with it! Out with it!" Lu glared.
> ". . . Tell you. In the old days our monastery was a fine one: plenty of land and many monks. But then those old monks took to drinking and whoring, spending temple funds on girls; and when the abbot tried to stop them they drove him out. That is why the monastery was given up. . . ."

Chin Sheng-tan comments: "A sentence here is unfinished." When it is completed further on, he comments on the fact again, ending with the praise: "Such brilliant sentence construction has not been written since ancient times." I suspect that these brilliant touches were the doing of Chin himself, for we find similar cases in his edition of *The West Chamber*. In the 100-chapter edition this passage runs:

The monk said: "Please sit down, brother, and let me tell you."

"Out with it! Out with it!" Lu glared.

And he said: "In the old days our monastery was a fine place: plenty of land and lots of monks. . . ."

In the 115-chapter edition there is no "Lu glared." Only: "The monk said: 'Brother, let me tell you. In the old days our monastery had plenty of land and lots of monks. . . .'"

Such abridgements were usually due to the fashions of the time. Thus Hu Shih says, "Chin Sheng-tan lived at a time when the country was overrun by brigands, he saw the havoc caused in the empire by bandits like Chang Hsien-chung[1] and Li Tzu-cheng,[2] and believed that brigandage should not be supported but attacked in works of literature." By the Ching dynasty the situation had changed, for then scholars considered: "Though these men made a false start, they repented, mended their ways and did good deeds. This was commendable and their military achievements should not be forgotten." So they took the last part of the 115-chapter edition, starting from Chapter 67, and published it as a sequel to the 70-chapter edition under the title: *The Suppression of Four Big Revolts.* This sequel has a preface dated 1792 by Shang-hsin-chu-shih (a gentleman seeking amusement).

Early in the Ching dynasty a 40-chapter *Sequel to Shui Hu Chuan* appeared by a writer who called himself a "Relic of the Sung dynasty," and with a commentary by Yen-tang-shan-chiao (a woodcutter of Mount Yen-

---

[1] 1605-1647.
[2] 1605?-1645. He and Chang Hsien-chung were leaders of peasant revolts.

tang). This is a sequel to the 100-chapter edition. It tells how after Sung Chiang died some of the brigand leaders fought for the state against the Golden Tartars without success; then Li Chun led some of the others out to sea and eventually he became King of Siam. This ending reminds one of the Tang dynasty romance *The Man with the Curly Beard.* The preamble says that the writer is unknown but was probably a contemporary of Shih Nai-an and Lo Kuan-chung. In fact he was Chen Chen, a native of Chekiang who lived at the end of the Ming dynasty. All his other works have been lost. Though this book was intended as an entertainment, it reveals his antagonism to the Manchus. During the reign of Tao Kuang (1821-1850) in the Ching dynasty there appeared another 70-chapter sequel to *Shui Hu Chuan* by Yu Wan-chun with an extra concluding chapter. This novel is called *The Suppression of the Rebels,* but it is the reverse of the other sequel. The author kills off all the brigand leaders, claiming that Sung Chiang never came over to the government side or helped to suppress Fang La, but that he was captured and executed by Chang Shu-yeh. This follows the abridged 70-chapter edition. Yu Wan-chun had the pen-name Hu-lai-tao-jen. The son of an official in Canton, he distinguished himself in a war to suppress an uprising of the Yao minority; then he became a physician in Hangchow, and later embraced religion, dying in 1849. He wrote this sequel between 1826 and 1847, taking twenty-two years over it, but died without having finally polished it. In 1851 his son Yu Lung-kuang edited the manuscript and had it printed. Some of the descriptions in this sequel come up to the standard of *Shui Hu Chuan,* and there are some remarkably good passages outside the range of the original. So this should be considered one of the more outstanding imitations of famous masterpieces.

Many other historical romances were written in the Ming and Ching dynasties. Some Ming dynasty romances dealt with the early times of Yao and Shun and the Hsia dynasty, others with the Chou dynasty and the Warring States, the Han dynasty, the Tsin, Tang and Sung dynasties. Even more such works appeared in the Ching dynasty. Some attempted to include all the past twenty-four dynasties in a single volume, while others were a patchwork of old records; but these were merely imitations of *The Romance of the Three Kingdoms* which fell far short of the original. Even the best among them were restricted by history and the dependence on old records; the language is crude and the authors dared not give free rein to their fancy or write detailed descriptions. Thus Tsai Ao, commenting on *The Romance of the States of Eastern Chou,* said: "You may call this history, yet it reads like fiction. . . . But if you call it fiction, all the stories in it come from classical records." He meant this as praise, but this is precisely the shortcoming of these historical romances.

Other romances about specific historical periods laid emphasis on one individual or group of people. In Wu Chih-mu's *Reminiscences of Hangchow* he tells us that in the second half of the thirteenth century a story-teller named Wang-liu-tai-fu drew crowds to hear his tales about famous generals and the recovery of territories in the Sung dynasty. These should be included as historical romances too. *Shui Hu Chuan* is a work of this kind, and later there were more novels of this type. One of the more important is *The Romance of Ming Dynasty Heroes.* This work came from Kuo Hsun's family and describes the generals who helped to found the Ming dynasty, paying special attention to the achievements of Kuo Ying who was Kuo Hsun's ancestor. Then there is the *True History of Ming Dynasty Heroes* which attacks Kuo Ying. There were stories about Yo Fei[1] by Hsiung Ta-pen, Yu Ying-ao and Tsou Yuan-piao,[2] all of whom described the achievements of this Sung dynasty general and his unjust death. Later there appeared *The Complete Story of Yo Fei*, elaborating on the earlier records. In the Ching dynasty there was the *Romance of the Witch Tang Sai-erh* by Lu Hsiung, dealing with the rebellion this woman raised in Shantung.[3] There was an anonymous romance about Wei Chung-hsien, an evil eunuch of the Ming dynasty. Then there were stories about brave generals in the Hsueh family during the Tang dynasty, and in the Yang family during the Sung dynasty, as well as General Ti Ching of the Sung dynasty and others. These stories, though crudely written, were popular. Other novels about historical figures, written for purposes of slander or on account of personal grudges, we can pass over in silence.

---

[1] The popular Sung dynasty general who inflicted several defeats on the Golden Tartars but was executed by the government in 1141.

[2] Three Ming dynasty writers.

[3] This revolt was suppressed in 1420.

16. MING DYNASTY NOVELS ABOUT GODS AND DEVILS

The Hsuan Ho period of the Sung dynasty was the time when Taoist worship and belief in alchemy and sorcery were at their height. During the Yuan dynasty, Buddhism was the most popular religion, though Taoism was also esteemed and faith in Taoist magic was widespread. Early in the Ming dynasty Taoism declined, but by the sixteenth century it was in vogue again. The alchemist Li Tzu and the Buddhist priest Chi-yao in the latter half of the fifteenth century and the Tartar Yu Yung at the beginning of the sixteenth became high officials thanks to their skill as magicians. They were famous, powerful and admired by all. Naturally there was much talk of magic lore which could not but leave its mark on literature. For centuries a struggle for supremacy raged between Confucianism, Taoism and Buddhism, till these three religions decided to tolerate each other and consider themselves as stemming from a single source. Then all concepts of right and wrong, true and false, good and evil, merged to be redivided into two main camps: orthodoxy and heterodoxy. I call this the struggle between gods and devils, though no special name for such literature existed. In the field of fiction, *The Sorcerer's Revolt and Its Suppression by the Three Suis* written at the beginning of the Ming dynasty, was one of the earliest novels of this kind and had many successors. After the Sung dynasty these stories were not necessarily based on

Taoist lore but on folk legends. Though often crude, uneven and hardly worth reading, they had a strong hold on the people. Some were polished and edited by scholars to form the base of later masterpieces.

One early collection of such legends is *The Four Romances of Wandering Saints*. This consists of four separate novels written by three men. The editor of this work is unknown, but judging by the editions still in existence it was probably published in the Ming dynasty. The first of these four novels, *The Eight Saints* or *The Voyage to the East*, is divided into two volumes and fifty-six chapters. The writer's name is given as Wu Yuan-tai. The story tells how the club-footed saint Li Hsuan attains sainthood and teaches the Truth to Chungli Chuan, who in turn teaches Lu Tung-ping. Both these men teach Han Hsiang and Tsao Yu; and Chang Kuo, Lan Tsai-ho and Sister Ho attain sainthood too. These are the eight saints. One day they all attend a feast in paradise. They are crossing the Eastern Sea on their way back, laden with precious objects, when a young dragon takes a fancy to Lan Tsai-ho's jade castanets and steals them. A great fight ensues. The eight saints set fire to the ocean and the defeated dragon king asks angels from heaven to help him, but they are vanquished too. Then the goddess Avalokitesvara comes to mediate; they go away and the world is at peace once more. The language is a mixture of classicisms and colloquial expressions, and the incidents are disjointed for this work is made up of folk legends strung together.

The second story, *Prince Hua-kuang* or *The Voyage to the South*, is in four volumes and eighteen chapters. The author is Yu Hsiang-tou, a publisher at the end of the Ming dynasty whose name appears in some editions of *The Romance of the Three Kingdoms*. This story is about the angel Miao-chi-hsiang, who offends Buddha by killing a demon and is sent down to be the son of Mother Horse-Ear. He is the Three-Eyed God with divine powers: he avenges his father and goes to Heaven to steal a golden spear but is killed by the Heavenly Emperor. Then he is reborn in the house of the Fiery Prince and while studying under the god he steals another gold sword and makes it into a gold brick, with which he plays havoc in Heaven. When the Heavenly Emperor defeats him with water, he is reborn on earth in the Hsiao family as Hua-kuang; but with the divine powers which he retains he fights against deities, causing great trouble on earth until the god pardons him. Because he has lost his gold brick now, he goes to find a gold pagoda, and meeting Princess Iron Fan he makes her his wife. He overcomes various monsters, proving invincible; then he searches for his mother in Hell and creates a great disturbance there too. He finds that his mother is a demon, Mother Chi-chih-to, who devoured Hsiao's wife and took her form in order to give birth to him; but because she still craved for human flesh she was captured by Buddha and sent to Hell to atone for her sins. Hua-kuang rescues her from Hell.

Hua-kuang was heartily glad when his third attempt to rescue his mother succeeded.

His mother Chi-chih-to said: "It was good of you, son, to let me out; but I want *Gya* to eat."

Hua-kuang asked: "What is *Gya*?"

She said: "If you don't know, ask Long-Sight and Sharp-Ears."

So Hua-kuang went to question them and they told him: "*Gya* means 'man.' She wants to eat men again."

When Hua-kuang heard this he said to his mother: "Mother, since you were suffering torment in Hell, I did all in my power to get you out. Why should you want to eat men again? This won't do."

His mother retorted: "But that's what I want. What a bad son you are! If you haven't got *Gya* for me, why did you get me out?"

Hua-kuang could do nothing but put her off by saying: "Wait a day or two and I'll find one for you to eat."

He advertises for a doctor to cure his mother, and being told that only a peach from paradise can help her he disguises himself as Monkey to steal a fairy peach. After that Mother Chi-chih-to stops devouring men, but when Monkey is suspected of theft and finds out from Buddha that the thief is Hua-kuang, he comes to fight him. Monkey is burned and defeated by the fire-weapon; but his daughter the Comet Maid has a skull which gives whomever it strikes a splitting headache and makes him die within two days. Hua-kuang falls a victim to this and is about to die when Buddha comes to make peace, Comet smooths out the mark on his bone and he revives. He goes back to worship Buddha.

Hsieh Chao-chih of the Ming dynasty compared the story of Hua-kuang to that of Monkey in *Pilgrimage to the West*, for both romances deal with the nature of the five elements. When fire is burning it destroys all in heaven and earth, but it is finally overcome by water. From the story of the mother who craved for human flesh as soon as she left Hell, Hsieh drew the moral that it is hard for a man to correct his faults. Obviously this novel was written before the last quarter of the sixteenth century. Shen Teh-fu in his anecdotes about the theatre describes the miracles of Hua-kuang as unduly fantastic, showing that these tales were used in dramas too.

The third novel, *The Dark God Chen-wu* or *The Voyage to the North*, is in four volumes and twenty-four chapters. This is also by Yu Hsiang-tou. The story tells how Chen-wu is born, attains divinity and conquers demons. In the Han dynasty the expression Dark God stood for Heaven, but this differed somewhat from the god in the later accounts. This Dark God Chen-wu grew out of Taoist lore in the Sung dynasty. *The Record of the Jade Calendar in the Primeval Cavern* states that when the god Yuan-shih (Beginning) expounded the Truth in the Jade Palace, he noticed that an evil wind had pervaded the earth below. So King Wu was sent to conquer the Shangs and the Dark God to conquer the demons. With dishevelled hair and bare feet, wearing golden armour and a black cape and bearing dark flags, the Dark God led his angels to earth and fought six demon kings in the wilderness. The demon kings conjured up a dark tortoise and a huge serpent out of the air, but the Dark God trampled them down with his divine power and locked up the demons in Hell so that the world was at peace. During the Yuan dynasty and even in the Ming, this Taoist god was worshipped. This novel is based to a great extent on these old legends, but has drawn additional material from Buddhist stories and popular lore, emphasizing the miracles in the style of village shamans or Taoist devotees. The novel relates that at a feast during the Sui dynasty the Jade Emperor expresses his desire to visit the world of men, and one of his three spirits becomes a son of the Liu family. Buddhist and Taoist gods teach him the Truth and he goes up to paradise. But longing for the earth again he is reborn as a prince in the lands of Kosha and Hsihsia. There a divinity teaches him the Truth and twice he gives up his throne to study religion. Returning to Heaven he is made the Pacifier of Demons and ordered to collect a host of angels. Then he is reborn on earth as the Prince of Chinglo, Mother North-Star teaches him the Truth and he goes to Wutang Mountain to study. Upon his return to Heaven, he sees an evil vapour on earth and knows that the angels he was to gather are causing trouble. He descends to earth, conquers the tortoise and the serpent and subdues various angels, including Chao Kung-ming, the Thunder God, the Comet Maid and others. He leads thirty-six of these spirits to Heaven, where the Heavenly Emperor makes them officers. There are still two demons, however, who have escaped to the Yangtse River: the Frying Pan and the Bamboo Rope. So the Dark God sends one of his spiritual bodies down to Wutang Mountain to control them. Towards the end of the story, in 1405, the Dark God assists the government to defeat its enemies. The text says: "More than two hundred years have passed since then," which suggests that this novel was written at the end of the Ming dynasty. But in earlier editions this passage is missing—it was probably a later interpolation.

The fourth novel, *Pilgrimage to the West*, in four parts with forty-one chapters, was written by Yang Chih-ho and edited by Chao Ching-chen. In this the Monkey, Sun Wu-kung, becomes a saint, the Tang emperor goes to Hell, and Hsuan-tsang the monk is ordered to search for Buddhist canons; after meeting many perils on the way he finally reaches the Western Regions, obtains the sutras and returns. The story of Emperor Tai Tsung's dream was told in the Tang dynasty. In Chang Tsu's *Anecdotes from Court and Countryside* we read:

At midnight Emperor Tai Tsung fell asleep and saw a man who said: "Come with me for a short time, Your Majesty. You shall come back by and by."
The emperor asked: "Who are you?"
He replied: "I am a living man serving the judge of Hell."
Then Emperor Tai Tsung went to see the judge, who questioned him about all that had passed on the fourth day of the sixth month,[1] after which he dismissed him. The man who had first appeared to him led him back.

A tale in the vernacular dealt with this story also, and an incomplete manuscript has been found in the Tunhuang Caves (see Chapter 12). In fact, Hsuan-tsang did not travel to India at the order of the emperor. His story is recorded in the *Tang Dynasty History*, and a biography of Hsuan-tsang entitled *Life of the Tripitaka Master of the Great Tzu-en Monastery* has been preserved among the Buddhist canons. No miracles are recorded here, yet the later legends abound in elements of the supernatural. Monkey, Sandy and monsters in various strange lands have already appeared in the chantefable version, while one early play of the Golden Tartar period also deals with Hsuan-tsang's travels. In the Yuan dynasty, Wu Chang-ling's play *Tripitaka Goes West to Find Buddhist Canons* contains such incidents as the

---
[1] When he killed his brothers in A.D. 626.

capture of Monkey and his conversion to Buddhism, as well as such characters as Sandy, Pigsy, the Red Boy and the Princess of the Iron Fan. Evidently the travels of Hsuan-tsang had gradually grown into a legend from the end of the Tang dynasty onwards, and as the plot became more and more involved later writers of fiction improved on it.

In Yang Chih-ho's version, the first nine chapters deal with how Monkey attains sainthood and is captured. First Monkey springs out of the rock, finds a water source and becomes the king of the monkeys; then he leaves the mountain to seek the Truth and with his magic powers plays havoc in Heaven until the Jade Emperor has to give him a title. After that he makes trouble at the feast on fairy peaches, the Jade Emperor sends the god Erh-lang to subdue him, and Monkey is taken prisoner after a fight. Here is an episode from the fight:

> When the small monkeys saw the god, they made haste to report his arrival to their king. The monkey king took up his gold-tipped wand and put on his flying slippers. The opponents made known their names and took up positions, then fought for a long time. After having attacked each other more than three hundred times, they transformed themselves into giants a hundred thousand feet high to fight among the clouds, leaving the cave. . . . While Monkey was resisting, he saw the monkeys of his mountain scatter in terror, whereat he himself turned and fled. The god followed with great strides in hot pursuit. In a flash the monkey king transformed himself and vanished into the water.

The god cried: "This monkey must have changed into some fish or shrimp. Let me turn into a cormorant to catch him."

When Monkey saw the god coming, he changed into a bustard and flew to a tree. Then the god with his catapult knocked the bird down on the slope, but though he made a search he could not find it. He went back to report that the monkey king had been beaten and disappeared without a trace.

The Heavenly Prince looked into his magic mirror and exclaimed: "The monkey has gone to your temple at Kuankou."

Then the god Erh-lang went back to Kuankou. Monkey quickly took the likeness of the god and sat in the main hall. Erh-lang thrust at him with his spear, Monkey warded off the blow, resumed his own form and started fighting again. Monkey wanted to return to his mountain but he was surrounded by angels, all chanting incantations. Suddenly Erh-lang appeared with other gods in the clouds and saw that Monkey's strength would soon be spent. Then the Patriarch threw down a magic ring which hit Monkey on the head so that he fell. Next Erh-lang's hound seized him by the chest and he stumbled. Finally Erh-lang and others with spears took him prisoner and put him in chains.

But since Monkey cannot be killed by fire or the sword, Buddha imprisons him under Five Elements Mountain, ordering him to wait for a monk who will pass this way in search of Buddhist sutras. The next four chapters relate how Wei Cheng kills the dragon, Emperor Tai Tsung visits Hell, Liu Chuan presents the melon and Hsuan-tsang is ordered to set out to find Buddhist sutras. From the fourteenth chapter onwards we read of the disciples the monk finds on the way and the perils they encounter, ending with their arrival at their destination and their return to the East after obtaining the sutras. There are three disciples: Monkey, Pigsy and Sandy, as well as a dragon-horse. They experience more than thirty dangerous adventures, the chief being at Wuchuang Monastery, Table Mountain, Fire-Cloud Cave, the River-Joining-Heaven, Poison Mountain, Lesser Thunder-Echo Monastery and during their encounter with the Six-Eared Monkey. Most of these stories are briefly told, but sometimes jokes are inserted for the readers' amusement. Here is the description of the battle at Fire-Cloud Cave:

Then the tutelary deities in the neighbourhood of the mountain gathered round to pay their respects and introduce themselves.

"This is Withered-Pine Valley," they said. "Near by is a mountain cave called Fire-Cloud Cave, where lives the son of the Ox Monster. His name is Red Boy and he uses divine fire which no one can withstand."

When Monkey heard this he dismissed the local deities . . . and went with Pigsy to the cave to find the Red Boy. . . .

The monster ordered his followers to bring out five-wheel carts and fall into battle formation. He came out with his spear and fought several rounds with Monkey, and Pigsy joined in. Then the monster whirled about and struck his nose so that flames spurted forth. All the carts started blazing fiercely.

Pigsy said: "Brother, let's go! I shall soon be completely roasted, and if he adds spice he will have a good meal."

Though Monkey was not afraid of fire, he could not stand smoke. So the two of them had to run back.

They persuade Avalokitesvara to help them, she changes swords into a lotus pedestal and catches the monster by a trick. The monster revolts and the gods imprison him with a gold ring and sprinkle sweet dew on him, after which he goes meekly off to Potalaka Mountain. One scene from Wu Chang-ling's drama, *Pilgrimage to the West,* "The Conversion of the Demon Mother," shows how the Red Boy was rescued and has this line: "Be merciful, Buddha, and I shall help Tripitaka in his pilgrimage to the West. If you spare Fire Boy, the god Erh-lang will help you." In this story the boy is the Ox Monster's son and is identified with Sudhana, the boy attending on Avalokitesvara.

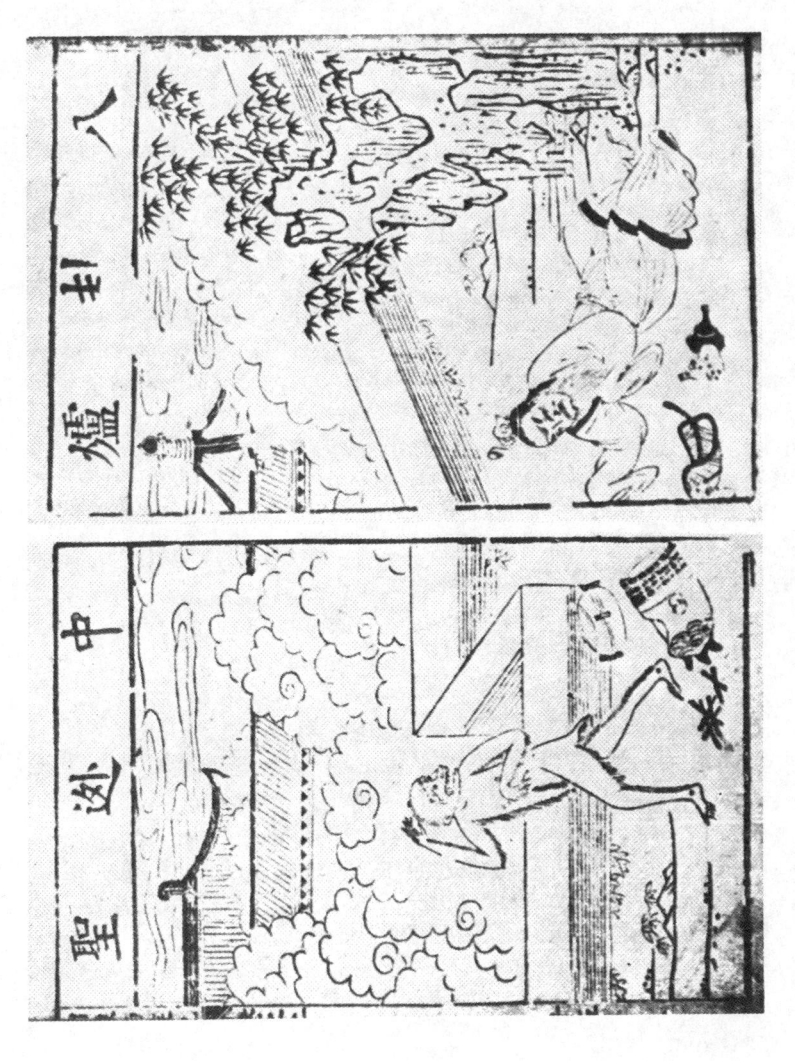

Two illustrations from an old edition of *Pilgrimage to the West* published about 1600

Illustration from an old edition of the *Pilgrimage to the West* published about 1635

17. MING DYNASTY NOVELS ABOUT GODS AND DEVILS *(Continued)*

There was a 100-chapter *Pilgrimage to the West* too, which appeared after the 41-chapter version and has become a popular classic. At one time it was attributed to Chiu Chu-chi, a Taoist priest who lived at the beginning of the Yuan dynasty. It is true that Chiu made the journey to Central Asia and his travels were recorded by Li Chih-chang in two books, *Chiu's Travels to the West*, which can still be found among the Taoist canon; and the two works were confused owing to the similarity of their titles. Early in the Ching dynasty, when certain publishers added Yu Chi's preface to Chiu Chu-chi's travels to the novel *Pilgrimage to the West*, confusion became even worse confounded.

But towards the end of the eighteenth century, Chien Ta-hsin wrote a postscript to Chiu's travels in which he made it clear that the novel *Pilgrimage to the West* had been written in the Ming dynasty. Chi Yun[1] in his *Notes of Yueh-wei Hermitage* also concluded that the novel must date from the Ming dynasty though he did not know who the author was, for: "All official names and titles in the novel — City Guards, the Board of Ceremony, the East City Garrison Headquarters, the Chancellor, the Imperial Academy, the Imperial Secretariat and so forth — are based on Ming dynasty institutions."

---

[1] 1724-1805.

But since scholars like to praise famous men of their own district, literati of Shanyang County like Ting Yen and Yuan Kuei-sheng discovered from old records that the author of the novel came from their district and his name was Wu Cheng-en. Another Shanyang scholar, Wu Yu-chin, confirmed this in his *Notes on Shanyang*, though he thought Wu Cheng-en based his novel on Chiu's travels just as Lo Kuan-chung had based his *Romance of the Three Kingdoms* on Chen Shou's history. This could only be because he had never read the book in question. Another theory was that Wu Cheng-en had written a sequel to Chiu's travels, but this is mere popular legend.

Wu Cheng-en had the pen-name Sheh-yang-shan-jen. He was an intelligent and witty scholar, well read and fond of a jest, who wrote several works of fiction and enjoyed quite a reputation in his lifetime. He became a senior licentiate in 1544, was appointed magistrate of Changhsin, returned to Shanyang at the beginning of the Lung Ching period (1567-1572), and died early in the Wan Li period. He lived from about 1510 to 1580. One of his works was the *Pilgrimage to the West*. We lack detailed information about his life, but know that he was a good poet. His poems were "restrained but clear, learned and profound." Indeed he was the best poet in Huaian during the Ming dynasty. Since he died a poor man and had no son, most of his writings were lost. Chiu Cheng-kang made a collection in five books of some of them, which Wu Yu-chin included among the works of Shanyang scholars. The *Shanyang County Records* edited in the Tung Chih period (1862-1874) omitted the information that Wu Cheng-en had written stories and novels, and his *Pilgrimage to the West* was left out of the bibliography. So Wu's fame was forgotten and few readers knew that he was the author of the novel.

The general outline of his book is more or less the same as the earlier Yang Chih-ho version. The first seven chapters describe how Monkey becomes a saint and is captured, corresponding to the first nine chapters in Yang's version. The eighth chapter, which tells how Buddha made the sutras, differs from the account in Buddhist records. The ninth chapter relates how Hsuan-tsang's parents are killed and how he avenges them; this again is not based on history or Yang's version but put in by Wu Cheng-en. The tenth to twelfth chapters, which tell how Wei Cheng kills the dragon and Hsuan-tsang is ordered to go to the West, correspond to the tenth to thirteenth chapters in Yang's version. The fourteenth to ninety-ninth chapters deal with the perils which Hsuan-tsang encounters on the way. Since nine was supposed to be the last of all numbers, and nine times nine makes eighty-one, there were eighty-one perils. In the hundredth chapter Hsuan-tsang returns to China and the book ends.

Though the skeleton plot already exists in the Yang Chih-ho version, the language is crude and the book hardly a proper novel. Wu Cheng-en, however, was a brilliant man of wide learning and he drew upon many sources including the stories about Hua-kuang and Chen-wu in *The Four Romances of Wandering Saints*, the earlier plays and chantefable about Tripitaka, miraculous happenings in the Tang dynasty tales, as well as satires based on current events. He rewrote and embellished the old version to such an extent that he produced what was virtually a new book. For example, the fight between Erh-lang and Monkey in Yang's version comes to some three hundred words only, whereas Wu Cheng-en makes it ten times as long. First he describes how the two opponents change their forms: Monkey transforms himself into a sparrow, an egret, a fish, a water snake, while the god changes into a kite, a stork, a cormorant and a crane. Then Monkey becomes a bustard and the god, scorning to contend with such a low creature, takes his own form again and knocks the bird off a cliff with his catapult.

Taking advantage of this opportunity, Monkey rolled down the cliff and crouching down changed himself into a wayside shrine. His mouth wide open was the doorway, his teeth were the door-flaps, his tongue the image of Buddha, and his eyes the windows. Not knowing what to do with his tail, he stuck it up behind like a flag-pole.

When Erh-lang arrived at the foot of the cliff in search of the bustard that he had just knocked over, all he found was this small temple. He stared at it hard till he noticed the flag-pole sticking up behind and said with a laugh: "That's Monkey! He's trying his tricks on me again. I have seen many temples, but never one with a flag-pole behind it. Depend upon it, this animal is up to mischief. If he gets me inside, he will bite me. Why should I go in? I'll clench my fist and knock down the windows first, then kick down the doors."

When Monkey heard this . . . he made a tiger-spring and disappeared into the air. Erh-lang searched hard up and down. . . . Half way up the sky he came across the Heavenly Prince, who was holding the monster-detecting mirror, his son Nocha at his side. He asked: "Prince, have you seen Monkey?"

"He hasn't been up here," said the prince. "I've been looking out for him."

Erh-lang told him what had happened, how they had changed into different forms and how he had caught the small monkeys, concluding: "He changed into a temple, but before I could smash it he disappeared again."

The prince looked in his mirror and burst out laughing. "Make haste, my lord!" he cried. "That monkey has made himself invisible to escape from the cordon and gone to your temple at Kuankou. . . ."

Now as soon as Monkey reached Kuankou, with one shake he took the form of Erh-lang, then descended from the clouds and went straight to the shrine. The guardian spirits, not knowing he was an impostor, bowed to welcome their lord. Monkey sat down in their midst to inspect the offerings, and saw that Li Hu had sent meat, Chang Lung had promised presents, Chao Chia had prayed for a son, and Chien Ping had asked to be cured of a disease. He was looking round when someone announced: "Another Lord Erh-lang is here!"

The guardian spirits turned hastily — and were amazed.

Erh-lang demanded: "Has a creature calling himself the Great Sage and Paragon of Heaven been here?"

"We've not seen any Great Sage," they said. "But there's another Lord Erh-lang inside inspecting the offerings."

The god rushed in and as soon as Monkey saw him he changed into his true form and said: "Don't shout, my lord! This temple is in my name now!"

Erh-lang raised his three-pronged, double-bladed magic lance and lunged at Monkey's face. Monkey dodged and took out his needle: one shake and the needle was as thick as a bowl. He darted forward and struck back. Cursing and shouting they fought their way out of the temple, through the mist and cloud, struggling as they went, till once more they reached the Mountain of Flowers and Fruit. The Four Heavenly Princes were keeping a strict guard, and now the Heavenly Generals Kang and Chang came to meet Erh-lang and surrounded Monkey, pressing in on every side.

But the most daring flights of fancy occur in the eighty-one perils such as the battle with the Rhinoceros Monster, the fight between the real and the false Monkey, and the battle of the Flaming Mountain, where the most miraculous and fantastic changes take place. The first two episodes appear in Yang's version also; the last, which borrows the Princess of the Iron Fan from a play and *Prince Hua-kuang*, and which includes the Ox Monster mentioned by name only in Yang's version, is even more strange and exotic. Here is the passage describing how the Ox Monster, defeated by the gods, tells his wife to give up the magic fan which will put out the fires of the Flaming Mountain so that Hsuan-tsang and his disciples may continue on their journey.

The Ox Monster lost his nerve completely . . . and started up the sky. But the prince and his son Nocha with all the yakshas and angels barred his way. . . . In desperation the Ox Monster shook himself and changed into a huge white ox to gore the prince with his iron horns. But the prince fell on him with his sword.

At this point Monkey came up . . . and said: "This fellow is not bad at magic if he can change into such a hulking creature. What shall we do with him?"

Nocha laughed and cried: "Don't worry! Just watch me catch him."

Then with a shout Nocha turned into a god with three heads and six arms, and leaping on the ox's back he swept his sword and cut off its head. Just as the Heavenly Prince had put down his sword to greet Monkey, another head sprouted from the neck of the ox, its mouth belching black smoke, its eyes throwing off gold sparks. Nocha hacked at it again, but as fast as one head fell another grew in its place. A dozen blows he struck and a dozen heads sprouted one after another. Then Nocha brought out his flaming wheel and hung it on the ox's horns, making the magic fire blaze so fiercely that the ox was burned and tossed its head and tail, bellowing with pain. But this time the Ox Monster could not change his shape again, for he was caught under the prince's magic mirror.

"Spare me!" he pleaded. "I surrender to Buddha!"

"If you want to be spared," said Nocha, "give us that fan without any more delay."

"My wife has it," said the Ox.

Nocha took a rope ... fastened the Ox by the nose and pulled him along. . . . As they approached the cave the Ox Monster called: "Wife! Bring out the fan to save me!"

At this the princess quickly divested herself of her jewels and coloured garments, and dressed in a white robe with hair knotted like a nun she came out holding the fan which was twelve feet long. At the sight of all the angels and the Heavenly Prince, as well as his son Nocha, she dropped to her knees and kowtowed saying: "Spare us, Buddha! We'll give this fan to Uncle Monkey to do as he wants with it. . . ."

Then Monkey took the fan and went up the mountain. He fanned with all his might till the flames on the mountain went out and it turned dark without so much as a spark. When he fanned a second time, a cool breeze sprang up. When he fanned a third time, the sky became overcast and a light rain started falling. As the following verse will testify:

> Far, far away the Flaming Mountain lies,
> Yet men the whole world over know its fame;
> No alchemist can brew elixirs here —
> The Truth is darkened in this smoke and flame.
> The borrowed palm leaf fan brings rain and dew,
> And help is sent by hosts of angels blessed;
> The rampant Ox returns to Buddha's yoke;
> The flames extinguished, all things are at rest.

Since Wu Cheng-en had a sense of humour, when describing supernatural beings or miracles he often slips in amusing touches, ascribing to the monsters human feelings and worldly wisdom. For instance, when Monkey is defeated by the Rhinoceros Monster and loses his gold-tipped wand, he asks the Jade Emperor for reinforcements.

The Four Heavenly Masters reported this to the court and Monkey was led to the steps where he bowed and said: "Excuse me for troubling you, old man, but I am helping a monk to find sutras in the West and I've had more than my share of trouble on the way. I won't go into that now. But since we came to Gold-Helmet Mountain a Rhinoceros Monster has dragged my monk into its cave — I don't know whether it means to eat him steamed, boiled or baked. When I went to fight it, the monster proved so powerful that it took away my wand and I couldn't beat it. Since it said it knew me, I suspect it is some fallen angel. So I have come to report this, and I hope you will be kind enough to order an investigation and send troops to conquer it. I await your answer in hope and trepidation." Then with a deep bow he added: "I beg to submit my humble report."

Saint Ko who was standing beside him burst out laughing. "What has humbled the proud Monkey all of a sudden?"

"Nothing has humbled me all of a sudden," retorted Monkey. "But I have lost my job. . . ."

Various appraisals of this novel were written in the Ching dynasty, including Chen Shih-pin's *The True Exposition of the Pilgrimage* with a perface by Yu Tung dated 1696, Chang Shu-shen's *The Correct Interpretation of the Pilgrimage* with a preface dated 1748, and Liu Yi-ming's *The Original Significance of the Pilgrimage* with a preface dated 1810. These critics argued that the book dealt with Confucian, Taoist or Buddhist philosophy, delving into its hidden meaning in detail and at great length. Actually, although Wu Cheng-en was a Confucian scholar, he wrote this book for entertainment. Its theme was not Taoism either, for the whole novel contains a few casual references only to the five elements; and the author was clearly no Buddhist, for the last chapter has some fantastic and utterly fanciful names of Buddhist sutras. Since there had long been talk about the common origin of the three religions, it was natural that a literary work should present readers with both Buddha and Lao Tzu, Buddhist concepts as well as Taoist, and that Buddhists, Taoists or Confucians alike should recognize their own philosophical views there. If we insist on seeking some hidden meaning, the following comment by Hsieh Chao-chih is quite adequate: "The *Pilgrimage to the West* is purely imaginary, belonging to the realm of fantasy and miraculous transformations. Monkey symbolizes man's intelligence, Pigsy man's physical desires. Thus Monkey first runs wild in heaven and on earth, proving quite irrepressible; but once he is kept in check he steadies down. So this is an allegory of the human mind, not simply a fantasy." The author himself wrote: "When the monks discussed the tenets of Buddhism and the purpose of the pilgrimage . . . Tripitaka remained silent, simply pointing at his heart and nodding again and again. The monks did not understand him . . . and he said: 'It is the mind that gives birth to monsters of every kind, and when the mind is at rest they disappear. I made a vow to Buddha in Huasheng Monastery and I must keep my word. I am determined to go on this pilgrimage to seek Buddha in the Western Paradise and obtain the true sutras so that our Dharma-wheel will turn again and our empire may for ever be secure.'"

There is a sequel to the *Pilgrimage to the West* in six books or forty chapters by an unknown author. It describes another monkey born in the Mountain of Flowers and Fruit who has magic power too and is known as the Lesser Saint. He accompanies a monk named Ta-tien to the West to seek for Truth, and on the way they meet another Pigsy and Sandy as well as various monsters; but after encountering a number of difficulties they reach the holy mountain and return safely. This sequel also has elements of both Taoism and Buddhism, but the language and plot are so inferior to Wu Cheng-en's polished style that it obviously cannot be by the same author. There was a *Supplement to the Pilgrimage* which I have not seen but Tung Yueh in *More About the Pilgrimage* comments: "The *Supplement to the Pilgrimage* is naturalistic and limited in scope, while the additional discourses on Buddhism are completely superfluous."

18. MING DYNASTY NOVELS ABOUT GODS AND DEVILS *(Continued)*

The current edition of the *Canonization of the Gods* in a hundred chapters has no author's name. According to Liang Chang-chu,[1] Lin Chiao-yin told him that the *Canonization of the Gods* was written by a well-known scholar in the Ming dynasty to form a trilogy with the other two celebrated romances the *Pilgrimage to the West* and *Shui Hu Chuan*. He happened on the theme by reading in the *Book of History* how the gods had assisted King Wu to overthrow the Shang dynasty. His stories about the gods were based on ancient military treatises, Ssuma Chien's *Historical Records*, the *Tang Dynasty History* and other sources, which he elaborated. This scholar's name is not mentioned, however. In the Ming dynasty edition preserved in Japan, the authorship is ascribed to Hsu Chung-lin; but not having read the book I cannot say when precisely it was written. Since Chang Wu-chiu's preface to *The Sorcerer's Revolt and Its Suppression by the Three Suis* refers to this novel, it probably dates from the second half of the sixteenth century. The book starts with a line of verse: "Tales of Shang and Chou have come down from ancient times." This suggests that the book is a historical romance, but it contains many elements of the supernatural and is

---

[1] Governor of Kiangsu in the middle of the nineteen century, and a good scholar.

Text and illustration from an old edition of *Canonization of the Gods* published about 1630

largely fictitious, merely using the fact of the overthrow of the Shang dynasty as the theme for an imaginary tale. As it lacks the realism of *Shui Hu Chuan* and the imaginative brilliance of the *Pilgrimage to the West* it has never been ranked equal with these romances. Ssuma Chien already mentions the cult of the eight deities which arose in the time of the Patriarch Chiang Shang, while ancient books of military strategy also speak of the divine power of the Patriarch of Chou, and Li Han[1] of the Tang dynasty alleges that Ta Chi the queen of Shang was a fox-fairy; so apparently legends about that period had existed from ancient times. The story of the canonization of the gods was also a popular Ming dynasty belief. One finds it in the tale of the god Chen-wu, without having to go back to the *Book of History*. When the novel starts, the last king of Shang is making offerings at the temple of the goddess Nu-kua; but he writes a poem which offends her and the goddess sends three monsters to bewitch him. Chapters two to thirty are concerned with the king's cruelty, Chiang Shang's early life before he rose to fame, King Wen's escape from death, King Wu's revolt against the Shang king, and the war between the Chous and the Shangs. Thence onwards the book is largely a catalogue of battles, with the orthodox gods and saints of Taoism and Buddhism helping the Chous, while a heretical sect called "Chieh" helps the Shangs. Both sides use magic to inflict casualties, but finally the heretics are defeated. The story ends when the last king of Shang kills himself in the fire, King Wu of Chou enters the Shang capital, the Patriarch Chiang Shang returns and canonizes the gods, and King Wu en-

---

[1] An imperial academician of the ninth century.

feoffs his barons. Thus living men are rewarded with fiefs, spirits with canonization, and all deaths are attributed to fate. Buddhist terms occur throughout the book and there are also comments in the style of the Confucian moralists, for the three religions are interwoven just as in the *Pilgrimage to the West,* though the whole is based on alchemist lore. Of the many battles described, the fiercest is that in which the leader of the heretics deploys the Myriad Fairies' Formation and the saints on the orthodox side break through his line.

Now Lao Tzu and Yuan Shih charged Master Tung-tien's formation and surrounded him. Mother Gold-Spirit, too, was beset by three holy saints. . . . She put up a stubborn resistance with her jade wand, but at last her golden crown slipped from her hair which hung dishevelled as she fought. The Priest of the Bright Lamp loosed his magic pearl which struck her in the middle of the forehead. Alas!

> Foremost among the stars she was canonized,
> For ever offerings shall be burned at her shrine.

So the priest dispatched Mother Gold-Spirit with the pearl. Then Saint Kuang-cheng let loose his Saint-Killing Sword, Saint Chih-ching his Saint-Slaughtering Sword, Lord Tao-hsing his Saint-Destroying Sword, Master Yu-ting his Saint-Murdering Sword, and black vapours whirled up to the sky enveloping the whole enemy formation. Those destined to be canonized were mown down like grass. The Patriarch raised his magic mace and struck out freely, while Yang Jen with his magic fan made a fire blaze ten thousand feet high on the battlefield till dense smoke hung black in the air. . . . And Nocha, the god with three heads and six arms, laid about him lustily . . .

When Master Tung-tien saw this massacre of his saints, he fell into a great rage and made haste to call: "Saint Long-Ear! Saint Long-Ear! Bring me the spirit flag!"

But Saint Long-Ear perceived that the Receiver of Spirits with his white lotus and bright Buddhist jewels and the angels with their tasselled golden lamps and holy auras were pure beings while his sect was heretical. So he left the battle by stealth, taking the spirit flag with him, to hide in the reeds.

> For he was a saint at heart,
> Who waited, hidden in reeds, to present the flag.

Master Tung-tien . . . loath to fight on . . . was eager to withdraw; but fear of his followers' scorn made him persist. When Lao Tzu dealt him a blow with his wand, in a passion Master Tung-tien hurled a thunderbolt at him.

Lao Tzu cried with a laugh: "You cannot harm me!" And a pagoda, appearing above his head, stopped the thunderbolt from descending. . . .

By now well-nigh all the angels of the zodiac had perished. When Chiu Yin learned their desperate plight, he tried to escape through the earth element. Lu Ya saw him, and fearful lest he could not overtake him, he bounded into the air and opened his gourd, releasing a white ray from which a weapon flew out. Lu Ya bowed and bade his magic weapon turn round, and that same instant Chiu Yin's head was severed. . . .

Then on the field of battle the Receiver of Spirits opened his heavenly wallet to receive the spirits of all fated to enter paradise. The god Cundi and Mayuraraja revealed themselves as gods with twenty-four heads and eighteen hands, holding pendants, parasols, garlands, gold bows, silver halberds, magic pestles, precious chisels, silver vases and the like to fight Master Tung-tien. At sight of the god, the master flew into a rage and swore: "How dare this confounded priest threaten me? So you want to spoil my formation again, do you?" He charged forward on his bull, brandishing his sword; but the god warded off the blow with his seven-gemmed magic bough.

> The Western Paradise and its infinite power
> Are but transformations of the lotus form.

The hundred-chapter *Expedition to the Western Ocean* edited by Erh-nan-li-jen has a preface by Lo Mao-teng written in the autumn of 1597. In fact, Lo was the author. This novel is set in the early part of the fifteenth century when the imperial eunuchs Cheng Ho and Wang Ching-hung went to thirty-nine foreign states and forced them to acknowledge China's suzerainty. According to the *Ming Dynasty History:*

> Cheng Ho . . . a native of Yunnan, was usually known as the Sanpao Eunuch. In the third year of Yung Lo (1405), the emperor ordered him to set out with Wang Ching-hung on an expedition to the Western Ocean at the head of 27,800 men. They were given large quantities of gold and silk and built a great fleet. . . . They set sail from Liuchia River in Soochow for Fukien, and from Wuhumen in Fukien they made their way to Cambodia and thence to other states, proclaiming the imperial edict and bestowing gifts on the princes and chieftains there, while those

unwilling to submit were awed by their military might. They went on seven expeditions to more than thirty countries and brought back innumerable rare and precious objects. The government, too, spent no inconsiderable sum. All emissaries sent abroad after Cheng Ho's time talked of his expeditions to foreign parts. Thus Cheng Ho's expedition to the Western Ocean was commonly described as one of the most brilliant events at the beginning of the Ming dynasty.

Since the story of Cheng Ho was so well known and popular in the Ming dynasty, towards the middle of the sixteenth century when China was harried by Japanese pirates and the people were indignant at the government's weakness, they longed not for able generals but for competent eunuchs, and this novel was made by combining different folk legends. Thus Lo says in his preface: "Today we have our hands full with fighting along the east coast. How different from the old times when western barbarians submitted to our rule! What would Lord Cheng Ho and Lord Wang Ching-hung think of this?" The novel itself, however, is mainly a farrago of miraculous events, not living up to the heroic tone of the preface. The first seven chapters tell how Abbot Pi-feng is born, becomes a monk and subjugates devils; Chapters eight to fourteen relate how he and the Taoist Master Chang compete in magic. The rest of the book recounts how Cheng Ho takes command and mobilizes troops for his expedition, how Abbot Pi-feng and Master Chang assist him to suppress evil forces so that all countries acknowledge China's suzerainty, and how a temple is built for Cheng Ho. Most of the fighting scenes are borrowed from the *Pilgrimage to the West* and the *Canonization of the Gods,* but they are inferior and rather involved. One feature of the novel is that it preserves such popular legends as the stories of the five ghosts who make fun of the Judge of Hell and the Five Rats who play havoc in the eastern capital. The latter story seems to have grown out of the fight between the true and the false Monkey in the *Pilgrimage to the West.* The five ghosts are the spirits of foreign chieftains slain in battles against the Ming forces, who make an uproar when they are sent to Hell. Here is part of their dispute with the judge:

> The five ghosts said: "You may not have taken bribes to return a verdict in their favour, but at least you have failed to make a proper investigation."
> The King of Hell demanded: "On what grounds do you make this accusation? Speak up!"
> Chiang Lao-hsing promptly answered: "I am a commander of Gold Lotus Elephant Land. I carried out my duty to the state — is that a crime? Was I wrong to defend my country?"
> Judge Tsui said: "Your country was in no danger — why did you have to defend it?"
> Chiang answered: "The Chinese came with a thousand ships, a thousand officers and hundreds of thousands of troops. We were in a very perilous position. Who says there was no danger?"
> Judge Tsui retorted: "The Chinese have never destroyed other states, annexed foreign territory or robbed other peoples. How can you say your position was perilous?"
> "Would I be here today, with so many deaths laid at my door, if my country had been in no danger?"

"All the Chinese wanted was recognition of their suzerainty. They never threatened you: you insisted on fighting. That is why we hold you responsible for all those deaths."

Yao-hai-kan put in: "The judge and the king are wrong. In our country, Java, five hundred sailors were cut in half and three thousand foot-soldiers were boiled in cauldrons. Yet you say we were the ones who wanted war!"

The judge said: "You brought it on yourselves."

Timour cried: "Our men were quartered! Yet you say we were the ones who wanted war!"

The judge repeated: "You brought it on yourselves."

The Third Prince said: "I fell on my own sword — would I have done that unless driven to it?"

"You brought it on yourselves."

Pai-li-yen said: "We were burned to cinders — wasn't that their doing?"

"You brought it on yourselves."

The five ghosts shouted angrily: "You lay the blame on us, but the proverb says: A murderer must pay with his life, a debtor must pay his debt. They killed us unjustly — why should you give judgement in their favour?"

The judge protested: "All the verdicts given here are scrupulously just. How dare you accuse me of favouring them?"

The ghosts retorted: "If you are so just, why don't you make them pay for our lives?"

"There is no reason why they should."

"If you say that, it shows you are prejudiced."

Then the five ghosts started shouting and bellowing together, creating a fearful din. The judge could do nothing but stand up and shout: "Silence! This is contempt of court. You accuse me of bias, but my iron brush here is impartial."

The ghosts rushed forward and snatched up the judge's brush. "Yes, an iron brush is impartial," they shouted. "But yours is made of cobwebs. No wonder all your arguments are so thin!"

More About the Pilgrimage is attributed by the commentator Tien-mu-shan-chiao to Monk Nan-chien. Nan-chien was the name Tung Yueh took after he became a Buddhist monk. Tung Yueh was born in 1620. He was a precocious child who chose to study the *Sutra of Perfect Enlightenment* before reading the Confucian classics. At the age of ten he could write essays and he passed the first examination at thirteen. The unsettled state of the country induced him to give up all thought of an official career and after the fall of the Ming dynasty he became a monk in Lingyen Mountain, taking the names Nan-chien and Yueh-han as well as various pen-names. For more than thirty years he set foot in no city, with no friends but fishermen and woodcutters, so that he was regarded as a saint. He left some poetry, prose and Buddhist dissertations. This novel opens with Monkey's attempt to get hold of the magic fan to put out the fire on Flaming Mountain. Monkey is begging for alms when the Ching Fish Spirit sends him into a trance and he dreams that he must borrow a bell from the First Emperor of Chin to remove the mountain. He wanders into the Pavilion of a Myriad Mirrors where he is thoroughly confused, for sometimes he sees the past and sometimes the future, changing now into a beautiful maiden now into the King of Hell. The Master of

Nothingness wakes him from this dream, and learns that the fish spirit and Monkey were born at the same time, but the fish spirit lives in an illusory world called "Ching-ching-shih-chieh," and since everything in this world is created by the spirit all things are illusory. "To apprehend the supreme Truth a man must first penetrate to the root of all desires, entering Desire itself to understand that all is vanity. Then only can he emerge to apprehend the reality of Truth." In the novel the Ching Fish Spirit, the "Ching-ching-shih-chieh," Prince Hsiao-yueh and other figures stand for "Desire." Some commentators believed that certain passages in the book referred to the Ching dynasty and that this was a satire written after the fall of the house of Ming. Actually the book contains more digs at Ming fashions than laments over the fate of the country, and I suspect that it was written before the end of the dynasty. There are casual references only to frontier troubles and though we find no complete renunciation of the world after the manner of Buddhists, the underlying idea is that of most Ming scholars, for the author makes the three religions one and gives Monkey three masters: the Taoist Patriarch, Tripitaka, and Yo Fei the Sung general. But the story is urbane and charmingly written, abounding in imaginative detail. Some of the fantasies are fresh and original and there are delightful touches of humour. In these respects Tung Yueh shows greater talent than any of his contemporaries.

Monkey (who had assumed the guise of Lady Yu) now took his own form again and, looking up, was delighted to find that he was at Nu-kua's gate.

"Yesterday after those sky-walkers sent by Prince Hsiao-yueh smashed heaven up I got the blame," he reflected. . . . "This goddess has a name for patching things up; I'll ask her to repair the damage so that I can go up to heaven to clear myself. This is a splendid opportunity." But going to the gate he found it shut, while pasted on the black-laquered door was a slip of paper saying: "On the twentieth I am going to visit the Yellow Emperor and shall be away for ten days. I apologize for not being here to welcome visitors." As soon as Monkey saw this he turned away. A cock near by crowed three times: it was nearly dawn. He went on for a few millions of *li* but could not find the First Emperor of Chin. All of a sudden, however, he saw a swarthy-faced man seated in a high pavilion. "So there are brigands in the ancient world too," thought Monkey with a smile. "Here's one on show with his face smeared with charcoal." A few paces further on he said: "No, this is no brigand. It must be a shrine to Chang Fei."[1] But then he mused: "If this were Chang Fei he ought to have a cap. . . . Instead he's wearing an emperor's crown and he looks amazingly dark. This must be Great Yu,[2] the Dark Emperor. If he will give me some charms to exorcize devils, I need not look for the Chin emperor." Drawing nearer, he saw a stone pillar before the pavilion with a white flag on it bearing an inscription written in purple: "Hsiang Yu[3] the Pre-Han

---

[1] A famous general of the Three Kingdoms period.
[2] The legendary pacifier of floods.
[3] The Lord of Chu who contended for the empire after the fall of the Chin dynasty at the end of the third century B.C. Lady Yu was his favourite.

Dilettante." Monkey burst out laughing and said: "The proverb is right: It doesn't do to count your chickens before they're hatched. So all my guesses were wrong. . . . This is simply Lady Yu's husband." Then it occurred to him: "I sneaked into this world of the past to find the emperor of Chin, to borrow something that would move the mountain. Here is Hsiang Yu, the conqueror of Chu, who comes after him in history: how is it I haven't found the Chin emperor yet? I know what: I'll go up there and ask Hsiang Yu where he is. That's the idea." He gave a leap and looked round . . . then shook himself and changed into Lady Yu. He mounted the pavilion step wiping his eyes on a silk handkerchief taken from his sleeve, and peeped from behind this handkerchief at Hsiang Yu, looking both angry and appealing. When Hsiang Yu threw himself on his knees, Monkey turned away. With swift strides Hsiang Yu came round and kneeled again, pleading: "My love, take pity on your husband! Give me a smile!"

Monkey said nothing till Hsiang Yu shed tears of despair. Then with a blush Monkey pointed at him and reproached him: "You scoundrel! You, a great general, could not even protect a weak woman. Aren't you ashamed to be sitting up so high?"

Hsiang Yu continued weeping and dared not reply. Monkey looked rather touched and helped him up, saying: "The proverb tells us that a man's knees are precious as gold. You mustn't kneel so easily in future."

19. NOVELS OF MANNERS IN THE MING DYNASTY

During the heyday of romances about gods and demons, novels about the affairs of men began to be written. These had the same themes as the *yin-tzu-erh* type of Sung dynasty stories: the joys and sorrows of human life, separations and encounters or sudden changes in fortune. Though the concept of divine retribution runs through a number of these works, since there is less stress on the supernatural than on the ways of the world and the vicissitudes of life, these books have been described as novels of manners.

The most famous of the novels of manners is *Chin Ping Mei*. At first this was circulated in manuscript only; but after Yuan Hung-tao[1] read a few volumes and adjudged this a classic second only to *Shui Hu Chuan*, the novel suddenly won a great reputation. These two books, with the *Pilgrimage to the West*, were styled "The Three Amazing Romances." *Chin Ping Mei* was first printed in Soochow in 1610. It was supposed to have a hundred chapters, but Chapters 53 to 57 were missing and those we have now were added at the first printing. The author is unknown. Since the Ming scholar Shen Teh-fu stated that the writer was an eminent scholar of the mid-sixteenth century, it was

---

[1] A famous seventeenth century scholar, magistrate of Soochow.

Illustration from an old edition of *Chin Ping Mei* published about 1636

Illustration from an old edition of *Chin Ping Mei* published about 1636

thought that he might be Wang Shih-chen[1] or one of his pupils. Then the legend was spread that when Wang wrote this novel he smeared the paper with poison in order to kill his enemy Yen Shih-fan, though others imputed this to Tang Shun-chih,[2] hence the edition published by Chang Chu-po in the second half of the seventeenth century began with an essay in praise of filial piety.

The central character in *Chin Ping Mei* is Hsimen Ching who appears also in *Shui Hu Chuan*. Hsimen Ching is a citizen of Chingho who neglects study and devotes all his time to pleasure. He has three concubines in addition to his wife, and is friendly with "a bunch of toadies, back-biters and upstarts." Becoming infatuated with Golden Lotus, he poisons her husband Wu the Elder in order to possess her. Wu's brother Wu Sung seeks to avenge him, but kills another man by mistake and for this crime is tattooed and exiled to Mengchow. Hsimen, confident that he is now secure, gives himself up to debauchery and makes love to Spring Plum, Golden Lotus' maid. He has another affair with Li Ping-erh, whom he makes his concubine too. By dishonest practices he acquires a fortune, Li Ping-erh bears him a son, Hsimen bribes Censor Tsai to give him the rank of a captain of the imperial guards, and he becomes an out-and-out profligate. He uses aphrodisiacs, indulges in licentious pleasure, takes bribes and breaks the law. Golden Lotus, jealous of Ping-erh, plays a cruel trick on her child so that it is killed and Ping-

---

[1] 1526-1590. One of the greatest writers of the Ming dynasty. His father was killed by the prime minister Yen Sung and his son Yen Shih-fan.

[2] 1507-1560. Another scholar who hated Yen Sung.

erh later dies of a broken heart. Then Golden Lotus does her best to please Hsimen, but one night he dies suddenly of an overdose of aphrodisiacs. She and Spring Plum become the mistresses of Hsimen's son-in-law, Chen Ching-chi, but when this is reported by another concubine, Hsueh-ngo, they are driven out of the house. Golden Lotus goes to live with Mrs. Wang until she can find another husband; but Wu Sung returns after an amnesty and kills her. Spring Plum is sold as a concubine to an official named Chou and having given birth to a son is made his wife. Hsueh-ngo is kidnapped and sold to Spring Plum, who vents her spite on her before selling her as a prostitute. Then Spring Plum pretends that Chen Ching-chi is her brother and takes him into her husband's house where they become lovers again. When Chou is appointed a garrison commander for his part in suppressing Sung Chiang's revolt, Chen Ching-chi is his aide-de-camp. Then the Golden Tartars strike south, Chou is killed in battle and Spring Plum, now having an affair with his son, dies one night after excessive debauchery. When the Golden Tartars approach Chingho, Hsimen's wife takes his son Hsiao-ko to Tsinan, on the way meeting Monk Pu-ching who leads them to Yungfu Monastery and reveals to them the divine retribution. Hsiao-ko becomes a monk, taking the name Ming-wu.

 The writer shows the most profound understanding of the life of his time, his descriptions are clear yet subtle, penetrating yet highly suggestive, and for the sake of contrast he sometimes portrays two quite different aspects of life. His writing holds such a variety of human interest that no novel of that period could surpass it. This is why it was attributed to Wang Shih-chen. It is not true to say that *Chin Ping Mei* deals only with the profligates and loose women of urban society, for Hsimen comes of a wealthy family and his friends include nobles, influential men and scholars. Hence this presentation of such a family is in effect a condemnation of the whole ruling class, not simply a story disparaging low society.

"You scoundrel!" said Golden Lotus. "You've reminded me of something I'd forgotten. Spring Plum, show him those slippers!" She turned back to Hsimen, "Do you recognize these slippers?"

"Indeed I don't," said Hsimen.

"What a picture of innocence!" jeered Golden Lotus. "A fine way you carried on with Lai-wang's wife behind my back, treasuring her stinking slipper like some jewel in your card-box with writing paper and incense in that cave in the garden. Are they such treasures? What use are they? No wonder that cursed bitch went to Hell when she died!" And pointing at Autumn Aster, she scolded: "This stupid creature produced them, thinking they were mine. I gave her a good beating!" She ordered Spring Plum: "Throw these objects away at once."

Spring Plum passed the slippers on the floor and said with a glance at Autumn Aster: "You can have them."

Autumn Aster picked them up, remarking: "Madam's slippers are so small, I can hardly get one of my toes in."

"You cursed slave!" exploded Golden Lotus. "Why say 'madam'? She must have been your master's mother in his last existence: otherwise why should he keep these as a treasure? No doubt it's a family heirloom. How disgusting!"

As Autumn Aster was walking out, Golden Lotus called her back. "Bring me a knife! Let me chop the bitch's slippers up and throw the bits into a piss-pot, so that she'll have to stay in Hell and never come to life again." She rounded on Hsimen: "The sadder you look, the smaller I'll cut them up."

Hsimen laughed. "You bitch! Just throw them away. I don't care a damn. . . ."

(Chapter 28)

When the time came to light the lamps, Censor Tsai said: "I have put you to a great deal of trouble today: let us call an end to this feast."

He stood up to leave the table, but before the attendants could light him out Hsimen interposed: "Wait a moment! Won't you have a rest in the back room, sir?" . . .

They went to Emerald Pavilion . . . and as the door closed two prettily tricked out singsong girls appeared by the steps and came forward to kowtow. . . . At sight of them the censor was loath to leave. "You are really too kind," he said. "But I can't accept this."

Hsimen replied with a chuckle: "This is no different from ancient times when Hsieh An[1] amused himself with girls in the Eastern Mountain."

"I fear I have not Hsieh An's talent," retorted Tsai, "but you are as cultured a gentleman as Wang Hsi-chih."[2] . . .

---

[1] A famous Tsin dynasty statesman.
[2] A celebrated scholar and calligrapher of the same period.

As they found paper and ink at the pavilion, Tsai decided to write a poem to mark the occasion. Hsimen told a boy to grind the ink well and hold the paper steady. This Censor Tsai was at least an accomplished scholar: he picked up the pen and dashed off a poem in a flash under the lamp. . . .

(Chapter 49)

The characters in Ming dynasty novels of exposure are usually based on real persons, for the writers used this means to get even with their enemies; but often the identification is difficult. According to Shen Teh-fu, *Chin Ping Mei* was also an attack on contemporary figures: "Tsai Ching and his son stood for Yen Sung and Yen Shih-fan; Lin Ling-su for Tao Chung-wen, Chu Mien for Lu Ping. The other characters, too, represented real persons." This being the case, the chief character Hsimen Ching must have stood for some particular individual. The start of the novel says: "There was a wealthy and noble family which came to a sorry end: all its craft and scheming came to nothing, all its kinsmen and connections proved broken reeds. After enjoying a few short years of splendour it left behind a dishonoured name. Those beauties who made the most of their charms to compete for their master's favour had their pleasure, but in the end their corpses lay in the shadow of the lamp and their blood was spilt in lonely chambers." The final section of the book delves into Buddhist lore. Hsimen's son is asleep in the monastery when the monk leads his mother and others in, and points with his wand; at once the lad turns into Hsimen Ching himself in a cangue and iron chains. When the monk points with his wand again the son reappears once more, fast asleep.

He is a reincarnation of Hsimen. By this rather unusual ending the author meant that the sins of the fathers are visited on their sons and can be dispelled only by knowledge of the Truth. Though the other fine-sounding theory that this book was written by a son to avenge his father adds piquancy to the tale, there is no genuine evidence to support it.

If we look at *Chin Ping Mei* from the point of view of literature, it is a novel of manners which gives a truthful and penetrating picture of life. Since it was written during the latter part of the Ming dynasty when things were not going well, the tone is harsh and bitter. Because there are numerous descriptions of private life and many amorous passages, later readers who concentrated on this aspect of the novel to the exclusion of others gave it a bad name, condemning it as pornography. Actually, at that time, such descriptions were the fashion. During the second half of the fifteenth century the alchemist Li Tzu and Monk Chi-hsiao rose to eminence by teaching the arts of love, while in the sixteenth century Tao Chung-wen won the emperor's favour by prescribing aphrodisiacs and for this was promoted to the rank of minister and ennobled. This decadent trend by degrees spread to scholars too: Chief Censor Sheng Tuan-ming and High Commissioner Ku Ko-hsiao became officials by passing the examinations, but achieved high rank by presenting recipes for aphrodisiacs. Since such sudden prosperity gave rise to envy, other men tried by every means to procure remarkable drugs and talk about the art of love and the use of aphrodisiacs was quite open. This vogue left its mark on literature: the honour in which alchemists were held and the general use of drugs were accompanied by moral laxity and debauchery. Thus the fiction of that period deals either with gods and demons or with amorous arts.

But *Chin Ping Mei* is so superbly written that, setting aside its pornographic descriptions, this is a remarkable novel in many ways; whereas later writers of this school laid stress on sex alone and dealt with such abnormal behaviour that their characters seem to be sex-maniacs. *The Human Hassock,* which judging by its style may be the work of Li Yu,[1] is comparatively good. But inferior works of this sort are pure pornography with no pretensions to the name of literature. They were printed in small volumes most of which, after being banned several times, are now lost.

During the reign of Wan Li (1573-1620) there appeared a novel called *Yu Chiao Li (Jade-Charming-Prune)* said to be by the author of *Chin Ping Mei.* Yuan Hung-tao, who was told its plot, describes it as a continuation of *Chin Ping Mei* in which different characters receive their due deserts. Wu the Elder in his next existence becomes a philanderer, Golden Lotus a wanton who is finally condemned to death, Hsimen a cuckold whose wife and concubines are unfaithful to him. Shen Teh-fu after reading the first part of this book condemned it as "utterly obscene and immoral. . . . The emperor is a Golden Tartar, the rivalry between the ministers Hsia Yen and Yen Sung is hinted at, while, curiously enough, other high officials of Chia Ching's reign appear under their real names. . . . But the style is spirited and lively, even better if possible than that of *Chin Ping Mei.*" This book has disappeared. Though a novel of the same

---

[1] A noted scholar and dramatist in the early Ching dynasty.

name exists, the contents are not as described here and it must be a later work.

There is another 64-chapter *Sequel to Chin Ping Mei* ascribed to a certain Priest Tzu-yang. Chapter 62 relates that during the Eastern Han dynasty there lived a saint in Liaotung named Ting Ling-wei and that five hundred years later there lived a saint at Hangchow named Ting Yeh-hao, who when he left the world predicted that after another five centuries there would appear a second reincarnation of Ting Yeh-hao. Accordingly, at the end of the Ming dynasty, a native of Tunghai with the same name came here, resigning his official post to become a priest calling himself Tzu-yang. This novel opens with a commentary on a Taoist tract by Ting Yao-kang of Chucheng in Shantung, and the preface says: "After an evil man burned my *Astrology* in the southern capital and a great change came about in society I ceased to speak of religious matters. Now our sagacious sovereign is propagating religion and has written a preface to the Taoist canon for the moral enlightenment of his subjects. . . ." From this it appears that this novel was by Ting Yao-kang and written at the beginning of the Ching dynasty. Ting Yao-kang as a government scholar in his youth belonged to literary societies in the Yangtse Valley, and failing to obtain any official position he wrote *Astrology* in ten books. In 1647 he went to Peking, became a senior licentiate, worked as a tutor, and won some reputation as a poet. Later he was appointed a county examiner and magistrate of Huian, but he did not go to this post. He lost his eyesight in his sixties and called himself the Indolent Priest. He died at the age of seventy-two, having lived from about 1620 to 1691. The works he has left include poems, essays and four plays. His treatise on astrology was a compilation of portents and omens from past dynasties, but we do not know how the book came to be burned: the *Records of Chucheng County* merely states that it was presented to Chung Yu-cheng of Yitu.

This sequel embodies rather simplified ideas about divine retribution. Monk Pu-ching is the reincarnation of a bodhisattva who one day distributes food to hungry ghosts, telling them the evil fates in store for them, and all his prophecies come true. Hsimen Ching is reincarnated as Chin-ko, the son of Shen Yueh, a rich citizen of Kaifeng. He lives opposite Shen's brother-in-law, Lieutenant Yuan, who has a daughter named Changchieh — Ping-erh's reincarnation. She is in Shen's house one day when the emperor's favourite, Li Shih-shih, is struck by her beauty and uses the imperial influence to carry her off, changing her name to Yin-ping. When the Golden Tartars take Kaifeng, the citizens of the capital scatter and Chin-ko becomes a beggar. Yin-ping is forced to turn prostitute and has a lover named Cheng Yu-ching; she becomes the concubine of Landlord Chai, but runs away with her lover and hangs herself after being tricked by Miao Ching. The second half of the novel tells the story of Mei-yu, the daughter of Captain Kung in Kaifeng. Longing for a life of luxury and comfort, she becomes the concubine of a Tartar, but his wife is jealous and treats her so cruelly that she determines to commit suicide. She learns in a dream, however, that she is the reincarnation of Spring Plum while the Tartar's wife is her old rival Hsueh-ngo; then she embraces religion and forgets her resentment in her worship of Buddha, thus atoning for her sins. Golden Lotus is reborn as Chin-kuei, daughter of Lieutenant Li of Shantung, and her husband, Liu the Club-Foot, is a reincarnation of Chen Ching-chi whose deformity is a punishment for his sins. Chin-kuei in her misery falls under a spell and dies after a long illness.

The rest of this novel is concerned with the punishment of sins interspersed with historical events. There are copious quotations from Buddhist, Taoist and Confucian works and commentaries, each running into hundreds of words; but the main preoccupation is with the philosophy of divine retribution. The author explains: "Before speaking of Buddhism, Taoism and Confucianism, we should start with the principle of retribution; but since empty talk unsupported by evidence is useless, we should start with the novel *Chin Ping Mei*." Ming dynasty authors of pornography used divine retribution to justify their writing. Thus the author says: "Many changes take place in the relations between husband and wife . . . for they have to atone for generation after generation of sins. So they drown themselves in the river of lust, or consume themselves utterly in the fire of passion. The whole of *Chin Ping Mei* deals with lust, while the sequel shows that all is vanity; and from lust and vanity we turn to the Buddhist Truth." This book is not entirely Buddhist, however, but contains Confucian and Taoist ideas as well, much in the same way as the novels about gods and demons. But since the author appears to lay special emphasis on good deeds and tolerance, he pokes fun at those who indulge in idle talk about the unity of the three religions or make vain attempts to compare their relative merits. The following extract describes how the Confucians and Taoists fight over Li Shih-shih's confiscated house which has been made into a convent.

In the Convent of the Great Awakening, Buddhism prospered. Then the Taoist priest of the Temple of Heaven and the students of the Confucian college started a dispute over this plot of land, and when the judge could not settle their dispute they appealed to the army headquarters of the Tartar prince. This mansion was a very large one, they contended, and both monks and prostitutes lived there. If it were simply made into a convent, there was danger of immoral conduct: it should therefore be turned into a government office with half the back-garden set aside for a Hall of Three Religions, where Confucian, Taoist and Buddhist sermons could be delivered. The prince granted this request, and all was well.

Once the Taoist priest saw that this place was divided up instead of coming entirely to him, he did not care for it. Then the scholars Wu Tao-li and Pu Shou-feng seized this opportunity to collect money — three silver cents for each subscriber — till they had between three and four hundred taels of silver and could build a hall with three chambers. They should have placed Buddha in the middle, with Lao Tzu on his left and Confucius on his right; but in order to give pride of place to their own religion they put Confucius in the centre, to show that Confucianism is the orthodox faith. They converted the pavilions in the garden into studies, as well as Yin-ping's dressing-room and bedroom. . . . Instead of studying religion, these fine gentlemen, dilettantes and hedonists, drank and wrote poems every day in the Hall of Three Religions and had a fine time studying feminine charms. They called the place the College of Triple

Nothingness, implying that all three religions amounted to nothing.

The novel *Flower Shadows on the Screen* in forty-eight chapters was also considered as a sequel to *Chin Ping Mei*. Actually it is simply a rehash of the last book in which the names and number of chapters are changed and all talk of retribution curtailed. This novel, which was never completed, was also called *Retribution in Three Generations*. Apparently there were more incidents to follow, unless the author counted the poisoning of Wu the Elder as retribution for sins in a previous life, making three generations in this way.

20. NOVELS OF MANNERS IN THE MING DYNASTY *(Continued)*

The popularity of *Chin Ping Mei, Yu Chiao Li* and other novels of this type gave rise to a host of imitations. Though these later works were not altogether the same, having different types of characters and adventures, the titles followed the established tradition; thus we have *Yu-Chiao-Li*,[1] *Ping Shan Leng Yen*,[2] and others. The stories dealt with talented scholars and beautiful girls, with refined, romantic actions, as well as failures and successes in the examinations and other changes of fortune. Since they started with many misadventures but always ended happily, they were known as "pleasant tales." Though the plots often seem reminiscent of Tang dynasty romances, there is no real connection. It was sheer coincidence that the heroes in both cases were nearly always scholars, making the stories appear similar though written in different ages. *Yu-Chiao-Li*[3] and *Ping Shan Leng Yen* have been translated into French, while another novel of this type, *Hao Chiu Chuan*,[4] has been rendered

---

[1] *Jade-Charming-Pear*. Though this has the same transliteration as the *Yu Chiao Li* mentioned above, it is not the same book.
[2] *Les deux jeunes filles lettrées*, Paris, 1860.
[3] *Les deux cousines*, translated by Abel Remusat, Paris, 1826.
[4] *L'Union bien assortée,* translated by Guillard d'Arcy, Paris, 1842. *Die Angenehme Geschichte des Haoh Kjoh*, translated by Christoph Gottlieb von Murr, 1766.

into French as well as German. So these works are better known abroad than in China.

Yu-Chiao-Li, a novel in twenty chapters, with no author's name, is also called *The Strange Story of Two Beauties*. It relates that towards the middle of the fifteenth century there lives an official, Pai Hsuan, who has no son. In his old age a daughter, Hung-yu, is born to him and proves a talented girl. She wins a reputation by writing a poem on chrysanthemums for her father, and Censor Yang Ting-chao instructs his son Yang Fang to ask for her hand. When the young man calls, Pai asks his brother-in-law, Academician Wu, to test his scholarship.

Academician Wu escorted Yang Fang to the pavilion, and raising his head the young man saw the inscription: *Fu Ku Hsuan*. Confident that he knew these characters, he scrutinized them intently.

When the academician saw this he remarked: "That was written by the scholar Wu Yu-pi. His calligraphy is spirited and masterly."

Yang Fang, eager to air his knowledge, said: "Masterly indeed! The last character *hsuan* is commonplace, but the first two, *fu kao*, are superb."

He pronounced the words *fu kao*, not realizing that in this quotation from the *Book of Songs* the *kao* should read *ku*. The academician, hearing this, was able to size him up but he merely made some ambiguous reply.

So Pai refuses the offer, and Yang in his resentment recommends that Pai be sent to the Tartar camp to bring back the abducted emperor. Pai leaves, entrusting his daughter to Academician Wu, who takes her to Nanking.

There he is so impressed by the poem written on a wall by Su Yu-pai that he wants to marry Hung-yu to him; but Su, mistaking some other girl for her, declines. Wu wrathfully urges the examiner to strike Su's name from the list of scholars, and since news has just come of Pai Hsuan's triumphant return and promotion the examiner obeys. Su sets off for the capital to find his uncle. On the way he falls in with some young men writing verses in imitation of Hung-yu's poem on the willow, who tell him that the best poet will win her hand. Su writes a verse too which is stolen by Chang Kuei-ju, who passes it off to Pai as his own and is taken on as Pai's secretary. Another suitor also poses as Su, but before long he and Chang expose each other. Now Su, impressed by Hung-yu's poem, starts north to ask Academician Wu's help in arranging a match with her. On the road he is robbed and taken in by a family named Li, in whose house he meets young Lu Meng-li, who is so struck by his talent that he begs Su to marry his sister. Su goes to the capital and does brilliantly in the examination; but on his return young Lu has disappeared. Little does he know that Lu is Hung-yu's cousin, who has gone to Nanking to join the Pai family. Unable to find a suitable son-in-law, Pai, travelling under an assumed name to Shan-yin, meets a brilliant youth named Liu in a temple there. He decides to marry both his daughter and his niece to Liu.

'There I happened to meet this young fellow Liu, who is from Nanking too and a true gentleman. . . . Struck by his good looks and learning, and sure that he would soon distinguish himself as a scholar in the Imperial Academy . . . I thought of marrying

Hung-yu to him — only I was afraid my niece might think that unfair. On the other hand, if I married my niece to him, my daughter might well call me an unnatural father. It is quite out of the question, though, to find another scholar as good as this one. In ancient times two sisters married the sage king Shun, and these two cousins are deeply attached to each other. They are bosom friends, quite inseparable. So I offered both girls to him. This has put me in a good humour over this."

Both girls are upset, however, because they want to marry Su. Then Liu comes to Pai's house and turns out to be Su, who was under an assumed name in Shanyin. And when Pai also discloses his real name, they are both surprised and delighted. So the marriage takes place. It emerges that Lu Meng-li is actually a girl, who travelled in disguise and, in offering her sister to Su in marriage, was really offering herself.

Ping Shan Leng Yen is a twenty-chapter novel by Tian-shan-jen. Sheng Po-erh[1] of the Ching dynasty said this was written by Chang Po-shan in his teens and finished by some older man. Chang Po-shan lived in Kang Hsi's reign. A poem he wrote on plum blossom at the age of nine greatly impressed his tutor; but though his precocity led Sheng to attribute this novel to him, the style seems rather that of a pedant than a boy. The novel speaks of the good old days, but since there is no indication of the date at which it was written, we do not know what period in the past is meant. In this story, the imperial astrologer reports that there are signs of

---

[1] Magistrate of Tzuchuan County and a scholar.

literary genius in the stars and the emperor joyfully orders a search to be made for talent. Happening to see a white swallow, he instructs his officials to write poems on it; and when the officials fail to satisfy him, Chancellor Shan Hsien-jen presents a poem by his daughter Shan Tai. This poem is as follows:

> A speck of white laments the setting sun,
> Her plumage mid white blossom does not show;
> She scorns to borrow pigments from the crow,
> Or feed herself on anything but snow.
> She leaves a shadow, flying through black night;
> She plucks red petals, but they make no stains;
> Within vermilion gates in wealth and pomp
> Immaculate and spotless she remains.

The emperor summons Shan Tai and asks her advice. Impressed by her intelligence, he presents her with a jade ruler "to measure the talents of the empire," and a gold wand "to command literature and protect herself against violence. When the time comes for her to marry, if any fool tries to win her by force she can strike him over the head with this wand and kill him without fear of punishment." The emperor also presents her with a placard bearing the inscription: "Talented Woman, Glory of Our Literature." At this time Shan Tai is no more than ten. Her father builds a Jade Ruler Pavilion to house the jade ruler and Shan Tai studies there. She is now exceedingly famous, and crowds come to ask for her calligraphy. After she writes a poem making fun of a young noble, her enemies spread the rumour that none of her writings are genuine; but when the emperor orders men of letters to compete with her they are all outdone, the slanderer is punished and her fame grows. A village girl, Leng Chiang-hsueh, who has also written poems since her childhood, offends Sung Hsin who contrives to sell her as a slave to the Shan family. On the way there Chiang-hsueh writes a poem and meets a young scholar of Loyang named Ping Ju-heng, but they are separated again. Arriving in the Shan household and revealing her gifts, she soon becomes such a favourite that her poems are shown to the emperor too. Ping Ju-heng, eager to find other talented men, makes friends with Yen Pai-han, a brilliant poet from a wealthy and noble family. These two scholars are recommended to the court, but not liking to receive official posts through recommendation they go to the capital for the examination and under assumed names ask for an interview with Shan Tai. Shan Tai reads some satirical poems by them and disguises herself and Chiang-hsueh to try them out. The girls outdo the two young men, who leave. Another man, Chang Yin, also comes as a suitor and is tested before the pavilion; but he is such a fool that they laugh at him, and when he tries to enter the pavilion he is beaten nearly to death. Chang later accuses Shan Tai through the Ministry of Ceremony of immoral conduct with young scholars. When the emperor investigates this charge, Chang names Ping and Yen as the two scholars concerned; but since the examination results have just been published and Ping and Yen are first and second on the list, the emperor is delighted. He orders Shan to marry his daughter and her maid Leng to these two scholars. So Shan Tai marries Yen and Leng Chiang-hsueh marries Ping. They have a splendid wedding.

The two girls mounted their sedan-chairs, accompanied by at least a hundred maids. All their way was gay with firecrackers and drumming, coloured banners and brilliant lanterns. They had imperial sanction for their marriage, and since one of the brides was the prime minister's daughter and the two grooms were imperial scholars, the splendour of the occasion surpassed anything heretofore seen. . . . If not for their true genius, how could they have hoped for this? Even today in the capital, Ping, Shan, Leng and Yen are known as "The Four Poets of Genius." While reading history at leisure, I was moved by my admiration to record their story.

(Chapter 20)

The central theme of both these novels is praise of talented women. The writers thought more highly of poetic gifts than of the ability to pass the examinations; they admired refinement and jeered at vulgarity. Yet though poetizing was their sole touchstone of talent, the verses quoted are third-rate doggerel reminiscent of the work of some country pedant. This novel also reflects the view that a man must pass the examinations in order to marry well, and such marriages must be decreed by the emperor. Here we see the limitations imposed on men's minds by the examination system. Unless a writer had outstanding gifts, he could not shake off these ideas.

Hao Chiu Chuan, a novel in eighteen chapters, is also called *A Tale of Romance and Gallantry*. The writer's name is given as Ming-chiao-chung-jen. In essence, this novel is similar to the two last, but the language is slightly superior and the hero is something of a new departure — a blend of handsome scholar and gallant man. He is Tieh Chung-yu, a scholar of Taming Prefecture.

... His fine, handsome features, like those of a beautiful girl, had earned him the nickname "Iron Beauty" in that neighbourhood. You might expect anyone so handsome to be gentle, but young Tieh was as unyielding as wrought iron. He had considerable physical strength and would pick quarrels on the least provocation, being seldom heard to make a joke. . . . His great virtue was that he would do all in his power to help anyone who asked him. . . . If men flattered him in the hope of future favours, he simply turned a deaf ear. Thus he was generally admired but without good reason no one dared approach him.

This young man's father Tieh Ying is a censor, and fearing that he may come to harm through his frankness, the youth goes to the capital to warn him. A noble named Sha Li abducts the wife of Han Yuan, and when Tieh manages to recover her his gallantry becomes known. But unwilling to remain in the capital he goes to study in Licheng in Shantung, where a retired Minister of War, Shui Chu-yi, has a beautiful daughter Ping-hsin, more intelligent than most men. Kuo Chi-tsu, the prime minister's son in the same district, is bent on marrying this girl and Shui dares not refuse him openly but tricks him into marrying his niece instead. When this is discovered, Kuo in his rage determines to ruin Shui and seize Ping-hsin, but by a clever ruse the girl escapes. Kuo urges the local magistrate to forge a government order compelling her to marry him, but Tieh who is present discovers the plot and thwarts it, earning Ping-hsin's gratitude. When Tieh suddenly falls ill, she takes him home and nurses him for five days. After Kuo's third attempt to seize Ping-hsin has failed, Tieh and Ping-hsin marry, but do not consummate their marriage. Kuo's father prevails on a censor to report: "This young man and girl are sharing one room and must be living in sin; yet her parents are condoning the matter — this is counter to all morality." When the case is investigated the emperor discovers the truth, and when Ping-hsin is summoned to court the empress finds that she is still a virgin. The slanderers are punished, Tieh and Ping-hsin are commended, ordered to go through the wedding again to uphold morality, and urged to cultivate even greater virtue.

The Iron Flower Fairy Tale in twenty-six chapters is by Yun-feng-shan-jen. It tells of a citizen of Hangchow, Tsai Chi-chih, who goes with his friend Wang Yueh to his ancestral garden to enjoy the flowers, staying there till the blossoms fade. Later they meet again in the capital and both have children. They pledge to marry their son and daughter to each other and become even closer friends. Wang's son Ju-chen is a clever child who can write poems by the time he is seven. He and Chen Chiu-ling pass the first examination while in their early teens. They are staying in the ancestral garden to enjoy the flowers and write poems when one night Chen meets a girl named Fu Chien-hua, who often appears there after dark. After the flowers are uprooted by a storm, however, she stops coming. Because Wang falls on evil days and his son fails to pass the higher examinations, Tsai decides to marry his daughter to a richer man, Hsia Yuan-hsu. Ju-chen's companion, Chen, who has passed the examination, urges his close friend Su Tzu-cheng to arrange a match between him and Jo-lan so that he can turn her over later to Ju-chen. But the girl runs away to stay in the household of Su's uncle. Hsia Yuan-hsu comes from a respectable family but is a worthless fellow. Hating his sister Yao-chih because she despises him, he arranges to present her to the palace; but on the way to the capital Yao-chih's boat capsizes and she is rescued by Su's uncle. This uncle makes Ju-chen his secretary and Tsai, lonely in his old age, makes him his godson, after which the young man marries Su's cousin, Hsing-ju. Chen asks for the hand of Yao-chih but is refused; however they elope together one night. By now Su has defeated some pirates and become a saint. One day he writes to Ju-chen and Chen telling them that the real Yao-chih is still in his uncle's house and Chen's wife is a monster: he must use the thunderbolt charm to destroy her. At this the monster flees and Su's uncle marries the true Yao-chih to Chen. One day, visiting Su's uncle, Ju-chen is amazed to see the former maid of Tsai's daughter Jo-lan. When the uncle realizes that she is betrothed to Ju-chen, he marries her to him. Both couples live to be over eighty, and after taking elixirs given them by Su die peacefully in their beds — it is commonly believed that they have become immortals.

This novel was written later than the others. The author apparently wanted to break the old pattern by introducing more miraculous incidents. That he was well satisfied with the result can be seen from his preface: "Earlier novelists aimed at describing the adventures of talented scholars and beautiful ladies for the readers' delectation. But they were often careless in the choice of titles: *Ping Shan Leng Yen* simply lists four surnames as the title, while *Yu Chiao Li* selects one character out of each one of three names. They used these slipshod methods not because they despised their characters but because this is an easy way to write a novel. This book is in a category apart. . . . Readers will find matter concerning iron, flowers and fairies, yet enfolding a tale of talented scholars and beautiful ladies. . . ." Unfortunately the style is rough and the plot confused. Moreover, by inserting accounts of war and the supernatural the author overstepped the bounds of this type of novel.

21. MING DYNASTY IMITATIONS OF SUNG STORIES IN THE VERNACULAR

Among the Sung dynasty stories in the vernacular those that exercised the greatest influence on later fiction were the historical romances. There were many such, as described in Chapters 14 and 15, and most of the Ming dynasty story-tellers were famous for their historical romances too. They also told religious tales based on Buddhist canons but there were few stories about ordinary people. By the end of the Ming dynasty, however, popular stories about urban life were revived; some were Sung tales retold, some new creations. These stories of urban life won wide popularity, but their old names were forgotten and they ceased to be known as "tales of the market-place."

The earliest important collection of forty of these tales was *Illustrated Stories Ancient and Modern*. The Tienhsu-chai Bookshop advertised this as follows: "Our bookshop has bought one hundred and twenty stories by famous men ancient and modern, and here as a start we are publishing one third of them." A preface by the Master-of-the-Green-Sky-Lodge stated: "Mao-yuan-yeh-shih has a fine collection of popular tales new and old. At the publishers' request he selected forty tales likely to have a beneficial influence on public morality and these are being printed in one collection." There was no mention of subsequent publications. Then three were other similar collections, the first two entitled *Stories*

Illustration from an old edition of *Stories to Warn Men* published in the seventeenth century

Illustration from an old edition of *Amazing Stories* published in the seventeenth century

to *Enlighten Men* and *Stories to Warn Men*. I have not read these but merely seen the table of contents. The first collection contains twenty-four tales, twenty-one of them from *Illustrated Stories Ancient and Modern*, and the three others also were included in the two other collections; so it seems to be based on an incomplete text of the *Illustrated Stories*. *Stories to Warn Men* has forty tales and a preface written in 1624 by Wu-ai-chu-shih. It contains seven tales from the *Popular Stories of the Capital*, showing that these collections include a number of old stories and are not all imitations by Ming writers. The third collection, *Stories to Awaken Men*, also has forty stories and a preface dated 1627 by Ko-yi-chu-shih who says: "Outside the Confucian canons and histories there are writings known as *hsiao-shuo*. But those that lay stress on theoretical arguments tend to be obscure, while those that concentrate on literary embellishments are often ornate and unable to appeal to ordinary readers. This is why *Stories to Awaken Men* is being published after *Stories to Enlighten Men* and *Stories to Warn Men*." Obviously *Stories to Awaken Men* was the last of the three collections. Since one of its stories, *Fifteen Strings of Cash*, is also found in *Popular Stories of the Capital*, this collection apparently contains old stories too.

In Sung-chan-lao-jen's preface to *Strange Tales New and Old* we find this remark: "Mo-han-chai edited and amplified *The Sorcerer's Revolt and Its Suppression by the Three Suis* in a skilful manner, rounding off the story. . . . His three collections, *Stories to Enlighten Men*, *Stories to Awaken Men* and *Stories to Warn Men*, contain excellent descriptions of society and manners, joy and sorrow, separations and reunions." Now *The Sorcerer's Revolt and Its Suppression by the Three Suis* has a preface by Chang Wu-chiu which states that this novel was completed by his friend Lung-tzu-yu. We know, then, that these three collections were by the same scholar, for Lung-tzu-yu was the pen-name of Feng Yu-lung or Feng Meng-lung, a citizen of Changchow and the Mao-yuan-yeh-shih mentioned in the preface to *Illustrated Stories Ancient and Modern*. At the end of the Ming dynasty Feng was a senior licentiate and magistrate of Shouning. He wrote some poems, but because he was fond of jokes and doggerel he was not highly regarded as a poet. He was a competent playwright, wrote *A Tale of Two Heroes* and compiled a collection of ten other plays which was well known and included his own "All Things Are Well," "A Romantic Dream" and "The Gardener." Having a special liking for fiction, he rewrote *The Sorcerer's Revolt and Its Suppression by the Three Suis,* compiled three collections of stories and asked Shen Teh-fu to make a copy of *Chin Ping Mei* for publication, though this edition never came out.

Five of the seven tales from the *Popular Stories of the Capital* deal with the reign of Kao Tsung in the twelfth century while the earliest is set in the eleventh century. As these stories were based on recent happenings they were fairly realistic. This is not the case in *Stories to Awaken Men*, which has two stories from the Han dynasty, eleven from the Sui and Tang dynasties, and many others based on early tales. Since customs and conventions had changed considerably in the intervening centuries, these early tales when padded out seem rather dull. Eleven stories set in the Sung dynasty are livelier, and it is possible that others, besides *Fifteen Strings of Cash*, were adapted from promptbooks also. The fifteen stories about the Ming dynasty are concerned with recent events, and since the social manners described are based on fact these are superior to the Han and Tang stories. The ninth tale, *Chen To-shou and His Wife*, describes two men, Chu and Chen, who like to play chess together and who arrange a marriage between Chen's son and Chu's daughter. When Chen's son contracts leprosy the Chu family wants to break the engagement, but the daughter insists on marrying the young man and nursing him. Three years later this unhappy couple poison themselves and die together. The passages describing the engagement and Mrs. Chu's subsequent complaints are simple and vivid.

When Old Wang and Chu Shih-yuan observed the steady way the lad walked, the clear way he talked and the polite way he bowed, they were loud in their praises.

Wang asked: "How old is your son?"

Chen Ching answered: "Nine."

Wang said: "It seems only yesterday that we celebrated his birth, yet nine years have passed in a flash. Time flies like an arrow: no wonder we are growing old!" Then he asked Chu: "Didn't you tell me that your daughter was born in the same year?"

"That's right," said Chu. "My daughter To-fu is nine too."

Wang said: "Don't be offended by my remark, but two of you have been cronies over chess all your life — why don't you become kinsmen by marrying your children to each other? In the old days there was a village called Chuchen where all the families were named Chu or Chen and their children intermarried. Now your two names are the same: this is surely fated.

They're a couple of fine children, as we've seen — they would make a good match."

Since Chu Shih-yuan had taken a fancy to the boy, without waiting for Chen to answer he said: "I'm all for it. I only hope Brother Chen agrees. If he does, I've no objection at all."

Chen said: "If Brother Chu doesn't think our poor family beneath him, as my child is a boy why should I refuse? I hope Mr. Wang here will be our go-between."

Old Wang said: "Tomorrow is the Double Ninth, so that won't do. The day after that is an auspicious day; I'll call on you then. You've given your word today and both of you are willing. All I'm hoping for is to drink some wine at the wedding: I don't expect any other thanks."

Chen said: "Let me tell you a joke. Once the Emperor of Heaven wanted to fix up a marriage with the Emperor of Earth. He thought: 'As we are both emperors, we must get another emperor for go-between.' So he asked the god of the hearth to do the job. When the Emperor of Earth saw the hearth god he cried out in astonishment: 'Why is this go-between so dark?' 'Dark?' said the hearth god. 'Can any go-between be fair?'"

Old Wang and Chu burst out laughing. Then Chu and Chen played chess till it was dark.

> From their liking for chess the whole business begun,
> And they fixed up a match for their daughter and son.

. . . .

When Mrs. Chu heard what manner of disease young Chen had, she wept and wailed about the house and reproached her husband: "Our daughter wasn't beginning to stink, yet you hurried to fix up her marriage when she was nine. Now what are we to do? I just hope that scurvy, scabby toad dies so as not to spoil my girl's life. But now he's neither dead nor alive and our daughter's growing up. We can't marry her to him nor yet break the engagement. Do you expect her to live like a widow all her life looking after that leper? This is all the fault of that old tortoise Wang, ruining our daughter's life. . . . "

Since Chu had always been afraid of his wife he maintained an unhappy silence, letting her run on cursing or scolding as she pleased. One day, turning out a cupboard, she came upon the chess set and flew into a passion.

"It was just because you played this accursed game together that you fixed up this marriage and ruined my daughter!" she raged. "Why should I keep the thing that caused all this trouble?" She flounced to the door, hurled the chess pieces into the street and smashed the board. Chu was a mild man who could do nothing when his wife was in a temper except keep out of her way. As for To-fu, she was too shy to say anything, so Mrs. Chu went on scolding till her tongue was tired. . . .

Amazing Stories has thirty-six stories. Like Feng's collections, it includes stories of previous dynasties, having six from the Tang, six from the Sung, four from the Yuan and twenty from the Ming dynasty. The preface to this work by Master of Chikung Lodge says: "The stories compiled by Lung-tzu-yu make good reading; they convey moral teaching, are unrestricted by present-day conventions and include nearly all the old tales of the Sung and

Yuan dynasties. . . . Now I am selecting various tales ancient and modern and rewriting them. I have chosen those which are fresh and amusing for these volumes." *Amazing Stories, Second Series* has thirty-nine stories, including one of the Chou, fourteen of the Sung, three of the Yuan and sixteen of the Ming dynasty, as well as five which cannot be dated and a play called *Havoc on the Lantern Festival*. This collection has a preface by the author dated 1632 which states: "In the autumn of 1627 . . . for my own amusement I chose some good stories and rewrote them. . . . There were forty in all. . . . As quite a few remained which I was reluctant to abandon, I made a second collection of forty tales. . . ." So it seems that when *Stories to Awaken Men* was published, *Amazing Stories* was produced to rival it. *Amazing Stories* is rather flat and uninteresting, however, falling below the standard of Feng's work. Master of Chikung Lodge was the pen-name of Ling Meng-chu, a citizen of Wucheng who also wrote poems and a drama *The Man with the Curly Beard*.

There was another collection of stories entitled *Second Series of West Lake Tales* and including a 200-line poem, "Autumn on the West Lake." The compiler's name is given as Ching-yuan. There are thirty-four stories, both ancient and modern, all of them concerned with the West Lake in Hangchow. Judging by the title there should be a first series also, but that I have never found. The preface by Hu-hai-ssu tells us that the author's surname was Chou and that he wrote an essay on the West Lake: this is all we know about him. There was a scholar named Chou Ching-yuan in the reign of Kang Hsi, but he was a native of Wuchin; there was another in Hangchow in the reign of Chien Lung; but both of these lived too late to have been the author. These stories also start with introductory tales, sometimes as many as three or four of them, differing in this respect from other collections. The language is fluent, but we find fulsome praise of the emperor, a plethora of moral teaching and some bitter asides which seem to indicate that the author was a disappointed man. The following passage from "Lord Han's Gifts" uses the story of a Tang dynasty poet to vent the dissatisfaction of an unsuccessful scholar:

Now one of Lord Han's subordinates was Jung Yu, prefect of Chehsi. Jung Yu was strikingly handsome, brilliantly gifted. He wrote with amazing speed, incredibly well. But priding himself on his talent he behaved with overweening arrogance. That was an age of tumult and disorder, however, when the arts of war were prized above the arts of peace. A man with outstanding physical strength — or even one who could handle one or two weapons, not to say all the eighteen different arms — could acquire an official cap with the greatest of ease. . . . Then attendants would clear the way for his horse and the fellow would have a retinue before and behind, with much pomp and glory and display of might, even if he were barely literate. Now Jung Yu set great store by his literary gifts, but in those days when soldiering was at a premium nobody would buy his wares, no one was impressed by his talents. Though he could write hundreds of poems, he could not fight battles, defeat invaders or suppress revolts, therefore he was unwanted. The only customer for Jung Yu's poetry was the sing-song girl Chin Feng. Nineteen and peerlessly lovely, a fine singer and dancer, she was quiet by nature, averse to all noise and bustle but passionately devoted to poetry. She was overjoyed to find a poet like Jung Yu. And since he was at a loose end and Chin Feng valued him, he displayed all the wares in his bag like any pedlar. From that day onward Chin Feng took no other lovers, and Jung Yu spent all his leisure hours with her on the West Lake. . . .

Making the Drunkard Sober is a collection of fifteen stories compiled by Ku-kuang-sheng of Shantung. All the stories date from the Ming dynasty except one about a man who changes into a tiger which is a Tang dynasty tale. Since some deal with events in the reign of the last Ming emperor, the book must have been written at the end of the dynasty. The writing is trenchant but oversimplified, showing the strong influence of the story-tellers' tradition. This collection is even more packed with moral teaching and admonitions than the *Second Series of West Lake Tales*. Though the story-tellers' tales of the Sung dynasty occasionally pointed a moral too, their main purpose was to entertain the townsfolk. The Ming imitators, however, are so concerned with moralizing that they seem to forget that their chief function should be to entertain. Moreover, they speak with relish of official honours from the viewpoint of the literati. So although the form is unchanged the spirit is worlds apart. Thus one fourteenth story in this collection tells how Mr. Mo of Huainan marries his daughter to a scholar named Su. Later she leaves her husband on account of his poverty and marries an innkeeper. Then the scholar passes the highest examination. Returning home in triumph past the inn, he catches sight of his former wife and descends from his chair to greet her. She passes the meeting off calmly, though at heart she feels very bitter. And finally, unable to bear the neighbours' jeers, she hangs herself. This story is obviously written in defence of poor scholars.

. . . Su saw sitting behind the counter a very pretty, proper woman — his former wife. He thought to himself: "I'll greet her and see how she treats me." He ordered his bearers to stop. With attendants holding a sunshade above him, dressed in his robes of office, he walked straight into the tavern. The innkeeper was counting money in a short jacket and breeches. At sight of an official he slunk out. The woman had recognized Su the moment he alighted from his chair, yet she neither blushed nor frowned but kept an impassive face. The scholar stepped forward to bow respectfully.

Without returning his bow, the woman said: "Get on with your job as an official while I get on with my job — selling wine."

> The scholar left with a smile.
> When water's spilt you can retrieve it never,
> And once divorced a pair must part for ever;
> If they should meet again, at most they'll smile
> Or linger side by side a little while.

I am sure the woman felt a pang; but after breaking with him so unjustly, even if she welcomed him now with a beaming face they could never be happily reunited; even if she sobbed pitifully and clutched at his garments, abasing herself, she could hardly expect him to take her back again. Her best course was to look unruffled and hold aloof. At heart, of course, she repented her hastiness, but there was nothing to be done.

> Now sick at heart she cursed her fate,
> Repenting her rash deed before,
> When she gave up the kingly tree
> For any plum beside the door.

The writer, concluding the story, comments that this woman was jeered at in life and had a bad name after death like the wife of Chu Mai-chen.[1] Then he declares more mildly that, even so, she is less reprehensible than those men who are not content with poverty and obscurity. None the less, he finds her fault unpardonable.

... Since a woman reads little and has little understanding, we cannot expect her to show great wisdom or great self-control. This is especially true when, cold and hungry, she compares her lot with that of others and finds it hard to endure their gibes and contempt. When her husband's name never appears on the graduate's list and he cannot discard his blue cloth gown but must rest content with a low and miserable position, how she must suffer! Of course such a woman complains. Yet death by starvation is preferable to loss of chastity, and how can she embrace another while the poor scholar still lives? How can she have no feeling at all for her husband? This is flagrant immorality! That is why Chu Mai-chen's wife has been a laughing-stock through the ages. ...

Feng Meng-lung's collections of stories were still popular at the beginning of the Ching dynasty. Thus

---

[1] Governor of Kuaichi in the Han dynasty, whose wife left him before he became an official on account of his poverty.

Wang Shih-chen wrote in his anecdotes: "There is a delightful tale in *Stories to Warn Men* about Wang An-shih's return to Nanking after he was dismissed from his post as prime minister, but this was actually based on the story of Lu To-hsun[1] who was exiled to the south." From this we can see that those collections were still fairly well known. Later they circulated less widely, though some of them were handed down in another popular selection of forty stories, *Strange Tales New and Old*. The preface to this says that since there were two hundred stories all told in the collections made by Feng Meng-lung and Ling Meng-chu, and to read so much was difficult, Pao-weng-lao-jen had made this selection. Eight of the tales are taken from *Illustrated Stories Ancient and Modern*, ten from *Stories to Warn Men*, eleven from *Stories to Awaken Men*, seven from *Amazing Tales* and three from the *Second Series of Amazing Tales*. The earlier collections are now rare, but we can see their general nature from this selection which must have been made at about the end of the Ming dynasty.

Hearsay Tales New and Old has twenty-two stories compiled by the Master of Tungpi Mountain Lodge. The contents are rather mixed, including four tales from *Stories to Awaken Men* and one from *West Lake Tales*, with others whose source I have been unable to trace. As mention is made of the "Taiping rebels," the book cannot have been compiled before the second half of the nineteenth century.

The *Sequel to Strange Tales New and Old* has thirty stories, but the compiler's name is not known. Since

---

[1] A minister of war in the tenth century.

twenty-nine of these stories come from *Amazing Stories* and one only from *Hearsay Tales*, it can hardly be called a selection. In 1868 when Ting Jih-chang, Governor of Kiangsu, prohibited the publication of licentious literature, *Amazing Stories* was among the books banned. It is therefore likely that this collection was produced by some publisher after the prohibition.

Manuscript copy of the *Strange Tales from Liao-chai* by Pu Sung-ling (1640-1715)

22. IMITATIONS OF CLASSICAL TALES IN THE CHING DYNASTY

Most collections of Tang dynasty tales were lost by the Ming dynasty, and though some were compiled in the *Tai-ping Miscellany* during the Sung dynasty this was never widely circulated. So when later scholars imitated certain classical tales, they aroused great interest and were considered highly original. At the beginning of the Ming dynasty, Chu Yu of Hangchow, who was known as a poet, wrote *New Anecdotes Under the Lamplight*. He modelled the language and form of these tales on those of the Tang dynasty; and though his style was rather weak, since he dwelt on love and other romantic themes his stories were popular and many writers followed his example. It took a government prohibition to end this fashion. By the reign of Chia Ching, early in the sixteenth century, Tang dynasty tales were published and book-sellers often made new collections of stories from the *Tai-ping Miscellany* and other tales. Thus genuine classical tales were mixed with later imitations. These collections were so popular, however, that scholars who had never tried their hand at fiction started writing about unusual characters, swordsmen, slaves, tigers, dogs or even insects, and included these tales in their works. So by the end of the Ming dynasty it was the fashion to write fiction and continued to be so in the new dynasty.

The most famous collection of tales was Pu Sung-ling's *Strange Tales of Liao-chai*. Pu Sung-ling (1630-

1715) was a citizen of Tzuchuan in the province of Shantung. He was a man of versatile gifts who did not distinguish himself in the examinations till old age, but spent most of his life as a licentiate and private tutor. Not till 1711 when he was eighty-two did he win the rank of senior licentiate, but four years later he died. His works include four volumes of essays, six of poems, eight of the *Strange Tales of Liao-chai*, as well as dissertations on the calendar, commonly used words and agriculture. His 431 tales were sometimes divided into sixteen volumes. He finished this collection when he was fifty, and wrote a preface saying: "I have not the talent of Kan Pao,[1] but I like collecting tales of the supernatural; and I share the tastes of Su Tung-po, who enjoyed hearing ghost stories. Each time I hear one I jot it down, and later write the material up into tales. For a long time, too, friends from different parts of the country have been sending me stories; so my collection is growing all the time thanks to our common interest." Obviously he had been collecting stories for many years, though some of them were based on Tang dynasty tales like "The Scholar of Fengyang" and "Sequel to the Dream." If he did not make this clear, it was probably because he did not want to disclose his plagiarism. There is one tradition that when he wanted to hear unusual stories he would keep tobacco and tea ready at his door and invite country folk to tell tales, later making use of those materials. This is nothing but a legend, however.

Though the *Strange Tales of Liao-chai*, like other collections of the period, are merely stories of the supernatural — of fairies, foxes, ghosts and goblins — the

---

[1] A Tsin dynasty writer of tales. See Chapter 5.

narratives are concise and meticulous in the tradition of the Tang dynasty stories, so that all these strange events appear very vivid. Sometimes the writer describes eccentrics, belonging not to the world of fantasy but to the world of men; and minor incidents are so well recorded that readers find them fresh and interesting. According to one account, because the great scholar Wang Shih-chen thought highly of this work and tried hard to purchase a copy it became more famous and many copies were made. Still the collection was not printed in Pu Sungling's time. It was published in Yenchow only at the end of Chien Lung's reign, and later annotated by Tan Ming-lun and Lu Chan-en.

The stories of marvels at the end of the Ming dynasty are usually so brief and fantastic as to seem incredible. The *Strange Tales of Liao-chai*, however, contain such detailed and realistic descriptions that even flower-spirits and fox-fairies appear human and approachable; but just as we forget that they are not human, the author introduces some strange happening to remind us that they are supernatural after all. For example, "The Fox's Joke" tells how a native of Pohsin named Wan Fu marries a fox-fairy in Tsinan who is good at making jokes and entertaining his friends. Later she leaves him as any wife might do. In "The Chrysanthemum Fairy," Ma Tzu-tsai marries a daughter of the Tao family named Huang-ying who is really a chrysanthemum spirit. She runs the house just like an ordinary woman till her younger brother gets drunk and changes into a flower. Then strange things begin to happen.

One day they had a drinking party at which Wan Fu was host. Sun and two other friends sat at the side while a couch was set for the fox at the bottom of the table. She said she could not drink but would join in the conversation, and to this they agreed. After the wine had gone round several times, they started throwing dice and played some drinking game. When one guest lost and it was his turn to drink he jokingly sent the cup to the fox-fairy, saying:

"Mrs. Fox is very sober. Won't you drink this cup for me?"

She answered with a smile: "No, I won't drink, but I'll tell you an amusing story."

. . . The guests warned her: "If you make fun of us, you'll be sorry!"

The fox laughed. "What if I make fun of a fox?"

"That's all right," they said, and cocked their ears to listen.

The fox told them: "Once upon a time a high official was sent as envoy to a foreign country. He was wearing a fox-fur cap when the king gave him audience. Intrigued by this cap, the king asked:

" 'What is that — so thick and warm?'

"The envoy told him it was fox fur.

"The king said: I have never heard of the animal. How do you write the word 'fox'?

"Sketching the character in the air, the envoy reported: On my right this is a big 'melon,' on my left a small 'dog.' "

All of them roared with laughter. . . .

A few months later she went back with Wan Fu. . . . After a year he returned to Tsinan on business and his fox-wife accompanied him. One day after she had been closeted for some time with several callers, she told her husband:

"I come from Shensi, but because we were fated to meet I put up here for a long time. Now my brothers are here and I must go back with them. I cannot stay with you."

He tried to keep her, but she left none the less.

("The Fox's Joke")

. . . Her brother Tao was a good drinker who had never been the worse for liquor. One day Ma received a visit from his friend Tseng, who had never found anyone to match his capacity, and he urged Tseng to compete with his brother-in-law. . . . They started drinking early in the morning and went on all day and all night till the fourth watch, each finishing a hundred pots of wine. Then Tseng, thoroughly drunk, fell sound asleep, while Tao started to his bedroom. Once out of the door he came to a bed of chrysanthemums. There he fell down, shed his clothes and changed into a chrysanthemum as tall as a man, with a dozen flowers as large as fists on it. In great alarm Ma told his wife, who ran to the spot, pulled up the flower and left it on the ground.

"How could he get so drunk?" she exclaimed.

Having thrown some clothes over the flower, she made her husband go away with her, warning him not to look. When he went back the next morning, he found his brother-in-law lying there drunk. Then Ma realized that they were chrysanthemum spirits, but this only made him love and respect her the more. After this Tao grew more careless and drank with even greater abandon. . . . At the Festival of Flowers, Tseng came again with two servants carrying a vat of wine in which herbs had been steeped to invite

Ma's brother-in-law to drink with him. . . . Once more Tseng became so drunk that he had to be carried home. And once more Tao fell to the ground and turned into a chrysanthemum. Not afraid this time, Ma pulled the plant up as before and stayed at hand to watch the transformation. But when he had waited for some time the leaves began to wither, and in dismay he went to tell his wife.

She cried out in horror: "You have killed my brother!"

Rushing to the spot, she found the plant had withered. Overcome with grief she plucked some stems, planted them in a pot and took it to her room, watering it every day. Ma was filled with remorse and resentment towards Tseng. A few days later, when they heard that Tseng had died of over-drinking, the flower in the pot began to sprout. In the ninth month it produced a small flower with white petals which reeked of wine, which they named Drunken Tao, and when watered with wine this grew more luxuriant. . . . Ma's wife Huang-ying lived to a great old age but no other marvels occurred.

("The Chrysanthemum Spirit")

Pu Sung-ling's descriptions of real life are neither exaggerated nor unnatural. His story "Ma Chieh-fu" describes a shrewish daughter-in-law in the Yang family who ill-treats her father-in-law, is rude to guests, and makes the Yang brothers so afraid of her that they cannot even entertain friends without trembling.

. . . Six months or so later, Ma, accompanied by his servants, paid a surprise visit to the Yang brothers. Outside the door he found an old man basking in the sun and catching lice. Taking him for a servant he bade him announce him to his masters. When the ragged old man had gone in, someone told Ma: "That was the old gentleman."

Ma had not recovered from this shock when the Yang brothers came out to lead him politely inside and they exchanged courtesies in the hall. Ma asked permission to pay his respects to their father, but Wan-shih declined, explaining that the old man was unwell. They sat and chatted pleasantly till evening; but though Wan-shih remarked several times that a meal was ready, it never came, and the two brothers went in turn to investigate. Then a scrawny slave came out with a pot of wine. They soon finished the wine and waited again interminably while Wan-shih, sweating with embarrassment, kept getting up to expedite matters. At last the slave brought out the food, but the rice and dishes were so badly cooked that they did not enjoy the meal. After dinner Wan-shih left unceremoniously, while Wan-chung brought out his bedding to keep the guest company. . . .

At the end of each volume Pu Sung-ling often adds brief anecdotes. Since these are much shorter than the other stories, consisting of only a few lines each, they bear some resemblance to the tales about the supernatural of the Six Dynasties. There are another twenty-seven stories in *The Last Tales of Liao-chai*, said to be compiled by later scholars, but none of these is up to a high standard. They are either stories rejected by the author himself or imitations written by others.

At the end of the reign of Chien Lung, Yuan Mei[1]

---
[1] 1716-1798.

of Hangchow wrote *New Tales* in twenty-four books and followed it up with a sequel in ten books. This collection was first named *What the Master Did Not Talk of* until Yuan Mei found that a Yuan dynasty scholar had written a book by the same title, whereupon he changed the name. In his preface he said: "This is simply idle gossip which I have jotted down and kept. It has no other significance." These simple, unadorned tales appear relatively natural, but as they are carelessly told the style is uneven. He was probably right in saying he had "written for fun." Many other scholars merely imitated Pu Sung-ling's style. One was Shen Chi-feng, who wrote *The Story-Teller's Clapper* in ten books with a preface dated 1791; but the language of this is trite and the contents trivial. Hopango, a Manchu scholar, wrote *Random Notes After Chatting at Night* in twelve books with a preface also dated 1791. This work is not entirely original, many of the tales being lifted from other books, and the language is often coarse; but we find good descriptions of the North China countryside and town life. Then there is *Strange Tales from the Glow-Worm Window* by Hao-ko-tzu in twelve books, apparently written during the reign of Chien Lung, with a spurious four-book sequel produced by some bookshop. There was also Kuan Shih-hao's *Gossip About Shadows* in four books with a preface dated 1801. Feng Chi-feng wrote *Tales of Hsi Liu* in eight books during the reign of Chia Ching. Considerably later there was *Tales to Cast Out Sorrow* by Tsou Tao-chih with a preface written in 1877. All these are tales of the supernatural in the tradition of Pu Sung-ling. A rather unusual book is *Miscellany Within and Without the Universe,* also known as *Crabbed Notes*, by Shu-yu-yi-sun in twenty books, probably written in the early part of Chia Ching's reign. The author strove for an original and erudite style concealing moral teaching; and the language is unusual though the contents are quite superficial and commonplace. According to Chin Wu-hsiang,[1] the author was Tu Shen of Kiangyin who also wrote anecdotes about poetry. These anecdotes, which are relatively easy to understand, do not all deal with strange happenings; but the style is similar.

The *Strange Tales of Liao-chai* remained popular for more than a hundred years and Pu Sung-ling's style was widely imitated and praised. Only Chi Yun criticized this work. Thus Sheng Shih-yen, in a postscript to Chi Yun's *Believe It or Not*, quotes him as saying:

The *Strange Tales of Liao-chai* is exceedingly popular, but while this is the work of a talented man it is not the way a serious scholar should write. Most ancient tales from the Han dynasty down to the Tang dynasty have been lost. Of those remaining there are two types: tales like Liu Ching-shu's *Garden of Marvels* and Tao Chien's *Sequel to the Records of Spirits*, and biographical literature like *The Private Life of Lady Swallow* and *The Story of Ying-ying*. Because the *Tai-ping Miscellany* contains different forms of fiction, it could include both types but it is extraordinary today to find two literary forms in one work. Tales which record things men have heard or seen should be pure narrative, not works of fantasy like plays on the stage. . . . Now Pu Sung-ling gives a vivid picture of the smallest details down to amorous gestures and the secrets whispered between lovers. It would be unrea-

---
[1] He wrote an account of the men of letters in Kiangyin County.

sonable to assume that the writer experienced these things himself; but if he was describing what happened to others, how could he have known so much? This is hard to explain.

Chi Yun was criticizing Pu Sung-ling for mixing the detailed descriptions of the Tang dynasty prose romances with the concise style of the tales of the Six Dynasties, producing something which was not biography yet had all its personal descriptions.

Chi Yun was a native of Hsien County in Chihli. His father Chi Jung-shu was prefect of Yao-an. Chi Yun was an intelligent youth who came first in the provincial examination at the age of twenty-four but did not pass the final examination till he was thirty-one. He was made a Compiler of the Imperial Academy, then a Reader; he was exiled to Urumchi on a charge of disclosing state secrets, but recalled three years later and once more appointed Imperial Compiler. Three years later he was promoted to the readership again and put in charge of the compilation of the Imperial Manuscript Library. For thirteen years he headed this bureau of compilation, and since all his energy went to cataloguing and writing brief introductions for the books, he left very little other writing. Later he became Minister of the Board of Rites and Lecturer. He was five times Chief Examiner and three times Minister of Rites. In 1789 he went to Jehol to edit some books in the Imperial Library. "When the work of compilation was over and there was nothing to do but watch the officers cataloguing the library," he jetted down from memory various anecdotes he had heard or events he had seen, and wrote *Summer Notes Made at Luanyang* in six books. Two years later he wrote another collection of anecdotes *What I Have Heard*, the year after, *Miscellanies of Huaihsi*, and the following year, *Believe It or Not*, all in four books each. In the summer of 1798, when he was seventy-five, he returned to Jehol and wrote another sequel to the *Summer Notes Made at Luanyang* in six books. Two years later his pupil Sheng Shih-yen published these collections as one work entitled *Notes of the Yueh-wei Hermitage*. In 1805 Chi Yun was transferred back to the Board of Rites and appointed Assistant Grand Secretary and Junior Guardian of the Crown Prince, in charge of the Imperial College. He died at his post on the fourteenth of the second month at the age of eighty-two, and was posthumously entitled "Wen-ta" (Cultured and Intelligent).

Though the tales in the *Notes of the Yueh-wei Hermitage* were written for pleasure, they followed strict literary rules. The author was for simplicity and against embellishment, in the style of the early tales. Thus in his preface he said: "Formerly writers like Wang Chung[1] and Ying Shao quoted classical allusions and showed erudition and profundity; others like Tao Chien, Liu Ching-shu and Liu Yi-ching excelled in a concise style and were lofty and natural. I dare not compare with these scholars of old, but in the main I try to follow our traditional style and teachings."

Since this was his aim, he followed a different path from Pu Sung-ling who had imitated the Tang dynasty prose romances; but his anecdotes contained more reasoning than the tales of the Six Dynasties, for he was not content to write pure entertainment but wanted his work to serve a moral purpose. Therefore the spirit of his

---

[1] A first century philosopher.

writing was inevitably different. Later imitators of his went a step further, turning out purely moralistic tales about divine retribution.

Chi Yun was a good writer, however, who had read extremely widely and had an enlightened, liberal outlook. He used his descriptions of supernatural beings, fox-spirits and ghosts, to express his own ideas; and he had a fine sense of humour; thus no writers after him could surpass his style. He was not an author who became well known simply on account of his high official position. Here are three fair samples of his work:

> When Judge Liu Yi-chai was a censor he rented a house at Hsihoyen, where every night he heard men beating the watchman's clapper and keeping up a din till dawn. . . . When he looked there was no one to be seen, but the phantoms made such a noise that he could not sleep a wink. Now Yi-chai was a bold man. He wrote a denunciation of these ghosts in large letters, pasting it upon the wall to exorcize them, and that same night he had peace. He exulted to think that in this he resembled Han Yu who drove the crocodiles away with an essay.
>
> I told him: "Your scholarship and rectitude are probably not up to Han Yu's standard yet; but as you are bold and have never done anything to be ashamed of, you could afford not to be afraid of ghosts. Besides, you were short of money after renting this house and in no position to move: you had no alternative but to tackle the ghosts. Since it was a final desperate fling on your part, the ghosts were generous enough to withdraw. . . ."

Yi-chai laughed and smote me on the back. "How sarcastic you are!" he said. "But I see you know me."

(*Summer Notes Made at Luanyang*)

Tien Pai-yen told me: "Once I was at a séance with some friends when a spirit called the True Hermit manifested itself, a gentlemanly recluse of the end of the Sung dynasty. This spirit was answering our questions pleasantly when two visitors were announced. At once it stopped writing. At another séance when this same spirit came back, we asked it why it had left so suddenly. It wrote: 'One of those two gentlemen is too polite and worldly, praising anyone he meets to the skies. I am too free and easy to cope with him, so it was better to avoid him. The other is too scrupulous and exacting, with a pettifogger's mind, who weighs every word you say most critically. Since I am too easy-going to stand such niggling ways, I made haste to escape.' When my father heard this he said: 'That spirit was rather narrow-minded. He should learn tolerance.'"

(*Miscellanies of Huaihsi*)

When Li Shang-yin wrote: "In vain the phantom sings the song of Tzu-yeh," he was using the Tsin dynasty allusion to the Tzu-yeh songs.[1] When Li Ho[2] wrote: "In the autumn graveyard the ghost chants Pao Chao's[3] poem," he was thinking of Pao Chao's funeral dirge and enlarging on the idea. And yet such

---

[1] Tsin dynasty love songs, popularly believed to be sung by ghosts at night.
[2] A Tang dynasty poet (790-816).
[3] A fifth century poet.

things do happen. According to Tien Hsiang-chin, he was studying in his lodge one night when the wind was hushed and the moon was bright and he heard someone singing a *kunchu*[1] air, clear, melodious, tender and ineffably moving. Listening carefully, he recognized the scene "Lamenting Before the Painting" from *The Peony Pavilion*.[2] He listened raptly to the end. Then he thought: "Beyond this wall is a rugged shore and wild bank where few people tread. Who can be singing?" When he opened the door and looked out, there was nothing outside but the autumn reeds.

(Believe It or Not)

According to Sheng Shih-yen's preface, Chi Yun was "upright and unassuming, averse to displays of learning and empty talk about the Mind and Nature." Naturally tolerant, he opposed the strict conventions and pedantry of the Sung dynasty Confucians. Indeed in his work, just as in his short introductions to the classics, he often criticized such scholars. He also challenged certain irrational conventions which had blinded men, exposing the fallacy of much conventional ethics. This is something we do not find in other works of fiction, but few readers recognized this and his tales were praised for their fine moral tone.

Wu Hui-shu told me this story. There was a doctor who was an honest fellow. One night an old woman came to him with a pair of gold hair-pins to buy some medicine for an abortion. The doctor was horrified

---

[1] A type of local opera popular in the late Ming and early Ching dynasty.
[2] A play by Tang Hsien-tsu.

and refused abruptly. The next evening, when she brought him two more pearl trinkets, the doctor was even more horrified and drove her away. Six or seven months later he had a dream in which he was haled before the Judge of Hell on a charge of manslaughter. When he reached the court he saw a dishevelled woman with a red scarf knotted tightly round her neck, who wept as she accused him of withholding medicine from her.

The doctor retorted: "Medicine is to save life — how could I kill a child for the sake of gain? You destroyed yourself by committing adultery. What has that to do with me?"

The woman said: "When I begged you for the medicine the child in my womb was still unformed. Had you helped to rid me of it I need not have died: you would have destroyed a senseless clot of blood and saved a woman's life. Not having the medicine, I had to give birth; whereupon the infant was cruelly strangled to death and I was forced to hang myself. So instead of saving one life, you destroyed two. Whom else should I blame but you?"

The judge sighed and said: "You are arguing according to expediency, the doctor according to what is considered right. Since the Sung dynasty many scholars have insisted on what is supposed to be right without taking the circumstances into account. He is not the only offender. Let the case be dismissed!"

As the judge banged on the table the doctor woke, shuddering.

(*What I Have Heard*)

Through Tungkuang County flows a river known as Wangman or Husu. Dry in time of drought, it rises in the rainy season till it is difficult to ford. My uncle Ma told me the following anecdote. Towards the end of Yung Cheng's reign a beggar woman attempted to ford this river, her infant son in one arm and her ailing mother-in-law on the other. In midstream the elder woman stumbled and fell. Then the mother dropped her son into the water and strained every nerve to save her mother-in-law.

Her mother-in-law reproached her bitterly: "I am an old woman of three score years and ten: what can my death matter to anyone? Why to save me did you abandon the child on whom generations of the Chang family depended for the continuance of their line? You wicked creature to put an end to our ancestral sacrifices!"

Kneeling before her mother-in-law, the woman wept and dared make no retort. Two days later the old woman died, having refused food in her grief for her lost grandson. The younger woman sobbed bitterly, and after remaining there for some days like one in a trance she died on the same spot. . . .

Some who heard this story commented: "A mother-in-law should come before a child, but the family line should come before a mother-in-law. Had the woman's husband or his brothers been alive, she would have been right to abandon her son; but since both she and her mother-in-law were widows with only this one child to continue the line, the mother-in-law was right. Though the woman died, she should be censured."

My father said: "How those scholars do delight in censuring others! In that rushing current which swept all away so swiftly, she could not give the matter careful thought. As she was unable to save both and abandoned her child to rescue her mother-in-law, she was doing what was right according to natural justice and human conventions. If her mother-in-law had died and her son survived . . . would she not have been accused of sacrificing her mother-in-law for the child? In any case, the infant was so small that its hold on life was uncertain. If she had let her mother-in-law drown and her son had died too, she would have been even more wretched. What she did shows remarkable good sense. It was unfortunate that her mother-in-law died and that this caused her death too — this is sad enough. Yet critics must needs wag their tongues, gloating over their own superior moral understanding. This is enough to make even the dead fume with rage in the nether regions. Sun Fu[1] in his *Studies of Orthodoxy in the Spring and Autumn Period* found fault with everyone, praising not one single man in those two hundred and forty years, while Hu Chih-tang in his *Notes on History* declared that there had been no perfect gentleman since the Hsia, Shang and Chou dynasties. These men may argue with eloquence, but I am simply not interested in such talk."

(*Miscellanies of Huaihsi*)

The *Summer Notes Made at Luanyang*, published as soon as completed, became as well known as the *Strange Tales of Liao-chai*. It was followed by *What I Have Heard* and the others, which won even greater popularity. After scholars began to imitate Chi Yun's style, Pu Sung-ling's influence declined and subsequent literature contained fewer detailed descriptions, reverting rather to the style

---

[1] A Sung dynasty Confucian scholar (992-1057).

of the tales and anecdotes of the Sung and Ming dynasties. Examples of such works are *Hearsay Tales* by Yueh Chun in twelve books with a preface dated 1792, and its sequel in eight books with a preface dated 1794; *Strange Tales* by Hsu Chiu-cha in two books with a preface dated 1846; *Collected Tales* by Tang Yung-chung in eight books with a preface dated 1848. Later came Wang Tao's *Wild Talk* written in 1862, his *Random Notes from Shanghai* written early in the reign of Kuang Hsu, and his *Shanghai Miscellany* with a preface dated 1887, all in twelve books. There was also Hsuan Ting's *Records of a Rainy Night by the Autumn Lamp* in sixteen books with a preface dated 1895. These later works were modelled on the style of the *Strange Tales of Liao-chai* again and enjoyed a certain popularity, but they dealt less with fox-spirits and ghosts than with love and singsong girls.

Nineteenth century works similar to the *Notes of the Yueh-wei Hermitage* were Hsu Yuan-chung's *Pen Gossip* in four books with a preface dated 1827 and Yu Hung-chien's *Anecdotes of Yinhsueh-hsuan* in four books with a preface dated 1848. The latter accorded high praise to Chi Yun's works but regretted that he was so hard on the Sung dynasty Confucians — apparently Yu Hung-chien held different views. In the reign of Kuang Hsu, Yu Yueh wrote *Anecdotes of Yutai Fairy Lodge* in sixteen books, simply recording strange happenings without drawing any moral. Under the pen-name Yang-chu-weng, he also wrote *Hearsay Tales* in four books, claiming to have done this purely for entertainment. We read in his preface: "The tales may contain ideas of reward and retribution, but in fact my purpose was to amuse rather than to edify or warn my readers." This was evidently in the tradition of Yuan Mei's tales, while Yu

Yueh's concise and elegant style is reminiscent of the *Notes of Yueh-wei Hermitage*, though the subject matter is different, few of the stories dealing with ghosts. There were in addition Chin Peng-chang's *Random Notes of a Traveller* in four books with a preface dated 1796, Liang Kung-chen's *Anecdotes of Chihshang Hermitage* in twenty-four books with a preface dated 1848, and Hsu Feng-en's *Village Talk* in ten books, also written during Tao Kuang's reign. These works consist of strange tales of the supernatural, but their purpose was to point a moral and educate men and they are not really works of fiction.

23. NOVELS OF SOCIAL SATIRE IN THE CHING DYNASTY

The element of social satire in anecdotes of the Tsin and Tang dynasties increased considerably during the Ming dynasty, especially in the novels of manners. However, the writers of such books usually slipped in descriptions of some low type of folly as a foil to the genius of some brilliant scholar. Hence these characters are seldom very true to life, serving merely as a peg on which to hang jokes. In certain of the better works, the characterization may be penetrating and the sarcasm sharper than a razor's edge, yet with the exception of the *Sequel to the Pilgrimage to the West*, the main object of satire always seems to be one particular individual or family. One suspects that the writer's bitterness springs from some private grudge rather than from public-spirited indignation which made him use his pen to attack social iniquities. The book which comes closest to criticizing society as a whole is *Chung Kuei the Ghost Catcher*, a story in ten chapters probably written in the Ming dynasty. The author takes all sorts and conditions of men and compares them to ghosts, analysing their characters thoroughly one by one; but his blunt attacks verge on downright abuse, for he did not know the fine art of innuendo. Wu Ching-tzu's *The Scholars* is the first novel in which a writer criticizes social abuses without any personal malice, directing his attack mainly on the literati. The

儒林外史第一回

說楔子敷陳大義　借名流隱括全文

人生南北多歧路　將相神仙也要凡人做　百代興亡朝復暮　江風吹倒前朝樹　功名富貴無憑據　費盡心情總把流光誤　濁酒三杯沈醉去　水流花謝知何處

這一首詞也是個老生常談不過說人生富貴功名是身外之物但世人一見了功名便捨著性命去求他及至到手之後味同嚼蠟自古及今那一個是看得破的雖然如

A comparatively early edition of *The Scholars* published in 1803

style is warm and humorous, gentle and ironical. This must rank as China's first novel of social satire.

Wu Ching-tzu was a native of Chuanchiao County in the province of Anhwei. A brilliant boy with a remarkable memory, he was elected to the government college. He had a good knowledge of classical literature and could toss off poems at a moment's notice; but his generosity and poor business sense made him run through his property in a few years' time, reducing him to relative poverty. In 1735, Chao Kuo-lin, governor of Anhwei, recommended him for the government examination for scholars, but he did not take it. He moved to Nanking and became the leader of the men of letters there. He and his friends raised money to build a temple to ancient sages at the Raining-Flowers Mount, where they sacrificed to two hundred and thirty worthies starting with Tai-po[1] of the Kingdom of Wu. When their funds were exhausted Wu Ching-tzu sold his house, becoming even poorer. In his later years he called himself Master Wen-mu and went to Yangchow to lead a Bohemian life, indulging in heavy drinking. There he died in 1754, the nineteenth year of Chien Lung, aged fifty-four. His works include some commentaries on the *Book of Songs*, five volumes of *Collected Writings*, and seven of *Poems*. None of these was widely known.

All Wu Ching-tzu's works were said to have an odd number of chapters. Thus *The Scholars* is in fifty-five chapters. This novel was probably written at the end of the reign of Yung Cheng (1723-1735), when the author was staying in Nanking. Less than a century had passed

---

[1] An ancient prince who relinquished his right to the throne in favour of his brother.

since the fall of the Ming dynasty and scholars still retained many of the old ways: they studied nothing but what was required for the examination essays, put on moral airs and imitated past sages. These were the men described by Wu Ching-tzu. Since he based his characters mainly on cases he had seen or heard of himself and succeeded in bringing these figures to life in his book, it is like a candle lighting up the dark, leaving nothing hidden. Officials, literati, scholars, hermits, sometimes humble townsfolk too, all stand vividly revealed in these pages, while a panorama of the whole country is unfolded before the reader's eyes. The novel has no central plot, however. Various characters are introduced in succession, their stories starting with their appearance and ending with their exit from the stage. So this long novel is like a group of short stories or a patchwork quilt of silk; though it lacks one great design, the rich and rare episodes which run through it make it entertaining and worthy of serious attention. According to his biographer, Cheng Chin-fang, Wu Ching-tzu took great pleasure in the company of genuine scholars and was most eager to meet them; he despised those who wrote nothing but examination essays, however, detesting those who were proficient at nothing else. Thus this novel makes a strong attack on the civil-service examination system and the scholars who gained office through the stereotyped examination essays. Let us look at the passage in which a compiler of examination essays, Ma Chun-shang, explains the importance of the *paku* essay:

> Ever since ancient times all the best men have gone in for the civil service. Confucius, for instance, lived during the Spring and Autumn Period when men were

selected as officials on the strength of their words and deeds. That is why Confucius said: "Make few false statements and do little you may regret, then all will be well." That was the civil service of Confucius' time. By the Han dynasty, examinations were designed to select men for their ability, goodness and justice, which explains why men like Kungsun Hung and Tung Chung-shu were appointed to office. That was the civil service of the Han dynasty. By the Tang dynasty, scholars were chosen for their ability to write poetry. Even if a man could talk like Confucius or Mencius that would not get him a post; so all the Tang scholars learned to write poems. That was the civil service of the Tang dynasty. By the Sung dynasty it was even better: all the officials had to be philosophers. That was why the Cheng brothers and Chu Hsi propagated Neo-Confucianism. That was the civil service of the Sung dynasty. Nowadays, however, we use essays to select scholars, and this is the best criterion of all. Even Confucius, if he were alive today, would be studying essays and preparing for the examinations instead of saying, "Make few false statements and do little you may regret." Why? Because that kind of talk would get him nowhere: nobody would give him an official position. No, the old sage would find it impossible to realize his ideal. . . .

(Chapter 13)

Practically all the characters in *The Scholars* are based on actual men, and their names are often puns on or allusions to their names in real life. By referring to the writings of the reigns of Yung Cheng and Chien Lung, we can identify nearly all these scholars. (See the postscript to this novel by Chin Ho.) Ma Chun-shang was actually the author's good friend Feng Tsui-chung of Chuanchiao, whose frank speech and respect for the ancient classics show that he is a genuine scholar, unlike those literati who study merely to become officials. His views none the less express the prevalent attitude to scholarship, and thoroughly expose the literati. Ma Chun-shang behaves throughout like an honest fellow. For example, during his trip to the West Lake, we see that he has no sense of beauty, but his aimless wandering and the snacks he eats are typical of an amiable pedant.

Ma Chun-shang set off alone through Chientang Gate, a little money in his pocket. He drank a few bowls of tea in a tavern, then sat before the triumphal arch overlooking the lake to watch boat after boat of countrywomen on pilgrimages. . . . The women were followed by their husbands. . . . Once ashore, they made their way to the various monasteries. Not finding much of interest here, Ma Chun-shang got up and walked nearly a mile further. The bank was lined with taverns. . . . But all these were beyond his means. . . . He walked into a noodle shop to have a bowl of noodles for sixteen cash; then, still hungry, went to the tea-shop next door for a bowl of tea and two cash's worth of dried bamboo shoots which he munched with relish. This snack eaten, he set out again. . . . After crossing the Six Bridges and rounding a bend, he found himself in fairly open country, where coffins coated with mud were awaiting an auspicious day for burial. He walked over half a mile yet still these coffins stretched ahead of him. Ma Chun-shang was quite disgusted. On the point of turning back he met a man.

"Is there anything worth seeing ahead?" he asked.

"The Monastery of Pure Compassion and Thunder Peak Pagoda are just round the corner," was the reply.

"They're worth seeing, aren't they?"

Ma Chun-shang walked on. . . . Passing Thunder Peak Pagoda, he caught sight of many buildings with glazed tiles in the distance, some high, some low. He pressed on to a huge gate on which was written in letters of gold: "The Monastery of Pure Compassion, founded by imperial decree." Beside this large gate was a smaller one, through which he entered. . . . Women from rich and noble families were strolling here in small groups. . . . Ma Chun-shang was tall and was wearing a high hat. With his swarthy face and massive paunch, he barged about in his shabby, thick-soled shoes, pushing his way through the crowd. The women did not glance at him, nor he at them. After a hasty tour of this monastery, he went back to the same tea-house . . . and drank another bowl of tea. On the counter were plates of preserved oranges, sesame sweets, dumplings, cakes, dried bamboo shoots, dried dates and boiled chestnuts; and Ma Chun-shang bought a few cash's worth of each to take the edge off his appetite, without worrying about their taste. Then, tired out, he limped back through Chingpo Gate to his lodgings, closed the door and went to bed. Stiff from too much walking, he spent the next day in bed. The day after, however, he got up to visit the Mountain of the Guardian Deity. . . .

(Chapter 14)

When Wu Ching-tzu describes the poverty of Fan Chin's family, its sudden affluence after his success in the provincial examination, and his observance of the proper mourning for his mother, without a single word of censure Fan's hypocrisy is made clearly evident. This is an excellent example of innuendo and a thoroughly biting attack:

First Mr. Chang paid his respects, then Fan Chin saluted his patron. The magistrate, having politely declined their homage, invited them to sit down and drink tea. After exchanging some remarks with Mr. Chang he praised Fan Chin's essay and asked, "Why did you not sit for the higher examination?"

"My mother has died," Fan Chin explained. "I am in mourning."

Magistrate Tang gave a start and hastily called for a plain gown to change into, after which he bowed them into an inner room. Wine was brought and the table spread. . . . They took their places. . . . The cups and chopsticks were inlaid with silver and Fan Chin hesitated to use them. The magistrate was puzzled until Mr. Chang told him with a laugh: "On account of his mourning, Mr. Fan is reluctant to use these cups and chopsticks."

The magistrate instantly ordered them to be changed for a porcelain cup and ivory chopsticks. Still Fan Chin would not eat.

"He does not use these either," said Mr. Chang.

Finally plain bamboo chopsticks were produced, and all was well. Seeing Fan Chin's strict observance of the rules of mourning, Magistrate Tang was afraid he would not eat meat — and there were no vegetable dishes prepared. But to his relief, he saw Fan Chin pop a large shrimp ball from the dish of birds' nests into his mouth.

(Chapter 4)

There are many other passages describing hypocrites and braggarts and attacking conventional morality. We are told that Wang Yu-hui was delighted when his daughter killed herself because her husband had died. But by the time he went to the temple to set her shrine in its place, he "was beginning to feel quite sick at heart." Later he remarked, "My wife's constant crying was more than I could bear." (Chapter 48) Here penetrating insight is shown into the clash between his conscience and moral conventions. It is remarkable the extent to which the author, who lived at the beginning of the Ching dynasty and was limited by the Confucian moral codes could revolt against them and express genuine feeling. The novel contains some positive characters too. Tu Shao-ching is a portrait of Wu Ching-tzu himself. Then there are Tu Shen-ching (the author's brother Chingjan), Yu Yu-teh (Wu Meng-chuan) and Chuang Shao-kuang (Cheng Mien-chuang). All these are fine characters. The climax of the novel comes with the sacrifice at Tai-po's temple. Some years later the scholars in Nanking die out and the temple falls into disrepair, but remarkable men appear among the townsfolk: a calligrapher, a vendor of spills, the owner of a tea-house and a tailor. Of these the tailor, Ching Yuan, is the most outstanding. He lives in Three Mountains Street. After the day's work is over, he plays the lyre and writes poems for his own amusement, occasionally calling on friends.

One day when Ching Yuan had finished his meal and was free, he walked to Chingliang Mountain. . . . He had an old friend there named Yu, who lived at the back of the mountain. Yu did not study or trade but owned a market garden worked by his sons. . . .

When Ching Yuan arrived Old Yu said: "I haven't seen you, brother, for some time. Have you been very busy?"

"I have," replied Ching. "Today was my first chance to get away to see you."

"I've just made a pot of tea. Do have some."

He poured out a cup and passed it to Ching, who sat down.

"This tea looks, smells and tastes delicious, uncle," said Ching. "Where do you get such good water?"

"We're better off than you folk in the south city. We can drink from all the wells here in the west."

"The ancients longed for a Peach Blossom Stream where they could escape from the world. I don't think any Peach Blossom Stream is needed. To live quietly and contentedly in a green plot in the city, as you do, uncle, is as good as being an immortal."

"Yes, but there's nothing I can turn my hand to. I wish I could play the lyre as you do, brother. That would help to pass the time. You must be more proficient than ever now. When will you let me hear you?"

"That's easy," said Ching. "I'll bring my lyre tomorrow."

After some more conversation he went home.

The next day Ching Yuan took his lyre. Old Yu was waiting for him with a censer of fine incense. After they had greeted each other and chatted for a while, Old Yu put Ching's lyre on a stone bench for him. Ching sat on the ground and Old Yu sat beside him. Ching slowly tuned his strings and began to play. The clear notes woke the echoes all around, and birds alighted on the boughs to listen. Soon he turned to a tragic air expressing grief and longing, and at the most moving passages the tears ran down Old Yu's cheeks. After this the two friends were constantly together.

(Chapter 55)

These men, however, do not care to mix with scholars and realize that the literati will not make friends with them either, for they belong to a different class. Whether good scholars appeared later or not, the author has not said.

This novel first appeared in manuscript form. Later it was printed in Yangchow, and then different editions came out. Someone listed all the literati in this book, saying that the famines and floods induced Emperor Wan Li to seek for Heaven's blessing by honouring these unknown worthies. These scholars were therefore given posthumous official titles and the officer in charge of rites was sent to sacrifice to them at the imperial college, while poetic phrases from the writings of Wu Ching-tzu were patched together into an elegy, forming one additional chapter. Thus one edition consists of fifty-six chapters. Another writer added four more chapters, with unconvincing incidents written in an inferior style, but this sixty-chapter edition is also widely circulated.

No other Chinese novel of social satire has since come up to the level of *The Scholars*.

24. NOVELS OF MANNERS IN THE CHING DYNASTY

Towards the middle of Chien Lung's reign, in about 1765, a novel called the *Tale of a Rock* appeared in Peking and within five or six years became extremely popular; but all the copies were handwritten and cost several dozen taels of silver apiece. There were eighty chapters only. The novel starts with an explanation of the origin of the story, saying that when the goddess Nu-kua mended the broken vault of heaven she left one rock unused, much to the rock's disappointment. Then a Buddhist monk and a Taoist priest came by, who told it:

"You appear to be a precious object but with no practical use. We shall carve an inscription on you so that all who see you will instantly know you for something unique. Then we shall take you to some prosperous and civilized country, to some cultured and noble family; in that land of romance and splendour, in that home of love and wealth, you may settle down in peace and happiness."

Thereupon they took the rock away. When many millenniums had passed, a Taoist priest named Illusion saw this rock, and at the rock's request copied down the inscription. This priest through nothingness apprehended beauty, beauty gave birth to love; then through the love of beauty he apprehended nothingness. So forthwith he changed his name to the Priest of Love, and renamed the *Tale of a Rock* the *Record*

Illustration from an edition of *Dream of the Red Chamber* published in 1791

Illustration from an edition of *Dream of the Red Chamber* published in 1791

of the *Priest of Love*. Later Kung Hai-hsi called this novel the *Precious Mirror of Romance*. Later still Tsao Hsueh-chin pored over this book for ten years in his Flower-Lamenting Studio, edited it five times and divided it into chapters with separate headings, entitling the book *Twelve Fair Women of Nanking*. He appended the following stanza:

> Pages of fantasy,
> Tears of despair,
> An author mocked as mad,
> None lays his meaning bare.

(See Chapter 1 in the eighty-chapter edition with Chi-liao-sheng's preface)

The story is set in the town of Shihtou, which does not necessarily refer to Nanking, in the house of Chia. There are two dukes in this family, Ning-kuo and Jung-kuo. The eldest grandson of Duke Ning-kuo, Chia Fu, dies young and the second grandson, Chia Ching, succeeds to the title; but since his heart is set on religion he relinquishes his title to his son, Chia Chen, and devotes his time to religious study. Chia Chen is a libertine. His son, Chia Jung, has a wife named Chin Ko-ching. Duke Jung-kuo's eldest grandson, Chia Sheh, has a son Chia Lien, whose wife is Madame Phoenix; another son Chia Cheng, and a daughter Chia Min who marries Lin Han but dies early leaving a daughter Black Jade. Chia Cheng marries a girl of the Wang family and has a son Chia Chu who dies young; then he has a daughter Primal Spring, who later becomes an imperial concubine. His third child, a boy born with a piece of jade in his mouth, is called Pao-yu (Precious Jade) and believed to be no ordinary child. His grandmother, in particular, dotes on him. At seven or eight, Pao-yu is most precocious, but he shows a preference for feminine company and often says that women are made of water, men of mud, giving the impression that he will grow up to be a philanderer. His father disapproves of him and controls him strictly, for he "does not understand the boy. . . . Only one who has read many books, studied the nature of things and grasped the mysterious Truth could understand him." (Chapter 2)

The Chia household is a vast one. In addition to members of the clan, there are many connections by marriage, girls like Black Jade and Precious Clasp who come to live there. There is also River Mist who visits them sometimes, and the nun Mystic Jade who studies in an inner courtyard. On the opposite page is a genealogical table of the family. The twelve girls whose names are marked with asterisks are those from whom this novel gained its name.

The story begins after Mrs. Lin's death when her delicate daughter Black Jade comes to live with the Chia family. She is eleven, the same age as Pao-yu. Mrs. Chia's niece Precious Clasp, a very pretty girl one year older, also joins the household. Pao-yu in his innocent fashion loves both girls equally, but whereas Precious Clasp is unconscious of this Black Jade sometimes grows jealous. One day Pao-yu, taking a nap in the room of his nephew's wife, dreams that he is in fairyland where he meets a goddess and reads the *Twelve Fair Women of Nanking*. He sees pictures and poems which he cannot understand. The goddess orders her maids to sing twelve songs, the last of which, "Birds Fly Back to the Woods," runs as follows:

ng-kuo

-shan
née Shih
above)

Mrs. Hsueh
née Wang
(sister of Mrs. Chia)

Chia Min
(female)

Hsueh Pao-chai*
(Precious Clasp)
(female)

Lin Tai-yu*
(Black Jade)
(female)

Shih Hsiang-yun*
(River Mist)
(female)

Miao Yu*
(Mystic Jade)
(nun)

> The high official's fortunes will decline;
> The rich man's gold and silver will melt away;
> The kind of heart will escape death;
> The heartless will receive his due deserts;
> He that takes life will pay with his own life;
> He that causes tears will weep till his eyes are dry. . . .
> One that sees through this world will enter holy orders;
> One enslaved by love will die a fruitless death.
> Even so, when all food is gone, birds fly to the woods,
> Leaving nothing but bare, naked earth behind.
>
> (Chapter 5)

Pao-yu does not understand this either, and after another dream he wakes up. When his sister Primal Spring is made an imperial concubine the family grows even more wealthy and powerful. They build the Takuan Garden to entertain her when she comes home for a visit, and the whole family feasts together in great happiness. As Pao-yu grows older he has good friends like Chin Chung and Chiang Yu-han outside the family, while at home he spends his time with his girl cousins and young maidservants — Fragrant Flower, Bright Cloud, Little Ping and Cuckoo. He is always eager to please. Because he is open-hearted and sensitive, he is constantly being distressed.

One day, when River Mist was better, Pao-yu went to call on Black Jade. She was having a nap and he did not like to disturb her, but he asked Cuckoo, who was sitting on the balustrade sewing:

"Was her coughing any better last night?"

"A little," answered the maid.

"Amida Buddha!" exclaimed Pao-yu. "I hope she will soon be well!"

Cuckoo laughed. "So you invoke Buddha too — this is something new!"

"In a serious illness a man turns to any physician," quoted Pao-yu, smiling too. He noticed that under a dark brocade bodice the girl was wearing nothing but a thinly padded grey silk jacket, and fingering this he said: "You are very lightly dressed to be sitting in the wind. This early spring weather is most treacherous. If you fall ill too, that will only make matters worse."

"Talk to me if you like, but don't touch me," protested Cuckoo. "You're growing up now. If you were seen it would make a bad impression, and you know now people love to gossip. You're so careless, you still behave as if you were a child. This simply won't do. Our young lady is always telling us not to joke with you. Can't you see that we're all trying to keep out of your way?" She stood up and flounced away, taking her needlework with her.

Pao-yu felt as if icy water had doused over his heart. He stood staring blankly at the bamboo grove. When Mrs. Chu came out to dig up some bamboo shoots and prune the branches, he hurried away to a rock where he sat down lost in thought. Tears welled from his eyes without his knowing it; and he remained in a brown study for some time, but could not think what to do. When Snow Swan passed by on her way from Mrs. Wang's room with some ginseng . . . she squatted down beside him and asked with a smile: "What are you doing here?"

"Why are you speaking to me?" demanded Pao-yu. "Aren't you a girl too? Aren't you afraid of gossip? If you're seen, there will be talk. You had better go away."

Snow Swan thought Black Jade must have been scolding him, but when she went in Black Jade was still asleep and she handed the medicine to Cuckoo....

"The young mistress is still asleep," remarked Snow Swan. "Who's been upsetting Pao-yu? He's sitting there, crying."

... Cuckoo hastily put down her needlework... and went to find Pao-yu. With a smile she told him: "I was only thinking of what's best for everyone. Why should you sulk and come to this chilly place to cry? I suppose you want to fall ill to frighten me."

Pao-yu smiled back and answered: "I wasn't sulking. I can see the sense in what you said, and if you feel like that others must too. That means it won't be long before none of you will have anything to do with me. That is what upset mê. . . ."

(Chapter 57)

Despite the outward magnificence of the ducal household, "There are more and more mouths to feed, more and more tasks to be done. Not one of the many masters and servants who live in such ease and dignity will exercise any forethought. They are so accustomed to their style of living that they cannot practise economy. So although outwardly the fabric is intact, the rot has set in inside." (Chapter 2) As the rot spreads more troubles arise. Pao-yu living in luxury is familiar with death: Chin Ko-ching hangs herself and Chin Chung dies young; Pao-yu himself comes under an evil influence and is nearly killed; Gold Bangle drowns herself in a well; Second Sister Yu commits suicide by swallowing gold; and his favourite maid Bright Cloud dies soon after being dismissed. Tragedy over-shadows the family's splendour, but Pao-yu is the only one conscious of this.

He took the two maids behind a boulder and asked them: "After I left, did Sister Fragrant Flower send anyone to look after Sister Bright Cloud?"
One of them answered: "She sent Auntie Sung."
"What did she say on her return?"
"She said Sister Bright Cloud kept calling out all through the night. This morning she closed her eyes, her cries stopped, and she fainted away. And then she breathed her last."
Pao-yu demanded: "Whom was she calling all night?"
The maid replied: "Her mother."
Pao-yu wiped his eyes. "Who else?"
"I don't think there was anybody else."
"Little fool, you can't have listened properly." . . . He thought: "Though I couldn't see her before she died, I must pay my respects at her shrine as a token of my love for her all these years." . . . He went out to the place he had visited that day, imagining that the coffin might be there. However, the girl's brother and sister-in-law had lost no time in reporting her death in the hope of getting a few taels of silver for the funeral. The old mistress had, indeed, given them ten taels with the instructions: "Take the body out at once and have it burned, for she died of consumption and must on no account be left here." Since they had hired undertakers to take her coffin straight to the furnaces outside the city . . . Pao-yu was unable to find her. . . . After standing there for a long time at a loss, he decided to go back to his own

quarters; but unhappiness made him look for Black Jade on the way. She was not in her room, however. . . . While he was debating with himself what to do, his mother's maid brought him a message: "The master is back and asking for you. He has a good subject for a poem. Go quickly!"

Pao-yu had to follow her. . . .

Chia Cheng was discussing the autumn scenery with his secretaries. "As we left, someone told me a charming anecdote that should be handed down to posterity," he said. "It deserves all the epithets 'romantic, beautiful, gallant and heroic.' It makes an excellent subject for a poem, and I want each of you to write a dirge for this heroine."

They immediately begged him to repeat the story.

He told them: "Prince Heng, the garrison commander of Shantung, was devoted to feminine beauty and gave all his leisure time to the arts of war. So he chose a number of beautiful girls to whom every day he gave military training. . . . One of his concubines, Lin, the fourth child of her family, was strikingly beautiful and excelled in the military arts. She was known as Fourth Mistress Lin. Since she was the prince's favourite, he set her in command over the others and gave her the title 'Sweet Warrior.' "

"Wonderful!" exclaimed the secretaries. "The epithet 'sweet' before 'warrior' is too romantic. It is simply superb! This prince must be a most gallant man."

(Chapter 78)

Though the ending of the novel is hinted at early in Pao-yu's dream, by Chapter 80 there is merely a suggestion of decline and the story is by no means finished.

In 1792 a printed edition with one hundred and twenty chapters appeared, in which the name of the novel was changed to *Dream of the Red Chamber* (*Hung Lou Meng*) and there were other minor alterations. In the preface by Cheng Wei-yuan we read: "The original table of contents mentions one hundred and twenty chapters. . . . I searched hard for the manuscript among book collectors and wastepaper heaps, yet it took me several years to find twenty-odd chapters, but one day I chanced upon another dozen or so on a bookstall which I bought at a high price. . . . Since the manuscript was in very poor condition, a friend and I made careful emendations, cutting out what was repetitious and filling in gaps before having the whole recopied. We had this printed for those who love the book, and so this novel is finally complete." The friend referred to was Kao Ngo, who wrote another preface dated the day after the winter solstice of 1791, one year before Cheng's preface was written.

The last forty chapters, which make up one third of the whole novel, contain accounts of many catastrophes: one character after another is ruined and dies. This is consistent with the prophecy: "When all food is gone, birds fly to the woods, leaving nothing but bare, naked earth behind." At the end, however, their fortunes improve a little. Pao-yu loses his precious jade and goes out of his mind. His father, appointed to some official post elsewhere, wants to see his son married before he leaves home; and since Black Jade is too delicate, Precious Clasp is chosen as bride. This marriage is secretly arranged by Phoenix; but when Black Jade hears of it she spits blood and sinks into a rapid decline, dying on the day of the wedding. Pao-yu goes happily to the wedding, assuming that his bride will be Black Jade, but when he finds himself married to Precious Clasp he starts pining away again. By this time the imperial concubine has died and Chia Sheh has been deprived of his rank for conspiring with provincial officials to take advantage of the weak. His properties are confiscated, and the house of Chia Cheng is involved. The grandmother dies, the nun Mystic Jade is kidnapped. Phoenix loses authority and dies an embittered woman. Pao-yu's illness grows steadily worse until he is on the point of death, when a monk appears with the lost jade. Pao-yu comes to himself, but faints away again at sight of the monk, only regaining consciousness after a nightmare. Then he changes his ways and determines to restore the fortunes of his house. The following day he takes the official examination, passing seventh on the list. His wife becomes pregnant, but he suddenly leaves her. Chia Cheng, on his way back to Peking after attending his mother's funeral in Nanking, puts up one snowy night at Piling station. There he sees a man with a shaved head and bare feet, in a red woollen cape, who bows to him. On closer inspection, he recognizes Pao-yu. Before he can speak to him, a Buddhist monk and a Taoist priest take Pao-yu away while someone chants a song about returning to the wilderness. He runs after them but they have vanished — all he can see is a snowy waste. A later reader of this story wrote four lines to follow up the author's verse at the beginning of the novel:

> This is a tale of sorrow
> And of fantasy;
> Our life is but a dream,
> Laugh not at mortals' folly.

(Chapter 120)

Though the events described in this novel are men's usual sorrows and joys, meetings and partings, a break has been made with the old conventions, so that this book is quite different from earlier novels of manners. As we read in the opening chapter:

So Illusion, the Taoist, said to the rock: "Brother Rock, in this matter of your story . . . in the first place, it seems to me, we have no means of knowing in which dynasty or year it took place. In the second, it records no deeds of virtuous or loyal men, no good rules of conduct or policy. There are merely a few unusual young women in it — some half crazed, some in love, some possessing minor accomplishments but lacking the virtues of the famous women of old. So even if I copy out your tale, I doubt if anyone will care to read it."

The rock laughed and retorted: "How can you be so dense, master? If this story belongs to no particular dynasty or year, can't you tag on some dynastic names like Han or Tang? However, since all past works of fiction appear to follow that convention, it would be more original not to use it. Let us content ourselves with these incidents. . . . Most of the old romances libel the sovereign or his ministers, slander men's wives and daughters, or give accounts of lewdness and cruelty. . . . Then there are works about talented scholars and beauties, all written according to one pattern, which usually include erotic descriptions. These books contain nothing but brilliant and handsome scholars and beautiful young ladies. . . . In fact, even the maids in them talk like pedants on classical literature and philosophy; but if you look more closely, they are all self-contradictory and beyond the bounds of reason. So it would be much better, it seems to me, to describe those girls whom I saw with my own eyes and heard with my own ears during my short lifetime. Though I cannot claim that they are superior to the heroines of earlier works of literature, at least their stories are of sufficient interest to banish boredom. , . . As for the scenes of prosperity and decline, joy and sorrow, separations and encounters, these are all set down as they happened with no embellishment or exaggeration to impress the credulous and depart from truth. . . ."

(Chapter 1)

It is because this novel keeps to the truth and is based on personal experience that it is so fresh and original, but past readers who failed to realize this tried to find some hidden meaning in it. Many theories were put forward. We can dismiss those which are too fantastic to be worth refuting, such as the claims that this novel is about Ho Shen[1] that it contains divine prophecies or that it explains the *Book of Change*. Let us simply examine those theories most widely held.

First, the theory that the book deals with the family of Nalan Hsing-teh. Quite a few scholars held this view. Chen Kang-chi in his anecdotes of Peking scholars, writing about Chiang Chen-ying who got into trouble in the official examination in 1675, mentions the theory of his teacher Hsu Shih-tung that "The *Hung Lou Meng* deals with the family of the former prime minister Ming Chu.[2]

---

[1] A powerful minister in the reign of Chien Lung, who was condemned to death in 1799.

[2] A minister under Kang Hsi, dismissed from office in 1688.

The twelve fair women are the scholars under his son's patronage, Precious Clasp stands for Kao Tan-jan, Mystic Jade for Chiang Chen-ying. . . ." Now Ming Chu's son was Nalan Hsing-teh, the poet. Chang Wei-ping[1] in his studies of the poets also says, "Pao-yu is Nalan Hsing-teh. The novel describes incidents in his youth." Yu Yueh[2] in his anecdotes comments that "Nalan Hsing-teh passed the examination at the age of fifteen and this coincides with the account of Pao-yu." However, many other incidents fail to fit. Hu Shih in his researches on this novel has pointed out many such discrepancies. The two most powerful arguments are: Chiang Chen-ying wrote an elegy after Nalan Hsing-teh's death, for they were greater friends than Mystic Jade and Pao-yu; and Nalan Hsing-teh died when only thirty-one, while the prime minister, his father, was still in office.

Secondly, there is the theory that this book is about Emperor Shun Chih (1644-1661) and his Lady Tung. Wang Meng-yuan and Shen Ping-an propounded this view, which is briefly as follows: "Old residents of the capital maintain that this whole novel is concerned with Emperor Shun Chih and his concubine Lady Tung, with some other princes and remarkable women of that time. . . ." They argue that Lady Tung was the famous Nanking courtesan Tung Hsiao-wan who married the well-known scholar Mao Hsiang, then was taken north by the Manchu troops after their advance south, whereupon she became a favourite of the emperor and was made an imperial concubine; when she died young, Emperor Shun Chih was so overcome with grief that he be-

---

[1] 1780-1859.
[2] 1821-1906.

came a monk on Mount Wutai. Meng Sheng in his *Study of Tung Hsiao-wan* points out the fallacy of this reasoning. His most forceful argument is that Tung Hsiao-wan was born in 1624; therefore if she went to the palace in 1650 she must have been twenty-eight when the young emperor was only fourteen.

The third theory is that the book deals with political events in the reign of Kang Hsi. This was first suggested by Hsu Shih-tung and more fully supported by Tsai Yuan-pei's researches. Tsai Yuan-pei[1] starts his thesis by saying: "This is a political novel of Kang Hsi's reign. The author, an ardent nationalist, wrote this book to lament the fall of the Ming dynasty, expose the iniquities of the Ching dynasty and deplore the surrender of those Han scholars who had accepted posts under the Manchus. . . ." He tried to prove his theory by various coincidences, such as the use of the word *hung* (red) in the title, a synonym for *chu* (vermilion) the surname of the imperial house of Ming; the fact that the novel is set in Nanking, the Ming capital; the resemblance of the surname Chia to the character *chia* meaning "false," referring to the Manchu dynasty. He also claimed that the twelve beautiful women were twelve well-known scholars at the beginning of the Ching dynasty; thus Black Jade is Chu Yi-tsun, Phoenix is Yu Kuo-chu, River Mist is Chen Wei-sung, while Precious Clasp and Mystic Jade are Kao Tan-jen and Chiang Chen-ying, according to the theory advanced by Hsu Shih-tung. Tsai Yuan-pei did his utmost to prove his case, but after Hu Shih published his studies on the author's life this theory fell to pieces. Hu Shih's most con-

---

[1] 1867-1940. President of Peking University.

vincing argument is that Tsao Hsueh-chin belonged to a Han family serving under the Manchus and the novel is autobiographical.

This theory that the *Dream of the Red Chamber* was autobiographical, as stated at the beginning of the book, actually appeared very early though it has not been proved until recently. At the start of Chia Ching's reign, the poet Yuan Mei pointed out: "During the reign of Kang Hsi, Tsao Lien-ting was in charge of the Silk Bureau in Nanking. . . . His son Tsao Hsueh-chin wrote the *Dream of the Red Chamber*, a novel describing the prosperous, romantic life of those days. His Takuan Garden was based on my garden 'Suiyuan.' " The last remark is sheer boasting. There were other minor inconsistencies: for instance, Tsao's name was Lien-ting with a "wood" radical, not Lien-ting with a "silk" radical, and Tsao Hsueh-chin was not his grandson but his son. Still it was quite clear that this statement was based on personal knowledge and that Tsao Hsueh-chin was the author. Not many people at the time believed this, however. Then Wang Kuo-wei[1] raised doubts, saying: "When the author said this book was based on actual happenings, he may have meant someone else's experiences, not necessarily his own." But Hu Shih's researches have cleared up this question conclusively. Now we know that Tsao Hsueh-chin was born into a rich family which later declined, that his life resembled certain episodes in this novel, that the book was written in the western suburb of Peking and left uncompleted at his death. The full version that appeared later was completed by Kao Ngo.

---

[1] 1877-1927. A historian and authority on the history of drama.

Tsao Hsueh-chin's family were Hans, some of whom served in the Manchu army. His grandfather Tsao Yin was in charge of the Nanking Silk Bureau in the reign of Kang Hsi. The emperor stayed five times in Tsao's official residence during his inspection tours in the Yangtse Valley, and Tsao Yin was present during the last four visits. Tsao Yin was fond of literature and won himself a name as a scholar by having more than ten ancient texts printed. He left some original writing too, including five volumes of poems, one of *tzu* lyrics and two plays. His son Tsao Fu, Tsao Hsueh-chin's father, also had charge of the Silk Bureau; and Tsao Hsueh-chin was born in Nanking at the end of Kang Hsi's reign. In 1728 Tsao's father was dismissed from his post and Tsao Hsueh-chin, then aged ten, accompanied him to Peking. The Tsao family suffered great reverses, the reasons for which are unknown. In Tsao Hsueh-chin's later years he lived in poverty in the west suburb of Peking, not always with enough to eat. Still he remained a proud scholar, who often drank heavily and composed poems. It was during this period that he wrote the *Dream of the Red Chamber*. In 1762 his son died and he fell ill of grief, dying on New Year's Eve in his early forties. He lived from 1719(?) to 1763, and left no more than eighty chapters of his unfinished novel.

That the last forty chapters were written by Kao Ngo can be seen from Yu Yueh's anecdote: "One of Wang Chuan-shan's poems is dedicated to his friend Kao Ngo. A line in it reads: 'All speak of the romance of the Red Chamber.' A note explains that all the chapters after the eightieth were written by Kao Ngo. It is quite clear that this novel was not by one single author. After the reign of Chien Lung, five-word verses were required in the official examinations, and in this novel writing poetry in an examination is mentioned, proving that the later chapters were added by Kao." However, all Kao Ngo writes in his preface is: "My friend Cheng Wei-yuan came and showed me the novel he had bought, saying: 'I have been to a great deal of trouble all these years to collect this manuscript, and I mean to have it printed for those who like it. As you are at leisure now, won't you help me edit it?' Since the book . . . did not appear to flout the rules of morality . . . I consented." Apparently he did not want to disclose his authorship of the later chapters, but some of his friends knew the truth. Kao Ngo came from a Han family which served in the Manchu army. After passing the provincial examination in 1788 and the palace examination in 1795, he entered the Hanlin Academy and became a Reader. In 1801 he was made Assistant Examiner of the Metropolitan Examination. He wrote the last forty chapters of the novel in 1791 or thereabouts, before he had passed the final examination. The fact that he was at leisure and slightly bored made him sympathize with Tsao Hsueh-chin's loneliness. However, he had not given up hope, unlike the author of Chapter 1, "beset by poverty and illness in his old age and sinking into decline." So although the sequel breathes an atmosphere of melancholy, the Chia family finally recovers its lost fortune instead of being left with nothing "but the bare naked earth."

Kao Ngo was not the only one to write a sequel to the eighty chapters. Yu Ping-po, studying the marginal notes in one of the first eighty-chapter editions, discovered that there was an earlier sequel of thirty chapters which apparently described how the Chia family broke up, Pao-yu became very poor and finally turned monk. We have no means of discovering more details. Then Chiang Jui-tsao in his studies on Chinese fiction says: "Tai Cheng-fu once saw another old version in which the sequel to the first eighty chapters was quite different. After the dukes' property was confiscated, the Chia family went downhill; Precious Clasp died early, Pao-yu had no means of support and became a nightwatchman; River Mist became a beggar and married Pao-yu in the end. . . . Such a version was said to be in the possession of Governor Wu Yun-sheng's family." Though these two sequels may not accord entirely with the author's intention, they both provide a gloomy, hopeless ending which agrees with the hints given early in the novel.

There have been many later sequels: *Hou-hung-lou-meng*, *Hung-lou-hou-meng*, *Hsu-hung-lou-meng*, *Hung-lou-fu-meng*, *Hung-lou-meng-pu*, *Hung-lou-pu-meng*, *Hung-lou-chung-meng*, *Hung-lou-chia-meng*, *Hung-lou-huan-meng*, *Hung-lou-yuan-meng*, *Cheng-pu-hung-lou*, *Kuei-hung-lou*, *Hung-lou-meng-ying* and so forth. Most of these resemble Kao Ngo's sequel in trying to bring about a more satisfactory ending; some, viewing all the chief characters as bad examples, find fault and make harsh strictures. Actually, according to the original novel, the author was merely relating true incidents and no sarcasm was intended, only regret over his misspent life. That is why readers like this novel, and why it is still so highly regarded and popular. On the other hand, this is rather unusual when viewed from the conventional stand; that is why some felt the conclusion was unsatisfactory and tried to give the book a happy ending. This shows the difference in men's understanding and Tsao

Hsueh-chin's greatness. Let me quote another passage in conclusion:

> ... The author says: After a certain dream, I concealed the true circumstances and borrowed the legend of the magic rock to write this novel. ... I have wasted my life in vain pursuits, and at the end of a windy and dusty road have found myself a complete failure. But when I think of all the women I have known and compared their qualities with mine, I realize their superiority in behaviour and understanding. I, with all my dignity of manhood, cannot measure up to those girls! Thoroughly ashamed as I am, regret is useless — there is nothing I can do. So now I mean to tell the world of my iniquities — how thanks to my sovereign's kindness and my ancestors' virtue I dressed in silk and fed on the fat of the land, but failing to profit from my elders' instructions and my friend's advice I squandered half a lifetime in riotous living without accomplishing anything. Though my wickedness is undeniable, there are many worthy characters in the women's quarters who must not remain obscure and unknown to conceal my own shortcomings. I live in a thatched and rudely furnished hut now; but neither the morning wind and evening dew, nor the willows and the flowers can check my imagination or stay my pen. Ignorant though I am and unskilled in writing, I can tell my story in simple colloquial speech to record the doings of these girls and to banish boredom. ...
>
> (Chapter 1)

25. NOVELS OF ERUDITION IN THE CHING DYNASTY

The earliest example of the Ching dynasty novels written to display erudition and literary talent, comparable to the moralistic tales but having a different purpose, was *A Rustic's Idle Talk*. Though this appeared at the beginning of the reign of Kuang Hsu (1875-1908), according to the preface its author was a certain Hsia of Kiangyin in the time of Kang Hsi (1662-1722). "A brilliant scholar who met with indifferent success in the government examinations, he consented to serve as a secretary to high officials, and in the process saw the whole of North China. . . . He travelled through Szechuan, Kweichow and Hunan to the Yangtse River before returning home. His rich experience gave an added distinction to his writing . . . but as by this time his hair was turning white, he abandoned all hope of prominence in the official world to concentrate on writing." He wrote this novel in twenty books for his friends, not for publication, and the work when later published was incomplete. There is one complete edition which is probably finished by another hand, but neither edition bears any author's name. According to Chin Wu-hsiang of Kiangyin, the author was Hsia Ching-chu. The *County Records of Kiangyin* published in the reign of Kuang Hsu describes him as follows: "Hsia Ching-chu was a county scholar, brilliant, learned and well-versed in history and the Confucian classics as well as the hundred schools of thought, ceremony, music, military science, law and punishment, astronomy and mathematics. . . . He travelled virtually all over China and made friends with famous and able men. . . ." Mention is made of other books by him on Confucianism and history, as well as poems and essays. This accords with the statement in the preface to the novel; but since Hsia is listed after Chao Hsi-ming, a scholar, under Chien Lung, he must still have been alive in Chien Lung's reign.

A Rustic's Idle Talk is a large work in 154 chapters. It is divided into twenty books, each bearing one word from the following pronouncement: "A truly remarkable work breathing the spirit of Confucianism by a gentleman peerless in the arts of war and peace." This was the author's own estimate. The work includes many topics, as listed at the beginning: "Narratives, philosophical dissertations, discussions of the classics and history, exhortations to loyalty and filial piety, teachings on policy and strategy, military science, prosody, medicine and mathematics, descriptions of the human emotions, advocacy of Confucian morality and attacks on heterodoxy." The hero Wen Po is:

A man of steel, prodigious genius, magnificent poet and profound scholar. He seeks no official post but possesses astounding political acumen, is no philanderer but a great lover. In his style he brooks comparison with the ancient masters, in military science he equals the finest strategists. He unites phenomenal physical strength with a gentle, frail appearance, combines extreme boldness with the utmost caution. As an astronomer and mathematician, he surpasses all other learned men; while in medicine, which to him is simply a hobby, he ranks with the best physicians. He is the most loyal of friends, a champion of Confucian morality; indeed he is the most sincere Confucian, a scholar of absolute integrity. The chief concern of his life has been to uphold orthodoxy and refute unorthodox views. With his unsurpassed intelligence he can solve problems which baffle other men and make pronouncements that no other can make.

(Chapter 1)

Because a sagacious sovereign is on the throne, Wen fulfils all his ambitions, wins rapid and high advancement and finds all his wishes granted. He exorcizes evil spirits and destroys monsters; barbarians are awed by his might and his family enjoys every blessing. He achieves tremendous feats in time of peace as well as in war till the emperor honours him with the splendid title of "The Patriarch." Furthermore, he possesses magic powers, is able to change his form and is adept in the art of love; thus he has many concubines, twenty-four sons, and a hundred grandsons with sons of their own. Since his mother, Shui, has reached the age of a hundred, there are six generations in his house and men of seventy nations come to offer congratulations on her birthday, while the emperor bestows on her the exalted title of "Grand Dame Who Pacifies the State and Defends the Confucian Faith." (Chapter 144) Every conceivable honour which a subject could desire is here — the one thing he dare not aspire to is the throne. The author lays special stress on attacking heterodox beliefs and comes down heavily on Taoists as well as Buddhists, leaving behind him shattered altars and ruined temples and pagodas while the Patriarch's family enjoys every happiness and is universally respected.

A Rustic's Idle Talk was written because the author "had great ambitions but could not attain official eminence or put any of his great schemes into practice." Clearly the main purpose of the work was to make a parade of learning and express the desire to be both saintly and powerful. Though this may differ somewhat from the Ming dynasty novels about gods and demons or talented young scholars and beauties, at bottom they are the same. Only Hsia substitutes heterodox doctrines for demons and a saint for a brilliant young man. This book with its boasts and its insipid language should not really rank as literature; but from it we can learn a good deal about the psychology of Confucian scholars at the time. At the end of Yung Cheng's reign, when Yang Ming-shih of Kiangyin County was the governor of Yunnan, his fellow-provincial Hsia Tsung-lan studied the *Book of Change* under him. Since Yang Ming-shih had been Li Kuang-ti's pupil, Hsia Tsung-lan too was influenced by Li Kuang-ti[1] and held even stranger views. At the beginning of the Chien Lung era, Yang Ming-shih was appointed Minister of Ceremony and Hsia Tsung-lan was recommended for the post of Assistant Tutor of the Imperial College and other academic posts. He consistently followed the teachings of Yang Ming-shih. Later on Hsia Tsu-hsiung, "another scholar steeped in the classics, especially in Confucian philosophy, decided that Yang Ming-shih and Hsia Tsung-lan were unduly lax in their views and attempted to introduce certain modifications." (*County Records of Kiangyin*) Evidently Yang Ming-shih had a considerable influence on the local scholars, and because Hsia Tsung-lan learned from him

---

[1] 1642-1718. A Confucian scholar and high official.

this tradition was handed down in the Hsia family. The ideas of these men conformed more or less to the dominant views of that time: the championship of the Neo-Confucianism of Chu Hsi and the Cheng brothers against the theories of Lu Chiu-yuan and Wang Yang-ming.[1] It was considered the proper thing to attack Taoism and Buddhism. So the sentiments and actions of the hero of the novel were not the ideals of the author alone. It has been suggested that Wen Po represents the author himself, and that the senior statesman in the book stands for Yang Ming-shih. Because the author admired the tradition of Hsia Tsung-lan, this novel has been wrongly attributed to Hsia.

A novel designed to reveal its author's virtuosity was *The Bookworm* by Tu Shen in twenty books. Tu Shen (1744-1801) came from a peasant family in Kiangyin and lost his father when a child. He was intelligent and passed the district examination at thirteen, the palace examination at twenty; then he was appointed magistrate of Shihtsung County in the province of Yunnan. Subsequently he became sub-prefect of Hsuntien. He was an examiner five times and passed a number of good scholars. Finally he served as sub-prefect of Canton. In 1801 he was waiting for a new appointment in Peking when he died of a sudden illness at the age of fifty-eight. Tu Shen was a gallant eccentric, a great admirer of the Ming dynasty dramatist Tang Hsien-tsu, a strict official, but a man with many concubines. He wrote in a style archaic and bizarre, which frequently becomes obscure. This is true both of his tales and notes on poetry. *The*

---

[1] Lu was a Sung and Wang a Ming scholar, both being influenced in their thought by Buddhist philosophy.

Bookworm is a full-length novel. The author's name is given as Lei-ko-shan-fang, but according to another Kiangyin scholar Chin Wu-hsiang, this was Tu Shen. The hero of the novel, Sang Chu-sheng, is the author's portrait of himself. He was born in the same cyclic year as Tu Shen. At the beginning of the novel the writer says: "While serving as an official in Canton after my fiftieth year, I made a trip along the coast and had certain interesting experiences. Now I am putting in one book the strange things I heard and saw." Thus since the plot of the novel centres mainly on the conquest of the Miao people by Fu Nai in 1795, the book could not have been written earlier than 1796 and must have been finished within the next few years; for there is a preface by Hsiao-ting-tao-jen written in 1801, and Tu Shen died soon after that.

The novel opens with a description of Sang Chu-sheng, a Fukienese who is shipwrecked and drifts to the bay of Chiatzushih. He is rescued by fishermen who take him to General Kan Ting. Since this general has just received orders to build a fortress against invasion and is looking for a good site, he is delighted to see Sang. He builds at Chiatzushih, according to Sang's plans, a magic fortress which no enemy can invade. In a cave they find three cases of divine oracles, and whenever they need guidance they open these and pray. Then a certain Kuang Tien-lung starts a rebellion, styling himself king of Canton. He is assisted by a magician, Lou Wan-chih. Kan Ting attacks the rebels and, aided by the dragon king's daughter, captures Kuang Tien-lung; but Lou Wan-chih escapes. In recognition of his services, Kan Ting is promoted to be a military governor. He sails against pirates and defeats marauders from Annam; but

Lou Wan-chih remains in Annam defying capture. Then Kan Ting is appointed commander-in-chief and sent to fight the Miao tribes in South China. He has many strange adventures but wins all battles. Here is one example:

... The Miao troops shouted: "Are the Han officers cravens who will not fight?" Chi-sun was leading five hundred men in a flanking movement when two of his flags pitched down and six cocks dripping with blood flew out of the ground to crow before him. At the same time six flame-coloured dogs appeared, uttering howls like hyenas. The soldiers turned deathly pale and stood stockstill, leaning on their weapons. As Chu-erh let fly with his pestles and broke the six heads, Mu-lan loosed his lizard and made it bite one cock which expired with gaping beak. At once the five other cocks cowered and ceased their crowing. Then they saw that these were drawings of cocks and dogs on potsherds scattered on the ground. . . .

They proceeded to Marshal Chin's camp, where they found six scabby oxen and six jaded horses, all suffering from mange. The troops gored and trampled by these beasts had died. One ox bit Marshal Chin's foot, sinking its teeth into his bone, and when Chu-erh swung two axes to chop off its head the teeth remained fastened in his foot. Mu-lan ordered the tiger-head god to hack them off, but the marshal's foot was crushed and men were ordered to carry him back to headquarters. No one could curb the stampeding oxen and horses till Mu-lan hurled his fish-scale kerchief at them. From each scale sprouted a sword which lunged at the beasts, but flames four or five feet in length spurted from their jaws and consumed the fish-scale swords. As the conflagration spread, the beasts bellowed in glee. But then a monkey plunged forward. Raising one paw it launched a thunderbolt, whereat a sudden downpour extinguished the fire, and water rising more than ten feet from the ground drowned all the oxen and horses. In lively gratitude Mu-lan exclaimed: "I knew the prince would find means to extinguish the fire."

When the flood abated, no oxen or horses could be seen, but only porcelain shards from a wall inscribed with the words "Ox" and "Horse," which the monster had conjured up. . . .

(Chapter 9)

Lou Wan-chih is also among the Miao tribesmen. When he learns that there will be trouble in Annam, he makes his way back there by stealth. Kan Ting comes to Canton and joins forces with General Ou Hsing to advance on Annam. Acting on wise advice, Ou Hsing storms the capital and captures the king, at which the Annamites surrender. Meanwhile Kan Ting goes by boat to deploy his forces north of the river.

. . . Lou Wan-chih pitted his wizardry against Long-Legged Li. . . . Li transformed himself into a golden well, and into this trap Lou fell. Then an iron spike thrust out, breaking the frame of the well. The boy led Ching-hsi thither, pulled out a white silk scarf and cast it over the spike, which disappeared with a crash. Li regained his original form and searched for Lou, whom he found crouching among the pebbles by the bridge. He conjured up a white pot and held it over Lou's head, chanting an incantation. . . . Then with his hand he fashioned a thunderbolt. Lou's spirit was carried away. He leaped into the water, hoping to escape down the river to the sea, but Mu-lan bade a hundred sea-warriors give chase, who raised a tumult wherever they found him. Lou was forced to change into a tiny crab and crept into an empty shell for refuge. A crab-catcher in Annam was overjoyed to find this shell the size of a winnowing fan, and he was endeavouring to prize the meat out when lo and behold this hidden creature emerged! It fell to the ground, grew larger and took a human form, changing into a blind monk! The crab-catcher asked his name, but received no answer.

Then up came a butcher with a chopper, who exclaimed at the sight: "How ludicrous that a monk or fairy should hide in the belly of a crab! There is no place here for this monster. If I do not kill him, endless calamities will descend on Annam." He struck off Lou's head.

By this time Kan Ting had entered the city. He was taking counsel with Ou about their return when troops brought in the head of the blind monk and reported the incident to the two generals.

At this Sang, the secretary, advanced and said: "This must be Lou Wan-chih's head. In the second picture in the oracle books I remember seeing a large crab floating in the ocean, and it was written that the evil-doer would perish. I foresaw that Lou Wan-chih would soon be killed, and now that has come to pass."

Then Long-Legged Li came to bid farewell and laughed to see the head. "This rascal worked black magic," he declared. "Now he has perished like a pig or dog by the butcher's knife, not by the sword. How could he be an immortal?"

(Chapter 20)

When all Annam is pacified Sang goes back to Fukien while Kan Ting resigns from his post to be a hermit in the mountains.

This novel seems a most unusual one, yet if we study it we find it rooted in the tradition of the Ming dynasty novels of gods and demons. The pornographic passages are due in part to the author's interest in the subject, in part to the Ming tradition. By coining strange, exotic terms and copying from ancient works, Tu Shen created an archaic style which helped to disguise the flatness and vulgarity of the book. Hung Liang-chi[1] compared Tu Shen's poetry to a crimson peony in a pot or goldfish in a pool, while Wang Chuan commented: "These poems which seem deep and abstruse are actually empty of content. . . . But his style is pleasantly bizarre." In other words, his writings are full of purple passages but lack all natural charm, being fantastic without being profound. This is equally true of this novel. The style alone is original, for a form not previously attempted was used.

Then an endeavour was made to write a novel in the euphuistic style, consisting of a string of parallelisms. This was Chen Chiu's *A Tale of Yenshan* in eight books. Chen Chiu was a licentiate of Hsiushui, a poor man whose profession was painting. Since he had the knack of writing euphuistic prose and liked romances, he wrote this novel. He claimed: "This is the first attempt at

---

[1] 1746-1809. A well-known scholar and poet.

a narrative in the euphuistic style. Such a venture is most audacious. . . . Yet since this is merely fiction, I hope to be forgiven." Apparently he had never read Chang Tsu's *The Fairies' Cavern* (see Chapter 8) and thought he was doing something new. The novel was written about the year 1810. Restricting himself almost entirely to euphuistic phrases, the author took Feng Meng-cheng's tale of the scholar Tou written in the Ming dynasty, and expanded it into a book of more than 31,000 characters. The story is as follows: During the reign of Yung Lo, Tou Sheng-tsu of Peking goes to study in Chiahsin and falls in love with a poor girl, Ai-ku, who becomes his mistress. Later his father forces him to marry the daughter of an official in Tzuchuan, and he leaves Ai-ku. Deceived by a merchant from Nanking, she becomes a prostitute till gallant Ma Lin enables her to go back to Tou as his concubine; but Tou's wife is such a jealous shrew that the situation becomes unbearable and Tou and Ai-ku run away. During the rebellion of Tang Sai-erh the lovers are separated. By the time Tou returns to his family, all his property has gone and his wife leaves him. But Ai-ku suddenly comes back, having hidden all this time in a nunnery. Tou passes the examination and becomes an official, then is promoted to the governorship of Shantung. Ai-ku is escorted to his official residence as a noble lady. They have a son, and the nurse they hire turns out to be Tou's first wife, reduced to poverty since her second husband and son have died. Though Tou treats her well she plots to kill Ma Lin, and Tou is involved in her crime. In the end, however, he is cleared and his official rank restored, after which he and Ai-ku become immortals.

This insipid and commonplace story follows the usual pattern of tales about talented scholars and beautiful women. The author no doubt chose this plot because its complexity enabled him to display his skill as a writer. The endless parallelisms hold up the action, and the descriptions of events and feelings are lifeless. The style not only falls far short of the euphuistic prose of the Six Dynasties, but lacks Chang Tsu's wit and liveliness. As an example, let us quote this description of how Tou is forced by his father to desert Ai-ku:

. . . The father, concerned at heart for his son, behaves outwardly in an overbearing manner. One who strikes at a rat does not care if a vessel is broken; one who chases a duck may frighten love-birds as well. The pig is driven back to its sty, the dog is ordered home. The sheep has gone astray and its pen must be mended; the tiger is locked up where it cannot escape; the rampant dragon is chained to an iron pillar; the agile monkey is humbled by a straw whip. The maiden knits sad brows by the rose trellis and pines away by the ivy-covered wall, for who can fathom her sorrow? The thoughts of her heart are known to her alone. Bitter are the lotus seeds; well-nigh dried the bamboo's tears; like a fall of snow the senseless willow catkins; like hanging thread the helpless cherry blossom. Spring has passed and summer is half gone. In vain she waits, their vows of love are ended. He enters her dreams and sorrow reigns in her breast. How can she forget her wrongs, how shake off her woe? When will her lyre's broken strings be mended? When will her lover return to her pavilion? He has left her far, far behind; she is waiting long, long in vain. Once they were separated in the same district; now mountains and rivers come between. In her fancy, he has departed for many years; she longs for him as for one in a distant land. . . .

(Chapter 2)

An abridged version of this novel annotated by Fu Sheng-ku of Yungchia appeared in 1879.

After the reigns of Yung Cheng and Chien Lung, scholars in the Yangtse Valley were so cowed by persecution that they avoided any reference to history and turned to textual criticism of ancient philosophical works and philology, or to the minor arts. They concentrated on factual details and were opposed to empty talk; thus erudition was the vogue. Later these men of letters assumed learned airs; and since fiction was considered trivial and unimportant, being based on hearsay and gossip, they would not stoop to it. However one scholar, Li Ju-chen, wrote the *Flowers in the Mirror*. Li was a native of Tahsing County in Chihli, born in 1763 or thereabouts. He showed intelligence at an early age and looked down on the fashionable *paku* essay. In 1782 he accompanied his brother to Haichow where he had Lin Ting-kan[1] as his tutor, and in addition to literature he studied phonology. According to him, he learned a great deal from Lin. He was then about twenty years old. Many of his friends were interested in phonology, and Li himself became most proficient in this science. Although he also distinguished himself in divination, astrology, calligraphy and chess, he never rose to prominence and ended his life as a licentiate. Towards the

---
[1] 1755-1809. A historian and authority on ancient music and phonology.

end, an impecunious, disappointed scholar, he wrote this novel for his own amusement, taking more than ten years over it. In 1828 a printed edition appeared, two years before he died in his early sixties. His work on phonology, *The Mirror of Sounds*, lays stress on the practical value of the science and on modern pronunciation, showing that he had the courage to challenge old conventions. Because he was an authority who dared to break the old rules, his erudition did not prevent him from writing fiction. In his novel, however, he devotes too much space to discussing the arts and the classics, spinning out these dissertations interminably. Thus his great learning proved a handicap too.

Flowers in the Mirror has one hundred chapters. The story, briefly, is as follows: Empress Wu, wanting to enjoy flowers in winter, gives orders for the hundred flowers to blossom. The flower goddesses dare not disobey, but they are punished by being sent down to earth as a hundred mortal women. The scholar Tang Ao, who has passed the highest examination, is accused of being in league with certain rebels and demoted. He longs to become an immortal and goes with his brother-in-law, Merchant Lin, on a voyage. They visit strange lands, meet strange people and see many curious customs and remarkable monsters. Tang is lucky enough to find a magic herb which makes him immortal, and goes into the mountains never to return. His daughter Hsiao-shan sets out in search of her father, but visits strange places and has many dangerous adventures without finding him. However, from a woodcutter in the mountains she receives a letter from her father in which he renames her Kuei-chen and promises that after she has passed the examination they will meet again. She goes on to a deserted grave called Flowers-in-the-Mirror, thence to Moon-in-the-Water Village, and finally to Lamenting-Fallen-Flowers Pavilion. Here there is a stone tablet with a hundred names on it, the first of which is Shih Yu-tan and the last Pi Chuan-chen. Her own name is eleventh on the list. Here is the comment which follows this list of names:

> The Master of the Pavilion comments: Shih Yu-tan (History-obscure-search) and Ai Tsui-fang (Lament-all-flowers) head the list because the Master has searched through the obscurities of history and found much interesting matter. He laments that all such flowers remain unknown and therefore records these stories. ... The list ends with the names Hua Tsai-fang (Flower-again-blossom) and Pi Chuan-chen (Completing all-virtue), because these flowers once unknown will gain immortality thanks to this story, which is as if they had blossomed again. Because these hundred maids were rare jewels, in this way all virtues are made complete.
>
> (Chapter 48)

Then Tang Kuei-chen abandons her search and goes home. She passes an examination set by Empress Wu for talented women. The successful candidates are the hundred girls listed on the tablet, who meet and feast together for some days, playing the lyre, composing poems, amusing themselves with chess and archery or other games, and discussing literature, prosody and the *Book of Songs*. Two other women arrive, claiming to be scholars, who are in fact the wind and moon goddesses. A quarrel ensues and the star of literary genius comes with another fairy to intercede. After this they write poems containing prophecies about these girls' future lives, and though some of these are very sad the feast ends happily. The final section of the novel deals with an attempt to restore the Tang dynasty, in which some of these women scholars join the army and some are killed. Empress Wu's forces are eventually defeated and Emperor Chung Tsung ascends the throne, but the empress is still held in great honour. She decrees another examination the next year for talented women, and all the women scholars are invited to a feast. At this point the story ends. This seems, however, to be only half of the whole story, for the author had indicated that more was to follow, but he never completed the work.

The purpose of the novel is explained by the Master of the Pavilion in the passage quoted above. Believing it would be a pity if these women were lost in oblivion, he wrote this novel to record their deeds. Since many views on women are expressed in this work, Hu Shih says: "This novel deals with the woman problem. The author believes that men and women should have equal opportunities, equal education, equal political rights." The author also introduces many episodes to express his criticisms of society, but since he was limited by his age he held certain conventional views too. Thus he praises conditions in the Land of Courtesy, though it seems sheer hypocrisy to quarrel out of politeness — that would be a troublesome place in which to live. Taken as fiction, such descriptions are quite entertaining:

By now they had come to the busy market-place where they saw a serving-man fingering some wares.

"Brother," he said to the vendor, "how can I buy such excellent goods for so little? You must raise the price before I can agree. If not, I shall know you don't really want to sell." . . .

Then they heard the shopman reply: "I appreciate your concern, but though I am blushing to have asked so much, you shame me further by calling it too little. It is not as if my goods have a fixed price that leaves no margin for profit. As the proverb says: 'The price asked is as high as heaven, that offered as low as the earth.' Yet instead of lowering it you want to raise it. If you refuse to show any consideration, I shall have to ask you to carry your custom elsewhere — I really cannot agree."

"With us it is always the customer who says 'The price is as high as heaven,'" Tang pointed out. "That applies to the other saying too. But here the shopman quotes them — how amusing!"

Then the serving-man went on: "It's hardly honest, is it, brother, to ask a low price for such good wares yet accuse me of being inconsiderate? Honesty is the best policy, and everyone has a sense of value. You can't make a fool of me."

Though they bargained for some time, the shopman refused to raise his price. Then the other sulkily paid what was asked but took only half of the goods. As he turned to go, however, the shopman barred his way, saying he had paid too much and taken too little. Two old men who came by acted as arbiters, and made the customer take four-fifths of the goods at the price agreed on. So a compromise was reached and the serving-man left. . . .

"The transactions we have seen certainly give a picture of gentlemanly conduct," observed Tang. "No further inquiries are needed. But let us stroll on a little. This is such a beautiful country, we may as well see more of its fine scenery. . . ."

(Chapter 11)

The novel sets forth much classical lore and describes various arts and games. The travels of Tang Ao and his daughter and the feasting of the hundred girls make up nearly seven-tenths of the whole book. The author delights above all in quotations from ancient books and a display of his knowledge of various arts, running on in this way for whole chapters at a time. Thus he makes Lin comment on his work:

"This book is written during the reign of a peaceful and sagacious sovereign, by a scholar of our celestial empire, a writer descended from Lao Tzu who wrote of mysteries in *The Way and Its Power*. The work is an entertainment yet contains moral lessons for men. In it we find the hundred schools of thought, men, flowers and birds, calligraphy, painting, lyre-playing, chess, medicine, fortune-telling, astrology, phonology and mathematics; there are also all manner of riddles and drinking-games, as well as games of dice and cards, ball games and shooting. These serve to banish boredom and to rouse laughter."

(Chapter 23)

The author obviously considered this book a storehouse of knowledge and art, but in this sense it is more like an encyclopaedia than a novel. Since he handled his materials adroitly, however, although a slave to classical lore he sometimes writes quite lively passages like the following one:

"If you are hungry, Brother Lin, there's something here you can eat," suggested To, plucking a dark plant growing in the green grass.

Lin took the plant which tapered like a leek, with green flowers on a tender stem. He put it in his mouth and nodded his approval. "Very fragrant and tasty. What is it? . . ."

"I once read that in Magpie Mountain across the ocean grows a dark green flower like a leek, which serves as a food. This must be it," said Tang.

To nodded several times and they went on. . . . The next moment Tang plucked a green plant from the roadside. It had a leaf like a pine-needle but was emerald green, and on it was a seed the size of a grain of mustard.

Removing this seed and pointing at the leaf, he said: "As you have just eaten one plant, brother, let me eat this to keep you company."

With that he swallowed the leaf, laid the seed in his palm and blew on it. At once there sprouted another green leaf like a pine-needle, about one foot in height. He blew again and it grew another foot. He blew three times till it was three feet high, whereupon he ate it.

"If you go on munching at this rate, brother, you'll soon have eaten all the plants here!" laughed Lin. "How does this seed change into a plant like that?"

"This is the herb called Soaring, otherwise known as Mustard-in-the-Palm," was To's answer. "When you hold the seed in your palm and blow on it, it grows a foot each time until it is three feet long. Anyone who eats it can soar aloft, hence its name."

"If it can do that, let me eat some too!" cried Lin.

"Then when I go home and thieves climb the roof of my house, I can soar through the air to catch them. Very useful, to be sure!"

But though they searched high and low they could find no more.

"It's no use your looking, Brother Lin," rejoined old To. "This plant only grows when blown on, and who is there on this bare mountainside to do that? What Brother Tang ate just now was probably some stray seed blown on by a bird in search of food, which fell to earth and took root. It is not a common herb — you can't possibly hope to find it. In all my years of travel overseas this is the first time I've seen it, and if our friend here hadn't blown on it I shouldn't have known that this was Soaring."

(Chapter 9)

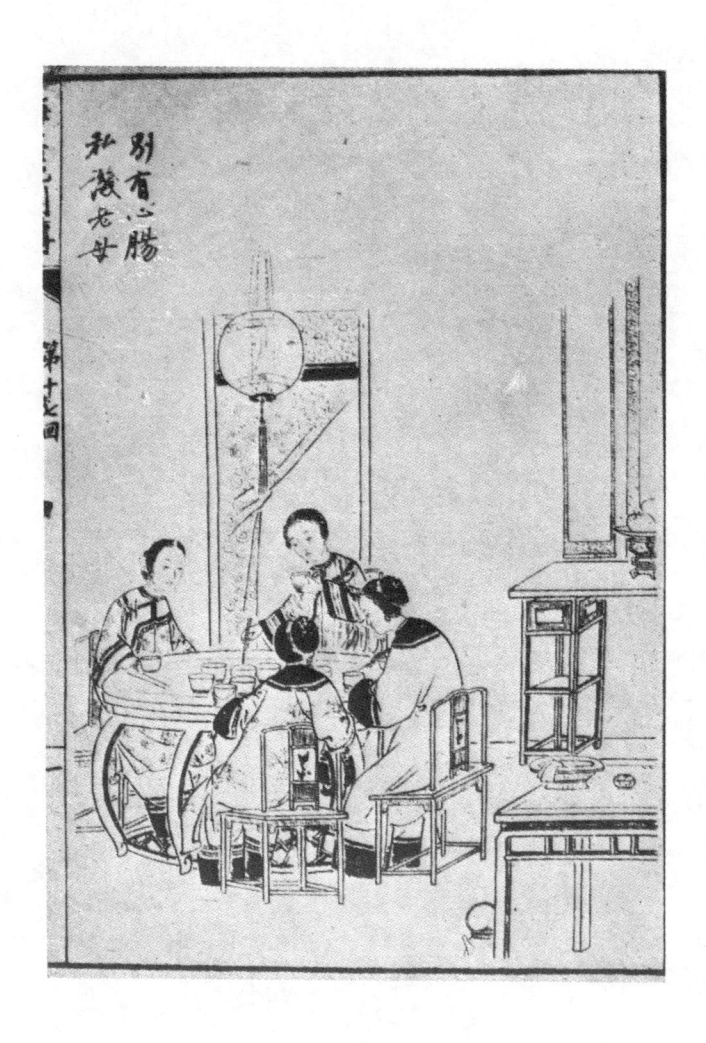

Illustration from an edition of *Lives of Shanghai Singsong Girls* published in 1892

26. NOVELS ABOUT PROSTITUTION IN THE CHING DYNASTY

During the Tang dynasty, to celebrate passing the government examinations scholars usually visited singsong girls or courtesans, and as this was handed down as a romantic tradition there is frequent reference to singsong girls in literature. We still have two such works from the Tang dynasty: *Accounts of the Singsong Girls' Quarters* by Tsui Ling-chin and *Records of the Courtesans' Quarters* by Sun Chi. During the Ming and Ching dynasties there were more stories about singsong girls, the best known being *Lotus in the Mud* by Mei Ting-tso of the Ming dynasty and *The Panchiao Miscellany* by Yu Huai of the Ching dynasty. Then came accounts of singsong girls in Yangchow, Soochow, Canton and Shanghai, and by degrees descriptions of actors were included in this category. These were miscellaneous anecdotes presented without any system, written as light reading to while away the time. The first long novel of this sort was *A Mirror of Theatrical Life* which comprised dozens of chapters though the characters in it were actors, not prostitutes.

There were quarters of ill fame in the Ming dynasty, but scholars were forbidden to frequent them or to hire singsong girls, although they could hire actors. In order, therefore, to keep within the law, officials and scholars often invited actors to their feasts, enjoying their singing, dancing and conversation. Once famous scholars had written in praise of this the thing became fashionable, growing more and more popular. At the beginning of the Ching dynasty this craze died down a little, to be revived later in a more licentious form with the actors known as "he-women" or "male prostitutes." *A Mirror of Theatrical Life,* printed in 1852, deals with Peking actors after the reign of Chien Lung, and a number of passages in it are obscene. The author apparently believed that some actors were respectable, some disreputable, just as their patrons might be cultured or vulgar. So he brought the different types together in this novel with a moral purpose, much as in certain novels of manners of the Ming dynasty. His aim was to give a picture of romance, culture and elegance; but since he could not shake off the tradition of the many romantic novels of the past, the finest characters in his book, idealized figures like Mei Tzu-yu and Tu Chin-yen, still belong to the school of "talented scholars and beauties," the actors being the "beauties" and their patrons the "scholars." The whole novel is filled with tender and romantic sentiments, the only difference being that the "beauties" are young men. Here is a passage describing how the famous actor Tu Chin-yen called on his patron Mei Tzu-yu who was ill.

Tu went to Mei's house in considerable apprehension, certain that he would be humiliated. But to his surprise Mrs. Mei instead of reproaching him seemed to pity him and urged him to go in and cheer her husband up. With mixed feelings of joy and sorrow, he wondered how serious Tzu-yu's illness could be and how best to comfort him. But doing as he was told, he went boldly to Mei's room. He found the curtains drawn, the desk covered with dust, and light gauze curtains hanging round a single hardwood bed. The maid parted the curtains and called:

"Here is Mr. Tu, sir!"

Mei muttered something in his sleep. Then Tu sat on the edge of the bed and saw how lean and haggard his friend had grown. He bent over the pillow and called out in a low voice, his tears falling ceaselessly on the scholar's face.

Then Mei laughed in his sleep and chanted: "On the seventh day of the seventh month in the Palace of Eternal Youth, we spoke in secret at midnight when no one else was near."

After chanting these lines he laughed again deliriously. Tu's heart contracted with pain and he shook him gently. He could not speak loudly, however, as Mrs. Mei was outside and he had to address his beloved friend formally. Mei was in fact dreaming of Tu in his longing to see him again on the Double Seventh to pour out his heart in Su-lan's house. So obsessed was he by this idea that he had chanted these two lines of Tang poetry. It seemed that nothing could wake him. Deep in his dreams, he laughed once more and declaimed: "I thought never to see him again in heaven or in hell. . . ." Still fast asleep, he turned his face to the wall. Tu's eyes were brimming with tears but all he could do was to look on helplessly, not daring to call out. . . .

(Chapter 29)

Most of the characters in *A Mirror of Theatrical Life* were based on real persons, and can be identified from their names and idiosyncrasies. But the central figures,

Mei and Tu, were fictitious, for the author could find no living men to use as models for these perfect lovers. The author himself appears in the novel too. He was Chen Shen-shu, a citizen of Changchow who lived in Peking during the reign of Tao Kuang and enjoyed the company of actors. He wrote thirty chapters from actual knowledge, then stopped and left the capital. In 1849 he returned to Peking from Kwangsi and completed the novel by adding another thirty chapters. Many copies were made by his friends, and three years later the book was printed.

The last chapter has an idealized ending, when all the talented scholars and famous exponents of women's roles gather in Nine Fragrance Garden. The actors are made up as flower-fairies and their patrons write poems to their beauty. Then the actors write complimentary lines for the scholars which are inscribed on stone in Nine Fragrance Pavilion. Since the actors have now given up their profession, they publicly burn their trinkets and women's clothes. But before the fire dies down, "A fragrant breeze sprang up and the ashes soared to the sky, glittering in the sunlight like thousands of petals and butterflies. Higher and higher they whirled, giving off a heady, intoxicating scent until they became mere dots of gold and vanished."

This novel was followed by *The Flower and the Moon* in sixteen books or fifty-two chapters by Mien-ho-chu-jen. There is a preface dated 1858, but the novel did not become known till the reign of Kuang Hsu (1875-1908). This book is not devoted entirely to prostitutes, but since it deals with them at some length, as well as with scholars, it belongs to the same category. Wei Chih-chu and Han Ho-sheng are talented scholars in Shansi who become good friends. They visit the singsong girls' quarter together and each has his favourite there. Wei's girl is Chiu-hen, Han's is Tsai-chiu. Although Wei is extremely able and his literary talent is well known, he has no luck and lives in straitened circumstances. Dearly as Chiu-hen loves him, they cannot get married. Then Wei's wife dies, Wei dies soon afterwards, and Chiu-hen follows him to the grave. Han Ho-sheng, however, is secretary to a high official and advises his employer on affairs of state. For the part he plays in suppressing a rebellion, he is appointed to the Ministry of War; and because he distinguishes himself in a campaign he is ennobled. Tsai-chiu, who has already married him, becomes a lady too; and when he returns in triumph, covered with honours, he gives feasts for three days at which his officers and men rejoice. Wei on the other hand leaves only a son who takes his coffin back to their home in the south. The plot aims at bringing out the contrast between the two men, and the tone is mainly sentimental. From time to time there are melancholy scenes, so that even moments of joy are tinged with sorrow. The novel is interspersed with poems and letters, and purple passages tend to obscure the story. Thus Fu Chao-lun commented: "The author was a talented poet but a novice in the writing of fiction. His most moving passages stem from his appreciation of poetry, and these are melancholy and beautiful. . . ." Though such praise is not entirely warranted, Fu has laid his finger on the main fault of the novel. The ending, in which the author describes the military achievements of Han Ho-sheng and introduces supernatural beings, is like a ghost story tacked on to a romance — totally incongruous and irrelevant.

Tsai-chiu said: ". . . Mystic Jade claims to have no worldly fetters while Pao-yu calls himself worldly. Mystic Jade lives in the Green Nunnery, Pao-yu in the Red Courtyard. . . . The novel describes Mystic Jade's purity while Pao-yu considers himself vulgar; but finally the one who is high-minded and pure comes to a shocking end and the one who is worldly and vulgar to a lofty end."

Wei sighed and chanted these lines: "One single slip brings eternal regret, and looking back your whole life has passed away." He continued: "When you examine the hidden meaning of the names of the characters in the book, you can see that Precious Clasp and Black Jade are both reflections of Pao-yu. That is why you find the first character of his name in 'Pao-chai' (Precious Clasp) and the second in 'Tai-yu' (Black Jade). In fact, these girls have no separate existence. But Mystic Jade is presented in direct contrast to Pao-yu. Whereas he becomes a monk, she becomes a nun. Don't you agree that a contrast is suggested?"

Tsai-chiu admitted that it was. . . .

Then Wei went on: "The form is non-existence, and non-existence is the form." Beating the table he chanted:

>The melody of a harp, the fragrance of incense
>Must arouse sensations of tenderness and sadness.
>Even though I know that all is vanity,
>I long for angels to dance and scatter flowers.
>I divined your heart in the lotus-gatherer's song;
>Now I see you again when cassia is in bloom.
>Why should I raise my whip and ride away?
>My heart has been here with you for the last ten years.

Before Wei had finished chanting, Han laughed and said: "Stop it! Let's drink."

They chatted and laughed till dawn. After breakfast Wei left first in Tsai-chiu's carriage, and at noon he received the following note from his friend:

"Just now I saw Chiu-hen, who wept when she spoke to me. I was very moved. I did my best to comfort her and urged patience. When I was leaving she begged me to advise you to rest well. She will find some way to express her feeling for you. As I know you are eager to hear of her, I am telling you this. I also enclose four short poems, and hope you will write some too."

Having read this, Wei started writing verses with the same rhyme:

Unhappily the flowers have faded fast;
Snapped twigs and falling petals are a sad sight.
I long for a clean end for all these blossoms,
Sorry the blustering wind has not blown them away.
The years slip by, the sun is sinking low.
For twenty years I have drifted past lakes and seas. . . .

As he was writing, his bald servant announced: "The Li house in Vegetable Market Street has sent a man to ask you to go over. He says Miss Chiu-hen is ill."

In alarm, Wei took the carriage to the house. He found Chiu-hen with a silk handkerchief tied round her head sitting up in bed with a few books beside her, lost in thought. She smiled at the sight of him and said in a low voice: "I knew you could not keep away for ten days. But what is the use?"

"They told me you were ill," said Wei. "How could I stay away?"

Chiu-hen sighed and answered: "Now that you have come when asked, there will be all sorts of complications."

With a smile Wei retorted: "Let the future take care of itself."

So he started seeing her again. That night he completed his poems. Two lines in the last stanza have become well known:

> To win my beauty gladly I court death,
> For she alone knows my worth.

(Chapter 25)

Hsieh Chang-ting, a scholar of Changlo, wrote three poems on the writings of Wei Tzu-an, and one of the works he mentions is *The Flower and the Moon*. So we know that the author's real name was Wei Tzu-an. From the same source we know that Wei was a native of Houkuan in Fukien. Though a precocious boy, he did not pass the local examination till he was twenty-eight; he took the provincial examination in 1846, but never had any success with the metropolitan examinations. He went to Shansi, Shensi and Szechuan, holding the post of dean of Fuyung College in Chengtu. When a local rebellion broke out he fled home and died in 1874 at the age of fifty-six. Of his many works, the only one widely known was *The Flower and the Moon*. While in Shansi he was tutor to the son of Prefect Pao Mien-chin of Taiyuan; since he had a good salary and plenty of spare time, he wrote this novel making Wei Chih-chu a portrait of himself. The prefect was impressed by the story and encouraged him to finish it. Another anecdote connected with this book is that a singsong girl in Taiyuan was attracted to Wei and wanted to marry him; but her owner demanded too high a price for her and she pined away.

Chiu-hen is probably based on this girl. Wei and Han are both reflections of the author himself. He imagined himself in prosperity and poverty, and split his own character to make the two scholars Han and Wei.

Another novel in sixty-four chapters about singsong girls is the *Dream of the Green Chamber*. According to the preface the author was Yu Yin-hsiang, whose penname was Mu-chen-shan-jen. A native of Soochow, he used to frequent the brothels and could not tear himself away. He died of a stroke in 1884. His writings include anecdotes, notes on ancient relics and poems. This novel was written in 1878 and the characters are based on prostitutes in Soochow. In it Yu attempted to portray an ideal man: an ideal patron of singsong girls who passes the government examinations, becomes a high official, is a filial son, good friend, exemplary husband, excellent father, loyal kinsman and helpful neighbour, abandoning worldly splendour to seek the Truth. It is clear that this is not a realistic novel. The hero is Chin Yi-hsiang of Soochow. He shows literary ability when young, and is intelligent and handsome, but does not marry because he wants to find a true lover. But "Where in all the world can such a one be found? The poor scholar is frustrated, for all his talent. Not one high official recognizes his worth. Only the singsong girls sometimes have the intelligence to recognize a great man before he achieves success." So Chin is a respected and popular figure in the singsong girls' quarter, and he orders the girls about as if he were a king.

When they reached the pavilion and looked round, they saw marks of excellent taste. Outside were rare and beautiful flowers, plants and trees, while in the pavilion itself a feast was spread. Yueh-su arranged the seating. The three patrons sat in the places of honour and the charming girls took their respective seats. The first girl was Chu Ai-fang, Mistress of the Hall of Love-Birds; the second was Wang Hsiang-yun, Recluse of Misty Willows; the third was Yuan Chiao-yun, the Iron-Flute Fairy; the fourth was Chu Su-ching, Lover of Fledgelings; the fifth was Lu Li-chun, Herald of Spring Flowers; the sixth was Cheng Su-ching, Seeker of Plum Blossom; the seventh was Lu Wen-ching, Bather of Flowers . . . the eleventh was Ho Yueh-chuan, Plum and Snow Beauty. When the Protector of Flowers herself had taken the last seat, four pairs of maids poured the wine. The beauties passed round the cups and were very merry.

Chin said to Huei-chiung: "At such a fine gathering we should have a set of drinking rules so that a good occasion will not be wasted."

"You are right," agreed Yueh-su. "Please give the order."

"The hostess should make the rules," protested Chin.

"Oh, no," said Yueh-su. "You must be the one."

Chin was forced to agree to this, and the girls insisted: "You must drink a round first before drawing up the rules."

Each of the twelve beauties filled a cup and passed it to Chin, who drained each in turn. Then he announced: "These drinking rules are stricter than martial law. Anyone who disobeys will be fined three big cups of wine."

All the girls assented. . . .

(Chapter 5)

This man Chin is most considerate too, and nurses the girls when they are ill.

One day at Liu Hsiang Pavilion Chin found Ai-chin indisposed and unable to eat. He was most concerned, and remembering that he had four volumes of Kuo Ching-tien's work on medicine on his shelves with many prescriptions in it, he went home to fetch it. He found *Hsiang-yu* powder suitable for her complaint. Having sent the maid to buy the ingredients, he attended to the preparation himself by the stove, giving up his tutoring for several days in order to nurse the patient day and night. Ai-chin was very touched and wrote a poem to express her gratitude. . . .

(Chapter 21)

Later on, Chin passes high in the examinations and makes five singsong girls his wife and concubines. In order to look after his parents, he takes a post in Yuhang and is promoted to a prefectship. Then his parents become immortals and fly from his yamen to heaven, after which Chin decides to go to the mountains to devote himself to religion.

He reflected: "I must not let them know that I am going to leave the dusty world. I shall have to keep it a secret and simply walk out."

The next day he wrote three letters to Pai-lin, Meng-hsien and Chung-ying to bid them farewell, asking Pai-lin to help to arrange Yin-mei's marriage. A few days later he took some dozen taels of silver and bought a priest's gown, a straw hat and sandals. Leaving these purchases outside, he went back to Plum Blossom Pavilion. Luckily all five of his womenfolk were there, and finding them in high spirits, quite unaware of his intentions, he felt a twinge of compunction. But after a little thought he said with a sigh: "Since I have seen through love, why should I care?"

(Chapter 60)

So he goes away and becomes an immortal in Tientai Mountain. Finally he comes home to make his wife and concubines immortals, so that two generations of the Chin family may all go up to heaven. (Chapter 61) By this time Chin's son has passed high in the examinations, and his old friends thanks to his help have become immortals too. Moreover, one by one, the thirty-six singsong girls he has known rejoin the ranks of the fairies; for they were goddesses in charge of different flowers, who fell from heaven because they longed for the world. Now that their time on earth is over, they become fairies again. (Chapter 64)

Soon after the *Dream of the Red Chamber* was printed many sequels to the novel appeared, all with a happy ending. This interest persisted for a long time; indeed it was not till the end of the Tao Kuang period that such books ceased to be written. And even then the influence of the *Dream of the Red Chamber* remained widespread. Since ordinary families had not so many members or such adventures and could not therefore be described in the style of the great novel, later writers wrote of prostitutes and brothels instead. While the three novels just mentioned differ in their treatment and artistic quality, their underlying spirit is the same: all describe handsome men and beautiful women in romantic situations, only the new characters and scenes were taken from the prostitutes' quarters, because readers were tired of meeting characters like Precious Clasp and Black Jade again and again in settings like the Takuan Garden. However, *Lives of Shanghai Singsong Girls* gives a realistic picture of brothels and exposes their iniquities; the author wanted to "teach a moral lesson based on his own experience," so that readers might "explore the secrets of the courtesans' quarters and understand its nature, thereby realizing that those who behave so admirably in his presence are worse than devils behind his back. Though today they seem dearer than wives, tomorrow they may spit poison more deadly than the venom of snakes and scorpions." (Chapter 1) Evidently the purpose of the book is different from that of earlier novels, and this marks the end of the romantic tradition in the literature dealing with singsong girls.

Lives of Shanghai Singsong Girls has sixty-four chapters. According to some scholars the author, whose penname is Hua-yeh-lien-nung, was Han Tzu-yun of Sungchiang. A good chess-player and an opium addict, Han spent many years in Shanghai, where he edited a newspaper. Since he squandered all his money on prostitutes and knew them well, he saw through all their tricks. This novel appeared in 1892, two chapters being published each week, and it was most popular. The chief character, Chao Pu-chai, comes to Shanghai at the age of seventeen to visit his uncle Hung Shan-ching. He goes to brothels and, owing to his inexperience, becomes more and more involved till Hung sends him home. He slips back to Shanghai, however, and goes from bad to worse, ending up as a rickshaw boy. The novel in its original form ended here. The twenty-eighth chapter was the last to appear in serial form. Though Chao is the main character, the stories about him do not amount to much: his adventures introduce us to other characters like the merchants in foreign concessions or other dissolute young men. There are many descriptions of brothels of every class. The construction is reminiscent of *The Scholars,* for a number of tenuously related stories are put together to form a novel. When the author describes the heartlessness of singsong girls — not that one would expect prostitutes to take love seriously — the descriptions are realistic with little exaggeration. So the writer was sincere when he said that his aim was to give a truthful picture as vivid as life. Here is a passage describing how Chao Pu-chai went with his friend Chang Hsiao-chun to a brothel just after his arrival in Shanghai:

> When Wang saw Hsiao-chun she rushed at him, crying: "Well! So you lied to me! You said you were going home for a couple of months, but this is the first time you've shown up since then. Is this a couple of months or a couple of years?. . ."
> Hsiao-chun smiled sheepishly and coaxed her: "Don't be angry. Let me explain." He whispered something to her.
> He had not had time to say much, however, when Wang leaped to her feet and said grimly: "How clever you are! You want to throw the wet blanket on someone else so that you can get away, isn't that it?"
> "No, no!" protested Hsiao-chun frantically. "That's not true. Let me finish explaining."
> The girl curled up on his knees to listen, and he spoke to her in a low voice. Presently he jerked his chin towards Chao, and Wang turned to give the young

man an appraising look while Hsiao-chun went on speaking.

"Then what about you?" she asked.

"The same as before."

Not till then did she forgive him. She stood up and trimmed the lamp. Then she asked Chao his name and looked him over carefully. Chao turned his face away pretending to be reading a notice. At this point a middle-aged maid came upstairs carrying a kettle in one hand and two cases of opium in the other. . . . Having put the opium on the tray, lit the opium lamp and made tea, she left with the kettle.

Leaning against Hsiao-chun, Wang started baking the opium. When she noticed Chao sitting all alone, she said: "Come and lie on the bed."

Chao, who had been hoping for this invitation, went over at once and lay on the other side. He watched the girl prepare the opium, fill the pipe and pass it to Hsiao-chun, who smoked it all in one breath. . . . When the third pipe was ready Hsiao-chun said: "I've had enough."

Then Wang turned round and offered the pipe to Chao. Since the young man was inexperienced, the pipe went out before he had smoked half. As the girl speared the opium with the needle to put it back on the lamp, Chao seized the chance to squeeze her wrist. She reached out and pinched his leg hard, sending a thrill of pain and pleasure through him. When Chao finished smoking he glanced at Hsiao-chun, who was lying with half-closed eyes between sleeping and waking. Chao called him twice in a low voice, but his friend simply waved one hand and would not answer.

"He's drunk with opium. Don't disturb him," said the girl.

Then Chao desisted.

(Chapter 2)

By 1894, sixty chapters of the novel had appeared. In the later half Hung happens to see his nephew pulling a rickshaw and writes to Chao's mother about it. Mrs. Chao does not know what to do, but her clever daughter Erh-pao comes with her to Shanghai to look for Chao. After finding him, they stay on. Though Hung urges them to go home they ignore his advice until he washes his hands of them. Before very long Mrs. Chao comes to the end of her money and the family cannot return home. Then Erh-pao becomes a celebrated prostitute and meets Third Master Shih who is very rich and takes a great fancy to her. She spends a summer in his house and he promises to marry her on his return from Nanking. Accordingly Erh-pao dismisses her other lovers and borrows a large sum of money to buy clothes and jewels for her wedding. Shih never comes back, however, and when Chao is sent to Nanking to make inquiries he finds that Shih has just arranged another marriage and gone to Yangchow to fetch his bride. Erh-pao faints away upon hearing this news. She is in debt to the tune of three or four thousand dollars and the only way out is to go back to her profession. So she becomes a prostitute again. The novel ends with a nightmare she has. According to the postscript, the author meant to write more but never did so. The second half of the book contains detailed but not too accurate descriptions of Shanghai celebrities, but the sections describing how men chased girls, frittered away their money and cheated each other are just as well done as in the first thirty chapters. The following passage, in which Mr. Lai runs after an actress, gives an excellent idea of the current fashion.

Wen-chun put on her costume and made her entry on the stage. One of Lai's men, hoping to please his patron, was the first to shout "Bravo!" At once many others joined in, shouting and cheering till the theatre was in utter confusion. . . . Only Mr. Lai was shaking with laughter, thoroughly pleased. In the middle of the performance he ordered his servant to distribute largesse. The man filled a basket with silver dollars and brought this for Lai to inspect, after which he scattered the money on the stage. With a clatter the glittering dollars rolled in all directions, while the theatre resounded with the cheers of Lai's men. Wen-chun's heart sank when she knew that Lai was after her, but soon hitting on a plan she was able to concentrate on her singing till it was time for her exit. . . .

She came to the feast with a smile. Without warning, Lai seized her and pulled her on to his knees. Wen-chun promptly pushed away his hands and stood up, making a show of anger. But caressing his shoulder she whispered a few words to him, at which Lai nodded several times.

"All right," he said. "I know. . . ."

(Chapter 44)

Though most of the characters in this novel were based on real people, only in the case of Chao Pu-chai is the true name used. It is said that Chao was a good friend of the author who often borrowed money from him; but when Chao stopped helping him Han wrote this book to blackmail /him, not stopping till twenty-eight chapters had been printed and Chao gave him a large sum. The chapters published were so popular, however, that after Chao's death Han went on with the book for financial considerations, even making Chao's sister a prostitute. As a matter of fact, he must have planned this from the start; for when Chao meets his uncle, Hung asks him: "Haven't you a younger sister? . . . Is she engaged yet?" And he answers: "Not yet. She is just fifteen this year." This was obviously paving the way for some later development. At the beginning of this century there were many such novels in Shanghai, which usually stopped after the publication of a few chapters when the blackmailer had succeeded. Similar novels were written not for purposes of blackmail but simply to expose the evils of prostitution. However, most of these exaggerate and introduce shocking or sensational incidents. None of them has the subtlety and natural style of *Lives of Shanghai Singsong Girls*.

27. NOVELS OF ADVENTURE AND DETECTION IN THE CHING DYNASTY

By the end of the Ming dynasty, *Romance of the Three Kingdoms, Shui Hu Chuan,* the *Pilgrimage to the West* and *Chin Ping Mei* were considered the "Four Great Novels." In the reign of Chien Lung during the Ching dynasty the *Dream of the Red Chamber* came to supersede the *Romance of the Three Kingdoms* in the estimation of scholars, although the general public continued to prefer the latter and *Shui Hu Chuan*. Men's tastes change with the times, and as readers grew tired of old books new trends developed. These new adventure stories, it is ture, had their origin in the early novels, but the spirit of these later books is completely different: they praise heroic deeds and acts of rough justice only if these accord with the feudal concepts of loyalty and right. When the literati lost interest in the *Dream of the Red Chamber*, a new type of novel appeared represented by *The Gallant Maid*; and when people could no longer understand the spirit of *Shui Hu Chuan*, books like *Three Heroes and Five Gallants* won favour.

The Gallant Maid originally had fifty-three chapters, only forty of which are left today. The writer described himself as "a man of leisure in Northern Yen." According to a preface by Ma Tsung-shan, he was Wen Kang, a Manchu of the Tao Kuang period (1821-1850) whose Manchu surname was Feimo and whose second name was Tieh-hsien. He was the second grandson of

Chancellor Leh Pao. "He bought the rank of secretary in the House of Dependencies and was subsequently appointed to the governorship of a province and promoted to the intendancy of a circuit. After resigning on account of his parent's death, he was appointed commissioner in Tibet; but illness prevented him from going to this post and he died at home." He came of a noble and wealthy family, but because his sons proved worthless their fortunes declined until they were in difficulties. In his old age he lived alone with only pen and ink for company and wrote this novel to amuse himself. Since he had known both riches and poverty, "He had a good understanding of changing fashions and human relationships." (These quotations come from the preface to the novel.) His position was not unlike that of Tsao Hsueh-chin, for the mood of this book is melancholy as a result of the decline in his fortunes. But whereas Tsao described real happenings and the *Dream of the Red Chamber* is partly autobiographical, the incidents in *The Gallant Maid* are imaginary and deal with quite different types of people. As the two authors led different lives, their writings differ accordingly. *The Gallant Maid* has a preface by Kuan-chien-wo-chai, dated 1734, which claims that this is a serious work to correct the evil trends of novels like the *Pilgrimage to the West* which deals with the supernatural. Another preface by Wu-liao-weng, dated 1794, says that he found this manuscript by an unknown author in the Peking market and after reading it through several times, "seeking its hidden meaning," discovered that it was based on real events. He therefore edited it, making certain emendations, and wrote this preface. In fact, both prefaces are by the author. At the start of the novel he says: "This book . . . was first entitled *Gold and Jade*. Because it dealt with events in the capital it was also called *What Is New Under the Sun*. Though the main message of a book is not what makes it good literature, at least this novel is free from obscenity and licence and does not deviate from what is right. It is therefore also called *Fifty-three Chapters of Holy Law* though it is not a Buddhist sutra. Later Wu-liao-weng re-edited the work, renaming it *The Gallant Maid. . . .*" By using these different names, Wen Kang was simply trying to impress his readers — a tradition started by the *Dream of the Red Chamber*.

According to the author, this novel was based on true happenings in Peking. The plot is as follows: Ho Yu-feng or Jade-Phoenix comes of a family of scholars but is remarkably intelligent and fearless. After her father has been killed by an enemy, she goes with her mother to live in the hills, waiting for a chance to avenge him. Since the enemy, Chi Hsien-tang, is a powerful official, she finds it hard to carry out her plan; but calling herself Thirteenth Sister she mixes with townsfolk and conceals her identity. During her travels she meets a young man named An Chi who is in trouble, and having saved his life becomes his friend. When her enemy is condemned to death by the court and her father's wrong is avenged, she wants to leave the world and become a nun. However, she is persuaded to marry An Chi instead. An Chi has another wife named Chang Chin-feng or Golden-Phoenix, who has also been rescued by this gallant maid. The two women become good friends and that is why this novel is also entitled *Gold and Jade*.

Many characters in this novel were based on contemporary figures or men from the previous century. Thus

Chi Hsien-tang was Nien Keng-yao,[1] according to Chiang Jui-tsao, and Nien's story certainly does coincide with the description of Chi. The young scholar An Chi is generally assumed to be either the author or the reverse of his unsatisfactory sons. Thirteenth Sister is no doubt a fictitious character. Because the author set out to combine heroism and the traditional feminine virtues in her person, the result is somewhat fantastic. In fact the gallant maid talks and behaves in an artificial way whenever she appears. For instance, when An Chi first meets her in a hostel, to stop her from entering his room he tells men to barricade his door with a stone roller. When the men cannot lift the stone, the girl carries it for them.

She said: "What is all this commotion about a stone?"

Chang San, pickaxe in hand, glanced at her and retorted: "All this commotion, eh? Take a look at it. Is there any other way to move it? This is no joke."

The girl walked over to look at the stone . . . which weighed at least two hundred and fifty catties. It was a roller with a hole drilled at one end. . . . She rolled up her sleeves . . . laid the roller on the ground, and revolved it with her right hand till she found the hole. Then she hooked two fingers into the hole and swung the whole thing up with one hand.

"Don't just stand gaping!" she cried to Chang and Li. "Come and wipe the mud off."

---

[1] Governor of Szechuan and Shensi early in the eighteenth century, he was ordered by the emperor to kill himself in 1725.

Hastily assenting, they wiped the roller clean. "It's all right now," they told her.

Then the girl turned with a brilliant smile to An, "Where would you like me to put it, sir?"

An flushed up to his ears and with eyes downcast mumbled: "Sorry to trouble you. Just inside the room."

Carrying the roller in one hand, the girl pattered up the stairs on her tiny feet, lifted the door curtain and stepped inside. Having set the stone lightly down in one corner of the room, she turned round — not out of breath or even faintly flushed. The spectators outside who had craned their necks to watch were all amazed.

(Chapter 4)

Later An Chi passes the highest examination, is appointed head of the Imperial College and promoted to be commissioner in Mongolia, though he does not go to this post. Eventually he becomes a provincial examiner and takes up this position without delay. "He solved some difficult cases of considerable importance and was commended for his ability, rising to be a very high official — we need not go into that now." Someone else wrote a sequel of thirty-two chapters, poor and unpolished both as regards language and contents, which was probably followed by yet another sequel. The name of the author of the sequel — some Peking bookseller — is not given in the preface which dates from about 1894.

Three Heroes and Five Gallants appeared in 1879. First called *A Romance of Loyal and Gallant Men*, it had one hundred and twenty chapters. The author was Shih Yu-kun, and according to the preface the manuscript was in the possession of Wen-chu-chu-jen and edited by

Ju-mi-tao-jen; but neither of these men are known. There were many stories of this type about brave and gallant men in towns or villages who championed the good, killed tyrants and achieved great deeds for the state. These gallants invariably worked for some outstanding official. In this case it was Pao Cheng, whose life is recorded in the *Sung Dynasty History*. Pao was a government scholar, later appointed vice-minister of the Ministry of Ceremony, who also served as adviser of Tienchang Pavilion, doctor of Lungtu Pavilion and prefect of Kaifeng. Strict, incorruptible and uncompromising, he was compared to the King of Hell. Many supernatural tales, however, crept into the legends which grew up about this popular judge. By the Yuan dynasty we already find such plays as *Restoring the Empress Dowager* and *The Ghost in the Black Pot*. By the Ming dynasty there were ten volumes recording Prefect Pao's cases including sixty-three cases of detection, omens or riddles revealed in dreams and disclosures made by ghosts. These books were written in crude language, apparently by barely literate men. Later they were combined into a long novel with a better plot, and this was the origin of *Three Heroes and Five Gallants*.

When this novel opens, Emperor Chen Tsung (998-1022) of the Sung dynasty has no son; but two of his concubines become pregnant and he decides that the one who gives him a son shall be made empress. Lady Liu plots with the eunuch Kuo Huai and when Lady Li has a son they take him away, leaving a skinned cat in his place and accusing her of giving birth to a monster. A maid is told to strangle the infant prince and throw him into the river. But instead she entrusts the child to Chen Lin, who hides it in the mansion of the Eighth

Prince, passing it off as his third son. So the child's life is spared. By means of slander Lady Liu procures Lady Li's dismissal and loyal officials are either banished or killed. Since Emperor Chen Tsung dies without an heir, the third son of the Eighth Prince succeeds as Emperor Jen Tsung (1023-1063). At this point we are introduced to Prefect Pao, told of his marriage, his official career, and the difficult cases he has solved. Many of these stories are based on legends of other famous historical figures. When Pao becomes prefect of Kaifeng, he meets Lady Li and clears up the old case of the cat substituted for the prince. The emperor learns who his mother is and invites her back to the palace. Prefect Pao's loyalty and honesty impress many gallant men, and at that time there are numerous brave outlaws in the country like the Three Heroes: the Southern Hero Chan Chao, the Northern Hero Ouyang Chun, and the Twin Heroes Ting Chao-lan and Ting Chao-hui. There are also the Five Rats: the Sky Rat Lu Fang, the Earth Rat Han Chang, the Mountain Rat Hsu Ching, the River Rat Chiang Ping and the Bright-Fur Rat Pai Yu-tang. Sometimes these men go to the capital to rob the palace for sport, and no one can stop them. But impressed by Prefect Pao they accept posts under him and help him to fight against evil-doers, bringing peace to the people. Later the Prince of Hsiangyang plots rebellion and a document signed by all the conspirators is hidden in his Chunghsiao Pavilion. The Five Rats go with Inspector Yen Cha-san to make an investigation, and Pai Yu-tang attempts to steal the document, only to perish in a copper-wire trap. Here the novel ends. As the only historical characters are Prefect Pao, the Eighth Prince and a few others, the story is mainly fictitious.

The Five Rats are mentioned in the Ming dynasty *Cases of Prefect Pao* and the novel *Voyage to the Western Ocean*, but there they are supernatural beings while here they are gallant men. Since no prince in the reign of Emperor Jen Tsung plotted rebellion, this episode was based on the rebellion plotted by Prince Ning[1] in the Ming dynasty. Though some of the incidents are rather naive, the gallant outlaws are vividly presented and the descriptions of town life and jests with which the book is interspersed add to the interest. Because men were bored with tales of the supernatural and with love stories, this picaresque story enjoyed an outstanding success.

Ma Han said: "Never mind about the wine. What sort of fellow is this Bright-Fur Rat?"

Chan Chao told them about the men at Hsienkung Island and how they came by their names. At this, Kungsun Tseh suddenly saw light. "This fellow is looking for you to pick a quarrel," he exclaimed.

"There has never been any bad blood between us," said Chan. "Why should he pick a quarrel?"

Kungsun said: "Use your head, brother. These fellows call themselves the Five Rats and now you are called the Imperial Cat. Cats catch rats, don't they? It's quite clear that your title annoys them: that's why he wants to pick a quarrel."

"There is something in what you say," rejoined Chan. "But my title was given me by the emperor: I didn't call myself the Cat in order to bully these Rats. If this is really the reason why he's come, I don't mind

---

[1] In 1519.

humouring him — I'll stop using the name. This isn't serious."

Chao Hu, who had been drinking heartily . . . was rather heated by now. Winecup in hand, he stood up and protested: "Brother! You are usually bolder than all the rest of us: what makes you so soft today? You got this title Imperial Cat from His Majesty — how can you change it? Never mind what sort of rat this is, he had better keep out of my way or I'll swallow him at one gulp to work off my feelings!"

Chan Chao hastily signed to him to be quiet, saying: "Hush! Someone may be listening outside the window."

At the same moment something flew in with a crash, smashing to pieces the cup that Chao was holding. He gave a start and the others were seized with panic. Chan leaped from his seat, banged the door shut and turned to blow out the lamp, pulling off his gown under which he was wearing a close-fitting jacket. He quietly picked up his sword and made as if to open the door again: at that something else crashed against it. Then he flung wide the door and in the same instant leaped through it. He felt a rush of cold air as some weapon slashed at him, but he warded off the blow with the flat of his sword. As he intercepted one blow after another, staring intently through the darkness lit only by stars he saw a man in a black, close-fitting jerkin who was very quick and light on his feet. It looked like the fellow he had met at Miao Market. The combatants said not a word: the clash of steel was the only sound. Content simply to defend himself, Chan observed that his assailant was attacking harder and harder with the most skilful and miraculous thrusts. He marvelled at this but thought: "What insolence! Here am I on the defensive so as not to hurt you — why should you press so hard? Do you really think I am afraid of you?" Then he decided: "I must at least give him a taste of my mettle." He held his sword level and as the next blow descended he made the cut known as "The stork sings through the sky," using all his strength. Clang! His opponent's sword was broken in two. The stranger dared not close with him but vaulted in one bound to the top of the wall. With a great leap Chan followed. . . .

(Chapter 39)

When Yu Yueh was in Soochow, Pan Tsu-yin, just home from Peking, showed him this novel. At first he thought it a commonplace tale but after reading it through was struck by "the remarkable plot and the romantic imagination revealed. The characters are drawn with a wealth of detail while the descriptions are apt and vivid. They remind one of Pock-Marked Liu Ching-ting's[1] description of how Wu Sung came to the deserted inn and with one shout set all the empty wine jars echoing. By deft and natural touches the writer has written a spirited novel." (Yu Yueh's preface to the novel) But Yu Yueh disliked the opening of the story on the score that the episode of the substituted cat was unhistorical; he therefore rewrote the first chapter to conform to history instead of to popular legend. He also contended that the Southern Hero, the Northern Hero and the Twin Heroes made four instead of three, while if the Young

---

[1] A celebrated story-teller at the end of the Ming dynasty.

Hero Ai Hu was added that made five. Moreover the list should include Chih Hua the Black Fox and Shen Chung-yuan the Wise Man, the former being the Young Hero's teacher and the latter "a gallant man who loved a jest." Accordingly he renamed the novel *Seven Heroes and Five Gallants,* wrote a preface in 1889 and had it published. Both the new and the old edition were popular, particularly in the Yangtse Valley.

In the fifth month of that year a sequel, *Five Younger Gallants,* appeared in Peking, followed by another sequel in the tenth month. These sequels had a hundred and twenty-four chapters each and according to their prefaces were also by Shih Yu-kun, whose pupil had preserved the manuscripts. The novel "in its original form consisted of more than three thousand episodes divided into three parts and called *The Romance of Loyal and Gallant Men.* Since the first part of the story dealt with five gallants it was known as the *Five Elder Gallants,* while the latter part dealing with a second generation was known as the *Five Younger Gallants.*" The sequel starts with Pai Yu-tang's attempt to steal the evidence of the prince's plot, repeating the last twenty chapters of the first book. It goes on to describe the Prince of Hsiangyang's conspiracy which the gallants try to expose. By now Pai Yu-tang is dead and his comrades-in-arms are growing old, but a younger generation appears to follow in their steps. Lu Fang's son Lu Cheng, Han Chang's son Han Tien-chin, Hsu Ching's son Hsu Liang and Pai Yu-tang's nephew Pai Yun-sheng all meet by chance during a journey, and when the Young Hero Ai Hu has joined them they became sworn brothers. In the course of their travels they kill some wicked men, then gather together at Wuchang and determine to thwart the prince's schemes; but the book ends before they can do this. The second sequel continues the story: the copper-wire trap is destroyed and the prince flees, after which the gallants deal with various evil characters in the countryside. Then the Prince of Hsiangyang is captured, the emperor distributes rewards and all the gallants receive their due deserts. So the whole story ends. Though the preface claims that both sequels were by Shih Yu-kun, the style of the first sequel is greatly inferior to that of the original work though the second sequel is somewhat better. It seems likely that both sequels might be by the same author but edited by different hands, resulting in this discrepancy in style.

Now Hsu Ching had such a temper that he would never stop to think carefully. If anything crossed him he flared up at once. So he pushed over the table with a crash, breaking all the dishes on it. Even if Chung Hsiung had been a thick-headed dolt, he must have taken offence.

"You are in my hands, yet I have treated you well and given you wine," he protested. "What do you mean by this?" No wonder he was angry! Wagging a finger at Hsu Ching he demanded: "What do you think you are doing?"

"Treating you better than you deserve," said Hsu.

"What do I deserve, then?"

"To be beaten up!"

With this, Hsu dealt Chung a blow. But Chung jerked a finger under his ribs and Hsu fell to the ground. Chung had used a method of stopping the circulation so that though Hsu was conscious he could not move. Chung kicked him and ordered his men to truss him up. After the kick Hsu found he could move again, but he was bound hand and foot. Then Chan Chao put his hands behind his back and said: "You can tie me too." The guards hesitated, but they had no choice. When Chung ordered their heads to be cut off at Red Phoenix Bridge, a shout was heard from the crowd: "Spare them!"

(Chapter 17 of the *Five Younger Gallants*)

Chih Hua the Black Fox and Shen Chung-yuan the Wise Man wanted to distinguish themselves by stealing the secret document from the prince's palace. . . . Crouching on the narrow ledge, he saw by the light of his torch a square box below . . . a hardwood box with gold handles. He reached out, grasped the handles and pulled it towards him. Crash! A crescent-shaped chopper came hurtling down! Chih Hua shut his eyes, not daring to move a step either forward or back, and the blade came down on his waist. He was certain that he must be cut in two. Slowly opening his eyes, he found that he was in no pain but was completely paralysed. Do you know the reason, reader? It was because the sword was crescent-shaped. Had it been an ordinary chopper, he would have been cut in half. The blade was curved, however, and since Chih Hua was slender and had removed his wallet his stomach was flat, while the leather sheath and sword on his back had protected his spine. . . .

In short, Chih Hua was fated not to die there, but Shen Chung-yuan was frightened out of his wits. . . .

(Chapter 1 of *Sequel to the Five Younger Gallants*)

After these sequels were published, a combined edition in two parts came out, with fifteen books or sixty chapters and a preface written by Hsiu-ku-chu-ssu in 1892. This edition cut out a certain amount of repetition and condensed the two novels into fifty-two chapters, adding another eight chapters describing the narrow escape of the Prince of Hsiangyang when he raised another army in Red Net Mountain, and his final death. This addition is actually quite superfluous. And though this version is clearer and more concise, by dispensing with many descriptive details it has lost some of the spirit of the original.

Prefect Pao and Inspector Yen were not the only legendary figures in detection. In 1838 appeared *The Cases of Lord Shih*, a novel in eight books divided into ninety-seven chapters, also known as *A Hundred Miraculous Cases*. The hero is Shih Shih-lun, prefect of Taichow and commissioner of Grain Transport in the reign of Kang Hsi. The story is poorly written, reminiscent of the Ming dynasty *Cases of Prefect Pao* but with a more highly developed plot: one case may fill several chapters, and there are other adventures apart from detection. So this was a precursor to the stories of gallant men. In 1891 appeared *The Cases of Lord Peng* in twenty-four books or a hundred chapters by Tan-meng-tao-jen. This deals with Peng Peng, magistrate of Sanho in the reign of Kang Hsi and later governor of Honan, who went to the capital and investigated important cases in Tatung and elsewhere. It is the same old story of a good official travelling incognito and gallant men stealing treasures, but written in atrocious, barely grammatical Chinese.

This is only one of many similar novels, perhaps the most popular being *The Reign of Eternal Peace* in ninety-seven chapters by Chang Kuang-jui of Luho, based on a tale told by Ha Fu-yuan. The story is about Emperor Kang Hsi's travels in disguise, and the suppression of evil cults and bandits. There was also a sequel in a hundred chapters by Tan-meng-tao-jen. *The Evergreen Prosperous Reign* in eight books divided into seventy-six chapters by an unknown writer describes how Emperor Kang Hsi entrusted the affairs of state to his ministers while he travelled down the Yangtse Valley, and contains stories of bad men and loyal, gallant subjects. The many other picaresque novels include *The Eight Elder Gallants, The Eight Junior Gallants, Seven Swordsmen and Thirteen Gallants* and *Seven Swordsmen and Eighteen Gallants*. Most of these appeared round about 1894. They were followed by *The Cases of Lord Liu, The Cases of Lord Li*, ten sequels to *The Cases of Lord Shih* and seventeen to *The Cases of Lord Peng*, as well as no fewer than twenty-four sequels to *Seven Heroes and Five Gallants*. These stories are repetitious and often written in abominable language, and one character may change completely in the course of the book. This was because these works were written by many hands and the editing was carelessly done, resulting in numerous inconsistencies.

Three Heroes and Five Gallants and its two sequels preserve the story-teller's style in their descriptive passages, as does *The Gallant Maid*. In Kuo Kuang-jui's preface to *The Reign of Eternal Peace* he says: "In my young days I travelled widely and often went to hear the story *The Reign of Eternal Peace* . . . which has circulated since the beginning of this dynasty. During the Hsien Feng period (1851-1861) a well-known story-teller named Mr. Chiang Chen-ming used to tell this tale, but no script was published at the time. Later I heard Mr.

Ha Fu-yuan tell it and learned it by heart. Then in my spare time I wrote it down in four volumes. . . ." The preface to *The Five Younger Gallants* also says that the book was based on a script by Shih Yu-kun like the novel *Three Heroes and Five Gallants*, and that the manuscript was kept by Shih's pupil. So probably Shih Yu-kun was a story-teller of the Hsien Feng period like Chiang Chen-ming, each of them specializing in one story. The author of *The Gallant Maid*, Wen Kang, was fond of listening to story-tellers too and imitated their style: This is why his novel has the same flavour. So the Ching dynasty novels about gallant men were directly descended from the Sung dynasty story-tellers' tradition: they were popular literature revived after more than seven hundred years. But since there were too many imitations and sequels, most of them badly written, this tradition declined again.

At the beginning of the Ching dynasty "bandits" were suppressed, but the people did not forget the previous dynasty and longed for gallant outlaws who would fight for the imperial house of Ming. Thus Chen Chen wrote a sequel to *Shui Hu Chuan* in which Li Chun left China and became King of Siam. (Chapter 15) During the hundred and thirty-odd years from the reign of Kang Hsi to the reign of Chien Lung, the new state authority established itself and men submitted to it: the scholars also became loyal to the new masters. This explains why when Yu Wan-chun in the reign of Tao Kuang wrote a sequel to *Shui Hu Chuan*, he killed off all the one hundred and eight outlaws. (Chapter 15) However, this was the viewpoint of a mandarin. *Three Heroes and Five Gallants* expresses the views of ordinary townsfolk, but though it appears to follow the tradition of *Shui Hu*

Chuan the similarity is a superficial one. A long time had elapsed since the fall of the Ming dynasty, and the story is set in the capital. Prior to this, several rebellions had been suppressed and rough soldiers who won some honour in the army would go home to boast to their friends and enjoy the respect of the villagers. So the heroes of such novels, though rough and gallant like the earlier outlaws, had to serve under some important official and considered it honourable to do so. This could happen only in an age when the people were completely subdued and subservient. Yet at that time men believed that "Here good citizens are rewarded and the wicked punished, the evil come to a bad end, but the righteous are blessed by Heaven. When these novels show this divine retribution clear and unerring, the readers clap their hands and applaud, instead of putting down the book with a sigh."

By this time the European influence was beginning to make itself felt in China too.

28. NOVELS OF EXPOSURE AT THE END OF THE CHING DYNASTY

After 1900 there was a rich crop of novels of exposure. During the nineteenth century, though many internal revolts were suppressed, including the White Lotus Rising and the Taiping, Nien and Hui rebellions, China was invaded by foreign powers such as Britain, France and Japan. Though the urban population might still listen with interest while sipping tea to romantic stories about the suppression of rebels, intelligent men realized that changes were necessary and started agitating for political reforms and patriotic action, emphasizing the need to make the country rich and strong. Two years after the failure of the 1898 Reform came the Yi Ho Tuan Movement,[1] a result of the people's complete loss of faith in the government. The trend in fiction was to expose social abuses and lash out at contemporary politics, sometimes at social conventions as well. Though this attack on abuses has something in common with the novels of satire, the criticisms were made openly without innuendo, sometimes even exaggerated to suit the popular mood, and the spirit of these works is intolerant. This is why I class these novels of exposure in a category by themselves. The most famous exponents of this school were Li Pao-chia and Wu Wo-yao.

---

[1] An anti-imperialist uprising in North China.

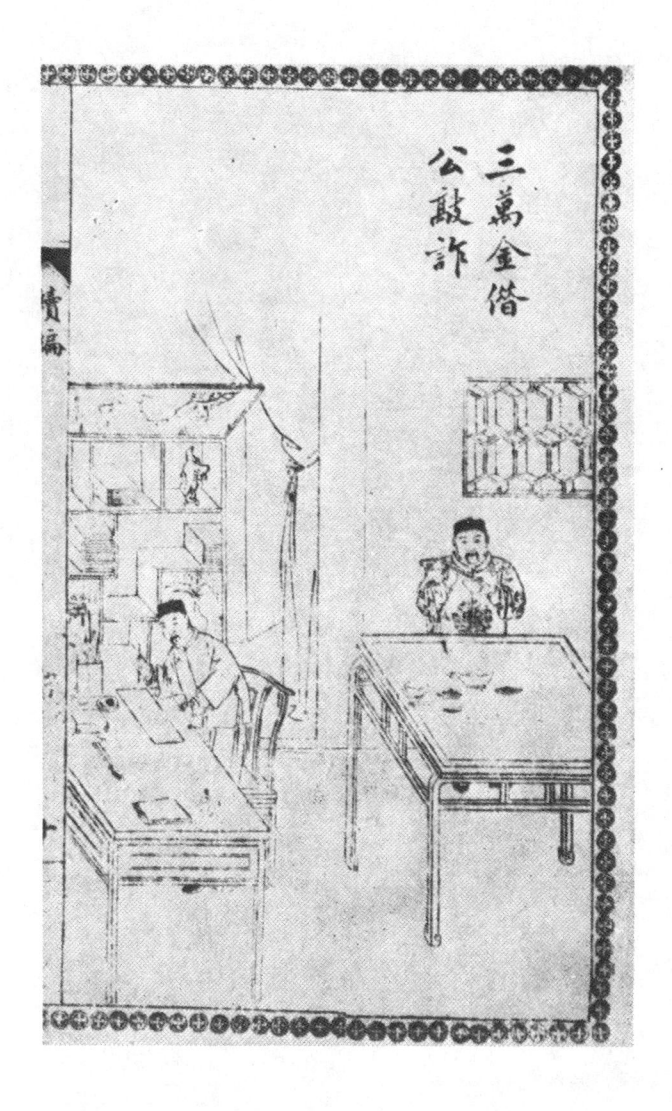

Illustration from an edition of *Exposure of the Official World* published in 1906

Li Pao-chia, who wrote under the pen-name Nanting-ting-chang, was a native of Wuchin County in Kiangsu. He showed a flair for the *paku* essays and for writing poems while still a boy, and passed first in the county examination; but failing in all subsequent examinations he went to Shanghai to start a paper *The Guide*. He gave this up to launch another called *Fun*, for which he wrote in a facetious, satirical vein. Later he sold this paper to a merchant and brought out the popular *Shanghai Sights* which carried news of actors and singsong girls, as well as poems and stories. His works include *Ballad of the Great Incident in 1900*, *Shanghai Impressions* in six books, *Li Lien-ying, A Dream of Splendour* and *Living Hell*. His novel *Modern Times*, published in serial form in the journal *Illustrated Stories*, was a well-known work of social criticism. In 1900 the government was so corrupt that men were in despair and everyone wanted to know the root of the trouble and who was responsible. Li Pao-chia was commissioned by a publisher for a novel called *Exposure of the Official World*. He planned to write this in ten books of twelve chapters each. Between 1901 and 1903 he completed three books and during the next two years another two; but in March 1906 he died of illness at the age of forty, his work unfinished. He had no son, and the actor Sun Chu-hsien attended to his funeral in gratitude for favourable notices in Li's papers. Li Pao-chia was generally respected because although recommended for a government post he declined the appointment. He was a skilled seal-engraver and published a book about seal-engraving.

The *Exposure of the Official World* has sixty chapters only. The third book was published in 1903 with a preface by the author saying: "I have seen officials whose sole work is to welcome visitors and see them off, whose sole ability is polite talk. They put up with hunger and thirst, with cold and heat, going to court or to call on their superiors at the crack of dawn and not returning till dusk. But they cannot tell you the purpose of these calls." In a year of famine when relief is granted, "They simply follow past precedents to win rewards; thus more and more of these bureaucrats appear and there is never any end." When the government decides on a retrenchment of staff, "They carry on as usual, concealing the true state of affairs from above and below, while the worst of them employ bad men to get them off by bribery. Thus the evil, instead of being checked, goes from bad to worse." The officials grind down the poor till they are desperate, yet no one dares remonstrate, and this makes the bureaucrats even more high-handed. "The author has wit and is thoroughly conversant with the filth and squalor of the official world, its ignorance and folly. By indirect means, keeping an open mind, he thoroughly reveals its secrets. . . . He has spent months and years, sparing no pains, to write this *Exposure of the Official World.* . . . This novel contains all manner of dark mysteries which Yu[1] could not record on his bronze tripods nor Wen Chiao[2] bring to light by burning the rhinoceros horn." Li Pao-chia tells of flattery, toadyism, cheating, exploitation and quarrelling among

---

[1] There is a legend that Yu, the pacifier of floods, made nine bronze tripods on which he depicted all manner of monsters.

[2] A Tsin dynasty scholar reputed to have used a rhinoceros horn as a torch and by its light to have seen many marvels in the river.

the officials; he shows the eagerness of scholars to obtain some government post, and discloses the secrets of officials' wives and concubines. There are many different episodes and characters, and each anecdote usually deals with a different individual. Thus the book as a whole consists of a number of loosely connected stories like Wu Ching-tzu's *The Scholars*. But many scenes are completely imaginary, not all is true to life, and there is far less innuendo than the author claims; hence the novel is not up to the standard of *The Scholars*. Moreover the tales collected were current gossip about official circles strung together into a novel, but without much variety. It was only the general interest in the subject at the time that made this novel famous overnight. It was followed by many imitations like the *Exposure of the Merchants' World, Exposure of the Teaching World* and *Exposure of the Women's World*. Let me quote a passage from the *Exposure of the Official World* as an example of this type of writing.

When it was nearly time to go to court, Chia rehearsed the ceremony in the ministry and all went according to the rules: but enough of this. On the appointed day he rose at midnight and drove into the city. . . . He waited till eight when some officer ushered him into the palace. When he and the others reached a certain court, the officer flapped his sleeve and they all fell to their knees at the steps, about twenty feet from the throne. It dawned on him that the man sitting there was the emperor! . . . Since he was a recommended scholar, he was ordered to wait for a summons the following day. . . .

Though Chia came from an official family, this was his first audience with the emperor, and despite the fact that he had asked advice on every side he still felt unsure of himself. So his first act on his return was to call on Minister Hua who had accepted ten thousand taels worth of curios from him, and naturally the minister talked with him cordially and showed friendly concern.

Chia said: "Tomorrow at court, in view of the fact that my father is Minister of Justice, should I kowtow to His Majesty or not?"

The minister was not listening carefully and caught only the word "kowtow." He promptly replied: "Kowtow a lot and say little: that is the way to be promoted."

Chia made haste to explain: "If the emperor asks after my father, of course I shall kowtow; but if he doesn't, should I kowtow or not?"

Minister Hua said: "If the emperor doesn't ask you anything, don't speak out of turn. But when it is right to kowtow, be sure to do so. Even kowtowing when it isn't strictly necessary will do no harm."

This advice left Chia more confused than ever. But before he could ask further questions, the minister rose to see him off and he had to leave. He decided not to trouble Minister Hua any more but to call on War Minister Huang . . . who might be able to enlighten him.

But when Chia had explained the purpose of his call, Minister Huang asked: "Have you seen Minister Hua? What did he say?"

Chia told him.

The war minister said: "Minister Hua is experienced. If he told you to kowtow many times and say little, this is the advice of an experienced man, absolutely correct. . . ."

Still at a loss, Chia called on Minister Hsu. This minister, who was elderly and rather deaf, sometimes pretended to be deafer than he was. He believed in peace at any price, and his mottoes were: "Take it easy!" and "Don't worry!" . . . All his colleagues had seen through him and called him "The Crystal Egg." . . . So today when they had greeted each other and Chia brought up this problem, Minister Hsu said: "Of course to kowtow a lot is the best, however, it is not absolutely necessary. After all, you should kowtow when kowtowing is called for, not otherwise."

When Chia told him what the others had said, Minister Hsu rejoined: "They are both right: you had better take their advice." He talked at length without committing himself to anything definite, till Chia had to take his leave. Later he found a minor official in the Ministry of War who happened to be a good friend of his father, and only then did he get a clear explanation of the ceremony. The next day when he was summoned by the emperor all went smoothly. . . .

(Chapter 26)

Wu Wo-yao (1866-1910), whose pen-name was Wo-fo-shan-jen, was a native of Nanhai in Kwangtung. He went to Shanghai in his twenties and started writing articles for newspapers. In 1902 Liang Chi-chao published a monthly magazine entitled *New Fiction* in Yokohama, and the following year Wu started writing novels for this magazine: *Strange Tales of Electricity, A Crime Involving Nine Lives* and *Strange Events of the Last Twenty Years.* He gradually won a considerable reputation, and his last novel was highly praised. He stayed in Shantung for a time before going to Japan, but not meeting with any success there he returned to Shanghai. In 1906 he became the chief editor of *Fiction Monthly*, for which he wrote *After the Disaster, The Way to Get Rich* and *Glimpses of Shanghai*. He wrote *A New Dream of the Red Chamber* for *The Guide*. The next year he was appointed principal of Kuangchih Primary School and devoted most of his time to educational work, writing less. In 1909 he completed twenty chapters of *Strange Events of the Last Twenty Years* and died in September 1910 at the age of forty-five. Two of his novels, *A Sea of Woe* and *Hu Pao-yu*, were printed not in serial form but as books. A merchant paid him three hundred dollars to write *The Return of the Soul*, advertising a drug, and he was criticized for this novel which is no longer extant. He was not particularly successful with his anecdotes and table-talk, but after he became famous several collections were made of his anecdotes, tales and jokes.

Strange Events of the Last Twenty Years was first published in serial form in *New Fiction*, and ended when that magazine stopped publication. In 1907 four volumes of this novel were published as a book, and in 1909 another four volumes came out, making one hundred and eight chapters in all. The central figure, "The man who barely escaped death," appears throughout the book and describes all the startling events he has seen in the last twenty years, starting from his childhood. He has collected a great deal of gossip, much in the style of the *Exposure of the Official World*. But since Wu Wo-yao had a richer experience of life than Li Pao-chia, he draws more types of people, including officials, teachers, scholars and merchants. Apart from stories current at the time, he also includes old tales from collections like *Chung Kuei the Catcher of Ghosts*. He says in the first chapter that "Thinking back over twenty years' experience of the world, he has met three types only: insects, beasts and goblins." From this we can tell the sort of people he describes. Wu is said to have been proud and honest, unwilling to submit to authority; therefore he remained poor all his life and was a cynic. But as he wrote hastily, often exaggerated and cared little for realism, his works fail to make a strong appeal, merely presenting some gossip as material for idle talk. Here is a passage describing how the hero's fellow-lodger ill-treats his grandfather.

That evening when the household had retired, lying in bed I thought I heard shouting in the east courtyard. . . . The noise subsided only to start again, and though I could not hear what was happening I was too disturbed to sleep soundly. . . . Not till three had struck did I manage to drop off. It was well after nine when I woke, got up, dressed quickly and left my sitting-room. Outside I found Wu and Li talking in low voices with two of the boys, the cook and a couple of servants. I asked what they were discussing. . . .

Li said: "Let Wang San tell the story. Then we needn't repeat it."

Wang said: "We were talking about what happened in Mr. Fu's family in the east courtyard. Last night I got up at midnight because I heard quarrelling there. . . . I groped my way to the back . . . and peeped inside. I saw Mr. Fu and his wife in the seats of honour with the old beggar who came here sitting below them. They were swearing at the old fellow, who just hung his head and wept without a word.

"Mrs. Fu said something very strange indeed. She said: 'When a man has lived to fifty or sixty, it is time for him to die. Yet here you are over eighty and still hanging on!'

"Mr. Fu went on: 'If you refuse to die, all right; but be satisfied with what you have, whether it's rice or porridge. Here you are complaining about your rice one day and about your porridge the next. Don't you know that a man must make himself useful if he wants to eat and dress well?'

"The old man said: 'Don't be hard on me! I'm not asking for good food, just for some salted vegetables.'

"When Mr. Fu heard this he jumped up and cried: 'Today you want salted vegetables, tomorrow you will be asking for salted pork, the next day for chicken, goose, duck and fish, and after that for bird's nest and shark's fin. I am just a poor official in the capital without a post in the country. How can I supply all these things?' He banged the table, kicked the benches and cursed. . . . After he had sworn at the old man for some time, a maid brought in wine and food and put them on the round table in the middle of the room. Husband and wife sat opposite each other drinking, laughing and chatting, while the old man sat there sobbing. Mr. Fu went on cursing over his wine, while his wife and her pet dog played with some bones. When the wretched old man muttered something, Mr. Fu lost his temper: he pushed over the table so that all the dishes crashed to the ground. Then he shouted:

"'All right! Now eat!'

"The old man was lost to shame. He took Mr. Fu at his word and got down on his hands and knees to find some scraps. Without warning Mr. Fu stood up, picked up the stool he had been sitting on, and hurled it at the old man. Luckily the maid was near enough to jump forward and try to catch it. Though she didn't succeed, at least she broke its force. The stool just grazed the old man's forehead. If not for her, the old fellow's head would have been broken!"

When I heard this I started sweating with horror and in silence reached a decision. During breakfast I told Li to lose no time in finding us some other lodgings: we couldn't stay here . . . .

(Chapter 74)

Three only of Wu's novels, *Sea of Woe*, *After the Disaster* and *Strange Tales of Electricity*, the latter adapted from some foreign novel, were what he called "romantic tales." All the rest were novels of exposure, though the degree of censure in them varied; this is because he made a living with his pen, so "his attitude had to be different in different places and at different times," but his main purpose was to "advocate a revival of the old morality."

The Travels of Mr. Derelict is a novel in twenty chapters by Liu Ngo (circa 1850-1910), who used the pen-name Hung-tu-pai-lien-sheng. It has a preface by the author written in the autumn of 1906 in Shanghai. Some say that the last few chapters were written by his son. Liu Ngo or Liu Tieh-yun was a native of Tantu in Kiangsu. He was a good mathematician as a youth, and well-read, but too much of a liberal to observe the usual conventions. Later he regretted his display of eccentricity and stayed at home to study for more than a year, after which he became a physician in Shanghai. Then he gave up medicine and went into business, only to lose all his capital. In 1888 the Yellow River flooded its banks at Chengchow and Liu Ngo, working under Wu Ta-cheng,[1] was successful in curbing the flood. He won a name for himself and was appointed to a prefectship. During his two years' stay in the capital he presented a memorial urging the building of railways and the opening of mines in Shansi, for which he was much abused and even called a traitor. At the time of the Yi Ho Tuan Movement he bought cheap grain from a state granary from the foreign troops occupying Peking, and with this he relieved the destitute, thereby saving many lives; but a few years later he was impeached for the purchase of government grain and exiled to Sinkiang where he died. His novel describes the travels, views and adventures of Tiehying or Mr. Derelict. The descriptions of scenery and incidents are often well-written. The author expresses his own views too and in many places attacks bureaucracy. One episode concerns an official, Kang Pi, who believes that a man named Wei and his daughter are responsible for the death of thirteen people. Wei's servant tries to save them by offering Kang Pi a bribe, but the latter considers this a proof of their guilt. This story aims to show that a strict official could be worse than a corrupt one. This was an original approach and the author prided himself on it. "All men know that corrupt officials are bad, but few know that strict officials are even worse. For whereas a corrupt official knows his own faults and dares not play the tyrant openly, a strict official imagines that since he never takes bribes he is

---

[1] 1835-1902. A high official and collector of ancient inscriptions.

free to do as he likes. Then self-confidence and personal prejudice may lead him to kill the innocent or even endanger the state. I have seen many such officials with my own eyes: Hsu Tung and Li Ping-heng are notable examples. . . ." Earlier novels of censure had exposed the faults of corrupt officials: this was the first to reveal the damage done by strict officials.

The runners dragged in Wei and his daughter, already half dead. They kneeled down before the judge and Kang Pi took from his pocket the bank order for a thousand taels of silver and the note of hand for five thousand five hundred taels. . . . These he ordered the runners to show them. When they denied any knowledge of this . . . he laughed sarcastically.

"So you don't understand? Let me tell you! Yesterday a scholar named Hu came to call on me and presented me with a thousand taels of silver, promising to pay me more if I let you off. . . . If you are not guilty of these murders, why should your family offer me bribes of several thousand taels of silver? That is my first piece of evidence against you. . . . I told Hu: 'If one life is reckoned as worth five hundred taels, you ought to pay me six thousand five hundred.' If you were not guilty your agent would surely have said: 'They had nothing to do with these murders. If you will help us, we don't mind paying you seven or eight thousand, but we can't pay six thousand five hundred.' Instead of this, though, he agreed to my estimate. That is my second piece of evidence against you. So take my advice: since you will have to admit your guilt sooner or later, you had better spare yourselves the agony of torture."

Father and daughter kowtowed again and again, pleading: "Your Honour, we are innocent! Indeed we are!"

Kang Pi banged the table and bellowed: "So you still won't confess, even after what I have said? Give them the finger-screws again."

Like a clap of thunder the runners shouted assent . . . and were just about to torture the prisoners when Kang Pi cried: "Wait! Come here, warders, and listen to me. . . . I know all your tricks. First you decide whether the case is serious or not. If your palms are greased, you apply the torture lightly so that the culprits do not suffer too much. But if a case is too serious to be pardoned and the prisoner has given you money, you kill him on the spot with sudden torture so that he need not have his head cut off and I shall be punished for killing men during questioning. I know your ways. Torture the girl first today, but don't let her lose consciousness. When she is fainting ease off, and tighten the screws again when she has recovered. We shall torture them slowly for ten whole days and see that they confess, however stubborn they think they are. . . ."

(Chapter 16)

A Flower in an Ocean of Sin was first published in the magazine *Forest of Fiction* in 1907. It was described as a historical novel "told by One-Who-Loves-Freedom and recorded by the Sick-Man-of-Eastern-Asia." In fact it was the work of Tseng Pu, a scholar of Changshu. The first chapter serves as a prelude, and it is said that sixty more will follow. The story starts with a scholar named Chin Chun who comes first in the palace examination, and goes on to describe the last thirty years of the Ching dynasty; it was probably intended to end with the 1911 Revolution but was left unfinished after twenty chapters. This scholar Chin is really Hung Chun of Soochow who was appointed chief examiner in Kiangsi. He passed through Shanghai on his way home because of one parent's death, and made the celebrated courtesan Fu Tsai-yun his concubine. Later he was appointed ambassador to England, and there was much gossip because he took her with him. After Hung's death in Peking, his concubine went back to Shanghai and returned to her old trade, changing her name to Tsao Meng-lan. Later still she went to Tientsin and took the name Golden Flower. During the Yi Ho Tuan Movement she was the mistress of Count Waldersee, commander of the allied armies,[1] and exercised considerable influence. This novel with its satirical approach to the scholar and his concubine gives excellent descriptions of the high officials and men of letters of the time. True, it often exaggerates like other novels of exposure; nevertheless it has the merits of a compact and well-conceived plot and an elegant style. Virtually all the characters are based on real persons. The scholar Li Chun-keh in the book has been shown to be the author's tutor Li Tzu-ming. Since this was a man whom he knew intimately, one would expect the characterization to be convincing; yet even here we find occasional exaggerations and episodes which appear unnatural. It was the fashion at that time to use hyperbole and not to be content with simple touches. Here is an example:

---

[1] Which occupied Peking in 1900.

Wearing civilian dress, Hsiao-yen hired a light carriage and ordered the driver to take him to Paoanssu Street in the south of the city. The autumn air was fresh, the horse raised a light dust; in no time at all he reached the gate and his carriage drew up in the shade of two great elms. The servant was about to announce him when he waved him aside, saying: "No need!" He jumped lightly down and walked in. On the gate was a new couplet written in an elegant yet flowing hand on two pink strips of paper:

> This house holds a collection of a hundred thousand books,
> And an official without a post staying idle for a thousand years.

Hsiao-yen smiled at this. Inside the gate was a spirit-screen, turning east he saw three rooms on the north corridor, and passing down this he came to a leaf-shaped gate. Beyond lay a small court and wistaria dark with foliage. Hibiscus was in bloom there, its brilliant red blossoms full-blown. From the three quiet chambers with their bamboo curtains no sound at all could be heard. A vagrant breeze brought Hsiao-yen the faint scent of herbs being brewed within, and lifting the curtain he stepped inside. A boy with his hair in a knot, a tattered fan in one hand, was watching the medicine by the east wall of the hall. He stood up at the sight of Hsiao-yen. Just then from the inner room a voice chanted:

> "Wearing a cap of silk under the lamp,
> I practise calligraphy in faint ink.
> In the light breeze, as bells tinkle,
> Comes the lady of my dreams."

Hsiao-yen walked in, asking with a laugh: "Who is this lady of your dreams?" He found Li Chun-keh in a shabby silk gown and straw sandals, tugging cheerfully at his short beard as he sat reading on his old bamboo couch. When Li saw him, however, he promptly lay down and breathed hard over his dog-eared volume, saying in a voice that quavered: "I am sorry I can't get up to welcome you — I am not well."

"When did you fall ill?" asked Hsiao-yen. "How is it that I never heard of this?"

"It started on that day when you all decided to celebrate my birthday. I didn't deserve such honour from you all. I'm afraid I shan't be able to join your party in Reclining-Cloud Garden today."

"I expect you just caught a slight chill. You should be all right when you have had some medicine. We still hope you will come, sir, and shall be most disappointed if you fail us." As Hsiao-yen was speaking he glanced round and saw a sheet of writing paper half under the pillow with many names on it; but strange to say none had proper titles attached, only the words "Silly fool." Hsiao-yen, puzzled, wanted to have a closer look when he heard two people coming in through the small gate. They were speaking in low voices and treading lightly. Before Li could speak, the bamboo curtain swished. But if you want to know who these visitors were, you will have to read the next chapter.

(Chapter 19)

There were sequels to this novel by other hands, such as *The Martyrs' Blood* and *Sequel to a Flower in an Ocean of Sin,* but these were inferior works.

Numerous other books of this type dealt with social abuses, but most of them were poor imitations of those we have described. There was a great deal of criticism of society but little genuine literature; the majority of these novels were hastily written and unfinished. There were also libellous works attacking private individuals, and some authors proved ingenious in writing invective but weak in narrative. Gradually this type of literature degenerated into mere material for gossip-columns.

POSTSCRIPT

The first fifteen of the twenty-eight chapters of this *Brief History of Chinese Fiction* were printed in October last year. From Chu Yi-tsun's *Collected Poems of the Ming Dynasty*, Volume 80, I subsequently found the name of the author of the *Sequel to Shui Hu Chuan*, while much additional material on this man appears in Hu Shih's preface to the novel. Again, from the first section of Hsieh Wu-liang's *Two Great Masters of Popular Literature*, I learned that one old edition of the *Romance of the Tang Dynasty* gives Lo Kuan-chung as the author and that the novel *Fen Chuang Lou* is also attributed to him. Unfortunately these discoveries came too late to be included in this work. The manuscript of Chapters 16 to 28 were on my desk for many months and I made certain corrections from time to time. But my ability is very limited and my reading by no means extensive. There are still many gaps in the section dealing with Ming and Ching dynasty novels, while I did not even have time to make a careful study of such recent writers as Wei Tzu-an or Han Tzu-yun. When a novel was first printed, there was usually a preface or postscript giving its date and the author's name; but old editions are rare, and I possess only later editions in which the careless printers have generally omitted all but the text itself. I fear the insufficient material at my disposal may have led me into mistakes: only by frequent corrections can I enable this book to pass muster. However, as time is pressing and this work is needed, I am letting it be printed with all its defects, for I have long wanted to help those attending my lectures and to save the copyists trouble.

Written on March 3, 1924,
after reading the proofs

APPENDICES

THE HISTORICAL DEVELOPMENT OF CHINESE FICTION

The following is a series of lectures delivered by Lu Hsun in 1924 at a Sian summer school to which he was invited by the Northwest University and the Shensi Bureau of Education. They were not generally known or included in The Works of Lu Hsun, for they came to light a few years ago only.

As they were given just after the publication of his Brief History of Chinese Fiction, these lectures may be considered a synopsis of that book. Certain views and arguments are actually expanded here, making this valuable material for students of our classical literature and of the history of Chinese fiction.

Many historians have told us that the history of mankind is evolutional, and China naturally should be no exception. But when we look at the evolution of China we are struck by two peculiarities. One is that the old makes a come-back long after the new has appeared — in other words, retrogression. The other is that the old remains long after the new has appeared — in other words, amalgamation. This does not mean there is no evolution, however. Only it is comparatively slow, so that hotheads like myself feel that "one day is like three autumns." The same applies to literature, including fiction. For instance, today we still find dregs of the Tang and Sung dynasties in modern writing, or even the ideas and behaviour of primitive man. In my talk I mean to ignore these dregs — popular as they still are — and try to find the trend of development in our regressive and chaotic literature.

I

FROM MYTH TO LEGEND

The expression *hsiao-shuo* was first used by Chuang Tzu, who spoke of "winning honour and renown by means of *hsiao-shuo*." But by this he simply meant trivial talk with no moral significance, something quite different from the modern meaning of the word. For Chuang Tzu considered the various schools of thought of Confucius, Yang Chu, Mo Ti and the others as "trivial talk." And the other philosophers no doubt considered Chuang Tzu's writing in the same way. When we come to the section on literature and art in the *Han Dynasty History*, *hsiao-shuo* means "the gossip of the streets," which is closer to what is called fiction today. Still, it was simply a collection of the talk of the common people made by the emperor's officers so that they could study popular sentiment and customs. It is not the same as modern fiction.

How did fiction first come to be written? According to the bibliographical section of the *Han Dynasty History*, "fiction writers were the successors of the officers whose job it had been to collect popular talk." Whether such an official function existed or not is another question. But even if it did, this can only explain the origin of such writing, not the origin of story-telling. Nowadays most students of the history of literature believe that story-telling grew out of mythology. When primitive men living in caves or in the wilderness were puzzled by such ever-changing phenomena of nature as wind, rain and earthquakes, which they could not account for, they attributed these things to supernatural beings, and made stories about the life and behaviour of the gods, as in the account of the creation of heaven and earth in Chinese mythology. So myths started. When these myths developed and became more human, demigods appeared — ancient heroes who achieved great deeds by means of superhuman attributes given them by the gods. Examples of these are Chien Ti, who ate a swallow egg and gave birth to Shang, and King Yao, who ordered Yi to shoot down the ten suns in the sky. These tales, which show the difference between demigods and ordinary men, are today called legends. Then these stories evolved further, and truthful accounts became history while other anecdotes became fiction.

It seems to me that poetry must have preceded prose stories. Poetry started with labour and religion. For men at work sang to forget their hardships and, beginning with monotonous chants, ended by expressing their feelings with a natural rhythm. Another origin of poetry was primitive man's fear of and subsequent respect for the gods, which made him sing their might and praise their achievements. As for story-telling, I suspect it originated during times of rest. Just as men tried to forget their troubles by singing while they were working, when at rest they told stories to while away the time. This is how fiction started. So poetry and song grew out of labour, and prose stories out of leisure.

In ancient times, however, poetry and story-telling alike were based on mythology. This was so in ancient India, Egypt and Greece, as well as in China. But in China we have no great mythological works, while even the few myths we have are not yet compiled in books; we have to search for them in the ancient classics. One of our most important source-books is *The Book of Mountains and Seas*. The myths here are not systematically arranged; but among the most noteworthy of them, important for its influence in later periods, is the story about the Queen Mother of the West. Here is an example of such writing:

> The Jade Mountain is where the Queen Mother of the West lives. She has a human appearance, the tail of a leopard and the teeth of a tiger. She can shriek, her hair is shaggy, and she wears trinkets. She rules over the avenging spirits and the five monsters of heaven.

There are many similar accounts. The Queen Mother of the West remained popular till the Tang dynasty, when the Mother of Li Mountain took her place. Then there is the story, discovered in an ancient tomb in the prefecture of Chi, about King Mu of the Chou dynasty who went to the Western Regions in a carriage drawn by eight wonderful horses. On the whole, though, there is a dearth of ancient myths in China, and what we do possess are fragmentary accounts rather than long narratives. Moreover, this is apparently not because many were lost but because there were always very few. To my mind, there are two main reasons for this dearth.

In the first place, life was too hard. The earliest Chinese lived in the Yellow River Valley where conditions were rigorous and men had to strain every nerve to wrest a living from nature. As this made them matter-of-fact, with a dislike for fanciful ideas, mythology could not develop or be handed down. Though labour gives rise to the growth of literature, it does so only under certain conditions. The work must not be too exhausting. Where you have toil and rest, or hard work but not too much of it, there songs and poetry will spring up and in leisure hours there will be story-telling. But too much labour and too little rest mean a man is constantly tired, and when he is short of food and sleep he will not think of literature.

In the second place, men's memories are short. In ancient times stories of gods, ghosts and men were often intermingled, so that primitive beliefs survived in the old legends. But as time went on these legends died out. For example, as Shen-tu and Yu-lei were famous deities who are supposed to have taken straw ropes to capture tigers and defend men against evil spirits, the ancients made door-gods of them. Afterwards, however, the two generals Chin Chiung and Yuchih Ching-teh became the door-gods, as we see from many historical accounts. So later generations forgot even the names of Shen-tu and Yu-lei, to say nothing of the stories about them. And there were many such cases.

As there are no full-length myths in China, let us have a look at the *hsiao-shuo* mentioned in the *Han Dynasty History*. Not one of all those listed there is left. Only fragments have survived. For example, the *Records of Rites* preserved by the Elder Tai quotes the following passage from *Ching Shih Tzu*:

> In ancient times, a boy would move to lodgings outside his home at the age of eight to learn the lesser arts and practise the lesser etiquette. When he bound his hair and undertook more advanced studies, he would learn the greater arts and practise the greater

etiquette. At home he would study ceremony and literature, abroad his jade pendants would tinkle, and when riding in his carriage he would hear harmonious bells. Thus no improper ideas could enter his heart.

Now *Ching Shih Tzu* was classified as *hsiao-shuo*, but judging by this quotation it seems to have been the same as the rest of the *Records of Rites*. It is hard to see why such a book was called *hsiao-shuo*. Perhaps because it contained many ideas alien to Confucian philosophy. Of the surviving *hsiao-shuo* said to date from the Han dynasty, the *Book of Deities and Marvels* and the *Accounts of the Ten Continents* are attributed to Tungfang Shuo. The *Tales of Emperor Wu Ti* and the *Private Life of Emperor Wu Ti* are attributed to Pan Ku. We also have *Penetrating the Mysteries* by Kuo Hsien, and the *Western Capital Miscellany* by Liu Hsin. The *Book of Deities and Marvels* is written in the same style as *The Book of Mountains and Seas*, and gives accounts of miraculous phenomena. Here is an example:

The Lying Beast lives in the mountains of the Southwest Wilderness. In appearance like a rabbit with a human face, it can speak like a human being. It often cheats men, saying east when it should be west and bad when it should be good. Its flesh is delicious, but eating it makes a man tell lies.

The *Accounts of the Ten Continents* contains what Emperor Wu is alleged to have heard from the Queen Mother of the West about these lands, and is also modelled on *The Book of Mountains and Seas*, although it is slightly more restrained in style. Both the *Tales of Emperor Wu Ti* and the *Private Life of Emperor Wu Ti* describe incidents from the birth to the death of that monarch. *Pene-*

trating the Mysteries deals with holy men, magic and prodigies in distant lands; while the *Western Capital Miscellany* records happenings in the world of men. The *Book of Deities and Marvels* and the *Accounts of the Ten Continents* are not mentioned in the *Han Dynasty History*, however, and cannot therefore have been written by Tungfang Shuo, but must be later works. The two accounts of Emperor Wu must also be by a later hand, for the style is not that of Pan Ku and they contain Buddhist ideas, although Buddhism was not widespread in China in the Early Han dynasty and the men of that time would not have used Buddhist concepts. As for *Penetrating the Mysteries* and the *Western Capital Miscellany*, these have been proved to date from the Six Dynasties period. Thus all these six *hsiao-shuo* attributed to Han dynasty writers are spurious. Only Liu Hsiang's *Account of the Saints* is genuine. Ko Hung of the Tsin dynasty also wrote about saints and fairies, and there were more such tales during the Tang and Sung dynasties which had a great influence on later ideas and fiction. When Liu Hsiang wrote, however, he was not aware that he was writing fiction, but thought he was recording facts. It is we who regard his work as fiction. The fragmentary legends in these books are still used as reading material for children today. As many people have asked whether they are suitable for boys and girls, I shall mention my view in passing. Some say that to teach children these legends will only make them superstitious and do much harm;. but others argue that these fairy tales are suited to childish natures and will interest without injuring them. It seems to me that the whole question hinges on the state of education in this country. If children can receive a good education, they will study science and know the truth and not be superstitious. In that case no harm will be done. But if young folk can have no better education and make no further mental progress, they will always believe the legends they heard when children, and this may be bad for them.

II
TALES OF MEN AND OF THE SUPERNATURAL DURING THE SIX DYNASTIES PERIOD

We can now go on to consider the *hsiao-shuo* of the fourth to the sixth centuries. The ancient Chinese believed in ghosts and deities who lived apart from men, and in order to communicate with them they had shamans or wizards. Later, these shamans split into two groups: priests and alchemists. The priests talked about spirits, the alchemists about making gold and attaining immortality. This was the fashion from the Chin and Han dynasties right down to the Six Dynasties. There was therefore much writing about the supernatural. Take this example from the *Records of Strange Things*:

Prince Tan of the state of Yen went as a hostage to the state of Chin. . . . When he asked the king's permission to return home the king would not hear of it and said jokingly: "You may go when the crow's head turns white and the horse grows horns." Prince Tan looked up and sighed, whereupon the crow turned white. He lowered his head and lamented, whereupon the horse grew horns. So the king of Chin was forced to send him back.

Tales like this show the influence of the alchemists of the time. Or take this anecdote from the *Garden of Marvels* by Liu Ching-shu:

During the Yi Hsi period (405-418), a serving-maid named Lan in the Hsu family of Tunghai turned unaccountably pale and wan, yet paid more attention to her appearance than usual. When the family kept a secret watch on her, they saw the broom go from its corner to the maid's bed. Then they burned the broom and the serving-maid recovered.

Evidently the men of that time believed all things had life. This was shamanism or animism. Such ideas still exist today. For example, we often see trees hung with placards announcing that all prayers will be granted. This shows that men of our generation still consider trees as gods, and are just as superstitious as the people of the Six Dynasties. As a matter of fact, in ancient times the men of all lands had similar ideas, only later they discarded them by degrees. But in China they are still prevalent.

In addition to the two books just mentioned, two more accounts of the supernatural during the Six Dynasties period are *Records of Spirits* by Kan Pao and its sequel by Tao Chien. Most of the former book is lost, however, what we have today being half genuine and half forged, with quotations from the original collected from various sources by Ming dynasty scholars together with other accounts. The sequel also deals with the supernatural; but as Tao Chien was an enlightened and intelligent man, he can hardly have written this. Some other writer probably made use of his name.

Another factor which encouraged the development of such tales was the coming of Indian thought. During the Tsin, Sung, Chi and Liang dynasties, Buddhism was extremely popular. Many Buddhist sutras were translated, and numerous tales were told about gods and ghosts, in which both Chinese and Indian supernatural beings figured. One example is this tale of the goose cage:

Travelling through the Suian hills, Hsu Yen of Yanghsien came upon a scholar . . . lying by the roadside, explained that his feet hurt and asked for a lift in the goose cage which Hsu was carrying. At first Hsu thought he was joking. But the scholar got into the cage . . . and sat down quietly beside the two geese and they appeared not to mind. Hsu picked up the cage again, but found it no heavier. Further on he stopped to rest under a tree and the scholar, coming out of the cage, offered to treat him to a meal. When Hsu accepted with pleasure, the scholar took from his mouth a copper tray laid with all manner of delicacies. . . . After several cups of wine the scholar told Hsu: "I have a girl with me. May I ask her to join us?" . . . Then from his mouth the scholar produced a girl . . . who sat down and feasted with them. Presently, slightly tipsy, the scholar went to lie down. . . . The girl confided to Hsu, "I have brought my lover with me and shall call him out." . . . Then the girl produced from her mouth an intelligent and charming man in his early twenties. . . .

Such stories were not of Chinese but Indian origin. Thus we can see the Indian influence in the tales of the supernatural of that period. We should bear in mind, however, that when writers of that time recorded supernatural happenings, they did so just as we record the daily news today. They were not deliberately writing fiction.

After dealing briefly with tales of the supernatural, let us turn to tales about men. During that period these tales were very simple too, rather reminiscent of the ghost stories. Here are two quotations from *Social Talk* by Liu Yi-ching of the kingdom of Sung:

When Yuan Yu was in Yen he had a fine carriage which he never refused to lend. A man wanted to borrow this carriage to bury his mother, but dared not ask for it. Yuan hearing of this sighed and said: "Though I have a carriage men dare not borrow it. Why should I keep it?" He had the carriage burned.

Liu Ling was often drunk and behaved wildly, sometimes throwing off his clothes to stay naked in his room. When someone saw this and laughed, Liu Ling retorted: "Heaven and earth are my home and these rooms are my breeches. Why should other gentlemen step into my breeches?"

That was how men behaved in the Tsin dynasty. From our modern point of view, the burning of the carriage and Liu Ling's abandoned ways seem rather peculiar, but they were not considered so then because the men of that time admired eccentric behaviour and philosophical talk. This philosophical talk started with the free discussion of the Han dynasty. As political life towards the end of the Han dynasty was corrupt, eminent scholars frequently discussed affairs of state. At first their views were widely influential; but later they offended the rulers and were persecuted. Men like Kung Yung and Mi Heng, for instance, were plotted against and killed by Tsao Tsao. So the scholars of the Tsin dynasty dared not discuss political affairs but talked of metaphysical subjects instead, and this became purely abstract talk. Such scholars still had a great influence, though. Moreover, a man who could not discuss metaphysics was hardly considered a scholar, and therefore *Social Talk* was looked upon almost as a textbook by the literati.

Before *Social Talk* other books had appeared like the *Forest of Sayings* and *Kuo Tzu*; but these are now lost. *Social Talk* was compiled from material dating from the Later Han to the East Tsin dynasties. Later Liu Hsiaopiao wrote a commentary for it, in which he referred to more than four hundred ancient works, most of which are also lost. This enhanced the value of the book for later generations, and it is still very well known today.

The *Forest of Jokes* by Hantan Chun of the kingdom of Wei also preceded *Social Talk*. Written in a simpler style, this book has disappeared too, though we can find quotations from it in Tang and Sung dynasty works. Here is one example:

> A man whose parents were living went to study in another district for three years. When he came back after that time his uncle asked what he had learned and observed that for long he had not seen his father. "Yes, I was more distressed than Duke Kang of Chin at Weiyang," said the youth. (Both Duke Kang's parents died.) His father reproved him, saying: "What good has your study done you?" "Unlike the son of Confucius," he replied, "in my youth I received no instruction from my father. That is why I have learned nothing."

Evidently this book consisted mainly of jokes.

The two types of writing represented by the *Forest of Jokes* and *Social Talk* did not exert an important influence because, though later writers imitated them, there was no further development of either genre. For instance, the popular collection of jokes *A Whole Forest of Jokes* is of course modelled on the *Forest of Jokes*; but whereas the bulk of the jokes in the earlier work are intellectual, those in the latter show a streak of vulgarity and are often concerned with men's appearance. This is a lower type of humour. There were even more imitations of *Social Talk*, like the *Sequel to Social Talk* by Liu Hsiao-piao, mentioned in the *Tang Dynasty History*, *Contemporary Sayings* by Wang Cho of the Ching dynasty and *New Sayings* by Yi Tsung-kuei in our own time. But as social conditions in the Tsin dynasty were completely unlike those of modern times, it is rather ridiculous to imitate that writing today. We know that between the Han dynasty and the Six Dynasties there was much fighting and social unrest. As men had a gloomy view of life, Buddhism and Taoism were popular and many escapist ideas were generally accepted. Under their influence, some men of the Tsin dynasty searched for means of becoming immortal and took drugs. Others tried to be intoxicated all the time in order to forget the troubles of this world, and drank a great deal of wine. It is known that one of the drugs commonly taken in those days consisted of five different minerals, which made men feel hot, parched and inflamed, so that they liked to wear old clothes, for new clothes chafed their skin. Because they seldom took baths most of them were lousy, and that is why they "chatted while catching lice." They also drank in a quite uninhibited manner, forgetting life and death. Those were the social conditions of that time, but since our way of life today is completely different, it would be the height of folly to try to imitate writing produced under such dissimilar circumstances.

As I have already pointed out, the scholars of the Six Dynasties did not consider their tales as fiction, for they believed those ghost stories and anecdotes. Hence the bibliographical section in the *Tang Dynasty History* does not classify writing about the supernatural as *hsiao-shuo*, but as history or biography. Not until the time of Ouyang Hsiu of the Sung dynasty was such literature considered as fiction. But anecdotes about real men were held to be more important than accounts of the supernatural, for they were closely bound up with achieving fame. If country scholars in those days wanted to become famous, they had to pay court to prominent men. In the Tsin dynasty they had to make up to statesmen like Wang Tao and Hsieh An. This is why the poet Li Po said: "Once a fish climbs past the Dragon Gate, its value increases tenfold." But to talk with such celebrities, suitable topics had to be found, and this meant reading books like *Social Talk* or the *Forest of Sayings*. Thus when Yuan Hsiu went to see Marshal Wang Yen, the marshal asked him what was the difference between the teachings of Lao Tzu and Chuang Tzu. Yuan answered: *"Chiang-wu-tung."* (Might-not-same.) This impressed the marshal, who made him an official, and he was known as the Three-Word Secretary. But what does *"chiang-wu-tung"* mean? Some interpret it as "They might not be the same," others as "Mightn't they be the same?" At all events, it was an ambiguous answer. If you wanted to learn this kind of verbal fencing, you had to read *Social Talk*.

III

THE PROSE ROMANCES OF THE TANG DYNASTY

In the Tang dynasty fiction underwent a great change. Whereas during the Six Dynasties period brief tales about real men and ghosts were recorded as facts, Tang scholars began to write fiction consciously. So this was a great step forward in the history of Chinese fiction. These stories were a good length and contained much detailed description, unlike the earlier concise anecdotes. This was therefore a great advance in writing too. But the men who wrote in the old style disapproved, and called such writing "*chuan chi*" — a name meant to be derogatory. Many of these stories are lost now, but in the *Taiping Miscellany* compiled at the beginning of the Sung dynasty we can still find some of them. (Incidentally, this book is a large collection of stories from the Six Dynasties period to the beginning of the Sung dynasty.) Wang Tu's *The Ancient Mirror*, written early in the Tang dynasty, tells about the miraculous adventures of an old mirror. Though fairly long, it consists of many strange incidents strung together, rather like the earlier tales. Then there is *The White Monkey* by an unknown author, about a general of the Liang dynasty named Ouyang Heh, who went to Changlo and penetrated into the mountains. His wife was carried off by a white monkey, but later he rescued her and she gave birth to a son who looked like a monkey. Ouyang Heh was killed by the first emperor of the Chen dynasty. His son Ouyang Hsun was prominent at the beginning of the Tang dynasty, but because he looked like a monkey his enemies made up this tale. So apparently as far back as the Tang dynasty men had started attacking each other by fictitious writing.

During the reign of Empress Wu, Chang Tsu wrote *The Fairies' Cavern* describing a journey to the northwest from Changan, during which he stopped to rest one evening at a house where he met two young women with whom he drank and amused himself. The plot is rather simple, but the tale is written in a euphuistic style not used previously for stories, and this makes it an exceptional piece of work. The Ching dynasty scholar, Chen Chiu, who wrote *A Tale of Yenshan* in the euphuistic style, though he was doing something new; but actually the innovator was Chang Tsu. *The Fairies' Cavern*, which was lost in China, can still be found in Japan. Chang Tsu enjoyed such literary fame and foreign travellers to China paid so much for his writing that it is quite conceivable that this tale was taken to Japan during his lifetime. As a matter of fact, his writing is rather flippant and not of the highest order, but he has a lively style.

Towards the middle of the eighth century the fashion changed, and there were many writers of fiction. Even those who despised short stories now started to write them. This was connected with certain developments in the civil service of that time. The candidates for the government examinations were in the habit of giving a sample of their writing to influential figures at court when first they reached the capital. If these compositions — usually their best poems — were praised, they would be highly regarded and have a better chance of passing the examinations. So this sample-writing was of great importance. The men of the later eighth century grew rather tired of poetry, and some scholars who used stories instead won fame through them. Then even those who disapproved of fiction felt constrained to write it, and short stories were all the rage. *The Story of the*

Pillow, written by Shen Chi-chi during the Ta Li era, was very widely known. The plot is briefly as follows: A man named Lu who was travelling to Hantan lamented his bad luck. Then he met an old man named Lü who gave him a pillow, and when he slept on this he dreamed that he married a girl of the Tsui family in Chingho. (As this was then a most illustrious family, such a match was a great honour.) He passed the government examinations and after repeated promotion became a minister and a censor, but other jealous officials had him demoted and banished to Tuanchow. A few years later he was appointed palace secretary with the title of Duke of Yen. Then he grew old and died after a long illness. At this point he woke up, and found that not enough time had passed to cook a pan of rice. This story was a warning against undue ambition and setting too much store by officialdom, wealth and fame. In the Ming dynasty Tang Hsien-tsu wrote *The Dream of Hantan*, and in the Ching dynasty Pu Sung-ling wrote *A Sequel to the Dream* which was included in the *Strange Tales of Liao-chai*. Both of these were based on Shen Chi-chi's story.

Another eminent writer of that time was Chen Hung, who with his friend Pai Chu-yi witnessed the rebellion of An Lu-shan during which the emperor's favourite, Lady Yang, died. They were so moved by this tragedy that Pai Chu-yi wrote *The Eternal Grief* and Chen Hung a tale to accompany this poem. His story had a great influence later, and in the Ching dynasty Hung Sheng based his drama *The Palace of Eternal Youth* on it. Pai Chu-yi's brother Pai Hsing-chien was also a famous writer. His *Story of a Singsong Girl* tells how the son of a noted Yingyang family went to the capital and led a life of dissipation. When he had spent all his money he had to earn his living as a professional mourner, helping to carry coffins and sing dirges. Later, a girl named Li rescued him and made it possible for him to study, so that he passed the examinations and became a staff officer. Pai Hsing-chien has an excellent style, and tells a moving story. This tale also exerted a considerable influence on subsequent literature, inspiring the Yuan drama *Chuchiang Pool* and the Ming drama the *Embroidered Jacket* by Hsueh Chin-yen.

The Tang scholars did not write much about the supernatural, and made it take second place. There are, of course, some collections of short ghost stories which were still influenced by earlier writings. Examples of these are *Accounts of Mysteries and Monsters* by Niu Sheng-ju, the *Yuyang Miscellany* by Tuan Cheng-shih, *More About Mysteries and Monsters* by Li Fu-yen, *Records of a Palace Chamber* by Chang Tu, the *Tuyang Miscellany* by Su Ngo, and *Strange Tales* by Pei Hsing. But these Tang dynasty tales have more elaborate plots and are better written than their Six Dynasties counterparts.

Apart from those already mentioned, two other Tang story-writers deserve special attention because they did much to shape the course of later literature. One is Yuan Chen, who wrote little but carried great weight and was well known. The other is Li Kung-tso, who wrote more and had a great influence too, but later enjoyed less fame. Now let us consider these two men separately.

Yuan Chen, or Yuan Wei-chih, was a famous poet and a contemporary of Pai Chu-yi. His only tale *The Story of Ying-ying* deals with a young man named Chang and a girl called Ying-ying and is so well known that we need not recapitulate it here. Yuan Chen's poetry and prose were greatly admired, but this story is not impressive, and at the end of it he makes Chang abandon Ying-ying, saying: "... As his virtue was not sufficient to withstand this wanton's blandishments, he had to break with her." In fact he excused Chang's heartlessness, writing a virtual essay of apology. Yet many later works were based on this story. Among them are the chantefable *The West Chamber* by a scholar named Tung in the Golden Tartar period, which was sung to an accompaniment of stringed instruments; the drama *The West Chamber* by Wang Shih-fu of the Yuan dynasty; the sequel to *The West Chamber* by Kuan Han-ching, and *The West Chamber of the Southern School* by Li Jih-hua and Lu Tsai of the Ming dynasty. Many plays were based on this story. But in these later versions the plot is slightly different: there is a happy ending to the romance. This change was made because the Chinese like a happy ending. I suppose we in China know that life is not perfect, but we do not like to admit it; for if you admit it openly, the problem arises: "How to remedy it?" Then men begin to worry and think of reforms, and that leads to trouble. As the Chinese do not like trouble and worry, readers are annoyed when a story describes the trials of life. So unhappy endings in history are generally changed into happy endings in fiction: all debts are repaid, and we deceive each other. This is one of the problems of our national character.

As for Li Kung-tso, little is known of him, and though he wrote many stories, only four are left today. *The Governor of the Southern Tributary State* is his most famous work. It tells of a man named Chunyu Fen, who had a large ash tree south of his house. One day after drinking he fell asleep in his eastern chamber, and dreamed that two men dressed in purple invited him to the Great Kingdom of Ashendon. There he married the king's daughter and served as governor of the Southern Tributary State. He did well and was promoted; but later he was defeated when he led an army against the kingdom of Sandalvine, and after his wife died he was sent home. He woke up to find that this was all a dream and that very little time had actually passed, though he seemed to have lived through a lifetime. When he went to look at the large ash tree, he found an ant-hill there and a swarm of ants, and these were the Great Kingdom of Ashendon and the Southern Tributary State. The moral of this story is much the same as that of *The Story of the Pillow*, but the excellent ending and the spell cast on the reader are far superior. Tang Hsien-tsu of the Ming dynasty based his drama *The Southern Tributary State* on this story.

Li Kung-tso's *Story of Hsieh Hsiao-ngo* tells about a girl whose father and husband, both travelling merchants, were killed by brigands. She dreamed that her father told her that his murderer's name was "Monkey in a carriage, grass at the east gate." And her husband told her that his murderer's name was "Walk among the grain, a man for a day." No one could solve this puzzle; but the writer explained that the first man was called Shen Lan, and the second Shen Chun. When the murderers were caught, this proved to be the case. Though this rather simple tale just used Chinese characters as a puzzle to catch murderers, it had a great influence on later fiction. For instance, in Li Fu-yen's *More About Mysteries and Monsters* there is a similar tale, *The Nun Called Miao-chi*. In the Ming dynasty a story on the same theme was written in the vernacular, and there were others in *The Cases of Prefect Pao*.

The third story, *Li Tang*, is about a prefect of Chuchow who heard from some fishermen that there was a great iron chain in the river at the foot of Tortoise Mountain. When he made his men pull out the chain with the help of oxen, a great storm sprang up and a monster like a monkey with white fangs and golden claws rushed up the bank, terrifying all who saw it. Then the monster disappeared again into the water with the iron chain. Li Kung-tso explained that this was the river-god Wu-chih-chi which "was stronger than nine elephants when it attacked, and could leap great heights and gallop like the wind." King Yu ordered Keng Chen to capture it, had it bound with a strong chain, and removed it to the foot of a hill at Huaiyin so that the River Huai could flow peacefully. This story also influenced much later writing. I suspect that Monkey Sun Wu-kung in the popular romance *Pilgrimage to the West* is modelled on Wu-chih-chi. However, Professor Hu Shih of Peking University says that Monkey comes from Indian mythology, and a Russian professor, Baron A. Von Staël-Holstein, also observes that there is a similar story in India. But I doubt Professor Hu Shih's theory for several reasons. First, Wu Cheng-en, the author of the Chinese romance, did not study the Buddhist canons; secondly, there is no such story in any Buddhist scripture translated into Chinese; thirdly, Wu was familiar with Tang stories, as his *Pilgrimage to the West* shows very clearly. Therefore I still believe that Monkey was derived from Wu-chih-chi. At all events, I still cannot agree with Mr. Hu Shih that Li Kung-tso was also influenced by Indian legends.

As the fourth story, *Old Woman Feng of Luchiang*, is very simple and of little literary value, we need not go into it here.

Many Tang stories were later made into dramas. This was the case with the story of the girl with a red whisk, the man with the curly beard, and the girl named Red Thread. In this way these tales became widely known and they are still very popular today. However, *chuan chi* or prose romances as a genre died out at the end of the Tang dynasty.

IV

SUNG STORIES AND THEIR INFLUENCE

I said last time that the *chuan chi* or prose romances died out at the end of the Tang dynasty, for though tales in this genre were written in the Sung dynasty they were quite different. Whereas the Tang scholars had for the most part described contemporary affairs, the Sung writers spoke mainly of the past. The Tang stories contained very little moral teaching, the Sung stories a great deal. Probably there was more freedom of speech in the Tang dynasty and writers did not get into trouble for discussing current events; but in the Sung dynasty there were more and more taboos, and in an attempt to avoid these the men of letters spoke of ancient things instead. Furthermore, because Neo-Confucianism was in such vogue during the Sung dynasty, even fiction acquired a Confucian flavour and stories without morals were thought rather worthless. But literature is not literature by virtue of its moral teaching. In fact if stories are made into textbooks for ethics, they cannot be literature. This is what I meant when I said that the *chuan chi* died out, although Sung writers did continue to produce some such stories.

The best thing the Sung scholars did was to compile the *Tai-ping Miscellany*. These five hundred volumes of fiction from the Han to the beginning of the Sung dynasty are a veritable treasure-house of stories. The scholars did not do this on their own initiative, however, but by order of the government. For at the beginning of the Sung dynasty, when the empire was united and at peace, scholars were summoned from all parts of the country, offered good salaries, and ordered to compile books. Then they produced *Choice Blossoms from the Garden of Literature, Tai-ping Imperial Encyclopaedia,* and the *Tai-ping Miscellany*. The government's aim was simply to gather the most prominent scholars together by this means, so that they would not turn against the state — it was not really interested in literature. But incidentally they left us a wealth of old stories. As far as original writing was concerned, the Sung scholars did not achieve much. But at that time another kind of story-telling arose among the people and took the place of the earlier tales. These stories were different in form as well as in language, for they used the vernacular — a tremendous change in the history of Chinese fiction. Though most of the literati of that time were interested in Neo-Confucian philosophy and despised fiction, the people still wanted their pleasure. It is therefore not strange that these popular stories appeared.

After Kaifeng became the capital, the country prospered and many different kinds of entertainment appeared. The townsfolk had a type of variety show which included story-telling. This was divided into four categories: "history," "Buddhist teaching for laymen," "story-telling," and skits or puns called *ho-sheng*. The "history" meant narrating episodes from history or the lives of famous men, and this later developed into historical romances. The "Buddhist teaching" was done in the vernacular too. The "story-telling" generally consisted of short tales. The *ho-sheng* usually started with an ambiguous couplet, after which a few more verses explained the meaning, and they were often satire against contemporary figures. Of these four categories, only the narrating of history and the story-telling had any bearing on the subsequent development of Chinese fiction. The professional story-tellers had their own organizations which were known as "Orators' Clubs." They also had certain prompt-books to help them, which were called *hua pen* (story-texts). At the beginning of the Southern Sung dynasty such prompt-books were still popular; but when the Sung dynasty fell and the Mongols conquered China these variety shows declined and most prompt-books were lost. Though there were still story-tellers during the Ming dynasty, some of them as well known as Liu Ching-ting, they were no longer the same. They were not attached to variety shows and had no organizations of their own. So now we know very little about the story-tellers of the Sung dynasty and their prompt-books. Luckily a few reprints have recently been made which serve as specimens.

One of these is *Popular Tales of the Five Dynasties*. This is a historical narrative, a type of recital which usually starts with the beginning of history and goes down to the period concerned. It begins with a verse, then follows the account itself, and it concludes with more verse. It is divided into sections, which are split up by verses. Unfortunately there is too much empty talk and too little on history itself. To my mind, the use of the verse shows the influence of the Tang dynasty, for the Tang people had great respect for versification, and writing poetry was considered cultured. In imitation of this, the story-tellers usually interspersed their stories with verses, and indeed this is still done by many present-day novelists. Another feature of the later historical romances is that each chapter usually ends with the same phrase: "If you want to know what happened afterwards, you will find the answer in the next chapter." I think this fashion also started with the story-tellers, because if they wanted the customers to come again it was necessary to leave some dramatic episode half-told in order to hold their interest. As for the fact that this is still done by modern novelists, that is just an anachronism like the human appendix — it serves no purpose today.

The other reprint is the *Popular Stories of the Capital*. This text is incomplete, only about ten stories being left. These *hsiao-shuo* are not novels. Very short, they often deal with contemporary affairs. They start with a sort of introduction, a long verse or an anecdote, which was called the "Triumphant Beginning" (*teh-sheng-tou-huei*) and was by way of a preamble to invoke good luck. The story itself follows, but this is hardly longer than the introduction, and could be told fairly quickly. So the Sung dynasty *hsiao-shuo* were actually short stories. And though the *Popular Stories of the Capital* is incomplete, from it we can see what these stories were like.

In addition to these two works, we have *Tales of the Hsuan Ho Period*. This story starts and ends with verses, and is interspersed with them like the historical narratives, though it is not in the vernacular. It also resembles the story-tellers' prompt-books in some respects, though not so short and concise. Since it tells of the outlaws of Liangshan, it is a precursor of the novel *Shui Hu Chuan*, a fact worth noting. Another recently discovered text is *Tripitaka's Search for Buddhist Sutras*, a chantefable. Long lost in China, this work came to light in Japan. This kind of chantefable is also a form of fiction punctuated by verses. Though it is a forerunner of the *Pilgrimage to the West*, the story is slightly different. For instance, in the chapter of the novel, "Stealing the Fruit of Immortality," Monkey wants to steal the fruit but the monk will not let him. In this early version the fruit is a fairy peach, and Tripitaka orders Monkey to steal it. This shows not so much a difference in age as a difference in the writers' ideas. For the author of the novel was a scholarly gentleman, while the writer of this chantefable was a common townsman. As the strict scholar felt a monk should not steal fruit, he put the blame on Monkey. The townsman was not so strict and did not mind if the monk stole a few fairy peaches; he came out with the facts quite bluntly, not troubling to hide them.

In short, the influence of these Sung story-tellers was very great, for most later fiction was based on their work. Certain stories of later ages like those in *Strange Tales New and Old* were modelled on them, while some long romances like the *Romance of the Three Kingdoms* were based on Sung historical narratives. This second category was the more influential, and ever since the Ming dynasty the history of earlier times has all been told in romances.

A famous writer of historical romances was Lo Kuan-chung, or Lo Pen. He was a native of Hangchow, who probably lived at the end of the Yuan and the beginning of the Ming dynasty. He wrote a number of novels, but unfortunately only four of them are left, and these have been so much changed by later editors that they are no longer authentic. (I suppose it is because the Chinese have always considered works of fiction trivial, unlike the Confucian classics, that they cannot resist making alterations.) Of Lo Kuan-chung's life we know nothing. Some say that because he wrote *Shui Hu Chuan* for three generations his descendants were deaf and dumb, but of course this is pure slander. His four works are: *The Romance of the Three Kingdoms, Shui Hu Chuan, Romance of the Sui and Tang History* and *The Sorcerer's Revolt and Its Suppression by the Three Suis*. The last novel describes how Wang Tse, a citizen of Peichow, started a rebellion by magic means but was finally vanquished by three men, all of whom had the character *"sui"* in their names. So the complete title is *The Sorcerer's Revolt and Its Suppression by the Three Suis*. The *Romance of the Sui and Tang History* relates historical incidents from the Sui dynasty to the reign of Emperor Ming Huang of the Tang dynasty. As neither the plot nor language of either these romances is outstanding, they are not very popular. The most widely read and influential works are the *Romance of the Three Kingdoms* and *Shui Hu Chuan*.

I. The *Romance of the Three Kingdoms*. Lo Kuanchung was not the first to tell the story of the Three Kingdoms. In the Sung dynasty some village storytellers specialized in tales about the Three Kingdoms period, and it was about this time that Su Tung-po wrote: "Wang Peng used to describe to me how children in the streets . . . would sit down to listen to old stories, including ones about the Three Kingdoms. When they heard of Liu Pei's defeat, they would fret and even shed tears. When they heard of Tsao Tsao's defeat, they would brighten up and applaud. This shows that even after a hundred generations good and bad men leave their mark." From this account we know that before Lo Kuan-chung's time there were already stories like that of the *Romance of the Three Kingdoms*. This is because the history of that period was not so confused as that of the Five Dynasties, nor so simple as that of the war between Chu and Han. It was exactly right for the subject of a romance. Besides, the heroes of that day were clever and brave and had most dramatic adventures; so men liked to use them as material for romances. Pei Sung-chih's very detailed commentary on the *History of the Three Kingdoms* also helped to interest readers in that period. Of course we cannot leap to hasty conclusions on the question of whether this romance was Lo Kuan-chung's own work or an adaptation from some earlier tale. In the Chia Ching edition of the novel we find this statement: "Lo Pen of the Ming dynasty compiled this romance from material in the history by Chen Shou, Marquis of Pingyang, of the Tsin dynasty." So it seems to have been based directly on the *History of the Three Kingdoms*. The romance as we know it today, however, has been altered so many times by later writers that it must be very different from the original. Critics think it has the following three defects:

(1) It is easy to mistake it for actual history. About seven-tenths of the episodes described are true, and three-tenths fictitious. Since there is more fact than fiction, it is easy for readers to believe the fictitious parts are real. For example, Wang Yu-yang, a well-known poet and scholar of the seventeenth century, wrote a poem

called "Lamenting Pang Tung at Phoenix-Falling Slope." Phoenix-Falling Slope appears only in the novel and has no basis in fact, yet Wang took it to be a real place.

(2) The characters are too black and white. A good character is described with no faults, while a bad man has no good qualities at all. Actually this is not true to life, for a man cannot be entirely good or entirely bad. Thus Tsao Tsao, from the political standpoint, has his virtues; while Liu Pei and Kuan Yu cannot be said to have had no shortcomings. But as the author did not trouble about this and made subjective judgements, his characters often appear unnatural.

(3) The finished result is not what the writer intended. In other words, what Lo Kuan-chung actually expressed is not what he imagined. For instance, he wanted to show Tsao Tsao's craftiness, but instead he gives us a picture of Tsao Tsao's wisdom and chivalry. He wanted to bring out Chuke Liang's wisdom, but the impression made is more one of craftiness. There is also some fine characterization, however, as in the dramatic and colourful passages which describe how Kuan Yu killed General Hua Hsiung and how he let Tsao Tsao escape on the Huajung Path — here he gives a lifelike picture of courage and justice. Many historical romances were written later, on the origin of the world, on the Han, Tsin, Tang, Sung and Ching dynasties; but none of these can compare with the *Romance of the Three Kingdoms*. Everyone likes this book, and it will remain highly valued in future too.

II. *Shui Hu Chuan*. This novel deals with the adventures of Sung Chiang and others. Lo Kuan-chung was not the first to tell this story either, for Sung Chiang was a historical figure, an outlaw whose exploits had been popular legends since the Southern Sung dynasty. During the Sung and Yuan dynasties, Kao Ju, Li Sung and others wrote about him. After the fall of the Sung dynasty Kung Sheng-yu wrote in praise of the thirty-six men headed by Sung Chiang. In the *Tales of the Hsuan Ho Period* it was already recorded that Sung Chiang captured the outlaw Fang La and was made a military governor. Thus such legends were already widespread, and some simple texts probably existed. Lo Kuan-chung collected the different versions of this story and rewrote them into a long novel. The original book is now lost, however, and we are left with two popular editions, one with seventy chapters only, the other with more. The latter starts with a Marshal Hung who accidentally let loose some evil spirits; then a hundred and eight men gathered at Liangshan and attacked landlords in the vicinity. Later they surrendered to the government and achieved great deeds by defeating the Khitans, putting down the rebellion of Tien Hu and Wang Ching, and capturing Fang La. But as the government did not trust them, Sung Chiang finally took poison and died, after which he became a god. This story of Sung Chiang's surrender reflects the ideas at the end of the Sung dynasty, when the country was in a turmoil and government troops were riding roughshod over the people. Those who kept the peace had to bear a heavy yoke, while those who were not so submissive were driven to revolt. The outlaws fought and defeated the government troops, and preyed on the people too. But when foreign troops attacked and the government was unable to resist, the people preferred to fight the invaders with the outlaws, who were stronger than the government forces. Thus outlaws became popular heroes. The account of

Sung Chiang's death by poison was added at the beginning of the Ming dynasty. After the first emperor of Ming united the country, he was suspicious of his supporters and had many of them killed. Few of his followers died a natural death. Since the people sympathized with these men, they made up this story of Sung Chiang's death and deification. This was the old tradition of Chinese fiction — change a sad ending into a happy one.

Shih Nai-an is often spoken of as the author of *Shui Hu Chuan*, because there were two editions with more than seventy chapters, and the one which contains additional episodes bears his name. In my opinion, however, Shih Nai-an may have lived after Lo Kuan-chung and written the longer version. When later readers saw his name to this, they assumed that the shorter version was an abridged text and that Shih had lived earlier than Lo. Chin Sheng-tan at the beginning of the Ching dynasty said that this novel was good down to the surrender of the outlaws, after which it deteriorated. He claimed to have found an old text which proved that the first part was written by Shih Nai-an, and the end added by Lo Kuan-chung. As he condemned the latter part he cut it out, leaving only the first seventy chapters — the popular edition which we have today. I doubt, however, whether he had any earlier version, and suspect that he made the abridgement to suit himself, justifying himself by this talk of an older text. It is true that there are certain discrepancies in the text, as he pointed out. Still, we have already noted that this novel was written by combining many legends and short accounts. Naturally it could not be consistent throughout. Besides, what happened to the rebels after their success would be more difficult to describe than their life as outlaws, and it is quite common for a long novel to have a weak ending. One cannot use this as evidence to prove that the end was added by Lo Kuan-chung. As for Chin Sheng-tan's reasons for cutting the latter part, I fancy they were due to the social conditions of his time. Mr. Hu Shih has said: "Chin Sheng-tan lived during an age when bandits were rising everywhere. He witnessed the depredations of brigands like Chang Hsien-chung and Li Tzu-cheng, and felt they should not be encouraged but condemned in literature." Because Chin Sheng-tan was unwilling to rely on outlaws to repel foreign invaders, he did not like the legend of Sung Chiang's valour.

After the fall of the Ming dynasty, however, when the foreign invaders became masters, those loyal to the fallen dynasty mourned in secret and forgot the sufferings caused by the outlaws, feeling a new sympathy for them. For instance, one such scholar, Chen Chen, under the pen-name of "Woodcutter in Yentang Mountain" wrote a sequel to the novel. In this he made the outlaws who survived Sung Chiang fight against the Golden Tartars. When they were defeated, Li Tsun took them across the sea and became king of Siam. This shows that Chen's sympathy for the outlaws was due to the conquest of China by foreign foes. Later, when circumstances changed again and men forgot their patriotism, during the Tao Kuang era Yu Wan-chun wrote another sequel to the novel, in which all the outlaws, including Sung Chiang, were wiped out by government troops. His style is spirited and he paints a vivid picture, but his ideas are rather depressing.

V

THE TWO MAIN TRENDS IN MING NOVELS

Though the Yuan dynasty was a splendid age for drama, there was little written in the way of fiction; we shall therefore pass on to the novels of the Ming dynasty. In the middle of this dynasty, during the first half of the sixteenth century, a number of novels appeared. These show two main trends: they deal either with wars between gods and demons, or else with human affairs. Let us examine them one by one.

Clashes between gods and demons became a common topic owing to the influence of religion and alchemy at that time. During the Hsuan Ho era of the Sung dynasty there was much Taoist worship; in the Yuan dynasty both Buddhism and Taoism flourished and alchemists were highly influential. In the Ming dynasty these religions began to lose ground, but during the Cheng Hua era they gained strength again and we read of the celebrated alchemist Li Tzu and the Buddhist monk Chi Hsiao, while in the Cheng Teh era there was the foreign priest Yu Yung. As all these men became officials, thanks to their religion or magic arts, there was an upsurge of superstition, the influence of which can be seen in literature. Through the ages the struggle between the three main religions of China — Confucianism, Taoism and Buddhism — has never been resolved. In general, however, they compromised and tolerated each other, until finally they were considered to stem from "one origin." When a new religion arose, it was regarded as heterodox and there would be arguments. But once it was looked upon as coming from the same origin, all persecution ceased. Not till the next new school appeared would those who prided themselves on being orthodox attack the unorthodox heretics again. Religious conceptions were very vague, and what was described as orthodox or unorthodox in fiction did not mean Confucianism versus Buddhism, Taoism versus Buddhism, or Confucianism, Taoism and Buddhism versus the White Lotus Cult. It simply meant a struggle between two beliefs not clearly defined. So I give it the general description of story about gods and demons. Let us take three novels to illustrate this trend: The *Pilgrimage to the West,* the *Canonization of the Gods* and the *Expedition to the Western Ocean.*

I. The *Pilgrimage to the West.* For a long time this book was wrongly attributed to a Yuan dynasty priest, Chiu Chu-chi; but Chiu's *Pilgrimage to the West* in three volumes is a travel account which can still be found in collections of Taoist canons. This confusion arose because the two books have the same name, and the novel was printed at the beginning of the Ching dynasty with the preface of Chiu Chu-chi's book. In fact the author of the novel was Wu Cheng-en of Shanyang County, Kiangsu. This was stated in the *Records of Huainan Prefecture* compiled in the Ming dynasty, but the Ching dynasty edition of these records omitted this fact. The novel as we have it now consists of a hundred chapters. First it tells how Monkey Sun Wu-kung reached sainthood, why the monk Tripitaka set out to look for Buddhist canons, how they passed through eighty-one perils and finally returned to China. This novel was not entirely Wu's creation, for earlier we have referred to the chantefable dealing with Tripitaka's search for Buddhist canons, which already contained such characters as Monkey and the river-god and accounts of various strange incidents. Some Yuan dynasty dramas also used material from this story, and in the early Ming dynasty there was another brief version of it. From this we can see that the story of Tripitaka's journey to the west in search of Buddhist canons grew by degrees into a legend between the end of the Tang and the Yuan dynasties, and was often written in simple story form. In the Ming dynasty, Wu Cheng-en gathered these legends together and wrote this long novel. Wu Cheng-en was an adept at humorous sketches, and he made the monsters in this story so human that everyone enjoys reading about them. This is his art. He also makes readers accept the story lightheartedly instead of feeling overjoyed or wretched, as they do when reading the *Romance of the Three Kingdoms* about the victories and defeats of Liu Pei. For in this novel all the characters are monsters, the entire thing is amusing, and no personal feelings obtrude to mar our enjoyment. That is another virtue of the book. As for the purpose of the novel, some say it is meant to encourage men to study, others that it is Buddhist, yet others that it is Taoist. There are many views on the subject, but to my mind the book was written solely to give pleasure. Because the author was influenced by China's three religions, he put in a little of them all: Buddha, Kuanyin, the Taoist supreme deity, Nature and so on and so forth. Thus Confucians, Buddhists or Taoists could read what they wanted into it. If we insist that the novel has a moral, the explanation given by the Ming dynasty scholar Hsieh Chao-chih is quite adequate: "Monkey represents the mind, and Pigsy the will. At first Monkey ran wild, ascending to heaven or descending to the earth just as he pleased. Then one incantation controlled him, and made him obedient and steadfast. This is simply a parable of the control of the mind." Later there were several sequels to this novel, but they were merely imitations. Tung Yueh's *More About the Pilgrimage* is really a satire, belonging to a different genre.

II. The *Canonization of the Gods* is another popular novel. Nothing is known of its author. Some say that he was a poor man, who wrote this book to provide his daughter with a dowry; but this story has no foundation. The ideas in the book seem to be vaguely influenced by the concept of three religions arising from one origin. According to the novel, Chou-hsin, the last king of the Shang dynasty, went to sacrifice to the goddess Nu-kua and wrote a poem which offended her. The goddess sent three vampires to lead him astray, and helped the Chous to overthrow him. There were many battles between gods and Buddhist saints. On the Chou side were the orthodox deities, while the Shangs were helped by the unorthodox ones. At all events, this book reveals the combined influence of the three religions, which represent the side of the gods, opposed to whom are the demons.

III. The *Expedition to the Western Ocean.* This novel, written during the Wan Li era, is seldom seen nowadays. It tells how the eunuch Cheng Ho led an expedition to the western ocean during the Yung Lo era and pacified thirty-nine foreign states, making them send tribute to China. According to the story, a monk named Pi Feng helped Cheng Ho to transport his expedition across the ocean and conquer other countries by means of magic art, so that he returned in triumph. This story belongs to the same category, for though it deals with wars between different states, China stands for orthodoxy and the gods, while the foreign lands stand for heresy and the demons. And this novel reflects something of the political situation of the time. Because Cheng Ho had great fame in the Ming dynasty and was a legendary figure, after the Chia Ching era, when Japanese pirates pillaged China's southeast coast and the empire was weak, the people naturally remembered the good old days. That is why this novel was written. A eunuch was made the hero instead of a general and magic relied on instead of military strength owing to the influence of traditional thought, and because eunuchs in the Ming dynasty often controlled the army and had great authority. This idea of defeating foreigners with magic was handed down to the Ching dynasty, and widely believed in. Indeed, the Yi Ho Tuan (Boxers) made such an experiment.

The second type of novel, which dealt with human affairs, was also written during the heyday of the novels describing wars between gods and demons. These books also grew out of the social conditions of the time, and some of them, like the first type, were closely connected with the ideas of the alchemists. Such books usually describe love and wanton lust, and in the episodes depicting happy encounters and sad partings considerable psychological insight is revealed. The most famous book of this kind is *Chin Ping Mei*. Hsimen Ching, a character who appeared in *Shui Hu Chuan*, is the hero, and the novel describes his adventures. This man had one wife and three concubines. Then he fell in love with Pan Chin-lien or Golden Lotus, poisoned her husband Wu the Elder, and made her his concubine. Next he had an affair with her maid, Chun-mei (Spring Plum), and another affair with a woman named Ping-erh (Vase), whom he made his concubine too. Then Ping-erh and Hsimen Ching died, Golden Lotus was killed by her first husband's brother Wu Sung, and Spring Plum died after excessive debauchery. When the Golden Tartars invaded Chingho, Hsimen's wife took his son to Tsinan. A monk meeting them on the way escorted them to Yungfu Monastery and converted the boy, who joined the order and took the name of Ming Wu. Because Chin-lien, Ping-erh and Chun-mei were the chief characters in the book, it was called *Chin Ping Mei (Gold-Vase-Plum)*. Most Ming pornographic novels were aimed at contemporary figures, for this was the writers' way of working off a grudge. So Hsimen Ching was probably a man whom the author hated, but we have no means of identifying him. We do not even know who the author was. Some say that Wang Shih-chen wrote this book to avenge his father, Wang Yu, who was killed by Yen Sung. Yen Sung's son Yen Shih-fan was all-powerful and suppressed all memorials to the throne which might injure his father. Wang Shih-chen is supposed to have found out that Yen Shih-fan was fond of novels, and to have written this so that he would forget all business while reading it; for then criticisms of Yen Sung could reach the court. That is why the early Ching editions had as preface an essay on filial piety. But this is simply a legend. The novel was attributed to Wang Shih-chen because it is well written and he was the foremost scholar of his day. Later editors adopted this view and inserted the essay on filial piety in order to forestall criticism of the pornographic nature of the book. There is no real evidence of the author's identity.

Another novel, more pornographic than *Chin Ping Mei*, was *Yu Chiao Li (Jade-Charming-Prune)*. This was lost, however, by the beginning of the Ching dynasty, and what we have today is not the original. A sequel to *Chin Ping Mei* by Ting Yao-kang of Chucheng County, Shantung, is different from the earlier book. It preaches transmigration, aiming to show that evil will be repaid in the next life. The story describes how in a later existence Wu the Elder becomes the amorous lover, while Golden Lotus becomes insatiable in lust and is killed in the end. Hsimen Ching becomes a fool and a cuckold, who lets his wife and concubines have lovers. All later such novels contained sermons. Stories like this about what happened to people in their different existences might go on for generations and never end. This is a strange and interesting phenomenon, but there were similar tales in ancient India, the *Angulimalya Sutra* being one example.

We see, then, that stories about human affairs could turn into moral talk about retribution. There was another kind: the "ladies and gentlemen" type. Examples of this are *Ping Shan Leng Yen, Hao Chiu Chuan* and *Yu-Chiao-Li (Jade-Charming-Pear)*. These titles are usually made up of names of different characters in the book, as in the case of *Chin Ping Mei*. Stories of this type deal not with amorous lovers and wanton women, but with talented young scholars and beautiful young ladies. The "talented" scholars can usually write poetry, which generally serves to bring the young people together. This seems counter to tradition and the idea that matches should be arranged by go-betweens according to the wishes of the parents. But as the final union usually takes place at the command of the emperor, the authors find a higher authority for this licence. None of these novels are well written, but some of them are well known abroad; for *Yu-Chiao-Li* and *Ping Shan Leng Yen* were translated into French, and *Hao Chiu Chuan* into both French and German. Thus all foreign students of Chinese literature know them, and include them in their histories of Chinese literature. Another reason is that in countries where monogamy is the rule, if several girls fall in love with one man there will be trouble; but in these novels it does not matter — they can all get married. From the Western point of view, this is most exotic and interesting.

VI

FOUR SCHOOLS OF FICTION IN THE CHING DYNASTY AND THEIR LATER DEVELOPMENT

We find more variety and greater changes in the Ching dynasty than in the Ming dynasty fiction; but since time is short I shall simply deal with it very briefly, dividing it into four schools: "classical," satirical, romantic and adventurous.

I. By "classical" I mean works modelled on the tales of the Six Dynasties or the Tang dynasty. As nearly all the Tang stories not in the large collections had been lost by the Ming dynasty, the occasional imitations appeared as great novelties. At the beginning of the Ming dynasty, a Hangchow scholar named Chu Yu wrote a number of pseudo-Tang stories entitled *New Tales Under the Lamplight*. Thanks to his erotic descriptions, these tales were popular though poorly written. He had many imitators until the government prohibited this type of writing and the fashion changed. But towards the middle of the sixteenth century the Tang stories became popular again and there were more imitations. Indeed most scholars wrote a few stories of this sort. The most famous collection is *Strange Tales of Liao-chai* by Pu Sung-ling, a native of Chihchuan in Shantung. It is said that before writing this book he had tea and tobacco ready at his gate every day, and asked passers-by to stop and tell him stories as material for his book. Most of these tales, however, he heard from friends or adapted from ancient books, especially from Tang stories like *The Scholar of Fengyang* and *A Sequel to the Dream*. That is why I place this book among the imitations of classical tales. Most of his stories are about spirits, fox-fairies, ghosts and other supernatural beings, like many other tales written in that period. Their superiority lies in the detailed descriptions, dramatic developments, fluent language, and the fact that the supernatural beings are depicted like men with a deep knowledge of the world, which makes them charming instead of frightening. The defect is that the author uses so many classical allusions that ordinary readers find the language rather difficult.

The *Strange Tales of Liao-chai* enjoyed tremendous popularity for a whole century, and were much praised and imitated. But towards the end of Chien Lung's reign a scholar named Chi Yun of Hsien County, Chihli, pointed out that this book had two serious faults. In the first place, he said, the language was too mixed. He objected to finding a medley of different styles in one book; some of the longer tales were imitations of Tang stories, while some of the shorter ones were modelled on the writing of the Six Dynasties. In the second place, there were too many detailed descriptions. Most of these stories were told in the third person, but there were a number of details which only the individual concerned could know, and many of which he would not disclose. How, then, could the author know them?

In order to avoid these shortcomings, Chi Yun modelled his *Notes of the Yueh-wei Hermitage* entirely on Six Dynasties tales. His plots were simple, his language concise and classical, unlike the Tang style. He made up most of his stories himself, using fox-fairies and ghosts to criticize the society of his time. To my mind, he did not believe in the supernatural but felt this was the best way to educate ignorant people. There is something very admirable about this man, who lived under the repressive rule of Chien Lung yet dared to write, attacking ridiculous conventions and social customs. He had great courage. His imitators, however, did not realize that his purpose was to criticize social conventions, and they simply aped his moralizing vein, until books of this type became virtually sermons.

Later imitators of classical tales took these two books as models. Even today in Shanghai, for instance, some so-called scholars are copying their styles. But far from achieving anything good, they have merely preserved the dregs. In fact, this school of fiction has been trampled to death by these disciples.

II. Satirical stories were written even before the Tang dynasty, and many of the Ming novels about human affairs were satires. In the Ching dynasty, however, we find very few satirical novels. The most famous and practically the only one is *The Scholars* by Wu Ching-tzu of Chuanchiao, Anhwei. As this author had a rich experience of life and was skilled in expressing his ideas, the different characters he draws are extremely lifelike. He portrays all sorts of scholars, including many strange types, in considerable detail. This novel was written within a century of the fall of the Ming dynasty, when the literati still retained some of the old characteristics: they studied nothing but the examination essays, and were good for nothing else. As a scholar himself who was familiar with this group, Wu could give very detailed exposures of their ludicrous ways. Though this novel is made up of different episodes which are not sufficiently well integrated, it offers us infinite variety and holds our interest. So it is the best satirical novel in China.

At the end of the Ching dynasty, when China was at the mercy of foreign powers, men wanted to find out why the country was declining. Novelists, too, tried to discover the reason. Li Pao-chia blamed bureaucracy, and under the pen-name of Nan-ting-ting-chang wrote his *Exposure of the Official World*. This novel was very popular at the time, but as literature it is much inferior to *The Scholars*. Besides, as the author was not too well-acquainted with the official world, certain passages are not entirely realistic. After him Wu Wo-yao of Nanhai, Kwangtung, laid the blame for China's decline on the disappearance of the traditional morality. Using the pen-name Wo-fo-shan-jen, he wrote *Strange Events of the Last Twenty Years*. Though this book also enjoyed great popularity, his descriptions of social evils are often exaggerated and superficial, for he wrote to give vent to his own indignation. He shared the faults of Li Pao-chia. Both these novels consist of separate episodes with no strong connecting thread or chief characters. In this sense they resemble *The Scholars,* but as writing they rank far below it. The most obvious difference is that *The Scholars* is a genuine satire, while these two books approach downright abuse.

Innuendo and subtlety are essential in satirical writing. If the author exaggerates or puts the case too bluntly, his work loses its literary value. But later novelists did not pay enough attention to this, with the result that after *The Scholars* we can say there was no real satire.

III. Romance. This type of fiction is best represented by the famous *Dream of the Red Chamber* or *Hung Lou Meng*. This novel was first entitled *Tale of a Rock*, had eighty chapters, and appeared in Peking during the reign of Chien Lung. The first copies were all handwritten. In 1792 the first printed edition was published by Cheng Wei-yuan with an additional forty chapters, making a hundred and twenty in all, and the name was changed to the *Dream of the Red Chamber*. According to Cheng, he collected various manuscripts from different families and street-vendors to obtain the complete novel. The early copies are hard to find today. A lithographic print exists, but we do not know whether it was made from the original or not. The novel is about the Chia family in Shihtou City, which may or may not be Nanking. Chia Cheng has a son named Pao-yu, who is very intelligent and fond of female company. There are many beautiful women in the household: the ladies and servants of the house, numerous relatives, and young guests like Black Jade and Precious Clasp; another girl, River Mist, also often visits them. Pao-yu loves Black Jade best, but his father chooses Precious Clasp to be his wife. When Black Jade hears of this she coughs blood and dies, and Pao-yu falls ill of unhappiness. Later, Chia Cheng's brother is demoted, his property is confiscated, and Chia Cheng is involved. So the family fortunes decline. Pao-yu becomes deranged for a time, then recovers and passes the government examination; but soon after that he disappears. When Chia Cheng passes Piling to bury his mother, a man with a shaved head and bare feet bows to him, and he recognizes Pao-yu. Before he can talk to his son, however, a Buddhist monk and a Taoist priest take the youth away, and he is left alone in the wild country.

We know that the author of this book is Tsao Hsueh-chin, for his name appears in the novel; but we have little information about him. Thanks to Professor Hu Shih's researches, some material is now available. Tsao Hsueh-chin was otherwise known as Tsao Chan or Tsao Chin-pu. Some of his ancestors served in the Manchu army. His grandfather, Tsao Yin, was in charge of the Silk Bureau in Nanking during the reign of Kang Hsi, and when the emperor travelled south he put up in this bureau. The author's father, Tsao Fu, held the same post. We know, then, that the novelist came from a wealthy family, was born in Nanking, and went to Peking at the age of ten with his father. Then for some reason the family suffered such a reversal that in his thirties he was reduced to living in the west suburb of Peking, not always with enough to eat. Still he continued to amuse himself with poetry and wine, and during this period he wrote the *Dream of the Red Chamber.* Unfortunately his son died young, and he himself died of grief in his early forties, having written eighty chapters only of his novel. Though Cheng Wei-yuan claimed to have compiled his edition of a hundred and twenty chapters from various manuscripts, it was actually completed by his friend Kao Ngo.

There has been much speculation about the purpose of this novel. Here are some of the chief theories.

(1) Some think this book refers to the Manchu poet, Nalan Hsing-teh, and the twelve beautiful girls in the

novel stand for his friends. For Nalan Hsing-teh was a poet who passed the government examination at an early age, whose family property was later confiscated. He therefore had much in common with Pao-yu. But the Chia property was confiscated during Pao-yu's lifetime, while in Nalan's case it was after his death. There are many other discrepancies, and not actually much similarity.

(2) Another theory is that the novel tells the story of Emperor Shun Chih and his concubine Tung. According to one tradition, Tung Hsiao-wan, a famous Nanking courtesan, was captured by the Manchu forces when they went south, and taken to Peking. She became the emperor's favourite and was made an imperial concubine; and at her death the emperor was so overcome with grief that he went to Wutai Mountain and became a monk. As Pao-yu also becomes a monk in the end, this might refer to the emperor's romance. But we know that the imperial concubine Tung was a Manchu girl, not the famous courtesan; and when the Manchus took the Yangtse Valley, Tung Hsiao-wan was twenty-eight while Emperor Shun Chih was only fourteen. As he could not have made her his concubine, that disposes of this theory.

(3) Another hypothesis is that this was a political allegory about Kang Hsi's reign, to lament the fall of the Ming dynasty and expose the corruption of Manchu rule. For example, the word *"hung"* (red) in *Hung Lou Meng* was a substitute for *"chu"* (red). Shihtou City meant Nanking. The name *"Chia"* means "false," and this was an attack on the Manchu regime. The twelve beautiful women in the novel represented the famous scholars who surrendered to the Manchus. This theory is too fantastic to be tenable. Besides, as we now know that the author's family joined the Manchu side from the start,

it is unlikely that he would regret the fall of the Ming dynasty.

(4) Others believe that the work is based on the author's own life. This was the earliest theory to be put forward, but it found little support in the past. Recently, however, more and more people are coming round to this view, for what we have now learned of the author's life seems to fit the incidents in the novel very well. His grandfather and father were in charge of the Silk Bureau in Nanking, and the family was a very wealthy one — like the Chia household in the book. Tsao Hsueh-chin in his youth was handsome and intelligent, rather like Pao-yu. And his family fortunes suddenly declined — their property may have been confiscated. So it does seem likely that the *Dream of the Red Chamber* is largely autobiographical.

As for the novel itself, it is one of the gems of Chinese literature. The author's greatest virtue is that he dares to describe life realistically without subterfuge or concealment, unlike earlier writers who made their characters either black or white. Hence all the people in this book are real. The most significant thing about this work is that it put an end to the traditional view of novels and how to write them, the beauty of the language is only of secondary importance. It has many opponents, though, who think it a bad influence for the young. This is because when the Chinese read a book they cannot enjoy it as a work of art, but must identify themselves with the characters in it. Boys and girls imagine they are Pao-yu or Black Jade, while their elders put themselves in the place of Chia Cheng, who has to control his son. Such limited views prevent them from seeing any more in the novel.

Many sequels were written to this novel, all designed to continue the love story and give it a happy ending. This went on till the Tao Kuang era (1821-1850), when readers tired of the subject. But as love stories set in ordinary families could not introduce so many attractive girls and romantic incidents, novelists started writing in the style of the *Dream of the Red Chamber* about actors and prostitutes; and so this type of novel underwent a change. Let us consider the two novels: The *Dream of the Green Chamber* and *A Mirror of Theatrical Life*. The latter is about actors in Peking after Chien Lung's reign. Though the characters have a very different social status from those in the *Dream of the Red Chamber*, they are all most romantic too, and the young actors and their lovers or patrons are described in the same way as the earlier scholars and young ladies. The *Dream of the Green Chamber* is a rather idealized story about prostitutes, which fails to carry conviction. The writer felt that singsong girls were the only people who could truly appreciate scholars, and after certain adventures a happy ending was reached. This was like the "scholar and beautiful girl" type of writing at the end of the Ming dynasty. Towards the middle of Kuang Hsu's reign (1875-1908), *Lives of Shanghai Singsong Girls* appeared. The girls in this book are not so idealized as those in the *Dream of the Green Chamber*. Some are good and some are bad, which is more realistic. At the end of the nineteenth century novels like *The Nine-Tailed Tortoise* were written. These are different again, as all the prostitutes are bad characters and all their patrons are rogues. So there have been three approaches to prostitutes: first there was undue praise, then a more realistic attitude was adopted, and finally the writers became hypercritical, using deliberate exaggeration and abuse, which sometimes amounted to slander and blackmail. It really is amazing how this type of novel evolved.

IV. Adventure. An example of this type of novel is *Three Heroes and Five Gallants*. A scholar heard this tale from some story-teller in a tea-house, and wrote it down; then it became well known. I suppose readers were tired of novels like the *Dream of the Red Chamber* which concentrated on love, or the *Pilgrimage to the West* which dealt entirely with supernatural beings. This novel about swordsmen and adventurers struck a fresh note, and therefore had immediate popularity. Pan Tsu-yin took the book from Peking to Soochow to show it to Yu Chu-yuan, who was greatly taken with it. But as he felt it was unhistorical, he rewrote the first chapter. And because there were really four chief characters — the Southern Hero, the Northern Hero and the Twin Heroes — the title *Three Heroes* was inaccurate. Accordingly he added two characters, Ai Hu and Shen Chung-yuan, and changed the title to *Seven Heroes and Five Gallants*. This revised edition is popular today south of the Yangtse. But this novel was not made up by one story-teller. Pao Cheng, the Sung dynasty prefect, was a strict and just official whose life is recorded in the *Sung Dynasty History*. Many legends about his miraculous adventures were popular in the Yuan dynasty and were written up as stories in the Ming dynasty to form the collection *The Cases of Prefect Pao*. Then further improvements were made in the plot and a big book was written, on which *Three Heroes and Five Gallants* was based. After this novel proved such a success, many similar books appeared: *Five Younger Gallants, A Sequel to Five Younger Gallants, Eight Elder Gallants, Eight Junior Gallants, Seven Swordsmen and Thirteen Gallants, Seven Swordsmen and Eighteen Gallants*. Most of these novels dealt with swordsmen and adventurers who killed bandits and rebels and were usually under the command of high officials. *The Cases of Lord Shih* and *The Cases of Lord Peng* were both widely read. The heroes of these books are for the most part adventurers, rather like the characters in *Shui Hu Chuan*. So though these stories developed from *The Cases of Prefect Pao*, we can also trace their origin back to the great classic. But the heroes in *Shui Hu Chuan* were rebels, while the characters in these books help the government. Presumably this big divergence in outlook was caused by different social conditions. For most of these books were written in the 1870s and '80s after several wars in China. The Taiping Rebellion had been suppressed; so had the Nien Rebellion and the rebellions of various religious sects. Many rough country fellows and rogues had joined the army, distinguished themselves and received official honours. Since these men and their "exploits" for the authorities were much talked about, the story-tellers in the tea-houses catered for the demand. There are already twenty-four sequels to *Seven Heroes and Five Gallants*, ten sequels to *The Cases of Lord Shih* and seventeen sequels to *The Cases of Lord Peng*. These books are so repetitious and badly written that we need not comment on them except to wonder how authors and readers can waste so much time on such trash.

These four types of fiction are still very popular today. There are other minor types, but I have no time to go into them now. As for the new fiction written since the republic was founded, this is still in its infancy and no really important works have yet appeared I shall not, therefore, speak of this either.

PREFACE TO THE JAPANESE EDITION

The news that a Japanese translation of my *Brief History of Chinese Fiction* is to be published is extremely gratifying, but it makes me very conscious of my decline. When I think back, it must be four or five years ago now that Mr. Wataru Masuda used to come nearly every day to my home to discuss this book, and occasionally we had pleasant chats about the world of letters at that time. In those days I still had enough leisure and ambition to study, but time speeds by: now even my wife and son are a burden to me, to say nothing of collecting books. So I shall probably never have a chance to revise this *Brief History of Chinese Fiction*. Doubtless my satisfaction is like that of some old man who has laid down his pen when he sees his complete works published.

But old habits are hard to forget, and sometimes my attention is still caught by the history of Chinese fiction. To speak merely of the more important discoveries: last year the late Professor Ma Lien's publication of the incomplete text of the *Stories of Ching-ping Hermitage* enriched our material on the Sung vernacular tales. Then Professor Cheng Chen-to's demonstration that the *Pilgrimage to the West* in the *Four Pilgrimages* was a condensation of Wu Cheng-en's novel and not a forerunner corrects the views I expressed in Chapter 16. His excellent paper on this appears in his collection *Chu Lou Chi*. Again, the discovery of the original version of *Chin Ping Mei* in Peking, though the language is rougher than that of the popular edition, proves beyond doubt that this novel could not have been written by Wang Shih-chen who was from Kiangsu, since the dialogue is in the Shantung dialect.

I have made no revisions, though. I have done nothing, despite all the book's shortcomings. I am merely delighted by the publication of this Japanese edition and hope there will be time in future to make amends for my sloth.

This book, naturally, is one fated to have few readers, yet Mr. Wataru Masuda has braved all difficulties to translate it, while Mr. Otokichi Mikame, the director of the Sairosha Press, is willing to have it published. To them I am truly grateful, just as I am grateful to those readers who will take this dry book into their studies.

Written by lamplight, June 9, 1935
Lu Hsun

INDEX

Account of the Saints （列仙传），399

Accounts of a Courtier （常侍言旨），174

Accounts of Avenging Spirits （冤魂志），61

Accounts of Emperor Ming Huang （明皇杂录），174

Accounts of Marvels （述异記），7, 44, 53, 54

Accounts of Mysteries and Monsters （玄怪录），113, 410

Accounts of the Ten Continents （十洲記），31, 32, 36, 398, 399

Accounts of the Singsong Girls' Quarters （教坊記），337

Advice to My Son （誡子拾遺），5

After the Disaster （劫余灰），378, 381

After the Invasion （南燼紀聞），162

Amazing Stories （拍案驚奇），107, 151, 261, 263, 268

Assembly of Ghosts, An （火蕫），150

Ancient Chronology （三五曆記），11

Ancient Mirror, The （古鏡記），86, 407

Anecdotes （小說），76

Anecdotes from Court and Countryside （朝野僉載），204

Anecdotes from Past History （卄一史識余），84

Anecdotes of Chihshang Hermitage （池上草堂笔記），287

Anecdotes of the Sui and Tang Dynasties （隋唐嘉話），174

Anecdotes of Yinhsueh-hsuan （印雪軒随笔），286

Anecdotes of Yutai Fairy Lodge （右台仙館笔記），286

Anecdotes on Books （書影），194

Anecdotes on Drama （顧曲尘談），192

Annals of the Seven States (II) or Yueh Yi's Victory Over the State of Chi （乐毅图齐七国春秋后集），163

Annals of Wu and Yueh （吳越春秋），18

Annexation of Six States by the Emperor of Chin, The （秦併六国），163

Bell of Anecdotes （說鈴），84
Boiling the Sea （张生煮海），110

Book of Deities and Marvels (神异径), 29-31, 32, 38, 398, 399
Book of Mountains and Seas, The (山海經) 7, 8, 19, 21, 27, 29, 31, 396, 398
Book of Supernatural Things, The (神异經), 7
Book of Tea (茶經), 5
Book Worm, The (蟫史), 322, 323-26
Canonization of the Gods (封神传), 220, 225, 428
Carriage-Load of Marvels, A (乘异記), 128
Cart-Load of Ghosts, A (媵車志), 128
Cases of Lord Li, The (李公案), 369
Cases of Lord Liu, The (刘公案), 369
Cases of Lord Peng, The (彭公案), 368, 442
Cases of Lord Shih, The (施公案), 368, 442
Cases of Prefect Pao, The (龙图公案), 368, 412, 441, 442
Chang Chun-fang (张君房), 128
Chang Feng-yi (张凤翼), 112
Chang Fu-kung (章撫公), 84
Chang Hua (张华), 5, 46, 47, 48, 118
Chang Kuang-jui (张广瑞), 369
Chang Po-shan (张博山), 248,

Chang Shih-cheng (张师正), 128
Chang Shu-shen (张書紳), 217
Chang Tai-ho (张太和), 112
Chang Tsu (张鷟), 87, 88, 89, 204, 327, 408
Chang Tu (张讀), 116, 410
Chang Wu-chiu (张无咎), 258
Chang Yung (张埔), 84
Chao Ching-chen (赵景真), 203
Chao Yu-shih (赵与时), 130
Chen Chen (陈忱), 195, 424
Chen Chiu (陈球), 326, 408
Chen Hung (陈鸿), 95
Chen Shen-shu (陈森書), 340
Chen Shih (陈实), 43
Chen Shih-pin (陈士斌), 217
Cheng Chung-kuei (郑仲夔), 84
Chi Hsieh (齐諧), 10
Chi Yun (紀的), 6, 209, 277, 278, 279, 280, 285, 286, 433
Chia Chuan (賈泉), 73
Chiang Fang (蔣防), 110
Chiang Kuan (江灌), 19
Chiao Hung (焦竑), 84
Chien Tseng (錢曾), 8, 9, 152
Chin Chai-ssu (秦再思), 128
Chin Chun (秦簹), 132
Chin Peng-chang (金捧閶), 287
Chin Ping Mei (金瓶梅), 232-239, 242, 245, 258, 355, 429-430, 431

Chin Sheng-tan （金圣歎），172, 192, 193, 194, 423, 424
Ching Shih-Tzu（青史子）,2, 3, 23, 28, 397, 398
Chiu Chu-chi （邱处机）, Putative Author of *Pilgrimage to the West*, 209, 426
Chou Liang-kung（周亮工）, 191, 193
Chou Mi （周密）, 143
Choice Blossoms from the Garden of Literature （文苑英华）, 90, 96, 123, 415
Chu Jen-hu （褚人穫）, 137, 173
Chu Yu （瞿佑）, 269
Chu Yuan （屈原）,18, 42-43, 69
Chuan chi or romance（传奇）, 85, 407, 414, 415
Chuchiang Pool （曲江池）, 98, 410
Chung Kuei the Ghost Catcher （鐘馗捉鬼传）, 288, 379
Collected Tales （翼駉稗編）, 286
Collected Tales of Miracles （集灵記）, 61
Collection of Marvels (括异志), 128
Compendium of Deities of the Three Religions, The （三教搜神大全）, 22
Complete Story of Yo Fei, The （說岳全传）, 197
Contemporary Sayings （今世說）, 84, 405

Correct Interpretation of the Pilgrimage, The （西游正旨）, 217
Corrections of Mistakes (刊誤), 5
Courtesan Named Yang, The （楊娼传）, 111
Crime Involving Nine Lives, A （九命奇冤）, 377

Dark God Chen-wu, The or *The Voyage to the North* （北方真武玄天上帝出身志传,即北游記）, 202
Discerning the Marvels （甄異傳）, 5, 53
Double Mirror, The （馮玉梅团圓）, 152
Dragon King's Daughter, The （柳毅传）, 104, 110
Dream of Hantan （邯鄲記）, 92, 409
Dream of the Green Chamber, （青楼夢）, 345-348, 440
Dream of the Princess of Chin, A （秦夢記）, 94
Dream of the Red Chamber or *Tale of a Rock* （紅楼夢又名石头記）, 298-315, 348, 355, 356, 436-439, 440, 441

Eight Elder Gallants, The （英雄大八义）, 369, 441
Eight Junior Gallants, The (英雄小八义）, 369, 441
Eight Saints, The or *The Voyage to the East* (八仙出处东游記）, 199

Embroidered Jacket （綉襦記）, 98, 410

Eternal Grief, The （长恨歌）, 95, 409

Evergreen Prosperous Reign, The （圣朝鼎盛万年青）, 369

Expedition to the Western Ocean （三宝太监西洋记）, 224, 428-429

Exposure of the Official World （官場現形記）, 373, 374, 375-377, 378, 435

Fairies' Cavern, The （游仙窟）, 88, 89, 327, 408

Fan Shu （范攄）, 117

Fang Chien-li （房千里）, 111
Feng Chi-feng （馮起凤）, 276
Feng Meng-lung （馮夢龙）, 177, 258, 266, 267

Filial Son Tung Yung, The （孝子董永传）, 139

Five Elder Gallants （大五义）, 365

Five Younger Gallants （小五义）, 365-367, 370, 441

Flower and the Moon, The （花月痕）, 340-344

Flower in an Ocean of Sin, A （孽海花）, 384-387

Flowers in the Mirror （鏡花緣）, 329, 330-336

Flower Shadows on the Screen （隔簾花影）, 244

Forest of Jokes (by Hantan Chun; 笑林), 79, 81, 404

Forest of Jokes (by Ho Chih-jan; 笑林), 83, 404

Forest of Marvels, Lu's （异林）, 53

Forest of Sayings （語林）, 72, 404, 406

Forest of Sayings (by Ho Liang-chun; 何氏語林), 84

Forest of Tang Dynasty Sayings （唐語林）, 84

Forgotten History of the Tang Dynasty （唐闕史）, 116

Forgotten Tales （拾遺記）, 48, 67

Forgotten Tales of the Kai Yuan and Tien Pao Periods （开元天宝遺事）, 174

Forgotten Tales of the Ta Yeh Period （大业拾遺記）, 134, 174

"Four Great Novels," The, 355

Four Romances of Wandering Saints, The （四游記）, 199, 211

Free Talk （劇談录）, 116

Gallant Maid, The （儿女英雄传評話）, 355, 356, 357-359, 369, 370

Garden of Anecdotes （說苑）, 28

Garden of Marvels, The （异苑）, 21, 54, 277, 400

Gems of Buddhist Literature （法苑珠林）, 61, 62, 63, 65

Girl with the Red Whisk, The (紅拂記), 112
Girl's Chamber, The (幽閨記), 192
Glimpses of Shanghai (上海游驂录), 378
Gossip About Shadows (影談), 276
Governor of the Southern Tributary State, The (南柯太守传), 104, 105, 411, 412
Grove of Gossip, The (談藪), 81

Han *Dynasty History* (汉書), fifteen works of *hsiao-shuo* mentioned in, 2-3, 23
Han Fei Tzu (韓非子), 28, 71
Han Hsin's Death at the Hands of Empress Lu (呂后斬韓信前汉書續集), 163
Han Tzu-yun (韓子云), 349
Hantan Chun (邯鄲淳), 79
Hao Chiu Chuan (好逑传), 245-246, 251-253, 431, 432
Hao-ko-tzu (浩歌子), 276
Hearsay Tales (by Yu Yueh; 耳郵), 286
Hearsay Tales (by Yueh Chun; 耳食录), 286
Hearsay Tales New and Old (今古奇聞), 268
Heart of Mysteries, The (玄中記), 21, 38
History of the Kings of Shu (蜀王本紀), 18
Ho Chih-jan (何自然), 83
Ho Liang-chun (何良俊), 84

Ho-sheng (合生), 142, 143, 416
Hopango (何邦額), 276
Hou Pai (Hou Chun-su; 侯白, 字君素), 5, 61, 81
Hsia Ching-chu (夏敬渠), 317
Hsiao Yi (萧綺), 67
Hsiao-shuo (小說), 1, 2, 3, 4, 5, 6, 7, 8, 23, 24, 26, 28, 29, 48, 55, 65, 142, 143, 151, 257, 394, 397, 398, 399, 400, 406, 417
Hsiao-shuo or *Yin-tzu-erh* (銀字儿), 142, 232
Hsiao-shuo, subdivided by Hu Ying-lin, 6
Hsiao-shuo, three categories of, 7
Hsin Chi-chi (辛弃疾), 162
Hsiung Ta-pen (熊大本), 197
Hsu Cheng (徐整), 11
Hsu Chiu-cha (許秋垞), 286
Hsu Chung-lin (許仲琳), 220
Hsu Feng-en (許奉恩), 287
Hsu Hsuan (徐鉉), 124, 126, 128
Hsu Yao-tso (許堯佐), 111
Hsu Yuan-chung (許元仲), 286
Hsu Wen Hsien Tung Kao (Sequel to Studies in Ancient Bibliographies; 續文献通考), 8
Hsuan Ting (宣鼎), 286
Hsueh Tiao (薛調), 111
Hsueh Yu-ssu (薛漁思), 116
Hu Pao-yu (胡宝玉), 378

Hu Ying-lin （胡応麟）, 6, 7, 67, 85
Hua pen （話本）, 143, 416
Huang Yun-chiao （黃允交）, 122
Huangfu Mei （皇甫枚）, 111
Human Hassock, The （肉蒲団）, 239
Hung Lou Meng （紅楼夢） See *Dream of the Red Chamber*
Hung Mai （洪邁）, 128-129, 130, 180
Hung Sheng （洪昇）, 96

Idle Talk （消言）, 84
Illustrated Stories Ancient and Modern （全像古今小說）, 256, 257, 258
Investigation of Spirits （稽神録）, 124
Iron Flower Fairy Tale, The （鉄花仙史）, 253-255

Jade-Sword Anecdotes （玉劍尊聞）, 84
Jen Fang （任昉）, 54
Jen the Fox Fairy （任氏传） 93

Kan Pao （干宝）, 43, 49, 52, 92, 270, 401
Kan Sun Tzu （干腆子）, 121
Kang Pien （康騈）, 116, 117
Kao Ju （高儒）, 8
Kao Ngo （高鶚）, 315
Kao Yen-hsiu （高彥休）, 116
King Wu's Conquest of the Shangs （武玨紂書）, 163

Ko Hung （葛洪）, 40, 41, 43, 44, 399
Ku-kuang-sheng （古狂生）, 264
Kuan Shih-hao （管世灝）, 276
Kung Ping-chung （孔平仲）, 84
Kuo Cheng-chih （郭澄之）, 73
Kuo Chih （郭湜）, 112
Kuo Hsien （郭憲）, 29, 38, 398
Kuo Hsun （郭勛）, 183, 185, 186, 189, 190, 196, 197
Kuo Pu （郭璞）, 19, 38
Kuo Tuan （郭彖）, 128
Kuo Tzu （郭子）, 73, 404

Last Tales of Liao-chai, The （聊斎志异拾遺）, 275
Laughter （解頤）, 81
Leisure Hours of a Secretary （幕府燕閑录）, 128
Li Chao-wei （李朝威）, 104, 110, 113
Li Chih （李贄）, 186, 188, 189
Li Ching （李清）, 84
Li Chiu-chin （李就今）, 122
Li Fang （李昉）, 124, 125
Li Fu （李涪）, 5
Li Fu-yen （李复言）, 107, 116, 410, 412
Li Ju-chen （李汝珍）, 329
Li Kung-tso （李公佐）, 100, 104, 107, 108, 109, 113, 410, 411, 412, 413
Li Pao-chia （李宝嘉）, 372, 373, 378, 435
Li Shang-yin (alias Li Yi-shan; 李商隱）, 121, 122

453

Li Shao-wen (李紹文), 84
Li Shu (李恕), 5
Li Tang (李湯), 107, 413
Li Yu (李漁), 110
Liang Kung-chen (梁恭辰), 287
Liang Wei-shu (梁維枢), 84
Lieh Tzu (列子), 10, 11, 71
Ling Hsuan (伶玄), 44, 133
Ling Meng-chu (凌濛初), 107, 267
Liu Cheng (柳珵), 111
Liu Ching-shu (刘敬叔), 54, 277, 279, 400
Liu Fu (刘斧), 152
Liu Hsiang (刘向), 28, 41, 68, 69, 74, 399
Liu Hsiao-piao (刘孝标), 74, 83, 405
Liu Hsiao-sun (刘孝孙), 5
Liu Hsin (刘歆), 2, 29 40, 41
Liu Ngo (刘鹗), 381-382
Liu Yi-ching (刘义庆), 55, 61, 73, 74, 279, 403
Liu Yi-ming (刘一明), 217
Liu's Anecdotes (次柳氏旧闻), 174
Lives of Shanghai Singsong Girls (海上花列传), 349-354, 440
Lo Kuan-chung (罗贯中), 166, 167, 168, 173, 183, 184, 185, 186, 188, 189, 191, 192, 195, 210, 418, 419, 423, 424
Lo Shih (乐史), 130
Lost Records (逸史), 174

Lost Records of Chou (遺周書), 8, 16, 26, 27
Lost Records of Yueh (越絕書), 18
Lotus in the Mud (青泥蓮花記), 337
Lu Hsiung (吕熊), 197
Lu Yu (陸羽), 5

Making the Drunkard Sober (醉醒石), 151, 264-266
Man with the Curly Beard, The (name of a play; 虬髯翁), 262
Man with the Curly Beard, The (name of a prose romance; 虬髯客传), 111, 195
Mao Tsung-kang (毛宗崗), 172
Martyrs' Blood, The (碧血幕), 387
Marvels in Loyang (洛中紀異), 128
Master of Tungpi Mountain Lodge (东壁山房主人), 267
Maudgalyayana's Descent to Hell (目蓮入地獄故事), 140
Meeting of the Dragon and the Tiger, The (龙虎风云会), 167
Mei Ting-tso (梅鼎祚), 337
Meng Yuan-lao (孟元老), 142
Ming Dynasty Social Talk (明世說新語), 84
Mirage, The (蜃中楼) 110
Mirror of Theatrical Life (品花宝鑑), 337, 338-340, 440

Miscellaneous Writings （百家）
2, 23, 28

Miscellany of Ai Tzu （艾子杂录）, 83

Miscellany of the Jade Hall （玉堂丛話）, 84

Miscellany of Yi-shan （义山杂纂）, 121

Miscellany Within and Without the Universe (also known as *Crabbed Notes;* 六合內外瑣言, （一名璅蛣杂录）, 276

Mistress Liu （柳氏传）, 111

More About Mysteries and Monsters （續玄怪录）, 107, 116, 410, 412

More About the Pilgrimage （西遊补）, 219, 228

More Social Talk （續世說）, 84

More Tales of Chi Hsieh （續齐諧記）, 5, 7

Mother Lamp-Wick (灯花婆婆), 8, 152

Nai-teh-weng （耐得翁）, 143, 149

New Anecdotes of Social Talk （世說新語）, 7, 74

New Anecdotes Under the Lamplight （剪灯新話）, 269

New Dream of the Red Chamber, A （新石头記）, 378

New Sayings （新世說）, 84, 405

New Tales (Originally *What the Master Did Not Talk of;* 新齐諧, 即子不語）, 276

New Tales Under the Lamplight （剪灯新語）, 432

Nieh Tien （聶田）, 128

Nine Admonitions of the Duke of Liang, The （梁公九諫）, **140**

Nine-Tailed Tortoise, The （九尾龟）, 440

Niu Sheng-ju (牛僧儒), 113, 410

Notes After Entertaining Guests （宾退录）, 130

Notes from the Green Latticed Window （青瑣高議）, 132, 137, 152

Notes of the Chief Sights in the Capital （都城紀胜）, 143

Notes of the Yueh-wei Hermitage （閲微草堂笔記）, 209, 279, 286, 434

Notes on the West Lake （西湖志余）, 192

Nun Called Miao-chi, The （妙寂尼）, 412

Old Man of the East City, The （东城老父传）, 95

Old Woman Feng of Luchiang （卢江馮媼传）, 107, 414

Opening of the Canal, The （开河記）, 136, 174

Origin of Things （事始）, 5

Original Significance of the Pilgrimage, The （西遊厚旨）, **217**

Pai Chu-yi (白居易), 95, 96, 98, 100, 409

Pai Chuan Shu Chih or *Hundred Rivers Bibliographical Notes* （百川書志）, 8

Pai Hsing-chien （白行簡）, 98, 409, 410
Palace of Eternal Youth, The （长生殿）, 96, 409
Pan Ku （班固）, 2, 3, 29, 33, 35, 36, 40, 398, 399
Panchiao Miscellany, The （板桥杂記）, 337
Pao-weng-lao-jen （抱甕老人）, 267
Pei Chi （裴启）, 72
Pei Hsing （裴鉶）, 117, 410
Pen Gossip （三昇笔談）, 286
Penetrating the Mysteries （洞冥記）, 33, 38, 398, 399
Peony Pavilion, The （牡丹亭）, 282
Pi Chung-hsun （毕仲詢）, 128
Pilgrimage to the West （西遊記）, 201, 220, 221, 222, 225, 226, 232, 355, 356, 413, 426-428, 441
Pilgrimage to the West (by Wu Cheng-en; 西遊記）, 109-110, 209, 210, 211-217, 220, 418,
Pilgrimage to the West (by Yang Chih-ho; 西遊記; 203, 205-208
Ping Shan Leng Yen （平山冷燕）, 245, 248-251, 254, 431, 432
Popular Stories of the Capital （京本通俗小說）, 144, 147, 152, 257, 258, 417
Popular Tales of the Five Dynasties （五代史平話）, 143, 144, 149, 164, 416
Popular Talk （俗說）, 76

Priest Tzu-yang （紫阳道人）, 240
Prince Huo's Daughter （霍小玉传）, 110, 134
Prince Hua-kuang or Voyage to the South, The （王显灵官大帝华光天王传，即南遊記）, 199, 214
Private Life of Emperor Wu Ti （汉武帝內传）, 35, 398
Private Life of Lady Swallow, The （飞燕外传）, 44, 133, 277
Private History of Lady Yang, The （楊太真外传）, 130, 131, 174
Pu Sung-ling（蒲松齡）, 269, 275, 276, 277, 278, 285

Random Notes After Chatting at Night （夜譚隨錄）, 276
Random Notes from Shanghai （淞隐漫录）, 286
Random Notes of a Traveller （客窗偶笔）, 287
Record During Office qt Luling （卢陵官下記）, 117
Record of Strange Men in the Yangtse and Huai River Valleys （江淮昇人录）, 126
Record of the Courtesans' Quarters （北里志）, 117, 122, 337
Records of a Palace Chamber （宣宝志）, 116, 410
Records of a Rainy Night by the Autumn Lamp （夜雨秋灯录）, 286
Records of Chou （周書，周考，周說）, 2, 16, 23, 27, 48

Records of *Divine Evidence* (宣驗記), 61
Records of *Ghosts and Spirits, Hsun's* (灵鬼志), 53, 59
Records of *Grievances*(窃愤录), 162
Records of *Jokes* (启颜录), 81
Records of *Light and Dark* (幽明錄), 5
Records of *Miracles* (神异記), 66
Records of *Mysterious Manifestations* (冥祥記), 61
Records of *Southern Beauties* (南部烟花录), 134
Records of *Spirits* (搜神記), 7, 20, 50, 92, 401
Records of *Strange Things* (博物志), 5, 7, 48, 118, 400
Reign of Eternal Peace, The (永庆昇平), 368, 369
Reminiscences of Hangchow (夢梁录), 142, 196
Reminiscences of the Eastern Capital (东京夢华录), 142
Repository of Fiction (說郛), 76, 78, 79
Retribution in Three Generations (三世报), See *Flower Shadows on the Screen*
Romance of Loyal and Gallant Men (忠烈俠义傳), 365
Romance of the Five Dynasties, The (殘唐五代史演义), 167, 176

Romance of the Ming Dynasty Heroes, The (皇明英烈传、一名云合奇踪), 196
Romance of the States of Eastern Chou, The (东周列国志), 151, 196
Romance of the Sui and Tang Dynasties (隋唐志传), 137, 151, 167, 173, 419
Romance of the Three Kingdoms (三国志演义), 8, 142, 167, 174, 184, 196, 200, 209, 355, 418, 419-421, 427
Romance of the Witch Tang Sai-erh (女仙外史), 197
Rustic's Idle Talk, A (野叟曝言), 317, 318-321

Sad Tale of the Hsiang River, A (湘中怨), 93
Saddharma-pundarika, Popular Version of (法华佳俗文), 40
Sakyamuni's Attainment of Buddhahood, (释迦八相成道記), 140
Samadhi-sagara-sutra (观佛三昧海經), 58
Samyukta-avadana-sutra (杂譬喻經), 58
Sayings of Monks (僧世說), 84
Sayings of the Han Dynasty (汉世說), 84
Sayings of the Ming Dynasty (明語林), 84
Sayings of Women (女世說), 84

Sayings of Yi Yin, The （伊尹說）, 2, 23-24
Scholar by the Roadside, The （阳羡鹅籠記）, 56
Scholar of Fengyang, The （凤阳士人）, 433
Scholars, The （儒林外史）, 288, 289-297, 434, 435, 436
Sea of Woe, A （恨海）, 381
Second Series of West Lake Tales （西湖二集）, 262-264
Secret Tales of the Han Palace （杂事秘辛）, 44, 133
Sequel to a Flower in an Ocean of Sin （續孽海花）, 387
Sequel to a Guide to Conversation （續談助）, 73, 76, 77, 79
Sequel to Chin Ping Mei （續金瓶梅）, 240, 244, 431
Sequel to Records of Spirits （續搜神記）, 52, 277
Sequel to Shui Hu Chuan （后水滸传）, 194, 195
Sequel to Social Talk (by Liu Hsiao-piao; 續世說）, 83
Sequel to Social Talk （續世說新書）, 83
Sequel to Strange Tales New and Old （續今古奇覩）, 267
Sequel to Tales of Chi Hsieh （續齐諧記）, 56
Sequel to the Dream （續黃粱）, 409, 433
Sequels to the Dream of the Red Chamber, 315
Sequel to the Pilgrimage to the West （后西遊記）, 218, 287
Sequel to the Yuyang Miscellany （酉阳杂俎續集）, 7
Seven Heroes and Five Gallants (revised edition of Three Heroes and Five Gallants; 七俠五义）, 365, 441, 442
Seven Swordsmen and Eighteen Gallants （七劍十八俠）, 369, 442
Seven Swordsmen and Thirteen Gallants （七劍十三俠）, 369, 442
Shang Chung-hsien （尚仲賢）, 110
Shanghai Miscellany （淞濱瑣話）, 286
Shen Chi-chi （沈旣济）, 90, 92, 93, 409
Shen Chi-feng （沈起凤）, 276
Shen Ya-chih （沈亚之）, 93
Shen Yueh （沈約）, 76
Shih Hui or Shih Chun-mei （施惠, 施君美）, 192
Shih Kuang （师曠）, 2, 23, 28
Shih Nai-an （施耐庵）, 185, 191, 192, 195, 423
Shih Yu-kun （石玉昆）, 359, 365, 370
Shui Hu Chuan（水滸传）, 8, 158, 167, 172, 183-194, 195, 196, 220, 221, 232, 233, 355, 370, 418, 419, 421-423, 429, 442
Singsong Girl Tan Yi-ko, The （譚意哥传）, 133
Social Talk （世說) See also New Anecdotes of Social Talk, 71, 74, 79, 81, 83, 403, 404, 405, 406

Social Talk, imitations of, 83
Sorcerer's Revolt and Its Suppression by the Three Suis, The （三遂平妖传）, 167, 176, 177, 198, 220, 257, 258, 419
Stories Exemplifying Marvels （旌異記）, 5, 61
Stories of Famous Swordsmen （劍俠传）, 117, 126
Stories to Awaken Men （醒世恆言）, 257, 258-261, 262
Stories to Enlighten Men （喩世明言）, 256-257
Stories to Warn Men （警世通言）, 257, 267
Story of a Singsong Girl （李娃传）, 98, 409
Story of An Lu-shan, The （安祿山事迹）, 112
Story of Chiu Hu, The （秋胡小說）, 139
Story of Eternal Grief, The （长恨歌传）, 95, 174
Story of Eunuch Kao, The （高力士外传）, 112
Story of Fei-yen （非烟传）, 111
Story of Green Pearl （綠珠传）, 130, 131
Story of Hsieh Hsiao-ngo, The （謝小娥传）, 105, 412
Story of Hsu Mai, The （許迈外传）, 130
Story of Lady Mei （梅妃传）, 137, 174
Story of Li Ching, Duke of Wei （李卫公别传）, 112

Story of Li Lin-fu, The （李林甫外传）, 112
Story of Li Po, The （李白外传）, 130
Story of Liu Yi, The （柳毅传書）, 110
Story of Prince Tan of Yen （燕丹子）, 4, 18
Story of Shang-ching （上清传）, 111
Story of the Labyrinth （迷楼記）, 174
Story of the Pillow, The （枕中記）, 90, 92, 105, 408
Story of the Prince of Teng, The （滕王外传）, 130
Story of the Three Kingdoms, The （三国志平話）, 163
Story of Ying-ying, The, or Encounter with a Fairy （鶯鶯传）, 100, 277, 410
Story-Teller's Clapper, The （諧鐸）, 276
Strange Dreams （异夢）, 93
Strange Events of the Last Twenty Years （二十年目睹之怪現狀）, 377, 378, 435
Strange Story of Two Beauties, The （双美奇緣） See Yu-Chiao-Li
Strange Tales (by Hsu Chiu-cha; 聞見异辭), 286
Strange Tales (by Pei Hsing; 传奇), 117, 410
Strange Tales from the Glow-Worm Window （螢窗异草）, 276

Strange Tales of Liao-chai
（聊斋志异）, 269-275, 286, 409, 433
Strange Tales of Electricity
（电术奇談）, 377, 381
Strange Tales New and Old
（今古奇覌）, 257, 267, 418
Su Ngo　（苏鶚）, 116, 410
Su Tung-po　（苏东坡）, 83, 122, 270, 419
Sui Dynasty History　（隋書）, discussion of *hsiao-shuo* in, 4
Sun Chi　（孙棨）, 117, 121, 337
Sung Dynasty History（宋史）, 5
Sung Tzu（宋子）, 2, 23
Supplement to the Pilgrimage
（續西遊記）, 219
Suppression of Four Big Revolts, The　（后水滸一名蕩平四大寇传）, 194
Suppression of the Rebels, The
（結水滸一名蕩寇志）, 195

Tai Tso　（戴祚）, 5, 53
Tai-ping Geographical Record
（太平寰宇記）, 52
Tai-ping Imperial Encyclopaedia（太平御覽）, 16, 17, 25, 27, 47, 60, 66, 67, 72, 73, 80. 123, 415
Tai-ping Miscellany　（太平广記）, 61, 72, 80, 81, 82, 83, 86, 87, 90, 96, 98, 113, 121, 123, 124, 125, 126, 129, 269, 277, 407, 415
Tale of a Rock　（石头記） another name of *Dream of the Red Chamber*

Tale of Chou and Chin, A
（周秦紀行）, 115
Tale of the Hot Spring　（温泉記）, 133
Tale of Lady Swallow（赵飞燕別傳）, 132
Tale of Li Mountain　（驪山記）, 133
Tale of Romance and Gallantry
（俠义风月传） See *Hao Chiu Chuan*
Tale of Two Heroes, A　（双雄記传奇）, 258
Tale of Yenshan, A　（燕山外史）, 326, 327, 408
Tales to Cast Out Sorrow（浇愁集）, 276, 409
Tales of Chi Hsieh（斋諧記）, 56
Tales of Divine Retribution
（感应传）, 5
Tales of Emperor Wu Ti, The
（武帝故事）, 53, 398
Tales of Hotung　（河東記）, 116
Tales of Hsi Liu　（昔柳摭談）, 276
Tales of Marvels　（列异传）, 5, 45
Tales of Seas and Mountains
（海山記）, 137, 174
Tales of the Hsuan Ho Period
（宣和遺事）, 152, 153, 157, 182, 189, 190, 191, 417
Tales of the Old Capital　（武林旧事）, 143
Tales of Yi Chien　（夷堅志）, 128, 129, 180

Tang Hsien-tsu （湯显祖），92, 176, 412

Tang Dynasty History （唐書）, bibliographical section of, 4-5

Tang Dynasty History, hsiao-shuo in, 5

Tang Emperor's Visit to the Nether Regions, The （唐太宗入冥記），139, 140

Tang Yung-chung（湯用中），286

Tao Chien （陶潛），52, 86, 277, 279, 401

"Three Amazing Romances," （三大奇書），232

Three Heroes and Five Gallants （三俠五义）,359, 360-364, 369, 370, 441

Three Dreams （三夢記），98

Tien Shu-ho （田叔禾），192

Tien-mu-shan-chiao （天目山樵），228

Tracing Marvels （祖异志），128

Travels of King Mu, The （穆天子传），7, 8, 15, 19, 27

Travels of Mr. Derelict, The （老殘遊記），381

Tripitaka Goes West to Find Buddhist Canons （唐三藏西天取經），204

Tripitaka's Search for Buddhist Sutras （大唐三藏法师取經記），152, 153, 418

True Exposition of the Pilgrimage, The （西遊真詮），217

True History of Ming Dynasty Heroes （真英烈傳），197

True Tales of the Kai Yuan and Tien Pao Periods （开天传信記），174

Tsao Hsueh-chin（曹雪芹），312, 313, 437

Tsao Pei（曹丕），45, 46

Tseng Pu （曾樸），384

Tsou Tao-chih （邹弢之），276

Tsou Yuan-piao（邹元标），197

Tsu Chung-chih （祖冲之），53

Tsu Tai-chih （祖台之），53

Tsui Ling-chin （崔令欽）, 337

Tu Kuang-ting （杜光庭），111

Tu Shen （屠伸），277, 322

Tuan Cheng-shih（段成式），40, 58, 117, 120, 126, 410

Tung Yueh（董說），219, 229

Tungfang Shuo （东方朔），29, 31, 32, 34, 38, 39, 398, 399

Tungyang Wu-yi（东阳无疑），56

Tuyang Miscellany （杜阳杂俎），116, 410

Village Talk （里乘），287

Vimalakirti-nirdesa, Popular Version of （維摩詰經俗文），140

Wang Chi （王圮），8

Wang Chia （王嘉），48, 67

Wang Cho （王晫），84, 405

Wang Chun-yu （王君玉），122

Wang Fang-ching（王方庆），84

Wang Shen-hsiu （王愼修），176

Wang Tao （王韜），286

Wang Tang (王讜), 84
Wang Tu (王度), 86, 87
Wang Wan (汪琬), 84
Wang Yen (王琰), 61
Wang Yen-hsiu (王延秀), 5
Way to Get Rich, The (发财秘訣), 378
West Chamber, The (西廂記), 103, 104, 172, 193, 411
Western Capital Miscellany, The (西京杂記), 7, 40, 41, 398, 399
Wei Kuan (韋瓘), 115
Wei Tzu-an (魏子安), 344
Wen Kang (文康), 355, 370
Wen Ting-yun (温庭筠), 121
White Monkey, The (补江总白猿传), 87, 407
Whole Forest of Jokes, A (笑林广記), 405
Wild Talk (遯窟讕言), 286
Wu Chang-ling (吳昌齡), 109, 204, 206
Wu Chun (吳均), 5, 40, 56, 58, 59
Wu Cheng-en (吳承恩), 109, 210, 211, 212, 216, 217, 219, 413, 426, 427
Wu Ching-tzu (吳敬梓), 288, 289, 290, 434
Wu Mei (吳梅), 192
Wu Ping (吳平), 18
Wu Shu (吳淑), 124, 126, 128
Wu Wo-yao (吳沃堯), 372, 377, 378, 435

Wu-shuang the Peerless (无双传), 111
Wu Tzu-mu (吳自牧), 142, 143, 147, 149, 196
Wu Cheng Tzu (务成子), 23
Wu Su-kung (吳肅公), 84
Wu Tzu-hsu Goes to the State of Wu (伍員入吳故事), 139
Wu Yuan-tai (吳元泰), 199

Yang Chih-ho (楊志和), 203, 205, 211
Yang Shen (楊愼), 133
Yang Sung-fen (楊松玢), 81
Yao Ju-neng (姚汝能), 112
Yeh Shih Yuan Shu Mu (也是园書目), 8
Yen Chih-tui (顏之推), 61
Yen Shih-ku (顏师古), 134
Yen Shu (晏殊), 74
Yen Tsung-chiao (顏从乔), 84
Yi Chien (夷堅), 10
Yi Tsung-kuei (易宗夔), 84, 405
Yin-tzu-erh (銀字儿), 142, 232
Yin Yun (殷芸), 41, 76
Ying Shao (应劭), 16, 279
Yotu Canon (古岳瀆經), 108
Yu Chiao Li (玉嬌李), 239, 245, 430
Yu-Chiao-Li (玉嬌梨), 246-248, 431, 432
Yu Chu (虞初), 16, 27
Yu Hsiang-tou (余象斗), 199, 202
Yu Huai (余怀), 337

Yu Hung-chien （俞鸿渐）, 286
Yu Lung-kuang （俞龙光）, 195
Yu Tzu （鬻子）, 24
Yu Yin-hsiang （俞吟香）, 345
Yu Ying-ao （余应鳌）, 197
Yu Wan-chun （俞万春）, 195, 370, 424
Yu Yueh （俞樾）, 286, 364
Yuan Chen （元稹）, 100, 103, 410
Yuan Kang （袁康）, 18
Yüan Mei （袁枚）, 275, 286
Yuan Yu-ling （袁于令）, 174
Yueh Chun （乐钧）, 286
Yun-feng-shan-jen （云封山人）, 253-255
Yung Lo Encyclopaedia, tales collected from （永乐大典）, 126
Yunhsi Miscellany （云溪友议）, 117
Yuyang Miscellany, The （酉阳杂俎）, 7, 40, 58, 117, 126, 141, 410